Tools of Critical Thinking

Metathoughts for Psychology

David A. Levy
Pepperdine University

WAVELAND
PRESS, INC.
Long Grove, Illinois

To my family—past, present, and future

For information about this book, contact:
  Waveland Press, Inc.
  4180 IL Route 83, Suite 101
  Long Grove, IL 60047-9580
  (847) 634-0081
  info@waveland.com
  www.waveland.com

ISBN 1-57766-316-0

Printed in the United States of America

7 6 5 4 3 2 1

Contents

Foreword

David Levy follows in the footsteps of classical philosophers who believed that knowledge of the Other begins with self-knowledge. Their perspective led to the grand humanist maxim, "Nothing human is alien to me."

Levy asks the readers to think, about thinking, and that they do so for themselves. He deviates from the dogma of psychological scientism that dictates studying the Other as a defective object, a perspective that generates the grand psychodiagnostic maxim, "Nothing alien is human to me." The fruits of this folly are now widely regarded as scientific progress. I think Ogden Nash's formula (made in a different context) applies: "We're making great progress, but we are headed in the wrong direction."

To be sure, accepting the invitation to think critically entails assuming the risk of living dangerously, the extent of the danger depending on what the thinker does as a result of, and with, his or her thoughts. Socrates thought for himself—and, for sharing his thoughts with others, was condemned as a criminal by the Athenian authorities. Zola thought for himself—and, for thinking and saying that Dreyfus was innocent, had to flee France. Official protestations to the contrary notwithstanding, we are not supposed to think. We are supposed to believe what the Authorities think, and define as Truth and Justice.

Lest we delude ourselves that that way lies security, we had better remember F. Scott Fitzgerald's fine insight in *Tender Is the Night*. "Either you think," he warned, "or else others have to think for you and take power from you, pervert and discipline your natural tastes, civilize and sterilize you." Unaware or unmindful of this risk, most people choose to abuse thinking or to avoid it altogether. According to Voltaire, "[People] use thought only to justify their injustices, and speech only to disguise their thoughts." And according to Aldous Huxley, "Most of one's life is one prolonged effort to prevent oneself thinking."

Because thinking is an arduous process of self-challenging, we are inclined to think only until we arrive at an understanding with which we are satisfied, that we call "explanation" and use as justification for ceasing to think further about the matter. Keeping our minds open to new explanations requires tolerating uncertainty, which, ironically is precisely the mental vexation we try to relieve by thinking.

Levy's style combines erudition with simplicity and earnestness with humor. *Tools of Critical Thinking* is devoid of psychobabble and avoids the pitfall of treating psychology as the pretentious demeaning of the Other by enrobing him in diagnostic deformations. The result is a clear and compelling book, accessible to lay persons and mental health professionals alike, that reaffirms Blaise Pascal's noble vision: "Man is obviously made for thinking. Therein lies all his dignity and his merit; and his whole duty is to think as he ought."

THOMAS SZASZ
Syracuse, New York

v

Introduction

In this era of so-called post-modernism, those of us who still try to teach enduringly useful modes of critical thinking often, in my own experience, feel themselves inundated and overwhelmed by multitudes of contemporary influences suggesting the propriety of more self-indulgent ways of rendering judgments about "the way things are." In the humanities and social sciences (the latter including the vast majority of issues relating to mental health and psychopathology), in particular, the task sometimes seems almost hopeless because the complexities and the value considerations involved routinely undercut the otherwise self-evident power of rigorous inductive and deductive logic applied to the realm of reliably established empirical observation. No less a figure than Carl Rogers, who in his appropriately revered earlier years had proclaimed "the facts are always friendly," and who was to learn otherwise in the tragic Mendota experience, eventually succumbed in his later writing to the considerable allures of a radically "humanistic" muddle-headedness.

But some help, at last, is on the way! In his *Tools of Critical Thinking: Metathoughts for Psychology,* David Levy has condensed both the wisdom of the ages and the findings of contemporary psychological science into a manageable set of principles ("Metathoughts") that will, where taken seriously, notably improve the general quality of thought not only in clinical psychology and cognate areas but across the broad expanse of scholarly and scientific endeavor. The work is remarkable in its successful reduction of certain extremely subtle and complex ideas to terms that should be accessible to and readily understood by the average college student. Indeed, the book is replete with compelling examples and suggested exercises that will be especially useful, I believe, to this level of reader.

It would not be a fair judgment, however, to suggest that the latter group is the exclusively appropriate audience for Levy's analysis. While his writing style is deceptively down-to-earth—even at times breezy—the central ideas examined are by and large profound ones, and they are engaged at an appropriately profound level. Accordingly, even "established" scholars will find much to ponder in this work, as did the present reviewer.

ROBERT C. CARSON
Professor of Psychology
Duke University

Preface

Man is only a reed, the weakest in nature, but he is a thinking reed.
—BLAISE PASCAL*

I think therefore I am. [Cogito ergo sum.]
—RENE DESCARTES**

Thinking—one of the most essential of all human characteristics. Thinking is an inexorable component of almost everything that we do. We use it to understand and control the world around us. It guides us in formulating problems and seeking solutions. It underlies our loftiest goals and our deepest fears. It is the very basis of learning and knowledge. It is fundamentally linked to language itself. In fact, it's nearly impossible to imagine any human experience that is completely void of the thinking process.

But do we ever *think* about *thinking?* Although we may focus on the content of our thoughts—that is, on *what* we think—what about the *way* we think? Or *how well* we think? Or *why* we think? In other words, how often do we subject our thinking process to critical analysis?

Educators rightfully profess that learning how to think is far more important than learning specific information, content, or facts. Throughout our schooling we are continually requested, urged, ordered, implored and harangued, coaxed and cajoled, begged and beseeched to "think critically." We are taught that critical thinking is one of the most vital and indispensable components of learning. Unfortunately, however, specific tools for critical thinking are rarely, if ever, provided to us. Thus, although we may be convinced of the value of critical thinking, we are left not knowing quite what to do about it.

Herein lies the impetus for this book, whose express purpose is to improve your thinking skills, to teach you to think critically, to help you think about thinking—in a word, to promote *metathinking*. Metathinking is not a magical, mystical, or mysterious abstraction. It is not an unattainable gift that is miraculously bestowed upon the intellectually elite. Rather, it is a *skill* (or more accurately, a series of skills) that can be successfully taught and learned. The thought principles, or *Metathoughts* (literally, "thoughts about thought") contained in this book are, in essence, cognitive tools that provide the user with specific strategies for inquiry and problem-solving. They serve, thereby, as potent antidotes to thinking that is prone to be simplistic, lethargic, myopic, biased, flawed, or otherwise just plain sloppy.

*1623–1662, *Pensées*: 200
**1596–1650, *Le Discours de la Method*, Pt. IV

For purposes of this book, each Metathought is illustrated primarily from the theory and application of contemporary social and clinical psychology.[1] Keep in mind, however, that these Metathought principles transcend the confines of any specific topic and can be utilized in a diverse array of fields, ranging from philosophy and theology to law, political science, history, sociology, anthropology, economics, journalism, business, medicine, biology, sports, the arts—in fact, in all areas of education and learning.

Acknowledgments

This book was over fifteen years in the making. It reflects a distillation and synthesis of my academic training in social psychology, my endeavors in conducting theoretical and empirical psychological research, my ventures in clinical psychology both as a therapist and a client in psychotherapy, my work as a clinical supervisor at a psychiatric hospital, my experiences teaching undergraduate and graduate psychology courses in the United States and the Soviet Union, as well as my observations of life around and within me.

Some of the ideas contained herein are centuries old, dating back to the ancient Greeks, whereas many are relatively new formulations. I am indebted to every person who has, wittingly or unwittingly, contributed to the creation, development, and illustrations of these Metathought principles. Consequently, I have made every effort throughout the book to give credit where credit is due by providing comprehensive reference citations for others' words, ideas, and research. In those instances in which I have inadvertently neglected to do so, or when I have been unable to locate a particular source, I offer in advance my apologies. For ethical reasons, in all clinical examples I have, of course, taken great care to protect the anonymity of any real persons (clients as well as therapists) involved.

I wish to take this opportunity to express my gratitude to my academic mentors at the University of California at Los Angeles for their guidance, insights, wisdom, and support. I am particularly grateful to Barry Collins, Shelley Taylor, Harold Kelley, Letitia Anne Peplau, Alex Caldwell, Bertram Raven, Christine Dunkel-Schetter, Harold Gerard, and James Coleman.

Although many authors have greatly influenced my thinking, those whose ideas I still find to be especially valuable include Thomas Szasz, R. D. Laing, Paul Meehl, Hans Eysenck, Viktor Frankl, Kurt Lewin, and Jay Haley (in my field), and Albert Einstein, Carl Sagan, Harry S Truman, and Blaise Pascal (from other fields of study and areas of life). Inspiration of a different kind was provided by the insights, humor, and wisdom of Matt Groening, Gary Larson, B. Kliban, Jules Feiffer, Jackie Mason, and "Vic."

I extend my thanks and appreciation to my esteemed colleagues, several of whom also happen to be my dearest friends, particularly Drew Erhardt

---

[1] See Epilogue for specific ideas and suggestions for students, instructors, clinicians, and researchers.

(*ontological chum extraordinaire*) and William M. Lamers. The same is true of some of my dearest friends, many of whom I wish were my colleagues, especially Vincent "Vinnie" DeStefano and Jonathan "J. P." Perpich. Thomas Greening, Elizabeth Loftus, Robert Carson, David Myers, Debora Carlin, Lynne Wetzell, Elizabeth Ann Snider, Mary J. Allen, Joseph Wolpe, Sandra Kaler, Charles Ramskov, Harold Chipman, and Eric Shiryaev also have my sincerest gratitude.

A special note of appreciation is due to Pepperdine University, an institution with which I am most proud to be affiliated and where I have consistently received the highest measure of academic freedom, respect, and courtesy. In particular, I want to thank Dean Nancy Magnusson Fagan and Associate Dean James Hedstrom for their years of encouragement and support. My gratitude goes not only to the administration and staff, but also to the truly remarkable faculty at Pepperdine's Graduate School of Education and Psychology and to my graduate students who have, over the years, supplied me with scores of fascinating examples and illustrations of these Metathoughts. In addition, Michele Nuzzo, Anre Venter, Parker Wilson, Stephen J. H. Kim, Rebecca Ishida, and Joe Lotta provided invaluable feedback and assistance on this project. I would also like to thank the therapy clients in my practice and at the hospital for teaching me more about the human experience than I ever thought possible.

I cannot imagine working with a finer, more dedicated, or more talented team of professionals. In particular, thank you to Laura Pearson and Alan Steinharter for the initial enthusiastic endorsements; to Bill Barke for your vote of confidence; to Sean Wakely for your input and guidance; to Joyce Nilsen for your magnificent and innovative marketing skills; to Marjorie Payne, Cynthia Newby, and Julia Penelope for your consummate professionalism and incredible attention to detail; to Suzanne Harbison for your creative contributions; to Erika Stuart for your diligence, kindness, and patience; and to Susan Badger for your extraordinary tenacity, honesty, insights, and wisdom.

My deepest appreciation goes to my immediate and extended family (especially my Mother and Father) and friends for their love, patience, and understanding, some of whom include (alphabetically): Marilee Bradford; Diana Brief; Dena Chertoff; Michael Christiansen; Lewis Colick; Kerry Hartjen; Rose Hasson; Terri Hayes-Clarke; Erin Holvey; the Levy family (Allegra, Carrie, Jacob, Leon, Lucy, LuJean, Rachel Rita, Robert, and Rosie); Anina Macchia; Brenda McKibben; Corrado Militi; J'Marie Moore; Steve Nevil; Dennis Palumbo; Nadine and Sterling Rachootin; Margot Ramirez; Bruce Shapiro; Colette Valette; and Anne Wharton. Although sheer numbers prevent me from listing everyone else by name, they all have my sincerest thanks.

I find myself virtually lost for words (a rare occurrence indeed) when it comes to expressing my heartfelt love, gratitude, and never-ending devotion to my wife, Beth. Suffice it to say, thank you Beth: "You're the One . . ."

DAVID A. LEVY

About the Author

Dr. David A. Levy has extensive experience as a teacher, psychotherapist, and researcher. He received his B.A. degree in theater arts at UCLA, an M.A. degree in psychology at Pepperdine University, a second M.A. degree in psychology at UCLA, and his Ph.D. in psychology at UCLA, where he specialized in social psychology, with minors in psychological assessment and personality psychology. He is an Associate Professor of Psychology at Pepperdine University, where he teaches graduate courses in Psychopathology, Theories of Personality, Clinical Practicum, and Marriage and Family Therapy. He served as a Visiting Professor of Psychology in the Soviet Union, where he delivered lectures and workshops in psychology and psychotherapy at Leningrad (now St. Petersburg) State University, the Leningrad Academy of Science, and the Bekhterev Psychoneurological Institute. He was honored as a Harriet and Charles Luckman Distinguished Teaching Fellow at Pepperdine, and was the recipient of the Shepard Ivory Franz Distinguished Teaching Award and Charles F. Scott Fellowship at UCLA.

Dr. Levy holds professional licenses both in psychology and in marriage, family, and child counseling. He conducts a private practice, supervises clinical interns, is certified in hypnotherapy, and works with the psychiatric population as a psychodrama consultant. He also served as the Executive Director of Crime Survivors Services, an agency which specializes in clinical work with victims of violent crimes. He utilizes his expertise in psychological testing (particularly the MMPI) in forensic settings, where he evaluates plaintiffs and provides legal testimony as an expert witness in cases involving allegations of emotional distress.

His numerous theoretical and empirical research studies have been published in scientific journals and presented at professional conferences. His areas of research focus include social cognition, interpersonal influence, psychopathology, and media psychology. His book, *Family Therapy: History, Theory, and Practice,* is the first complete textbook on family therapy available in Russian to clinicians, researchers and educators of that country. His *Levy Optimism-Pessimism Scale (LOPS)* has been translated into several foreign languages (including Russian, Slovak, Italian, Japanese, and Spanish) and has been utilized internationally in a wide variety of research contexts. He is also the author of numerous satirical articles, including "How to Be a Good Psychotherapy Patient," "Psychometric Infallibility Realized: The One-Size-Fits-All Psychological Profile," and "A Proposed Category for the Diagnostic and Statistical Manual of Mental Disorders (DSM): Pervasive Labeling Disorder."

Dr. Levy is a member of the Board of Editors for the *Journal of Humanistic Psychology,* he has served as a reviewer for the *Journal of Social Behavior and Personality,* he is a consultant for the Russian-American Center for International Education, and he is listed in *Who's Who in California* and in *International Leaders of Achievement.* He has appeared on over two dozen television and radio programs, where he was interviewed on his research findings, as well as on current issues, problems and trends in the fields of psychology and mental health.

P a r t **One**

*Conceptualizing
Phenomena*

$$Chapter \quad 1$$

I. The Evaluative Bias of Language: To Describe Is to Prescribe

Description is always from someone's point of view.
—RHODA KESLER UNGER*

Preferring a nonjudgmental term to a judgmental
one is itself a judgment.
—THOMAS SZASZ**

Language serves many functions. Certainly one of its most common and most important purposes is to help us *describe* various phenomena, such as events, situations, and people: "What is it?" Another purpose is to *evaluate* these same phenomena: "Is it good or bad?" Typically, we consider descriptions to be objective, whereas we consider evaluations to be subjective.

But is the distinction between objective description and subjective evaluation a clear one? The answer, in the vast majority of cases, is no. Why? Because words both describe *and* evaluate. Whenever we attempt to describe something or someone, the words we use are almost invariably value laden, in that they reflect our own personal likes and dislikes. Thus, our use of any particular term serves not only to describe, but also to *prescribe* what is desirable or undesirable to us.

*Unger, 1983
***The Therapeutic State*, 1984

This problem is not so prevalent in the physical sciences, as compared to the social sciences. Let's take, as an illustration, the terms *cold* and *hot*. In the field of physics, both terms refer, in a relatively neutral sense, to the rate of molecular vibrations (or temperature): "That liquid is very cold," or "That liquid is very hot." When we use these same terms to describe an *individual,* however, they take on a distinctly *evaluative* connotation: "That person is very cold," or "That person is very hot."

What are the consequences of the evaluative bias of language? The words that we use can, with or without our intent, become powerful instruments of change. In those instances where we are deliberately attempting to influence others to agree with our point of view, we intentionally select words that most persuasively communicate our values. In many cases, however, the process is tacit or unintentional. Our best attempts to remain neutral are constrained by the limits of language. When it comes to describing people it is nearly impossible to find words that are devoid of evaluative connotation. Incredible as it may seem, we simply don't have neutral adjectives to describe personality characteristics. And even if such words did exist, we still would be very likely to utilize the ones that reflect our own personal preferences.

The evaluative bias of language is illustrated in the following table and accompanying exercise. Let's say that two different observers (Person A and Person B), each with a different set of values, are asked to describe the same person or event. Notice how the words they use reveal to us their own points of view.

**TABLE 1-1   The Same Phenomenon as Described
from Two Different Perspectives**

Person A	Person B	Person A	Person B
pushy	assertive	oversensitive	vulnerable
greedy	ambitious	cowardly	self-protective
manipulative	persuasive	pushover	flexible
ruthless	driven	spineless	cooperative
stubborn	tenacious	immature	childlike
intrusive	concerned	naive	idealistic
exhibitionistic	outgoing	old	mature
reckless	brave	overly emotional	passionate
troublemaker	feisty	obsessed	committed
cheap	frugal	manic	enthusiastic
rigid	steadfast	weird	interesting
unfeeling	nerves-of-steel	wimpy	sweet

TABLE 1-1 *Continued*

Ready to try some on your own? Remember that you are to select words that best reveal Person B's personal attitudes and values, which are clearly and consistently more "positive" than Person A's. (Some suggestions appear in Appendix 2.)

Person A	Person B	Person A	Person B
obstacle	_____	rationalization	_____
problem	_____	resistance	_____
issue	_____	defense	
failure	_____	mechanism	_____
terrorist	_____	psychotherapy	_____
murder	_____	therapy patient	_____
handout	_____	psychiatric	
conformity	_____	institution	_____
hostage	_____	Dependent	
brainwashed	_____	Personality	
		Disorder	_____
perversion	_____	Avoidant	
slut	_____	Personality	
promiscuous	_____	Disorder	_____
idiot savant	_____	Paranoid	
retarded	_____	Personality	
developmentally	_____	Disorder	_____
disabled		Narcissistic	
		Personality	
anal retentive	_____	Disorder	_____
egocentricity	_____	Histrionic	
thought disordered	_____	Personality	
irresponsible	_____	Disorder	_____
psychotic	_____	Obsessive–Compulsive	
catatonic	_____	Personality	
codependent	_____	Disorder	_____

This Metathought also underscores the reciprocal influence of attitudes and language. That is, not only do our attitudes and perceptions affect our use of language, but our use of language in turn influences our attitudes and perceptions (see Metathought XI, Bi-Directional Causation).

Because of the evaluative bias of language, we must be careful both to become aware of our own personal values and to communicate these values as openly and fairly as possible. In other words, we should avoid presenting our value judgments as objective reflections of truth. It also should alert us to the value judgments inherent in *other* people's use of language, and that in many cases the words they use tell us at least as much about *them* as the events and individuals they are attempting to describe.

Glossary Terms

The following terms (or variations) are defined in the Glossary:

affect
attitude
bias
connotation
consequence
defense mechanism
description
disorder
evaluation
event
intentionality
judgment
neutral
objective
perception

personality
personality disorder
phenomenon
physical
prescription
psychosis
psychotherapy
rationalization
reciprocal
resistance
science
social
subjective
truth
value

C h a p t e r 2

II. *The Reification Error: Comparing Apples and Existentialism*

The world is a unity of the given and the constructed.
—*GEORG WILHELM FRIEDRICH HEGEL**

*It is difficult to determine what is "given"
and what are our "constructions."*
—*R. D. LAING***

*Mental illnesses do not exist; indeed, they cannot exist,
because the mind is not a body part or bodily organ.*
—*THOMAS SZASZ****

It is tempting but misleading to regard abstract concepts as if they were concrete objects. This error in thinking is called *reification*.[1] To reify is to invent a concept (or "construct"), give it a name, and then convince ourselves that such a thing objectively exists in the world.

As an example, consider the term "self-esteem." It is easy to forget that self-esteem isn't something that someone actually "has." Rather, it is nothing more than a concept which we have created to help us organize and make sense out of other people's (as well as our own) behavior. Unfortunately, however, many well-intentioned individuals persist in reifying this construct, for

---

*1770–1831
***The Politics of the Family*, 1969
****The Therapeutic State*, 1984

7

instance, by advising others, "You know what your problem is? You need to get a whole lot more self-esteem," (as if self-esteem were some kind of commodity that can be purchased at one's local hardware store!).

The litany of constructs that are commonly reified in the field of psychology is never-ending. To list but a few:

the mind	emotions
intelligence	complexes
motivation	archetypes
cognition	personality traits
personality	personality disorders
the unconscious	mental illnesses
the self	

In fact, the traditional usage of the term *mental* represents one of the most pervasive and chronic reification errors in the entire "mental health" (!) field. Remember that *mental* is a metaphorical construct, not an objective entity, like a tree or a stone. It is thus linguistically fallacious to pose the question, "Is the patient's problem *physical,* or is it *mental?*" To ask such a question is to compare a concrete thing to an abstract concept. The brain is a thing; the mind is a concept. Apples and oranges are things; existentialism is a concept. Thus, asking the question, "Is the patient's problem physical or mental?" is as senseless as comparing apples and existentialism.

Consider, as another illustration, Freud's depiction of the human psyche. In using the terms *id, ego,* and *superego,* Freud (1933/1964) did not mean to imply that these are concrete entities that have a specific location in the brain. Rather, they were Freud's shorthand way of designating various hypothetical personality processes. Freud *created* these constructs as "useful aids to understanding," which assisted him in depicting his view of how people work. In like fashion, the unconscious was not "discovered," it was *invented;* resistance was not "encountered," it was *conceived;* neuroses were not "detected," they were *declared.*

Exercise: Differentiating Events and Constructs

To give you some practice at honing your ability to differentiate concrete (observable) phenomena from abstract (hypothetical) phenomena, try the following exercise. For each pair of terms below, indicate which refers to a physical event (E) and which refers to a theoretical construct (C). (Answers appear in Appendix 2.)

humor: _____

laughter: _____

tearfulness: _____

sadness: _____

smiling: _____

happy: _____

nervous: _____

fidgety: _____

restless: _____

anxious: _____

energy: _____

activity: _____

talkative: _____

extraverted: _____

quiet: _____

introverted: _____

personality type: _____

blood type: _____

muscular strength: _____

ego strength: _____

disordered psyche: _____

disordered desk: _____

housing complex: _____

inferiority complex: _____

drunkenness: _____

alcoholism: _____

heartburn: _____

heartache: _____

rotten egg: _____

rotten attitude: _____

sea sickness: _____

love sickness: _____

broken dream: _____

broken nose: _____

lost toothbrush: _____

lost soul: _____

healthy outlook: _____

healthy spleen: _____

Ready for a few more?

free will: _____

motionless: _____

love: _____

disorganized: _____

heavy: _____

self-concept: _____

self-actualization: _____

deviant: _____

unseen: _____

hepatitis: _____

schizophrenia: _____

repression: _____

intuition: _____

suicide: _____

The Reification of Theory

We are also subject to committing errors of reification when it comes to creating, testing, and evaluating certain types of theories. Let us begin by defining some key terms. First, what is a theory? Briefly stated, a theory is a proposed explanation of observed phenomena. We may further differentiate two types of theory: *Event Theory* and *Construct Theory*.

Event (or "Type E") Theories provide explanations that lend themselves to direct measurement. Thus, given the proper circumstances, an Event Theory can be verified or proven. When this occurs, it is no longer a theory—it is a *fact*.

Event Theories seek to answer a wide variety of questions, ranging from the mundane to the profound. For example:

"Why does my car stall at stoplights?"
"What happened to the money in my desk drawer?"
"How did the patient acquire an infection?"
"Who is responsible for committing these serial murders?"
"How many assassins were involved in shooting President Kennedy?"
"Did human beings evolve from apes?"
"What caused dinosaurs to become extinct?"
"When did life first appear on earth?"

Under the assumption that there are actual, objective answers to all questions of this type, Event Theories are intended to ascertain these solutions, irrespective of whether or not we currently possess the methods to do so. In other words, Type E Theories are, *in principle*, confirmable.

Construct (or "Type C") Theories, by contrast, provide explanations that, by their very nature, are *not* directly measurable. As a consequence, even under ideal conditions, a Construct Theory can *never* be "proven." This is because the explanations are, in themselves, intangible abstractions.

Construct Theories abound in many areas of study. In the field of physics, for example, there are theories of gravitation, magnetism, electricity, sound, light, and energy. In psychology, we have theories that attempt to explain everything from cognition, emotion, memory, and perception to motivation, maturation, personality, and numerous forms of psychopathology, to name but a few.

In all of these instances, although the phenomena under investigation may be observable, their underlying explanations are not. An apple falling from a tree to the ground can be seen directly; "gravitation," however, cannot. Similarly, behavior can be directly measured; but "motivation," "personality," or "psychopathology" cannot.

Now, how do we go about evaluating a theory? The answer depends on the *type* of theory in question. Specifically, Event Theories should be evaluated in terms of their *accuracy*. In other words, they can be judged as true or false, right or wrong, correct or incorrect. This is because Type E Theories are, in principle, provable (and therefore refutable).

This is not the case, however, for Construct Theories, which are *never* capable of being proven directly. As such, it is pointless to subject a Construct Theory to the criterion of accuracy. How, then, are we to evaluate Construct Theories? Simply put, in terms of their *utility*. Is the theory *useful*, for example, in helping us to describe, predict, or control various phenomena? Is Einstein's theory of gravitation more *useful* than Newton's theory of gravitation in accounting for the motion of celestial bodies? Is one theory of psychopathology more *useful* than another in helping us to alleviate human suffering? To the extent that a Type C Theory is useful, it should be pursued, cultivated, and applied; to the extent that it is not useful, it should be revised, reworked or, if need be, discarded.

Why are these distinctions important? Because we create nothing but conceptual (not to mention methodological) havoc for ourselves when we confuse these two types of theory. In particular, we must be especially careful not to reify Construct Theories by treating them as if they were Event Theories. Whenever we naively set out to "prove" if a Type C Theory is true or false, our mission is doomed at the outset as we embark on a pointless journey through an impossible maze in the futile pursuit of an exit that does not exist, and encounter only one blind alley after the next. Why? Because the question we are asking is unanswerable; it is, in fact, quite meaningless.

For instance, because we can neither prove nor disprove directly the existence of the unconscious, it is inappropriate to ask whether Freudian theory is true or false. The same may be said of so-called "laws of nature." Gravity, for example, isn't an actual "law" that must be "obeyed" and never "violated." Rather, it is nothing more than a hypothetical model—a fiction—that various theorists, from Newton to Einstein, have created and re-created to assist them in explaining why every object in the universe appears to be attracted to every other object in the universe. Once again, the issue with Type C Theories isn't one of truth; rather, it is one of usefulness.

One very unfortunate consequence of this confusion is that the field of psychology is teeming with outdated and empirically unsupported theories that have long overstayed their welcome. Why do such theories persist? Perhaps the most important reason is that they have never been directly disproven, which some people mistakenly take as evidence of their veracity. Could it be that these theories are, in fact, true? Not once we realize that they are, by and large, Type C Theories and thus are not *capable* of being proven or disproven. In other words, "correctness" is an *inappropriate criterion* for evaluating these theories. They should be judged, instead, solely in terms of their usefulness (or lack thereof), an endeavor that is all too rare.

What is the lesson to be learned here? Don't make the mistake of reifying Construct Theories. Remember that Type C Theories are not objective facts "somewhere out there," just waiting to be stumbled upon. (Einstein did not *discover,* so much as he *invented,* "E = mc². ") Rather, they are human-made con-structions—fragile and imperfect—that represent our best attempts to explain the world around us.

Glossary Terms

The following terms (or variations) are defined in the Glossary:

abstract
assumption
attitude
behavior
category
chronic
cognition
concept
concrete
consequence
construct
Construct (Type C) Theory
criterion
description
disorder
emotion
empirical
evaluation
event
Event (Type E) Theory
existence
existentialism
explanation
extraversion
fact
fallacious
hypothetical
introversion

intuition
judgment
measurement
mental
mental illness
metaphor
mind
motivation
objective
perception
personality
personality disorder
personality trait
phenomena
physical
psyche
psychology
psychopathology
reification
repression
resistance
theoretical
theory
thinking
truth
unconscious
utility
veracity

Notes

[1] Gilbert Ryle, the British philosopher, referred to such errors as "category mistakes" (see Ryle, *The Concept of Mind,* 1949).

III. Multiple Levels of Description: The Simultaneity of Physical and Psychological Events

*Body and soul are not two different things, but only two differ-
ent ways of perceiving the same thing. Similarly, physics and
psychology are only different attempts to link our perceptions
together by way of systematic thought.*
—ALBERT EINSTEIN*

*Two errors: 1. to take everything literally,
2. to take everything spiritually.*
—BLAISE PASCAL**

What is the relationship between mind and body? Which comes first? Does
one cause the other? If so, which is the cause and which is the effect? Can one
exist without the other?

   These questions (and countless versions thereof) have plagued philosophers for centuries. More recently, social scientists have picked up the gaunt-

*1879–1955, quoted in Dukas & Hoffman, *Albert Einstein: The Human Side,* 1979
**1623–1662, *Pensées:* 252

let and grappled with new variations of this age-old theme by asking, "Are psychological events the cause or the effect of biological events?" More specifically, for example, does neurochemical activity (such as the release or inhibition of neurotransmitters) cause changes in psychological events (such as thoughts or feelings)? Or, conversely, do psychological events cause changes in neurochemical activity?

Perhaps nowhere is this debate better illustrated than in the clinical psychologist's primary diagnostic question, namely, "Is the patient's problem *physical* or *mental?*" As I pointed out in Metathought II (the Reification Error) this question is linguistically senseless because, in this context, *physical* and *mental* are noncomparable terms. It is, in other words, an error in reification to treat a theoretical construct (mental) as if it were a concrete event (physical).

An even more profound flaw, however, lies in the implication that mental events are somehow not physical. The artificial and fallacious dichotomy inherent in the "physical-or-mental" question does not take into account the principle of *multiple levels of description*.[1] By this I mean that any given event can be described at different levels of analysis. At one level, for example, events can be described in terms of physical phenomena. At another level, these same events can be described in terms of theoretical constructs.

The physical level of description refers to concrete events that are directly and objectively observable, quantifiable, or measurable.[2] With respect to human behavior, we have a multitude of terms that describe phenomena at the physical level of analysis, such as *biological, biochemical, physiological, anatomical, organic, neurological, neurochemical,* and *neurophysiological*.

By contrast, the construct level of description refers to abstract events that are *not* directly or objectively observable, quantifiable, or measurable. Rather, they involve *subjective* phenomena that are theoretical, conceptual, or metaphorical. In describing human behavior at this level of analysis, we typically use such terms as *psychological, perceptual, experiential, cognitive,* and *mental*.

What, then, is the relationship between these two levels of description? Does one cause the other? If so, which is the cause and which is the effect? Before we can address these questions, we first must take a step back and define some key terms and concepts.

In order to say that there is a cause and effect relationship between two events (let's call them Event A and Event B), two conditions must be satisfied, each of which is necessary and both of which are sufficient:

1. Event A must occur before Event B.
2. When Event A changes or is manipulated (like a switch being turned on), then Event B changes accordingly; similarly, when Event A stops changing or ceases to be manipulated (like a switch being turned off), then Event B changes accordingly.

Pay particular attention to the first condition, namely, the *temporal relationship* between the events. If Event A does not occur before Event B, then by definition A cannot cause B. Thus, if Event A occurs *after* Event B, then A does not cause B. Further, if Event A and Event B occur *simultaneously,* then A does not cause B (and, of course, B does not cause A). Again, if two events occur simultaneously, then they do not (in fact, they *cannot*) constitute a cause and effect relationship. For instance, if a biological event occurs simultaneously with a psychological event, then one does not cause the other; rather, they constitute a singular phenomenon, simply described at two different levels of analysis.

Let's take this a step further. Can a physical event occur in the absence of a psychological event? Of course. Even after death, biochemical activity exists in the deceased's body.

But is the converse also true? That is, can a psychological event occur in the absence of a physical event? This supposition is groundless. In fact, it is safe to assume that *every* mental event has some corresponding physical correlate. Thinking, happiness, and creativity, for example, are no more or less biochemical than delusions, depression, or schizophrenia. They are *all* reflected or "mapped" in some form physically, whether or not we know how to measure them. In other words, psychological and biological phenomena are linked, but not causally; rather, they occur *simultaneously* as one "psychobiological" event.

Keeping these ideas in mind, let us now return to the clinical question of determining whether a patient's problem is "physical or mental." The question rests on the assumption that disorders have causes that are *either* physical (biological, neurochemical, organic,) *or* mental (psychological, psychogenic, functional). Put another way, it assumes that physical and mental events are independent phenomena.

In one sense, the patient's problem is *always* physical, if one chooses to explain it at that level of description. In fact, the patient's problem *may* be *entirely* physical, since biological events can occur in the absence of psychological phenomena. However, if the patient's problem is mental, then by definition it is *also* physical, since all psychological events have biological correlates. Further, the patient's problem can *never* be *entirely* mental, since psychological phenomena cannot exist in the absence of biological activity. In sum, mental and physical phenomena are not independent events; rather, they are inexorably intertwined.

Where does this leave us? With a clinical pseudo-question that rests on faulty premises and that almost invariably results in misleading conclusions. Specifically, in the course of formulating a diagnosis, when clinicians are not able to locate any specific physical malfunction, they sometimes jump to the conclusion that, "Since the patient's problem isn't physical, it therefore must be mental." When we consider the simultaneity of psychological and physical phenomena, this is, as you can see, a senseless (and in fact, a patently absurd) deduction.

As an illustration of this Metathought, let us analyze the phenomenon of "anxiety" using this dual-level model of description (refer to Figure 3-1). At the biological level (B_1), anxiety involves specific neurochemical activity (namely, arousal of the sympathetic division of the autonomic nervous system along with other particular neurological configurations). *Concurrently,* at the psychological level (P_1), anxiety involves the subjective perception and experience of apprehension or fear. Thus, neurochemistry doesn't cause fear, and fear doesn't cause neurochemistry; they are *equivalent* and *simultaneous* phenomena, merely described in two different ways and at two different levels of analysis. (Put another way, B_1 doesn't cause P_1, and P_1 doesn't cause B_1; rather, they occur together as a singular P_1/B_1 event.) The same is true for *all* psychological phenomena, pathological or otherwise: the relationship between "physical" and "mental" is, by definition, not concretely causal but conceptually correlational.

To elaborate on this example, let's say that a person's anxiety (Event 1) causes him to want to feel better (Event 2). This event consists of the motivation to alleviate his emotional discomfort (P_2), which is accompanied by the biological correlate (or "map") of this psychological drive state (B_2). Event 2 then leads to Event 3, namely, the formulation of a plan of action for anxiety reduction (P_3); these cognitive strategies, again, coincide with (and are reflected in) particular neurochemical activity (B_3).

Now, let's postulate that the person decides to assuage his misery by taking an antianxiety medication. The outcome is Event 4, which consists of the occurrence of B_4 (activation of the parasympathetic division of the autonomic nervous system along with a new neurological configuration) and P_4 (subjective feelings of relief and relaxation).

Alternately, let's say that, rather than ingesting pills, the person opts to seek the assistance of a psychotherapist, who promptly offers soothing words of comfort and support. What is the outcome? Theoretically, Event 4 can be essentially *equivalent* to the one produced by taking tranquilizers. Thus, two different courses of action (tranquilizers or psychotherapy) may lead to the same (P_4/B_4) effect (see Metathought XIV, Multiple Pathways of Causation). Further, note that either course of action involves *both* biological *and* psychological phenomena. In this way, contrary to common intuition, psychotherapy is *no less biochemical* than medication.

To enhance and consolidate your understanding of these ideas—which can be somewhat elusive at first glance—try analyzing a different phenomenon (for instance, insomnia, anger, sexual arousal, depression, or any original example of your own choosing) using this dual-level model of description. You also may find it helpful to map out graphically the sequence, utilizing Figure 3-1 as a template.

Notice in the figure illustration how the causal sequences at each level of description run *parallel* to each other; the arrows do not cross diagonally between the two levels. In other words, if we choose to analyze a sequence of events purely at the conceptual level, we could say that one psychological

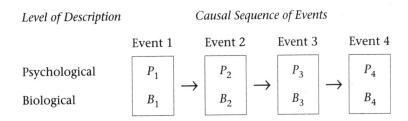

Level of Description   *Causal Sequence of Events*

(*Note:* P = Psychological; B = Biological.)

FIGURE 3-1   A Causal Sequence of Events Analyzed
at Dual Levels of Description

event causes another psychological event (for example, P_1 causes P_2). Similarly, if we were to analyze the same sequence solely at the physical level, we would not be mistaken in saying that one biological event causes another biological event (for example, B_1 causes B_2).

However, we must be careful not to confuse these two different levels of description. Specifically, psychological events do not, strictly speaking, cause biological events. Put another way, *a theoretical construct can't produce a physical symptom.* In like manner, biological events do not cause solely psychological events. In terms of the figure above, for example, P_1 does not cause B_2 nor does B_1 cause P_2. Once again, the key point is that psychological and biological events are linked, as a unit, in their simultaneous occurrence.

Why is all of this important? Because we must not allow ourselves to be seduced into believing that once we have located a biological *correlate* to a psychological event, we have therefore discovered its biological *cause* (see Metathought X, Correlation Does Not Prove Causation).[3] Even worse, we must not equate a biological *correlate* with a biological *disease*. To take an example, if we find neurological differences between those persons whom we diagnose as schizophrenic and those whom we consider normal, it should come as no great surprise. After all, we are also likely to discover neurological differences between those persons whom we call creative and those whom we do not. But what does this prove? Only that we've located the biological correlates for different types of psychological processes. However, this criterion alone doesn't prove that schizophrenia is a medical disease any more than it proves that creativity is not. Even if we were to find the physical correlates to *every* psychological phenomenon, it still leaves us with the formidable and complex task of defining and differentiating illness from health (see Wakefield, 1992, for the one such attempt). In other words, evidence of physical *difference* is not, *per se,* scientifically valid proof of medical *disease.*

All things considered, it isn't surprising that the "physical or mental?" question has not yet been answered. What's surprising is that it's still being *asked.*

Glossary Terms

The following terms (or variations) are defined in the Glossary:

abstract	fallacious
assumption	intuition
attitude	measure
behavior	mental
belief	metaphor
causal	mind
cause	motivation
clinical	normal
cognitive	objective
concept	pathological
concrete	perception
construct	*per se*
correlate	phenomenon
correlation	physical
criterion	premise
deduction	psychological
delusion	psychotherapy
description	quantify
diagnosis	reification
dichotomous variable	scientific
disease	social
disorder	subjective
effect	symptom
event	temporal
experience	theoretical
explanation	thinking

Notes

[1] Portions of this Metathought originally appeared in my essay, "Is the Remedicalization of Psychiatry Good for the Mental Health Field? No." (Levy, 1994), published in *Controversial Issues in Mental Health*.

[2] In stating that physical events are measurable, I am referring to all phenomena that, by definition, lend themselves to the possibility of direct measurement, irrespective of our actual ability to do so. In other words, the property of "measurability" should not be determined by the current (or even future) limits of our technology, instrumentation, or resources. By contrast, theoretical constructs (such as thoughts, attitudes, or philosophies) are, by definition, *never* capable of being measured directly.

[3] For an examination and integrative analysis of some of the principles discussed in this Metathought, see Cacioppo and Berntson's (1992) article, "Social Psychological Contributions to the Decade of the Brain: Doctrine of Multilevel Analysis."

IV. The Nominal Fallacy and Tautologous Reasoning: To Name Something Isn't to Explain It

Just because your doctor has a name for your condition doesn't mean he knows what it is.
—ARTHUR BLOCH*

There must be something the matter with him
because he would not be acting as he does
unless there was
therefore he is acting as he is
because there is something the matter with him
—R. D. LAING**

The Nominal Fallacy

Words are so important to us that if we can find, formulate, or invent a special *name* for something, we easily fool ourselves into believing that we have *explained* it. This error is called the *Nominal Fallacy*. Given that descriptive labels are an essential component both of science and of everyday life, we need

*Murphy's Law, Book Two, 1980
**Knots, 1970

to be aware that *naming* any particular behavior (such as with a diagnostic label) does not, therefore, *explain* the behavior. Here are some examples of the Nominal Fallacy in action:

> "Why does she have difficulty falling or staying asleep?"
> "Because she's got *Insomnia.*"

> "Why is that boy chronically disobedient toward authority figures?"
> "Because he's got *Oppositional Defiant Disorder.*"

> "Why does the patient have a persistent, irrational fear of heights?"
> "Because she's got *Acrophobia.*"

> "Why is she completely preoccupied with the unfounded fear that she has a serious disease?"
> "Because she's got *Hypochondriasis.*"

> "Why does that man get sexually aroused by rubbing up against nonconsenting people?"
> "Because he's got *Frotteurism.*"

Tautologous Reasoning

The Nominal Fallacy typically involves circular or tautological reasoning. A *tautology* is the needless repetition of an idea, statement, or word, wherein the phenomenon is true by virtue of its logical form alone. Put another way, it is circular reasoning in which one conclusion rests upon another, which in turn refers back to the first. Thus, a tautology can never be falsified.

For example: "People who hit others are aggressive; therefore, people who are aggressive hit others," or "People who display gross impairment in reality testing are psychotic; therefore, people who are psychotic display gross impairment in reality testing."

Here are some other illustrations of tautologous reasoning:

> "Why is that guy so sociable?"
> "Because he's an extravert."
> "How do you know that he's an extravert?"
> "Well, can't you see how sociable he is?"

> "Why is she completely suspicious of everybody's motives?"
> "Because she's got Paranoid Personality Disorder."
> "How do you know that she's got Paranoid Personality Disorder?"
> "By the fact that she's so suspicious of everybody's motives."

> "Why did the defendant do what he did?"
> "Because he is insane."
> "How do you know that he's insane?"
> "Because only an insane person would do what he did!"

These kinds of circular explanations are, of course, no explanations at all. It's like "explaining" a bright child's low grades by declaring that he or she is an "underachiever." Similarly, a diagnosis of Depression does not explain profound sadness; a diagnosis of Alcohol Dependence does not explain drinking problems; a diagnosis of Schizophrenia does not explain delusions and hallucinations; a diagnosis of Narcissistic Personality Disorder does not explain extreme grandiosity; and a diagnosis of Borderline Personality Disorder does not explain someone's severe problems in their interpersonal relationships.

As an exercise, try your hand at completing the following tautological dialogues:

"Why does she firmly cling to her false beliefs, despite obvious evidence to the contrary?"
"Because she's got Delusional Disorder."
"How do you know that she's got Delusional Disorder?"
"_____."

"Why does that man persistently have an absence of any sexual drive?"
"Because he's got Hypoactive Sexual Desire Disorder."
"How do you know that he's got Hypoactive Sexual Desire Disorder?"
"_____."

"Why does that woman have difficulties in achieving a sexual climax?"
"Because she has Inhibited Female Orgasm Disorder."
"How do you know that she has Inhibited Female Orgasm Disorder?"
"_____."

"Why is he intentionally producing symptoms for the sole purpose of assuming the patient role?"
"Because he's got Factitious Disorder."
"_____?"
"_____."

"Why does the patient have a persistent, irrational fear of train travel?"
"Because she's got Siderodromophobia."
"_____?"
"_____."

"Why does the patient have a persistent, irrational fear of the number 13?"
"Because he's got Triskaidekaphobia."
"_____?"
"_____."

For a final illustration of this Metathought, do your best to navigate through the mind-bending tautologies in the following "Catch 22"-like discourse:

The man who has just been found guilty of first-degree murder is asking for the death penalty. He must be crazy, therefore, since only someone who is crazy would ask for the death penalty. We don't administer the death penalty to people who are crazy. Therefore, since he asked to be executed, we cannot have him executed. If, on the other hand, he had asked not to receive the death penalty, then we could give him the death penalty, since we only execute people who aren't crazy, and anybody who doesn't want to be executed obviously isn't crazy. Thus, if he requests the death penalty, that proves he's crazy, so we can't sentence him to death (since people who request the death penalty are crazy, and we do not give the death penalty to people who are crazy). But if he requests not to have the death penalty, that proves he isn't crazy, so we can sentence him to death (since people who request not to have the death penalty aren't crazy, and we do give the death penalty to people who are not crazy). In conclusion, if he's not crazy, then we can execute him; but if he is crazy, then we cannot execute him. Therefore, if he wants to be executed, he should say that he doesn't want to be executed; then we can sentence him to death. But if he doesn't want to be executed, he should say that he does want to be executed; then we cannot sentence him to death.

In summary, be sure not to confuse a name with an explanation. Remember that labeling something does not, *per se*, explain it. Finally, learn to recognize tautologous reasoning. Remind yourself that although tautologies may have the appearance of being logical, they are, in fact, a completely invalid method of proof.

Glossary Terms

The following terms (or variations) are defined in the Glossary:

behavior	interpersonal
belief	motive
chronic	Nominal Fallacy
delusion	*per se*
description	personality disorder
diagnosis	phenomenon
disease	psychotic
disorder	reasoning
explanation	science
extraversion	symptom
fallacy	tautologous (tautological)
intentionality	reasoning

V. *Differentiating Dichotomous Variables and Continuous Variables: Black and White, or Shades of Grey?*

In approaching the subject of mental disorder, I must empha-size that, in my view, persons showing mental disorder do not manifest anything specifically different in kind from what is manifested by practically all human beings.
—*HARRY STACK SULLIVAN**

Sanity is a matter of degree.
—*ALDOUS HUXLEY***

Some phenomena in the world may be divided (or *bifurcated*) into two mutu-ally exclusive or contradictory categories. These types of phenomena are *dichotomous variables*. For example, when you flip a coin, it must turn up either heads or tails—there is no middle ground. Similarly, a woman cannot be "a lit-tle bit," "somewhat," or "moderately" pregnant—she is either pregnant or not pregnant. Here are some other examples:

A light switch is either on or off.
A toilet is either flushed or not flushed.

**Clinical Studies in Psychiatry,* 1956
**1894–1963, quoted in Rowes, *The Book of Quotes,* 1979

A golf ball either ends up in the hole or it doesn't.
A neuron either fires or does not fire (the *all-or-none principle*).
A person is either male or female (with some rare exceptions).

Other phenomena, by contrast, consist of a theoretically infinite number of points lying between two polar opposites. These types of phenomena are *continuous variables*. For example, between the extremes of black and white there exists a middle ground consisting of innumerable shades of grey. Consider also the measurement of distance, weight, volume, motion, or temperature. In these cases, the results may fall at any point along a range, spectrum, or dimension, and are expressed in terms of quantity, magnitude, or degree.

The problem is that we often confuse these two types of variables. Specifically, we have a natural tendency to dichotomize variables that, more accurately, should be conceptualized as continuous. In particular, most person-related phenomena (especially psychological constructs) are frequently presumed to fit into one of two discrete types (*either* category A *or* category B), rather than as lying along a continuum. In the vast majority of cases, however, continuous variables are more accurate (and therefore more useful) representations of the phenomena we are attempting to describe and explain.[1]

What are some examples of continuous psychological variables that frequently are assumed to be, or treated as if they were, dichotomous?

normal–abnormal
mental health–mental illness[2]
introvert–extravert
autonomous–dependent
trust–mistrust
functional–dysfunctional
adaptive–maladaptive
therapeutic success–therapeutic failure
scientifically useful–scientifically not useful

The following exercise will give you some hands-on practice at differentiating dichotomous and continuous phenomena. For each of the terms below, indicate those that refer to dichotomous phenomena (D) and those that refer to continuous phenomena (C). (Answers appear in Appendix 2.)

conscious–unconscious: _____
feminine–masculine: _____
gun fired–not fired: _____
optimist–pessimist: _____
married–single: _____

present–absent: ____
emotionally secure–emotionally insecure: ____
published–not published: ____
airborne–grounded: ____
day–night: ____
good mood–bad mood: ____
licensed–unlicensed: ____
honest–dishonest: ____
morning person–evening person: ____
neurotic–nonneurotic: ____
mailed–unmailed: ____
subjective–objective: ____
alcoholic beverage–nonalcoholic beverage: ____
successful basketball shot–unsuccessful shot: ____
psychological trait–psychological state: ____
tenured–untenured: ____
"Type A" personality–"Type B" personality: ____
guilty verdict–not guilty verdict: ____
power on–power off: ____
addicted–not addicted: ____
therapeutic–nontherapeutic: ____

Theoretical and Clinical Applications

In terms of psychological theory, the process of false dichotomization is illustrated in the ego defense mechanism of *splitting*. In explaining early childhood development, some neo-Freudians (e.g., Klein, 1937; Mahler, Pine, & Bergman, 1975) have theorized that the child both wishes for, yet is hostile and fearful toward, the maternal object. According to these theorists, the child attempts to resolve this conflict by categorizing or "splitting" the world into good versus bad components by treating them in an all-or-none fashion. Adults, too, may manifest this same defense mechanism, which these theorists interpret as representing fixation at a more primitive level of psychological development.

This Metathought also has applications to the practice of psychotherapy. An important goal of cognitive therapy approaches, for instance, is to help clients modify their "black-or-white" thinking into seeing more "shades of grey" (see Ellis, 1984; Ellis & Bernard, 1985). A person with an eating disorder, for example, may be encouraged to recognize and to moderate such dichotomous thinking patterns as "fat *or* thin," "perfect *or* imperfect," and "mature *or* immature." By learning to view their life situation in less absolute (and therefore more realistic) terms, clients can presumably gain a greater sense of acceptance, flexibility, and control over their lives.

Glossary Terms

The following terms (or variations) are defined in the Glossary:

bifurcate	measurement
category	mental
clinical	mood
cognitive	neurotic
cognitive therapy	normal
cognitive–behavioral therapy	objective
conscious	personality
construct	phenomena
continuous variable	psychological
description	psychotherapy
dichotomous variable	scientific
dimension	splitting
disorder	subjective
dysfunction	theoretical
e.g.	theory
ego defense mechanism	thinking
explanation	trait
extraversion	unconscious
interpretation	variable
introversion	

Notes

[1] This principle is discussed in depth by the eminent social psychologist Kurt Lewin in his article, "The Conflict Between Aristotelian and Galileian Modes of Thought in Contemporary Psychology" (1931). Lewin's article is noteworthy in that it also pertains to several other Metathoughts, in particular the Belief Perseverance Effect (Metathought XXV), Deductive and Inductive Reasoning (Metathought XX), and the Nominal Fallacy and Tautologous Reasoning (Metathought IV). Lewin's essay serves as a foundation for Robert Carson's superb commentary and critical analysis of contemporary approaches to conceptualizing psychopathology, "Aristotle, Galileo, and the *DSM* Taxonomy: The Case of Schizophrenia" (in press). This Metathought is related as well to some of the ideas expressed in Bart Kosko's book, *Fuzzy Thinking: The New Science of Fuzzy Logic* (1993).

[2] This Metathought is directly relevant to the ongoing debate between *categorical* versus *dimensional* approaches to clinical assessment and diagnosis.

Chapter *6*

===============

VI. *Consider the Opposite: To Contrast Is to Define*

There can be no reality without polarity.
—CARL G. JUNG*

A great truth is one whose opposite is also true.
—NIELS BOHR**

The lady doth protest too much, methinks.
—WILLIAM SHAKESPEARE***

In order to define or understand any given phenomenon, its theoretical opposite also should, whenever possible, be addressed and explored. How can we possibly define the concept of "mental illness," for example, without also addressing what we mean by "mental health"? How can we define introversion in the absence of defining extraversion? Can we ever truly understand conformity without also understanding dissent? This same principle holds true for scores of other psychological opposites: depression and happiness, optimism and pessimism, intelligence and stupidity, selfishness and altruism, responsibility and irresponsibility, infidelity and faithfulness, adaptive and maladaptive, functional and dysfunctional.

As these examples illustrate, to contrast a phenomenon with its polar opposite is to give definition to both terms. Just as thesis and antithesis can't be understood in isolation from each other, all polar opposites are dependent upon each other for their very conceptual existence. What, for instance, is the meaning of feminine without masculine? Unconscious without conscious?

*1875–1961, *Aion: Researches into the Phenomenology of the Self*, 1951/1959
**1885–1962, physicist and creator of quantum theory
***Hamlet*, Act III, Scene 2

Exciting without dull? Pain without pleasure? Dark without light? Order without chaos? Simple without complex? Empty without full? Strong without weak? Active without passive? Good without bad? Without one, conceptually speaking, its opposite ceases to exist.

The concept of polar opposites in the human condition is a theme that runs throughout the writings of the Swiss psychiatrist Carl G. Jung. According to Jung, within every personality there is a multiplicity of conflicting, sometimes complementary, but usually opposing forces. Jung (1921/1971) utilized the term *enantiodromia* (taken from the fifth century Greek philosopher, Heraclitus) to refer to these polar opposites. Jung (1943/1953; 1951/1959) believed that the failure to recognize the opposite tendencies within ourselves leads inevitably to the feeling of being torn apart; thus to live a whole and healthy life, we must learn to accept and integrate our inherent enantiodromia.

The historical development of psychological theory and research on attitude change provides a very interesting illustration of this Metathought. Beginning in the 1940s, and subsequently for many years, the predominant theme in social psychology was, "How can we cause attitude change?" In the late 1950s, William McGuire shed a different light on this problem and inspired a new direction in thinking simply by posing the opposite question: "How can we *resist* attitude change?" This led McGuire to develop his *inoculation theory* of attitude change, which essentially proposed that people are more resistant to the effects of persuasive communications after having been exposed to weak counterarguments (see McGuire & Papageorgis, 1961). Had McGuire not bothered to "consider the opposite," his innovative insights and important contributions might never have been realized.

Sigmund Freud most certainly considered the opposite when he conceptualized the ego defense mechanism of *reaction formation,* which involves the unconscious transformation of unacceptable impulses into their opposite, and thus more acceptable, forms (A. Freud, 1936). For instance, a mother who unconsciously harbors aggressive feelings toward her son may become excessively concerned for his welfare and safety. Or, a man who appears to be vehemently anti-pornography may be unconsciously motivated by the very sexual desires against which he is publicly crusading. In like manner, a person who fervently professes an ardent aversion to homosexuality may be using this attitude as a barrier against his or her own unconscious homosexual desires.

Considering the opposite also has a number of useful applications in the clinical setting. In particular, many techniques in Gestalt therapy (Perls, 1969) are designed to help clients confront (and thereby integrate) their inner opposites or polarities. For instance, if a psychotherapy client feels torn between his desire for change versus his fear of change, the Gestalt therapist might ask him to role play a dialogue between these opposing sets of feelings. When faced with a client who protests ("...too much, methinks") that she has no need whatsoever for an intimate relationship, the therapist may gently ask her to explore the part of herself that might, in fact, have such a need. Similarly, a client who adamantly professes nothing but disdain for his mother may be encouraged to examine what he likes about his mother. In these cases (and countless more), taking a few moments to consider the opposite frequently leads to very important therapeutic discoveries.

A fascinating illustration of this Metathought is the clinical technique of *prescribing the symptom* or *paradoxical intention* (see Frankl, 1959; Haley, 1976), in which a therapist gives the client a directive that he or she actually wants *resisted;* the resulting change takes place as a consequence of the client defying the therapist. This technique is utilized to undermine clients' resistance to change by, paradoxically, instructing them *not* to change, or even to deliberately engage in the unwanted or undesirable behaviors. In effect, the therapist's directives are precisely the opposite of the desired goal. For instance, a paranoid patient might be urged to become even *more* suspicious. Or, a married couple entering therapy with the complaint that they fight too much may be directed to go home and argue for three hours, twice daily, for one week. Similarly, a client who is afraid of being alone may be instructed for the next two weeks not to spend *any* time alone.

To take another example, how might we caution a person of things to *avoid* as a patient in psychotherapy? Utilizing this technique, we might prescribe the exact opposite behavior by imparting the following (paradoxical) instructions:

BOX 6-1

<u>How to Be a Good Psychotherapy Patient</u>[1]

There is a multitude of books and articles devoted to teaching people how to become effective psychotherapists. However, there is a dearth of literature on how to become good psychotherapy patients. The purpose of this essay is to offer you some practical guidelines, suggestions, and techniques that can help you to make the most out of your psychotherapy experience.

<u>Conducting Yourself in the Psychotherapy Session:</u>
<u>Twenty Easy "Dos" and "Don'ts"</u>

By far, the most challenging (and yet potentially the most entertaining) aspect of being a psychotherapy patient concerns your relationship with your psychotherapist. It is crucial, from the opening moments of that first phone call, that you get your therapist to like you, to become dependent on you, and to become convinced that only he has the power to cure you. While your therapist is busy delving deep into the inner recesses of your psyche, just follow these twenty easy-to-learn techniques and in virtually no time at all, you'll have him or her eating out of the palm of your hand.

continued

BOX 6-1   *Continued*

1. *Do* attribute all of your successes to your therapist, and all failures to yourself.
2. *Do* gaze reverently into your therapist's eyes as he pontificates about the nature of the human condition.
3. *Do* occasionally confuse something that your therapist said with something that Freud said.
4. *Do* complain about insensitive and judgmental parents, teachers, and, especially, prior psychotherapists.
5. *Do* apologize profusely to your therapist for not showing faster improvement.
6. *Do* casually inform your therapist that you're due to come into large sums of money in the near future.
7. *Do,* at random moments, say to your therapist, "You *really care* about me, don't you?"
8. *Do* tell your therapist that you passed up a week in Tahiti, just so you wouldn't have to miss your therapy session.
9. *Do* tell your therapist that when you win the Nobel Prize, you will announce to the world that you owe it all to him.
10. *Do* tell your therapist that you're totally committed to sticking with therapy—even if it takes fifty years.
11. *Don't* point out that your therapist constantly contradicts himself.
12. *Don't* embarrass your therapist by waking him up when he dozes off in the middle of your session.
13. *Don't* tell your therapist that his mind is obviously on everything else in the world, other than what you're saying.
14. *Don't* tell your therapist that his interpretations of your dreams are about as helpful as last year's horoscope.
15. *Don't* say to your therapist, "So, tell me something I *didn't* know."
16. *Don't* say to your therapist, "For *this,* I'm paying you money?"
17. *Don't* say to your therapist, "At least a plumber guarantees *his* work!"
18. *Don't* say to your therapist, "What's the matter? Not smart enough to get into law school?"
19. *Don't* say to your therapist, "Is doing therapy the *only way* you can get your intimacy needs met?"
20. *Don't ever* say to your therapist, "But what should I *do* about my problem?"

<u>Secondary Gains and Fringe Benefits:</u>
<u>Getting the Maximum Mileage from Being a Psychotherapy Patient</u>

Irrespective of what actually happens (or doesn't happen) in the course of psychotherapy, the very fact of being a psychotherapy patient can proffer you powerful leverage in all of your interpersonal relationships. Here are four easy pointers:

1. <u>Hide Behind Diagnostic Labels.</u>
     You can deftly absolve yourself of all personal responsibility for your annoying habits and obnoxious behavior by cloaking yourself in psychological diagnoses. For example, if someone is, in any way, critical of something you've done, just retort: "Hey, what do you *expect* from me? I'm a passive-dependent personality type with low-grade, uncrystallized borderline personality features!"

VI. Consider the Opposite

2. <u>Use Therapy against Your Mate</u>.

Having an argument with your mate? No problem! Regardless of the content of the argument, you're sure to render your opponent powerless by smugly delivering the line: "Well, at least *I'm* in therapy. What are *you* doing to help this relationship?"

3. <u>Get Back at Your Parents</u>.

When your parents ask you why you're in therapy, you have your choice of two very powerful strategies, either of which is guaranteed to leave them speechless and riddled with feelings of guilt and self-doubt.

a) <u>The Passive–Aggressive Maneuver</u>:

To execute this maneuver, simply follow this prescribed sequence: (1) Look confused and disappointed; (2) Emit a mildly exasperated, "some-people-never-learn" sigh; (3) Walk away, slowly shaking your head and muttering under your breath.

b) <u>The Direct Frontal Attack</u>:

For this tactic, just look them both straight in the eyes and shout with great vehemence, "*I'll give you two guesses!*"

4. <u>Impress Your Friends</u>.

When in the company of your friends, make a habit of using psychological terms that you've picked up in your psychotherapy sessions and from watching television shows. Show them how deep you are by talking glibly about faulty introjects, repressed libido, inflated personas, irrational belief systems, incomplete gestalts, maladaptive learning patterns, ontological insecurity, dysfunctional family systems, your critical "inner-parent," your battered "inner-child," and your obnoxious "inner-aunt." Occasionally, squint your eyes, tilt your head, and ask people, "Don't you think you're projecting?"

<u>A Final Word</u>

Remember that it's *not easy* to become a good psychotherapy patient. Millions of people never learn. But, *don't get discouraged!* Trust that *you can do it!* Make these strategies a part of your life, and you're well on the way to complete recovery and true mental health.

Exercise: Toward the Resolution of Interpersonal Conflict

In the broader social context, the principle of considering the opposite can be utilized to increase one's understanding of—and empathy for—other people's point of view. As an exercise, select three specific issues (whether political, ethical, moral, legal, cultural, professional, familial, or intimate) about which you feel particularly strong. Now, for each issue, take the perspective of someone with the *opposite* attitude or opinion, and write out, as persuasively as you can *from their vantage point,* the reasons, arguments, and feelings pertaining to their position.

Issue #1:_____

Your attitude: _____

Opposite perspective: _____

_____

_____

_____

_____

_____

_____

Issue #2: _____
Your attitude: _____
Opposite perspective: _____

_____

_____

_____

_____

_____

_____

Issue #3: _____
Your attitude: _____
Opposite perspective: _____

_____

_____

_____

_____

_____

_____

In reflecting on your responses to this exercise, briefly enumerate the potential value(s) of viewing these issues from opposing perspectives.

_____

_____

_____

_____

_____

Last, identify some particular instances or situations in which utilizing this method of considering the opposite may contribute to the successful resolution of interpersonal conflict.

_____

_____

_____

_____

_____

Glossary Terms

The following terms (or variations) are defined in the Glossary:

attitude
attribution
behavior
belief
cause
clinical
concept
conscious
consequence
diagnosis
dysfunction
effect
ego defense mechanism
ethics
existence
experience
extraversion
Gestalt therapy
insight
interpersonal
interpretation
introversion
mental
ontological

opinion
paradox
paradoxical intention
personality
phenomenon
prescription
projection
psyche
psychological
psychology
psychotherapy
reaction formation
repression
resistance
social
subsequent
symptom
theoretical
theory
thinking
truth
unconscious
value

Notes

[1] This essay originally appeared in the *Journal of Polymorphous Perversity* (Levy, 1991). (Yes, this journal actually *does* exist.)

VII. The Similarity-Uniqueness Paradox: All Phenomena Are Both Similar and Different

The more things change, the more they remain the same.
—ALPHONSE KARR*

There is no new thing under the sun.
—[THE] BIBLE**

You can't step twice into the same river.
—HERACLITUS***

By way of introducing this Metathought, let's examine the following problem: Which of the following four words does not belong with the other three?

A. knee
B. eye
C. mind
D. rock

The correct answer to this question is *C*, because *mind* is the only term that represents a theoretical construct, rather than a physical object.

---

*1808–1890, *Les Guepes;* cited in *The New International Dictionary of Quotations*, Miner & Rawson, 1994
**Ecclesiastes 1:9
***c.540–c.480 B. C., *On the Universe;* cited in *The New International Dictionary of Quotations*, Miner & Rawson, 1994

But, wait...the correct answer is *D,* because *rock* is the only term not related to a living organism.

Then again, the correct answer is *B,* because *eye* is the only word that isn't comprised of four letters.

Is that it? Not quite. The correct answer is *A,* because *knee* is the only word that contains a silent letter.

So, which is it? Can it be that all four answers are correct? If so, how can every term be both similar to and different from the others?

The solution to this apparent paradox lies in the cognitive schema or perceptual set with which one initially approaches the problem (see Metathought XXIII, the Assimilation Bias). More specifically, it is a function of the particular dimensions or variables on which one has elected to evaluate the response options.

For example, if you were "on the lookout" for grammatical phenomena, you would process the information in a manner that leads you to notice things like spelling, parts of speech, verb tense, abbreviations, the number and arrangement of letters, and even the presence of silent letters. By contrast, if you were to examine the same question with a mindset for semantical phenomena, you would be paying attention to definitions, synonyms, antonyms, and homonyms; you may attempt to group the terms into conceptually useful categories; and you might recognize and distinguish metaphorical versus literal word meanings.

Thus, as you can see, determining the similarities and differences between any set of events depends almost entirely on the perspectives from which you choose to view them. In this way, phenomena can be seen as both unique from and, at the same time, similar to other phenomena.

Keeping these principles in mind, let's try another problem:

A. heroin
B. cocaine
C. amphetamines
D. caffeine

Now, if you were to approach this question with an interest in identifying chemical substances that are likely to boost your energy level, the correct answer would be *A.* This is because heroin, in contrast to the other three drugs, is not a central nervous system stimulant.

If, on the other hand, you were to look at the same four choices but this time with legal issues foremost in your mind, the correct answer would be *D* (caffeine), because the other three drugs are either completely illegal, or are illegal as to their purchase, distribution, and usage without proper authorization.

Third, suppose that you are attempting to categorize substances in terms of their currently sanctioned, legitimate medical usage. Here, the correct answer would be *C*, because, of the four drugs, only amphetamines are commonly prescribed by doctors (typically for Attention–Deficit/Hyperactivity Disorder, weight reduction, and occasionally for depression).

Finally, let's say that you are conducting research into the derivation of product names given to popular soft drinks. From this vantage point, the correct answer is *B*, because cocaine ("coke") was originally an ingredient in one of the world's most famous sodas, Coca-Cola ("Coke"). (And no other term appearing on this list can boast of such a claim!)

Let's take a step back now and examine in greater detail the interlocking processes of comparing and contrasting phenomena. First, how do we determine the degree to which phenomena are similar? To begin with, any two phenomena in the cosmos share at least one fundamental commonality: namely, they are both phenomena. With this as a starting point, they may subsequently be compared along a virtually infinite array of dimensions or "sorting variables," ranging from the broadest of universal properties to the minutest of mundane details.

For instance, are the phenomena in question observable ("physical") or theoretical ("conceptual")? If theoretical, in which conceptual domain? If observable, of what chemical or molecular composition? Are the phenomena living or nonliving? Terrestrial or extraterrestrial? If living on earth, which phylum? Genus? Species? Sex? If human, what are the physical features (height, weight, hair and eye color, health, strength, attractiveness)? Demographic characteristics (age, race, nationality, culture, religion, income, occupation)? Social context (competitive, cooperative, structured, restrictive, supportive)? Personality attributes (intelligence, behavioral patterns, maturity, psychological problems, coping skills, cognitive and attributional style, creativity, motivation, insight, awareness, values, beliefs, attitudes, goals, interests, preferences in art, music, food, and wallpaper)?

When comparing any two phenomena on these (and a multitude of other) dimensions, initially they will "match" with respect to their mutual similarities. But no matter how many features they might share in common, there is no escaping the inevitable fact that at some point there will be a conceptual fork (or *bifurcation*) in the road, where the phenomena will differ. We may refer to this juncture as the *point of critical distinction* (PCD), before which the phenomena are similar, and after which they are different.

Clearly, then, when we are attempting to define, compare, and contrast any two phenomena, it is imperative that we identify and examine the PCDs which are relevant to the particular events under scrutiny. If, for instance, we are interested in exploring the *similarities* between the events, we should examine the variables that appear *before* the PCD; if, by contrast, we wish to analyze the *differences* between the same two events, we should focus on the variables that appear *at and after* the PCD. (Of course, to gain a full and comprehensive understanding of their relationship, we should examine the variables that appear *both before and after* the PCD, with particular attention to the PCD itself.)

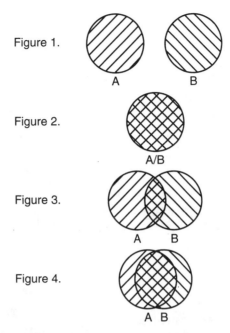

Figure 1.

Figure 2.

Figure 3.

Figure 4.

FIGURE 7-1   Four Relationships between Phenomena A and B

*Figure 1) Two different phenomena with absolutely nothing in common.

*Figure 2) Two different phenomena that are completely identical.

Figure 3) Two different phenomena with very little in common (that is, a low similarity-to-difference ratio).

Figure 4) Two different phenomena with a great deal in common (that is, a high similarity-to-difference ratio).

(*Note that Examples 1 and 2 cannot, by definition, actually occur.)

Some examples of these relationships are depicted in the Venn diagrams above. In interpreting these figures, note that overlapping areas indicate commonality between the two phenomena. Thus, a relatively large area of overlap indicates a high similarity-to-difference ratio (that is, more similarities than differences), whereas a relatively small area of overlap indicates a low similarity-to-difference ratio (more differences than similarities).

The following exercise will give you some practice at comparing, contrasting, and identifying points of critical distinction from a diverse array of phenomena. First, browse through the list below and select several word pairs that, for whatever reason, capture your interest. Then, utilizing any dimensions or sorting variables that might be useful, for each pair, answer the questions: (1) "How are they similar?" and (2) "How are they different?"

-God and Satan

-heaven and hell

-predestination and free will

-religion and art

-religion and science

-religion and slavery

-religion and freedom

-religious conversion and cult indoctrination

-Catholicism and Protestantism

-Judaism and Christianity

-religious leaders and political leaders

-television evangelists and television salesmen

-philosophy and science

-astronomy and astrology

-chemistry and alchemy

-neurology and phrenology

-cause and effect

-correlation and causation

-Event Theory and Construct Theory (see Metathought II)

-deductive reasoning and inductive reasoning (see Metathought XX)

-good and bad

-hot and cold

-dark and light

-pain and pleasure

-life and death

-any phenomenon and its opposite (see Metathought VI)

-fire and water

-earthquakes and hurricanes

-volcanic eruptions and anger

-rain and sadness

-brain and mind

-physical illness and mental illness

-physical abuse and emotional abuse

-depression and anxiety

-depression and death

-psychosis and creativity

-hypnosis and prayer

-psychotherapy and science

-psychotherapy and art

-psychotherapy and medicine

-psychotherapy and religion

-psychotherapy and friendship

-psychotherapy and prostitution

-men and women

-platonic love and romantic love

-love and psychosis

-sadism and masochism

-rape and consensual sex

-date rape and stranger rape

-rape and robbery

-sex and power

-sex and intimacy

-sex and aggression

-sex and dancing

-sex and pizza

-Spanish culture and Mexican culture

-Japanese art and Chinese art

-Israeli music and Arabic music

-Italian food and French food

-poverty and racism

-ignorance-based racism and hostility-based racism

-prejudice against blacks and prejudice against Jews

-affirmative action and discrimination

-discrimination and reverse discrimination

-racial inequality in 1955 and racial inequality in 1995

-Democrats and Republicans

-Communism and Naziism

-cult indoctrination and psychoanalysis

-apples and oranges

-apples and existentialism

-dogs and people

-wolves and gangs

-infancy and old age

-bullies and cowards

-actors and athletes

-sports and war

-Beethoven and Einstein

-ant colonies and human societies

-emotions and the stock market

-school and prison

-parents and jail wardens

-physician-prescribed medication and illicit street drugs

-your mate/spouse and your opposite-sexed parent

-yourself and any other person

-yourself now and yourself five years ago

-yourself now and yourself ten years ago

-yourself now and yourself when you were a young child

Word pair: _____

Similarities: _____

_____

_____

_____

_____

Differences: _____

_____

_____

_____

_____

Word pair: _____

Similarities: _____

_____

_____

_____

_____

Differences: _____

_____

_____

_____

_____

Word pair:_____

Similarities:_____

_____

_____

_____

Differences: _____

_____

_____

_____

_____

Word pair:_____

Similarities:_____

_____

_____

_____

Differences: _____

_____

_____

_____

_____

What is the purpose of this exercise? First, it illustrates that any two phenomena in the universe, no matter how seemingly disparate at first glance, always share at least some similarities. Second, phenomena invariably are differentiated by various points of critical distinction, which, in essence, define the boundaries delineating one phenomenon from another. Third, by utilizing this method of comparing and contrasting phenomena, you probably gained new insights and discovered some fresh perspectives into these relationships that you heretofore might not have considered. Fourth, given the fact that any two events are similar *and* different, it is crucial to take them *both* into account in your assessment of the phenomena.

This same method (of comparing and contrasting phenomena by analyzing relevant PCDs) also may be utilized to evaluate the relative appropriateness, usefulness, or merit of analogies and metaphors. Remember that, by definition, an analogy never can be "perfect"; there always exists *some* difference between the original phenomenon (e.g., addiction to a drug) and its analogue (e.g., addiction to a job, game, or person). However, by focusing on what they *do* share in common, specifically, their similarities prior to the PCD (such as feeling overwhelmed by irresistible urges to perform certain behaviors), the analogy's applicability or value may be judged in terms of how well, on the whole, it seems to "fit." Thus, whether we are drawing a metaphoric parallel between physical illness and mental illness, between a broken machine and a broken family, or between repairing a damaged computer and repairing a damaged psyche, we must be alert not only to avoid committing errors of reification (see Metathought II), but also to identify and scrutinize all relevant PCDs, thereby acknowledging the limits inherent in our metaphoric representations.

Similarly, we should bear in mind that all conceptual divisions (such as categories, classifications, diagnoses, and taxonomies) are human-made simplifications that, by their very nature, are fundamentally flawed. Thus, although we need to accept such simplifications as "necessary evils" in science, we also should never forget that they are artificial, contrived, and to varying degrees distorted, inaccurate, and erroneous. Here again, a systematic examination of similarities and differences provides us with a useful method of understanding and coming to terms with this dilemma. As noted by social psychologists Susan Fiske and Shelley Taylor (1984), "Life is not a series of boxes connected by arrows. Although the boxes are a convenient fiction, . . . you would not want to live in them" (p. 306).

Sources of Error

In the course of evaluating similarities and differences between any phenomena, we are subject to committing errors in two directions: first, by allowing genuine differences to be obscured by similarities, and second, by allowing genuine similarities to be obscured by differences.

Differences Obscured by Similarities

In these situations, the person makes the mistake of permitting similarities between phenomena to eclipse their differences. For instance, someone who routinely engages in stereotyping members of particular groups (based on, for example, their sex, race, ethnicity, religion, profession, political affiliation, and so on) is prone to habitually, systematically, and automatically overestimate within-group similarities, while minimizing (or even ignoring) within-group variability (Fiske & Taylor, 1984). In other words, the individual perceives group members to be more alike than they really are and, at the same time, does not recognize many of the ways in which they are different from one another. As you can readily discern, in its most extreme form, this process is a fundamental component underlying prejudice, bigotry, chauvinism, racism, classism, sexism, ageism, and so on, wherein all members of the "outgroup" are seen as essentially the same, while their individuality goes virtually unnoticed.

In the context of psychotherapy, some therapists make this error when they fail to respect (or even recognize) the uniqueness indigenous to each individual client. Unfortunately, these therapists tend to perceive one client as basically the same as every other client. In this way, clients are viewed *not* as distinct and varied individuals, each possessing a separate and unique constellation of life experiences, memories, thoughts, feelings, perceptions, values, beliefs, goals, hopes, fears, and dreams. Instead, they are spontaneously filtered through the therapist's own cognitive "client role schema" (see Metathought XXIII, the Assimilation Bias), from which they emerge as a relatively undifferentiated, homogeneous, amorphous, two-dimensional "client-type." In this less-than-therapeutic environment, then, irrespective of individual clients' unique situations, problems, or needs, they all receive essentially the same procrustean, "cookie-cutter" approach to clinical assessment and treatment.

As a final example, let's examine the act of killing a human being. Here, regardless of any other factors, the outcome is invariant, unambiguous, and unequivocal: death. Thus, when viewed solely in terms of its consequences, all forms of killing are equivalent. What if, however, we were to consider other dimensions on which to compare and contrast various acts of killing? Suppose, for instance, that we could take into account such variables as social context, motivation, intentionality, and the target of the act. Without a doubt, substantial and meaningful differences (based on a wide range of PCDs) would immediately ensue. Specifically, we would now be confronted with relatively clear differentiations between: premeditated murder, self-defense, manslaughter, legal execution (capital punishment), symbolic acts of retribution, wartime combat, killing for food, killing for sport, killing out of jealousy, gang initiation rites, political assassination, physician-assisted or self-induced suicide, and even euthanasia ("mercy killing").

Similarities Obscured by Differences

How many times have you heard someone make the following pronouncement (or any derivation thereof): "You can't compare these two things because they're totally and completely different from each other!" Here we have a vivid illustration of a person who is making the converse mistake of allowing similarities between phenomena to be overshadowed by their differences. Thus, the individual who staunchly and adamantly maintains that, "One should *never* stereotype," is effectively blinding him or herself to authentic commonalities that actually do exist within specific subgroups. However, by obstinately clinging to this position, such individuals practically ensure that they will remain oblivious to true similarities within (as well as between) groups of people.

Similarly, psychotherapists who tenaciously cling to their belief that, "Every client should be viewed and treated as totally unique and without regard to other clients," run the risk of allowing true (and potentially helpful) similarities between persons to be overlooked, neglected, or omitted. Unfortunately, the therapist's overemphasis on individual differences typically is realized at the expense of minimizing interpersonal commonalities (see Metathought XXX, Every Decision Is a Trade-Off). As a consequence, deeply powerful and universal life experiences that appear to be intrinsic to the human condition—themes, for example, related to needs for love, acceptance, empathy, esteem, or success—are prone to be minimized, disregarded, or even rejected outright.

How might this Metathought be constructively applied in the clinical setting? The following brief vignette provides one such example.

Client: "There's no way that you can understand how I feel. After all, you're white, and I'm black. And you've never been discriminated against because of your race."

Therapist: "You're right. I can never know exactly what that feels like. We are truly different in that respect. But at the same time, I know what it's like to be discriminated against because of my gender. And I have had the experience of being persecuted out of ignorance and hatred. To that extent, we do share a common experience. We are indeed both similar and different."

To briefly summarize this Metathought, all phenomena are both *similar to* and *different from* each other, depending on the dimensions or variables that have been selected for purposes of evaluation, comparison, and contrast. Further, no phenomenon is *totally identical* or *totally unique* in relation to other phenomena. Finally, the degree of similarity or uniqueness revealed between any two events is a function of the relevant *points of critical distinction* (PCD).

What are some antidotes to this Metathought? First, when comparing and contrasting any two phenomena be sure to ask yourself, "In what ways are they similar?" *and* "In what ways are they different?" Even before you ask these questions, however, make certain that you are clear as to the specific *purpose* of your analysis. Next, carefully select the most relevant dimensions and variables on which you will base your evaluation. Despite what may be an overwhelming number of similarities between two phenomena, don't neglect to search for and take into account their differences; conversely, regardless of what may appear to be a virtual absence of commonality between the phenomena, be sure to identify and scrutinize their similarities. (For one application, see Levy & Nail, 1993.)

Keep these principles in mind whenever you are faced with the task of comparing and contrasting any phenomena. You are likely to be more than just a little surprised each time you realize that the dimensions or variables you select for purposes of evaluation ultimately will determine just how "similar" or "unique" the phenomena turn out to be!

Glossary Terms

The following terms (or variations) are defined in the Glossary:

ambiguous	intentionality
analogy	interpersonal
antidote	judgment
attitude	mental illness
attribution	metaphor
behavior	mind
belief	motivation
bifurcation	paradox
category	perception
causation	personality
cause	phenomenon
clinical	physical
cognitive	point of critical distinction (PCD)
concept	procrustean
consequence	psyche
construct	psychoanalysis
Construct (Type C) Theory	psychological
correlation	psychosis
deductive reasoning	psychotherapy
diagnosis	reification
dilemma	schema
dimension	science
disorder	semantic
effect	social
e.g.	stereotype
emotion	subsequent
erroneous	taxonomy
evaluation	theoretical
event	treatment
Event (Type E) Theory	universal
existentialism	value
experience	variable
fact	vignette
inductive reasoning	vivid
insight	

Chapter 8

VIII. The Naturalistic Fallacy: Blurring the Line between "Is" and "Should"

We can, and must, distinguish clearly between facts and rules.
—THOMAS SZASZ*

It is of fundamental importance not to make the positivist mistake of assuming that, because a group are "in formation," this means they are necessarily "on course."
—R. D. LAING**

One very important way in which our personal values can bias our thinking is when we equate our description of what *is* with our prescription of what *ought* to be. This occurs, for instance, whenever we define what is good in terms of what is observable. This error in thinking is called the *Naturalistic Fallacy*.

Let's examine the following statements: "What's typical is normal; what's normal is good. What's not typical is abnormal; what's abnormal is bad." Notice how, in each case, a *description* of what exists becomes converted into a *prescription* of what we like or dislike.

As the Scottish philosopher David Hume pointed out over 200 years ago, values, ethics, and morality are based not on logic or reason, but on the sentiments and public opinions of a particular society. Thus, no description of human behavior, however accurate, can ever ordain what is "right" or "wrong" behavior. It makes no difference whether we are studying people's

*The Therapeutic State, 1984
**The Politics of Experience, 1967

political beliefs, religious customs, work performance, recreational activities, family upbringing, sexual practices, or table manners. If most people do something, that does not make it right; if most people do not, that does not make it wrong.

Of course, the converse also is true: If most people do something, that does not make it wrong; if most people do not, that does not make it right. In other words, there is no need to idealize someone just because he or she is different from the crowd. Likewise, we need not condemn someone solely for doing what others do. The point is that, in any case, we must be careful not to confuse *objective description* with *subjective value judgment*.

As an exercise, try to think of examples from everyday life that people may place into each of the following four categories:

Common, therefore good: _____
Uncommon, therefore bad: _____
Common, therefore bad: _____
Uncommon, therefore good: _____

Application 1: Maslow's Theory of Self-Actualization

No one is immune to making this error, not even social scientists. A case in point is Abraham Maslow's (1970) theory of motivation. Maslow, a pioneer of Humanistic psychology, proposed that humans have a number of innate needs, which are arranged in a hierarchy in terms of their potency. Malsow grouped these needs into five categorical levels: physiological, safety, love, esteem, and self-actualization. Once an individual has satisfied the cluster of needs at a particular level, he or she is able to progress to the next hierarchical level. Thus, for example, people typically are not prompted to seek acceptance and esteem until they have met their needs for food, water, and shelter.

TABLE 8-1   Abraham Maslow's Hierarchy of Needs

Level 5:	*Self-Actualization Needs*
Level 4:	*Esteem Needs*
Level 3:	*Belonging and Love Needs*
Level 2:	*Safety Needs*
Level 1:	*Physiological Needs*

Maslow noted that as one ascends the hierarchy of needs, one becomes less animal-like and more human. If the person has been able to satisfy adequately the needs in the first four levels, he or she is in a position to fulfill the highest-order needs, namely, to actualize one's fullest and unique potential. According to Maslow, once a person enters the realm of self-actualization, he or she becomes qualitatively different from those who are still attempting to meet their more basic needs. The self-actualizing person's life is governed by the search of "being-values" (B-values), such as Truth, Goodness, Beauty, Wholeness, Justice, and Meaningfulness.

In contrast to most personality theorists who preceded him, Maslow created his theory by studying healthy and successful people, rather than clinical cases of psychopathology. His interest in self-actualizing people began with his great admiration for Max Wertheimer (one of the founders of Gestalt psychology) and Ruth Benedict (the renowned cultural anthropologist). After discovering that these two individuals had many characteristics in common, Maslow began to search for others with the same qualities. The group that he finally isolated for more detailed study included Abraham Lincoln, Thomas Jefferson, Albert Einstein, Eleanor Roosevelt, Albert Schweitzer, Benedict Spinoza, Adlai Stevenson, and Martin Buber.

Based on his informal research, Maslow developed a composite, impressionistic profile of the optimally functioning, mature, and healthy human being. Maslow concluded that self-actualizing persons exhibit a number of similar characteristics, including: an accurate perception of reality, a continued freshness of appreciation and openness to experience, spontaneity and simplicity, a strong ethical awareness, a philosophical (rather than hostile) sense of humor, needs for privacy, periodic mystical ("peak") experiences, a democratic leader structure, deep interpersonal relations, autonomy and independence, creativeness, a problem-centered (rather than self-centered) orientation, a resistance of enculturation, and an acceptance of self, others, and nature.

Critics of Maslow's theory question whether such characteristics truly are a valid depiction of the fully-functioning person, or, instead, are a reflection of Maslow's own subjective value system. In other words, Maslow has been criticized for mixing ethical and moral considerations with his logic. Consider, for example, his portrayal of self-actualizing people as open, realistic, spontaneous, possessing a democratic leader structure, and accepting of self, others, and nature. Is this an objective description of human fulfillment? Or is it a *pre*scription, masked as a *de*scription, of Maslow's own subjective ideals? As noted by M. Brewster Smith (1978), perhaps Maslow simply selected his personal heroes and offered his impressions of them.

Let's explore this notion by conducting a little thought experiment. Imagine that some other theorist, with a distinctly different set of values, were to utilize Maslow's method of delineating the characteristics of self-actualization by studying *his* own heroes, who, for the sake of argument, happen to be Napolean Bonaparte, Alexander the Great, and General George S. Patton. In this alternative scenario, *now* what are some of the qualities that define the "self-actualized, optimally-functioning, healthy human being?" How about *totalitarian leader structure? Egocentric orientation? Obsessed with power? Need to conquer? Love of war?*

In defense of Maslow, he acknowledged that his theorizing and research on self-actualization lacked the rigor of strict empirical science. He fervently believed, however, that it was imperative to begin the process of rounding out the field of psychology by attending to "the highest capacities of the healthy and strong man as well as with the defensive maneuvers of crippled spirits" (1970, p. 33). Further, Maslow maintained that it would be misleading to believe that science is value free, since its methods and procedures are developed and utilized for human purposes.

Application 2: Erikson's Theory of Healthy Ego Functioning

As another illustration, let us consider Erik H. Erikson's theory of psychosocial development. Erikson (1950) theorized that all humans pass through a series of eight developmental stages, which stretch from birth to death. Each stage is characterized by a developmental conflict, problem, or *crisis*. If the crisis has a positive resolution, the person's ego is strengthened by gaining a *virtue*, which results in greater adaptation and a healthier personality. But, if the crisis has a negative resolution, the ego loses strength, resulting in inhibited adaptation and an unhealthier personality. For instance, if a young child's conflict between initiative and guilt has a positive resolution, he will emerge with the virtue of purpose; a negative outcome, however, would result in a sense of unworthiness.

TABLE 8-2   Erik H. Erikson's Stages of Psychosocial Development

Stage	Ego Crisis	Age	Positive Outcome
1	Basic Trust versus Mistrust	0–1	Hope
2	Autonomy versus Shame and Doubt	1–3	Will
3	Initiative versus Guilt	3–5	Purpose
4	Industry versus Inferiority	5–12	Competence
5	Ego Identity versus Role Confusion	adolescence	Fidelity
6	Intimacy versus Isolation	young adult	Love
7	Generativity versus Stagnation	adulthood	Care
8	Ego Integrity versus Despair	maturity	Wisdom

Erikson thus defined the healthy or mature personality as one that possesses the eight virtues (namely: hope, will, purpose, competence, fidelity, love, care, and wisdom) that emerge from a positive resolution at each stage of development. It was Erikson's belief that the outcome of every crisis resolution is reversible. The goal in his approach to psychotherapy, therefore, was to encourage the growth of whatever virtues the client happened to be missing.

As was the case with Maslow, Erikson has been criticized for mixing objective description with subjective prescription. Specifically, the virtues he uses to define the healthy individual are clearly in accordance with Western, Judeo-Christian ethics, values, and social institutions. In other words, Erikson, like many social theorists, may have been describing what he believes *should* be, rather than what *is*.

Caveat and Conclusion

I wish to emphasize that it is not my intention to impugn the value judgments implicit in the theories of Maslow and Erikson; in fact, I find myself closely aligned with many of their beliefs. However, *values and veracity are not synonymous*. Further, we must remember that our perceptions of the world are inescapably colored by our personal beliefs, and that the distinction between description and prescription frequently is a jumbled one indeed.

Glossary Terms

The following terms (or variations) are defined in the Glossary:

behavior	normal
belief	objective
bias	opinion
category	perception
clinical	personality
description	prescription
empirical	psychology
ethics	psychopathology
experience	psychotherapy
fact	resistance
fallacy	science
Gestalt psychology	social
Humanistic psychology	subjective
interpersonal	theory
judgment	thinking
logic	value
motivation	veracity
Naturalistic Fallacy	

IX. *The Barnum Effect: "One-Size-Fits-All" Personality Interpretations*

A good circus should have a little something for everybody.
—ATTRIBUTED TO P. T. BARNUM*

There's a sucker born every minute.
—P. T. BARNUM**

A *Barnum statement* is a personality interpretation about a particular individual that is true of practically all human beings; in other words, it is a general statement that has "a little something for everybody." The *Barnum Effect* refers to people's willingness to accept the validity of such overly inclusive and generic interpretations.

Barnum statements pervade the popular media (from television and radio shows to books, newspapers, and magazines) in the form of self-help primers, astrological forecasts, psychic hotlines, biorhythm and numerology readings, and interpretations of your dreams, palms, or favorite colors. To find Barnum statements, you need look no further than the contents of *Dianetics*, the *I Ching*, or your most recent fortune cookie. Unfortunately, however, they are also commonly proffered to an eager (and frequently gullible) public by media psychologists. Worse yet, Barnum statements sometimes parade in the guise of psychological assessments or clinical diagnoses at professional psychotherapy treatment planning meetings and case conferences. For instance, a therapist

---

*1810–1891
**Cited in Bartlett, *Familiar Quotations*, 1968

may confidently announce to his colleagues, "My patient's problem is that he has self-esteem issues." (*Who doesn't?*) Or, "My patient is sensitive to criticism." (*Who isn't?*) Or, "My patient doesn't want to be rejected." (*Who does?*)

The variations on this theme are virtually infinite. To list but a few:

>"He has ambivalent feelings about his parents."
>"Deep down, she craves love and approval."
>"He has control issues."
>"She has boundary issues."
>"He has trust issues."
>"She has issues around intimacy and commitment."
>"He has intrapsychic conflict."
>"She's afraid of being hurt."
>"He struggles with feelings of insecurity."
>"She doesn't like being overly dependent."
>"He's trying to find a balance between autonomy and closeness."
>"She just wants to be understood."
>"He's his own worst enemy."
>"She is holding a grudge that she really ought to let go."

In a number of experiments, researchers have presented subjects with Barnum-like personality descriptions, such as those in Box 9-1 (which was constructed from a horoscope book).

BOX 9-1

<u>Are any of these statements untrue?</u>

"You have a strong need for other people to like and admire you. You have a tendency to be critical of yourself . . . At times you have serious doubts as to whether you have made the right decision or done the right thing. You prefer a certain amount of change and variety and become dissatisfied when hemmed in by restrictions and limitations. You pride yourself on being an independent thinker and do not accept other opinions without satisfactory proof. You have found it unwise to be too frank in revealing yourself to others. At times you are extraverted, affable, sociable; at other times you are introverted, wary, and reserved. Some of your aspirations tend to be pretty unrealistic" (Forer, 1949).

When subjects in the experiments were led to believe that the bogus feedback was prepared especially for them, and when it was generally favorable, they nearly always rated the description as either "good" or "excellent" (Dickson & Kelly, 1985). In fact, when given a choice between a fake Barnum description and a *real* personality description based on an established test, people tended to choose the *phony* description as being more accurate![1]

The moral? *Be careful* about making—and accepting—such Barnum statements. Though they might (and in fact often do) have *prima facie* validity, they are not particularly helpful in telling us anything *distinctive* about a specific person, such as when we are attempting to arrive at a differential clinical diagnosis.

In fact, to stretch the point just a bit, I have constructed what I believe to be the ultimate Barnum description: "The One-Size-Fits-All Psychological Profile."[2]

BOX 9-2

<u>The One-Size-Fits-All Psychological Profile</u>

<u>Developmental History</u>

You are the kind of person who was biologically conceived by two, opposite-sexed parents. However, no one, including your parents, ever asked you if you wanted to be born. For a period of time, you were totally dependent on others for providing food, shelter, and safety. Your vocabulary was extremely limited, you found it impossible to stand up without assistance, and you were incapable of accomplishing even minor tasks, such as brushing your teeth. In fact, for a while there, you didn't even *have* any. On more than one occasion, your cries went unheeded.

Things are different for you now than they used to be. You are not as young as you were. You've had numerous experiences in your life. You've had some problems and suffered some disappointments in your past. When things didn't work out the way you wanted them to, you wished that they had. You are more likely to remember those things that you don't forget.

<u>Physiological Processes</u>

You're the type of person who has a variety of bodily needs. For example, when deprived of oxygen, you are likely to experience feelings of suffocation. Sometimes you are thirsty; at other times, you just aren't. When you are thirsty, you crave something to drink. When you are hungry, you crave something to eat. During periods of intense hunger, you are likely to seek, procure, and ingest food. When you've eaten too much food, you usually don't feel hungry for a while. You are prone to have very little appetite when you are in the act of vomiting.

If you were to go without sleep for several days in a row, you would be prone to experience feelings of fatigue, weariness, or even exhaustion. The longer you go without sleep, the more tired you are likely to become. When you are asleep, you don't know it. In fact, it's only after you've woken up that you know that you were.

You're the kind of person who derives pleasure from scratching an itch. Pain hurts you. In fact, you typically attempt to avoid pain. When you are too cold, you have a strong tendency to seek heat. When you are too hot, you try to cool down. When you feel sick, you experience a desire to get well. When having sex, you're the type of person who prefers to have an orgasm, rather than not have one. You experience a sense of relief, or even pleasure, after relieving your bladder or bowels. You prefer the smell of your own excreta to that of other people's (see Levy & Erhardt, 1988).

Many of your bodily processes have an "automatic" quality to them. For example, when you are engaging in strenuous physical activity, your heartbeat, blood pressure, and respiration increase, whether you like it or not. When your skin is cut, you are very likely to bleed. You're the type of person who experiences a "gagging" sensation whenever a foreign object (such as a stick, screwdriver, or cooking utensil) is shoved down your throat.

Personality Characteristics

You're a person who has many different sides to your personality. There are parts of your personality that you like more than others. Deep down, you have some pretty deep feelings. These feelings are likely to be much deeper than those feelings that are closer to the surface. When your feelings are hurt, you're the kind of person who doesn't like it. Given the choice, you'd rather feel good than bad. Sometimes you are happy; sometimes you aren't. You like feeling happy, but you don't like feeling lonely, depressed, or anxious. In fact, the more miserable you are, the more you dislike it.

Interpersonal Functioning

You are similar to other people in some ways, but not in other ways. There are many people whom you just do not know. You enjoy having the respect of others. You like some people more than others. When you lose someone dear to you, you are likely to feel sad. You are the kind of person who prefers not being ridiculed, mocked, or tortured by others.

Goals and Expectations

You wish that you could be more the kind of person who you really want to be. You wish that you had more control over your life. You want to accomplish more. You would prefer to be successful rather than unsuccessful.

Diagnostic Impressions (Check as many as desired, depending on the clinician's theoretical orientation.)
_____You have maladaptive learning patterns.
_____You have inner-child issues.
_____You have codependency issues.
_____You have repressed introjects.
_____You have unfinished business.
_____You are searching for meaning in life.
_____You come from a dysfunctional family.
_____You have a biochemical imbalance.

Future Prognosis

If you continue to live, you will grow older. The longer you live, the more experiences you are likely to have. You will always be older than your younger siblings. At some point in your future, you will be completely unable to talk, walk, or even breathe. And this condition will last for a very, *very* long time.

As an historical note, Donald G. Paterson once warned clinicians about a "personality description after the manner of P. T. Barnum" (cited in Meehl, 1956), who remarked that "a good circus should have a little something for everybody." Paul Meehl (1956, 1973) subsequently coined the term "Barnum effect," in honor of the renowned circus-master.

Barnum was also famous for declaring that, "There's a sucker born every minute." This observation may have been more prophetic than Barnum ever intended, both of clients who accept uncritically the validity of Barnum statements about themselves, and of clinicians who delude themselves into believing the veracity of their own pseudo-incisive personality interpretations.

Exercise: De-Barnumizing Barnum Interpretations

Begin this exercise by selecting a few Barnum interpretations from this chapter, or come up with some of your own. Then, "de-Barnumize" each statement by incorporating any potentially useful qualifiers, modifiers, or adverbs. To get you started, here are two examples:

Barnum statement: <u>My patient is sensitive to criticism.</u>
De-Barnumized statement: <u>My patient is moderately sensitive to criticism.</u>

Barnum statement: <u>She's afraid of being hurt.</u>
De-Barnumized statement: <u>She's profoundly afraid of being hurt.</u>

Barnum statement: _____
De-Barnumized statement: _____

Barnum statement: _____
De-Barnumized statement: _____

Barnum statement: _____
De-Barnumized statement: _____

Barnum statement: _____
De-Barnumized statement: _____

Barnum statement: _____
De-Barnumized statement: _____

Glossary Terms

The following terms (or variations) are defined in the Glossary:

Barnum Effect	description
Barnum statement	diagnosis
belief	differential diagnosis
clinical	dysfunction
decision	effect

expectation	personality
experience	*prima facie*
experiment	psychological
extraversion	psychotherapy
generic	repression
interpersonal	subsequent
interpretation	theoretical
intrapsychic	treatment
introversion	validity
opinion	veracity

Notes

[1] See Snyder, Shenkel, and Lowery (1977) For an excellent review of research in this area.

[2] The complete version of "The One-Size-Fits-All Psychological Profile" originally appeared in the *Journal of Polymorphous Perversity* (Levy, 1993).

P a r t **Two**

Explaining Phenomena

X. Correlation Does Not Prove Causation: Confusing "What" with "Why"

ROGERS'S LAW:
As soon as the stewardess serves the coffee,
the airliner encounters turbulence.
DAVIS'S EXPLANATION OF ROGERS'S LAW:
Serving coffee on aircraft causes turbulence.
—ARTHUR BLOCH*

President Bush taking credit for the collapse of Communism
is like a rooster taking credit for the arrival of the dawn.
—SOURCE UNKNOWN**

A *correlation* is a statement about the relationship or association between two (or more) variables. Correlations thus enable us to make predictions from one variable to another. For example, if two events are correlated, then the presence of one event provides us with information about the other event. A correlation does not, however, necessarily establish a *causal* relationship between the variables.[1] In other words, cause-and-effect can't be proven simply by virtue of a correlation.

As an example, let us consider the empirically validated correlation between creativity and mood disorders (see Andreason & Canter, 1974; Andreason & Powers, 1975; Jamison, 1993). Based on this correlation, what

**Murphy's Law, Book Two,* 1980
**1992 Presidential campaign

may we conclude? That mood disorders cause creativity? Perhaps. But maybe creativity causes mood disorders. Then again, is it possible that creativity and mood disorders form a bi-directional causal loop? To complicate matters further, what about the possibility that some other variables, such as a genetic predisposition, cause both creativity and mood disorders?

Put another way, given a correlation between A and B, does A cause B? Does B cause A? Do A and B cause each other? Does C cause A and B? (See Figure 10-1.) Could there be some combination of these causal relationships? Unfortunately, a correlation alone does not (in fact, *cannot*) provide us with the answers to these questions.

Now, in some cases it is relatively safe to infer the direction of causation from a correlation. For example, there is a known positive correlation between rainfall and traffic accidents—the more it rains, the greater the number of traffic accidents. Clearly, rainfall causes accidents. (It is improbable that accidents cause rainfall!) To take another example, there appears to be a correlation between gender and aggressive behavior, in that boys typically are more aggressive than girls. Obviously, aggressiveness cannot cause gender; gender must, in some way, be causing aggressiveness.

Unfortunately, however, in most areas of life in general, and psychology in particular, there are very few circumstances in which causal explanations can be clearly determined from a correlation. The following are some examples of correlated variables about which people frequently (but erroneously) infer causality.

Example 1: Research indicates that watching violent television programs appears to be mildly but positively correlated with aggressive behavior (see Huesmann, 1982). This correlation does not prove, however, that TV violence causes aggressiveness. Perhaps aggressive people prefer to watch violent TV programs. Maybe aggressiveness and TV violence feed off each other in a "vicious cycle" (see Metathought XI, Bi-Directional Causation). Or, consider the possibility that family conflict causes both aggressive behavior and the watching of TV violence.

$$A \rightarrow B \qquad A \rightleftarrows B$$

$$A \leftarrow B \qquad \begin{array}{c} C \\ \swarrow \quad \searrow \\ A \qquad B \end{array}$$

FIGURE 10-1   A Correlation between Event A and Event B with Four Possible Causal Relationships

Example 2: People who are depressed tend to have low self-esteem. In other words, depression and self-esteem are negatively (or inversely) correlated. But this doesn't prove the causal link (or links) between these two variables. Depression might cause low self-esteem. Conversely, low self-esteem might cause depression. Further, depression and low self-esteem may cause each other. Or, some other variables, such as chronic failure, distressing events, and learned helplessness might cause both depression and low self-esteem (see Metathought XII, Multiple Causation).

Example 3: Studies show that there is a positive relationship between "authoritative" (as opposed to "authoritarian" or "permissive") parents and socially competent children (Baumrind, 1983; Buri, Louiselle, Misukanis, & Mueller, 1988; Coopersmith, 1967). This evidence, however, is primarily correlational in nature. Thus, we must be very tentative regarding the conclusions we attempt to draw. We should take into account, for example, the possibility that other variables, such as high socio-economic status, a happy marriage, and/or common genes, also might be responsible for producing social competence.

Example 4: Most heroin addicts started on marijuana; thus, there is a positive correlation between heroin use and the previous marijuana use. But this correlation does not prove that marijuana use causes subsequent heroin use. Why not? Consider the fact that virtually all heroin addicts *originally* started on *milk*! Now, what does this correlation "prove"? That drinking milk in infancy eventually leads to hard drugs?

Consider also the correlations between homelessness and mental illness; obesity and the number of hours spent watching television; receiving poor grades in school and being in trouble with the law; dopamine and schizophrenia; kissing and pregnancy. In all of these instances (and countless more), *beware* of concluding causation based solely on correlation. Further, when a correlation is observed, be sure to consider all plausible pathways and directions of causation.

To give you some practice at applying these principles, try to identify some of the possible causal relationships, pathways, and explanations that could account for each of the correlations presented below.

Exercise 1. "Eveningness" and optimism appear to be negatively (inversely) correlated (Levy, 1985); that is, people who are "evening types" tend to be more pessimistic than "morning types." Why might this be true?

   1. <u>Optimism may cause "morningness."</u>
   2. <u>"Morningness" may cause optimism.</u>
   3. <u>Optimism and "morningness" may affect each other.</u>
   4. <u>Satisfying job may cause both optimism and "morningness."</u>

Exercise 2. Riots tend to occur with greater frequency during the hot, summer months than during other seasons of the year; thus there is a positive correlation between riots and summertime. Why? (*Hint:* Be sure to consider variables such as unemployment and vacation from school.)

1. _____
2. _____
3. _____
4. _____

Exercise 3. There appears to be a negative correlation between the neurotransmission of serotonin and depression. Why?

1. _____
2. _____
3. _____
4. _____

Exercise 4.a. A psychotherapist reports that, "Before the patient started seeing me for therapy, his life was a total mess. Since he's been in treatment with me, however, his life has completely turned around." Why?

1. _____
2. _____
3. _____
4. _____

Exercise 4.b. A psychotherapist reports that, "When the patient was seeing me for therapy, he was doing great. But since he terminated treatment, he's really gone downhill." Why?

1. _____
2. _____
3. _____
4. _____

Superstitions, Magical Thinking, and the Contiguity–Causation Error

Let us conclude with an interesting application of this Metathought to a particular type of faulty reasoning, the *Contiguity–Causation Error.* This mistake involves arriving at the erroneous conclusion that a cause and effect relationship exists between two events simply because the events occurred next to each other in time (that is, based on their *temporal contiguity*).[2]

For example, in the middle of a group therapy session, a member of the group starts to sob uncontrollably and then bursts out of the room. In attempting to explain his behavior, the other group members very likely would be tempted to rely on temporal contiguity by asking themselves, "What happened in the group just before he got upset?" In point of fact, however, the man's behavior could have been due to any number of causes, none of which necessarily occurred within the group immediately before he became upset.

Harry Stack Sullivan (1954) referred to this form of thinking as the *parataxic mode of experience.* Parataxic reasoning also may be seen as a kind of "magical thinking," because events that occur close together in time are construed as causally linked. As it turns out, most superstitions are based on parataxic reasoning. For example, if a football coach doesn't shave before a game, and his team then wins, he might assume that not shaving somehow caused the success. As a result, he may adopt this superstitious behavior for future games. Similarly, a gambler may be on a losing streak at the roulette table. If, however, she suddenly strikes it lucky, the Contiguity–Causation Error may lead her to conclude that the gentleman who just sat down nearby was the cause of her change in luck.

As these examples clearly illustrate, although correlations may provide us with accurate—and frequently very useful—information regarding *"what"* relationships exist, they cannot be counted on to answer the question, *"why?"* Even in those circumstances when a correlation strongly *implies* causation, remember that it does not *prove* causation.

Glossary Terms

The following terms (or variations) are defined in the Glossary:

behavior
belief
bi-directional causation
causal
causal loop
causality
causation
cause
chronic
Contiguity–Causation Error
correlate
correlation
disorder
disposition
effect
empirical
erroneous
event

experience
explanation
fact
infer
mental illness
mood
parataxic reasoning
post hoc
prediction
psychology
psychotherapy
reasoning
social
subsequent
temporal contiguity
thinking
treatment
variable

Notes

[1] For a definition and discussion of causal relationships, see Metathought III, Multiple Levels of Description. More comprehensive definitions and examples may be found in *Dictionary of Philosophy* (Angeles, 1981).

[2] This error in logic also is known as *post hoc, ergo propter hoc:* that is, the belief that because Event *B* follows Event *A,* then *B* must have been caused by *A.*

XI. Bi-Directional Causation: Causal Loops, Healthy Spirals, and Vicious Cycles

The ancestor of every action is a thought.
—RALPH WALDO EMERSON*

Thought is the child of Action.
—BENJAMIN DISRAELI**

See this egg. It is with this that the schools of theology and all the temples of the earth are to be overturned.
—DENIS DIDEROT***

Although we typically tend to think of causal relationships as being *uni-directional* (Event *A* causes Event *B*), frequently they are *bi-directional* (Event *A* causes Event *B, and* Event *B* causes Event *A*). In other words, variables may, and frequently do, affect each other. This relationship also may be referred to as a causal loop or, depending on our subjective evaluation of the particular situation, either a "healthy spiral" (if we happen to like it) or a "vicious cycle" (if we don't). (In this regard, see Metathought I, the Evaluative Bias of Language.)

*1803–1882, *Essays,* First Series
**1804–1881, *Vivian Grey*
***1713–1784, *Le Rêve d'Alembert,* pt. 1

$$A \rightleftarrows B$$

FIGURE 11-1   Bi-Directional Causation

As a prominent illustration of this Metathought, let's look at the endlessly debated question in psychology, "Does thought cause emotion, or does emotion cause thought? Which comes first? Which is the cause and which is the effect?" (see Berscheid, 1982; Mandler, 1975; Weiner, 1980; Zajonc, 1980). When viewed as a bi-directional relationship, however, the argument may be moot: clearly, thoughts and feelings affect each other.

To take another example, research indicates that the relationship between aggressive behavior and watching television violence is bi-directional (Huesmann, Lagerspetz, & Eron, 1983). That is, aggressive children are prone to watch violent TV programs, and television violence, in turn, results in aggressive behavior.

Consider also the bi-directional relationship between mental illness and one's social environment. Specifically, it is quite probable that cold, rejecting, and hostile parents can cause emotional and behavioral problems in their children. At the same time, don't ignore the possibility (and frequently the likelihood) that children with emotional and behavioral problems also might cause their parents to become cold, rejecting, and hostile!

Bi-directional relationships are as interesting as they are plentiful: hostility and rejection; weight gain and physical immobility; drug use and depression; optimism and success; pessimism and failure; self-esteem and popularity; thinking and language.

As an exercise, consider the bi-directional relationship between anxiety (Event *A*) and sexual dysfunction (Event *B*). First, describe some ways that anxiety (*A*) might impair sexual performance, thereby leading to sexual dysfunction (*B*). _____

_____

_____

_____

_____

_____

Next, describe some ways that sexual dysfunction (*B*) can lead to anxiety (*A*). _____

_____

_____

_____

_____

_____

Is it possible to determine which is (or was) the "initial" cause? If so, how?_____

_____
_____
_____
_____
_____

Under what circumstances might it be important to identify which was the initial cause? _____

_____
_____
_____
_____
_____

Under what circumstances might it be *unimportant* to identify which was the initial cause? _____

_____
_____
_____
_____
_____

For some more practice, select another bi-directional relationship (either from the list above or an original example from your own experience). First, describe the ways that Event *A* affects Event *B*.

_____
_____
_____
_____
_____

Then describe the ways that Event *B* affects Event *A*. _____

_____
_____
_____
_____
_____

Is it possible to determine which is (or was) the initial cause? If so, how?

_____
_____
_____

Under what circumstances might it be important to identify which was the initial cause? _____

_____

_____

_____

_____

Under what circumstances might it be unimportant to identify which was the initial cause? _____

_____

_____

_____

_____

As you can see, "cause" and "effect" are relative terms: a cause in one instance becomes an effect in another. From this perspective, asking the question, "Which comes first?" although interesting, may be unnecessary, irrelevant, even unanswerable. Thus, when faced with such chicken-and-egg questions, remember that your answer may depend entirely on where you happen to enter the causal loop!

Glossary Terms

The following terms (or variations) are defined in the Glossary:

affect
behavior
bi-directional causation
causal
causal loop
causation
cause
dysfunction
effect

emotion
evaluation
event
psychology
social
subjective
thinking
uni-directional causation
variable

Chapter *12*

XII. Multiple Causation: Not "Either/Or," but "Both/And"

It is very remarkable how often a symptom is determined in several ways, is "overdetermined."
—JOSEF BREUER & SIGMUND FREUD*

An effect may be, and usually is, the result of *several* causes, which are operating concurrently. Virtually every significant behavior has *many* determinants, and any single explanation is almost inevitably an oversimplification.

To take an example, what causes depression? Is it caused by early childhood trauma? Or a vital loss? Or a faulty belief system? Or a perception of failure? Or unresolved mourning? Or internalized anger? Or learned helplessness? Or a biochemical predisposition?

Now try replacing each *or* with *and*. Depression thus may be seen as caused by a *combination* of factors, including early childhood trauma, *and* a vital loss, *and* a faulty belief system, *and* a perception of failure, *and* unresolved mourning, *and* internalized anger, *and* learned helplessness, *and* a biochemical predisposition.

As another example, what causes aggression? Taking into account the principle of multiple causation, aggression appears to be due to some *combination* of profound frustration, and suppressed rage, and low self-esteem, and the reinforcement of aggressive behaviors, and the use of extreme punishment, and faulty role modeling, and social rejection (Feshbach & Weiner, 1986).

*Studies on Hysteria, 1895

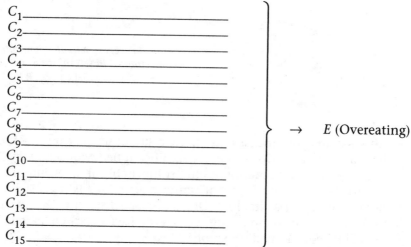

FIGURE 12-1   Multiple Causation

(*Note:* C = cause; E = effect.)

As an exercise, consider the multiple determinants of overeating. In the spaces below, list as many possible causes as you can think of. (Suggested answers appear in Appendix 2.)

C_1 _____
C_2 _____
C_3 _____
C_4 _____
C_5 _____
C_6 _____
C_7 _____
C_8 _____   } → E (Overeating)
C_9 _____
C_{10} _____
C_{11} _____
C_{12} _____
C_{13} _____
C_{14} _____
C_{15} _____

How might you put this Metathought into direct practice? First, in attempting to explain why an event occurred, don't limit your search to *one* cause. Instead, explore *multiple* plausible causes, *all* of which may be responsible for producing the effect. Second, every time you are faced with a question, issue, or problem that is presented in terms of *"either/or,"* stop for a moment. Now, try replacing *either/or,* with *both/and*. For example, the statement, "Prejudice is caused by either ignorance or hatred," becomes "Prejudice is caused by both ignorance and hatred." Then ask yourself, "Is this new formulation *useful*?" In a great number of situations, you are very likely to find that it is.

Gestalt therapists (see Perls, 1969) also would agree with this approach. In fact, it is common for the Gestalt psychotherapist to ask his or her client to replace the word *but* with *and*. For instance, "I like myself but I want to change" is replaced with "I like myself *and* I want to change." "I enjoy being alone but I need to be with people" is replaced with "I enjoy being alone *and* I need to be with people." "I love my mother but she drives me crazy," is replaced with "I love my mother *and* she drives me crazy." What is the rationale for this therapeutic technique? *But* is seen as divisive and thereby leads to fragmenting, splintering, and "disowning" parts of oneself. The result is psychological maladjustment. In contrast, *and* is integrative, thus fostering synthesis, unity, and a sense of wholeness—in short, psychological health.

Advanced Applications of Multiple Causation: Linear and Non-Linear Combinations

In a *linear* (or "additive") combination, even though an effect is due to several causes, the effect can theoretically be explained in terms of just one of the causes. In other words, each cause is, in itself, *sufficient* to produce the effect. Thus, a linear combination requires making a statement about only two variables—one cause and its effect. Consider, as an illustration, the causes of depression described above. Although depression involves multiple determinants, each cause alone may be sufficient to produce the same effect. Thus, depression appears to be due to a linear combination of causes.[1] To represent this concept algebraically (where C_1 and C_2 are causes and E is the effect): When $C_1 + C_2 \rightarrow E$, either C_1 or C_2 alone is sufficient to produce E. The same principle holds true, irrespective of the number of causes. Thus, when $C_1 + C_2 + C_3 + C_4 \rightarrow E$, the effect can be due to C_1 or C_2 or C_3 or C_4 independently.

In a *non-linear* (or "multiplicative") combination, by contrast, the effect *cannot* be explained without necessarily taking into account *at least two* causes. In other words, a non-linear combination *requires* making a statement about a third variable. Thus, where $C_1 \times C_2 \rightarrow E$, neither C_1 nor C_2 alone can produce the effect. In a non-linear combination, each causal factor is *necessary but not sufficient* to produce the effect. The statistical concept of an *interaction* (so named because the causes affect each other, or "interact") is, by definition, a non-linear combination.

Multiple Causation:
Linear Combination

$$C_1 + C_2 + C_3 = E$$

Multiple Causation:
Non-Linear Combination

$$C_1 \times C_2 \times C_3 = E$$

FIGURE 12-2

Note: C = cause; E = effect.

Examples of non-linear combinations include:

Heat × Oxygen = Fire
Blue × Yellow = Green
Ability × Motivation = Performance

In each of these non-linear examples, neither cause *alone* is capable of producing the effect; instead, they *must interact* with each other, or the effect cannot be achieved.

Glossary Terms

The following terms (or variations) are defined in the Glossary:

affect	event
antecedent	explanation
behavior	Gestalt therapy
belief	linear
causal	perception
causation	psychological
cause	reinforcement
concept	social
determinant	symptom
effect	variable

Notes

[1] As an historical note, Freud (1900/1953) used the term *overdetermination* to refer to a linear combination of causes, in which a number of different antecedent events (such as trauma, loss, and failure) combine to produce a psychological symptom (such as depression or anxiety).

Chapter *13*

XIII. *Degrees of Causation: Not All Causes Are Created Equal*

Genius is one percent inspiration and ninety-nine percent perspiration.
—*THOMAS ALVA EDISON*[*]

'Tis the last straw that breaks the camel's back.
—*ANONYMOUS*[**]

In many situations, it may be overly simplistic to ask the question, "Is this a causal factor or not?" As discussed in Metathought XII, an effect may be (and usually is) the result of multiple causes. And these causes are likely to *vary in the degree to which they are responsible* for producing the effect. In other words, one cause may be more influential than another. This doesn't mean, however, that a cause with less weight is not responsible for the effect. In other words, it would be erroneous to conclude that a cause which contributes only a nominal proportion to the effect is therefore a "non-cause."

As an example, let's say a man wakes up early one morning, stumbles into the bathroom, and, while brushing his teeth, runs out of toothpaste. He becomes mildly annoyed. Before he leaves for work that morning, his wife scolds him for not earning enough money. His anger mounts. On the way to work his car breaks down, so he has to catch the bus. Now, he's furious. He finally arrives late for work, dashes into his office, and begins his assignments for the day. Then, his boss casually walks over to his desk and fires him. The guy is stunned. He tries to keep working, but he is in a daze. Then, when he inadvertently breaks a pencil lead, he suddenly loses all control, grabs his boss by the lapels, and launches him out of the sixteenth-story window.

[*]1847–1931, newspaper interview, quoted in *The Golden Book of Quotations,* 1964
[**]Quoted in Barber, *The Book of 1000 Proverbs,* 1876/1971

Now, why did the man kill his boss? What caused his behavior? To varying degrees, probably *all* of these events (and certainly more). Without a doubt, getting fired was one of the most important causes. And the pencil lead may have been tantamount to the proverbial straw that broke the camel's back. But can we completely rule out *any* of these events—including running out of toothpaste—as a "non-cause"? Certainly not.

This Metathought relates directly to the concept of personal—as well as legal—responsibility. For instance, a man may be seen as "more responsible" for deliberately throwing a glass against a wall, causing it to shatter, than he might be for lending his damaged bicycle to a friend, who subsequently has an accident on it. But that's not to say that the man has *no responsibility* for the bicycle accident. Rather, it is a matter of *degree*, however small.

Similarly, let's say that you choose to drive late at night through a section of the city which you know full well to be exceedingly dangerous. And, sure enough, no sooner do you enter the area than you are attacked by a gang of thugs. Now, where does the responsibility lie? Who should be held accountable? Without question, your assailants. But what about *you*? Based on the same line of reasoning, it would be both illogical and naive to maintain that you bear absolutely no responsibility, as small a proportion as it might be, for your ordeal.

To give you some practice at applying this Metathought, try the following exercise. First, select a situation involving multiple causation, either from examples in this book or, better yet, from your own personal experiences. You may wish to examine, for example, the factors that account for your decision to break off a romantic relationship, or for your choice of which college to attend, or even for your current mood. Second, list all plausible causal factors that could be contributing to the effect. Third, rank order the factors in terms of their relative impact on the final outcome. Fourth, assuming (for the sake of this exercise) that together they total 100% of the effect, assign relative weights, in the form of percentages, to each factor.

$$\left. \begin{array}{l} C_1\ (x\%) \\ C_2\ (y\%) \\ C_3\ (z\%) \end{array} \right\} \rightarrow E$$

$$C_1(x\%) + C_2(y\%) + C_3(z\%) = E \text{ (linear combination)}$$
$$C_1(x\%) \times C_2(y\%) \times C_3(z\%) = E \text{ (non-linear combination)}$$

FIGURE 13-1   Degrees of Causation

(*Note: C* = cause; *E* = effect.)

As an illustration, let's say that you are interested in analyzing the factors that are causing your irritable mood. After completing the four steps outlined above, your responses might look something like this:

C_1 (50%) financial worries
C_2 (20%) pressure of final exams
C_3 (15%) tense relationship with roommate $\Bigg\} \rightarrow E$ (Irritable Mood)
C_4 (10%) an annoying baby pimple inside your lip
C_5 (5%) life in general

Do you have the idea? Now, try a couple on your own.

C_1 (%) _____
C_2 (%) _____
C_3 (%) _____ $\Bigg\} \rightarrow E$ (   )
C_4 (%) _____
C_5 (%) _____

C_1 (%) _____
C_2 (%) _____
C_3 (%) _____ $\Bigg\} \rightarrow E$ (   )
C_4 (%) _____
C_5 (%) _____

What are the primary lessons to be learned from this Metathought? First, remember that causation is not necessarily a dichotomous variable (that is, "causal" versus "non-causal"). Instead, causation can lie on a continuum with regard to its degree, magnitude, or weight (see Metathought V, Differentiating Dichotomous Variables and Continuous Variables). Next, attempt to assess the approximate proportion that each cause contributes to the outcome, keeping in mind that not all causes are equal. Finally, don't automatically disregard, ignore, or rule out causes solely because they possess less relative weight. In short, before reaching your conclusions, consider the contribution of *all* possible causes.

Glossary

The following terms (or variations) are defined in the glossary:

behavior	effect
causal	erroneous
causation	event
cause	linear
concept	mood
continuous variable	reasoning
decision	subsequent
dichotomous variable	variable

C h a p t e r **14**

XIV. Multiple Pathways of Causation: Different Causes, Same Effects

Whether we force the man's property from him by pinching his stomach, or pinching his fingers, makes some difference anatomically; morally, none whatsoever.
—JOHN RUSKIN*

All roads lead to Rome.
—JEAN DE LA FONTAINE**

Any road leads to the end of the world.
—EDWARD FITZGERALD***

A number of different antecedent conditions may lead to the same outcome. Put another way, the same observed result may spring from different causes. To take an example, the factors that cause a mother to become an alcoholic in one family may be completely different from the factors that cause a mother to become an alcoholic in another family, or from those factors that cause a mother to become an alcoholic in a third family. In other words, there are multiple routes or pathways[1] to alcoholism.

---

*1819–1900, The Two Paths, V, quoted in The Pocket Book of Quotations, Davidoff, 1952
**1621–1695, Fables, XII, quoted in The Pocket Book of Quotations, Davidoff, 1952
***1809–1883, Polonius, quoted in The Pocket Book of Quotations, Davidoff, 1952

$$C_1 \rightarrow E_1$$
$$C_2 \rightarrow E_1$$
$$C_3 \rightarrow E_1$$

FIGURE 14-1   Multiple Pathways of Causation

(*Note:* C = cause; E = effect.)

Here are some further illustrations of this Metathought:

LAUGHTER may be produced by a number of independent pathways, such as humor, nervousness, happiness, embarrassment, or physical tickling;

TEARS may be caused independently by sadness, joy, pain, frustration, anger, allergies, or direct ocular irritation (such as exposure to onions, soap, or smog);

MALE GENITAL ERECTION may be brought about by direct physical stimulation, by visual exposure to erotic photographs, by sexual fantasies, as a correlate of the REM sleep cycle, as a side effect of some antidepressant medications, or by being hanged by a rope from the neck until dead.

An extremely useful application of this Metathought involves identifying and examining the etiology of various types of psychopathology. Depression, for example, may be produced by numerous independent pathways, including:

>the ingestion of certain drugs (such as reserpine, methyldopa, oral contraceptives, or barbiturates);

>withdrawal from drugs (such as amphetamines or cocaine);

>vitamin deficiencies (such as pellagra, pernicious anemia, or thiamine deficiency);

>starvation;

>physical illness (such as hypothyroidism, Cushing's syndrome, or mononucleosis).

Depression also may be the result of "psychological" phenomena,[2] such as:

>faulty belief systems (unachievable expectations or goals);
>loneliness;

>helplessness;
>loss;
>failure;
>trauma;
>a sense of existential futility and meaninglessness.[3]

As an exercise, identify independent causal pathways that can produce anxiety (suggested responses appear in Appendix 2):

> _____ ;
> _____ ;
> _____ ;
> _____ ;
> _____ ;
> _____ ;
> _____ ;
> _____ ;
> _____ ;
> _____ ;
> _____ .

The notion of multiple causal pathways applies not only to the etiology of problems, but to their potential *resolution* as well. Specifically, in terms of psychopathology, there are *multiple pathways of treatment*. For example, depression may be successfully alleviated by psychopharmacology (such as heterocyclic antidepressants or Monoamine oxidase inhibitors), electroconvulsive therapy (ECT), cognitive psychotherapy, insight-oriented psychotherapy, emotional catharsis (such as the ventilation of anger), success experiences, supportive interpersonal relationships, or finding meaning and purpose in life.

Anxiety, too, may be reduced by a number of pathways, including psychopharmacology (such as benzodiazepines), cognitive therapy, insight-oriented psychotherapy, behavioral therapy (such as relaxation training, systematic desensitization, implosion, or flooding), exercise, a vacation, hypnosis, meditation, biofeedback, a change in jobs, supportive and comforting interpersonal relationships, or spiritual faith.

The moral of this Metathought? First, never assume *a priori* that similar outcomes must be the product of similar causes. Second, when exploring avenues of causation, always be on the lookout for alternate routes.

Glossary Terms

The following terms (or variations) are defined in the Glossary:

antecedent	existentialism
a priori	expectation
belief	experience
causal	insight
causation	interpersonal
cause	phenomena
cognitive	physical
cognitive therapy	psychological
cognitive–behavioral therapy	psychopathology
concept	psychotherapy
correlate	syndrome
effect	theory
etiology	treatment
event	

Notes

[1] The concept of multiple pathways of causation is synonymous with the philosophical *principle of the plurality of causes* (see Angeles, 1981) and also is similar to the general systems theory term, *equifinality* (see Bertalanffy, 1968).

[2] In using the term *psychological,* I do not mean to suggest that these events are, in any way, "non-physical." I am, of course, assuming that *all* psychological phenomena necessarily have physical (biological, physiological, neurochemical, neuroanatomical, and other) components or correlates. (See Metathought III, Multiple Levels of Description.)

[3] This Metathought does not imply that pathways of causation are mutually exclusive. Causal pathways can (and typically do) exist simultaneously; that is, *multiple pathways may involve multiple causation.* The point here is that each causal pathway alone is *sufficient,* and does not depend on the presence of another pathway, to produce the effect. This, in fact, is the distinction between the two Metathought principles, Multiple Causation (Metathought XII) and Multiple Pathways of Causation. Multiple Causation, by definition, always involves at least two causes that together produce a given effect. In Multiple Pathways, by contrast, there may be a single cause that is sufficient to produce the effect

Part Three

Common Misattributions

Chapter *15*

XV. *The Fundamental Attribution Error: Underestimating the Impact of External Influences*

Don't call a man honest just because he never had the chance to steal.
—YIDDISH PROVERB

One unable to dance blames the unevenness of the floor.
—MALAY PROVERB

How do we explain the causes of people's behavior? We typically attribute their actions either to their personality or to their circumstances. Put another way, we ascribe dispositional attributions or situational attributions. Dispositional attributions involve assigning the causes of behavior to people's personality traits, characteristics, or attitudes, that is, to "internal" influences. Situational attributions, in contrast, involve assigning the causes of behavior to people's circumstances, surroundings, or environment, that is, to "external" influences.

In reality, of course, behavior is due to a combination of many factors (see Metathought XII, Multiple Causation), both internal and external, that vary in the degree to which they are responsible for causing a person's actions (see Metathought XIII, Degrees of Causation). However, in arriving at causal attributions, we have a tendency to overestimate people's dispositions and to underestimate their situations. In other words, we are prone to weigh internal determinants too heavily, and external determinants too lightly. We are thus likely to explain others' behavior as resulting predominantly from their personality, while we often minimize (or even ignore) the importance of the particular situations in which they find themselves. This mistake is so prevalent, in fact, that the social psychologist Lee Ross (1977) termed it the Fundamental Attribution Error (see also Heider, 1958).[1]

What are some illustrations of this attributional bias? If people don't tip a waiter, we may conclude that they are stingy. If they don't go to work, they are lazy. If they say nice things, they are friendly. If they don't return phone calls, they are rude. If they cry, they are sensitive. If they don't smile, they are aloof. If they help you, they are caring. If they hurt you, they are cruel.

Notice how these attributions essentially disregard any external or situational factors that might be responsible for producing these behaviors. Consider, for instance, that people may not tip a waiter because the service was atrocious; they may not go to work because of a family emergency; they may say nice things because their behavior is being monitored; they may not return phone calls because they haven't received any messages; they may cry because they are in the midst of a tragedy; they may not smile because it's been "one of those days"; they may help you because their paycheck depends on it; and they may hurt you because you have hurt them. Remember that at any given time, how people behave depends *both* on what they bring to the situation ("who" they are), *as well as* the situation itself ("where" they are). Thus, we must guard against our tendency to minimize or discount the impact of external influences.

To take another example, imagine that a patient sits in your office for a clinical intake interview. During the interview, you observe that she is extremely quiet, she speaks in hushed tones, she squirms and fidgets in her chair, her hands tremble, and she avoids making direct eye contact with you. What is causing her to behave this way? If you are like most people, your first inclination probably would be to explain her behavior in terms of her personality characteristics. You might conclude, for instance, that she is an introverted, high-strung, insecure, or emotionally unstable person. You are liable, moreover, to overlook any number of situational factors that also could account for her behavior. For example, the patient's demeanor may be a consequence of the formality of the interview, an argument that she just had with her boyfriend, her just having received distressing news, the demands of her time schedule, or possibly even your own behavior. In short, the *circumstances themselves* may be stressful.

As another illustration, consider the dilemma of the homeless. An observer is likely to explain homeless people's condition as being due to characterological or personality factors, such as laziness, moral weakness, alcoholism, or mental illness. These attributions, however, fail to take into account the situational factors that can (and do) perpetuate homelessness, such as a lack of affordable housing, job scarcity, discrimination, and a depressed economy.

The following exercise serves to underscore the enormous, yet typically unnoticed, power of the social situation in influencing our feelings, attitudes, and behavior. Imagine yourself in the following scenarios and how you might respond to the simple question, "So, how are you doing?" For each situation, indicate not only what you might say, but also provide a brief description of your probable demeanor, body language, and the emotional tone of your response.

With your parents: _____

With your sibling:_____

With your grandparent: _____

With your child: _____

With your best friend: _____

With your current "significant other": _____

With your ex-"significant other":_____

With someone whom you know dislikes you: _____

With someone whom you dislike: _____

With an eight-year-old child: _____

With an eighty-year-old adult: _____

With your teacher: _____

With your therapist:_____

With your minister/priest/rabbi:_____

With your boss: _____

With your physician: _____

With a police officer: _____

With a used car salesman: _____

With a friendly waitress: _____

With a crabby receptionist: _____

With a beggar on the street:_____

While exercising: _____

While cramming for a test:_____

While doing the laundry: _____

At a party: _____

At a funeral: _____

At a job interview: _____

At a singles bar: _____

On a first date:_____

While having sex: _____

In looking over your answers, observe that *all* the variability in your responses is attributable to the situations themselves, because both you and the initial question were fixed and held constant. Before we move on, one final point deserves mention. Can you determine which of these responses reflects the "real" you? Notice that this question is, in itself, virtually unanswerable without also taking into account the *context* of the situation.

One of the most intriguing aspects of the Fundamental Attribution Error is that it frequently becomes *reversed* when people attempt to explain *their own* behavior. In other words, persons perceiving their own actions tend to overemphasize the impact of situational factors, while underestimating the impact of their own dispositional characteristics. The term *Actor–Observer Bias* (Jones & Nisbett, 1972) refers to the tendency for observers to overestimate the importance of another person's dispositions, but for that person (the "actor") to overestimate the importance of the situation in explaining his or her own behavior.

To take an example, let us return to the scenario of the clinical intake interview described above. An observer (in this case, the clinician) would be inclined to explain the patient's behavior primarily in terms of her dispositional characteristics ("This patient has an Anxiety Disorder with Avoidant Personality Features"). The patient, in contrast, is likely to explain her own behavior principally in terms of the circumstances that she is experiencing ("This therapist is so pushy, intrusive, and obnoxious that he's making me nervous"). In other words, the observer (clinician) overemphasizes dispositional causes, while the actor (patient) overemphasizes situational causes.

What is responsible for these attributional errors? Social psychologists have identified two principal sources: *cognitive biases* and *motivational biases*.

Cognitive biases refer to systematic mistakes that derive from limits that are inherent in our capacity to process information. Because of our intrinsic cognitive limitations, we attempt to simplify our thinking by utilizing various mental "shortcuts" that permit us to process information more rapidly and efficiently (albeit less accurately). For instance, because we are not capable of perceiving everything in our environment, our focus is automatically drawn to the most prominent, conspicuous or "eye-catching"—that is, *perceptually salient*—stimuli. Further, we rely heavily on salient information to help us explain the world around us. Unfortunately, however, perceptual salience leads us to formulate biased and inaccurate causal attributions (Taylor & Fiske, 1975). Specifically, we are prone to equate the most *perceptually salient* stimuli with the most *causally influential* stimuli.

How does this relate to the Fundamental Attribution Error? When somebody behaves, our attention is focused, almost instinctively, on the *person*, not on his or her *environment*. As noted by the eminent social psychologist Fritz Heider (1958), "Behavior... has such salient properties that it tends to engulf the field." In other words, the person's behavior so dominates our perceptions that the situation itself fades into relative obscurity. Thus, the salience of the person's behavior leads us to ascribe dispositional attributions of causality.

The Actor–Observer Bias also can be explained as a function of perceptual salience. That is, when *we* behave, our attention is focused not on ourselves, but on our *situation*. Because our environment is most salient to us, we are apt to perceive it as more causally influential. Thus, in explaining our own behavior, we are prone to arrive at situational, rather than dispositional, attributions.[2]

In sum, the observer focuses on the actor, which leads to dispositional attributions; by contrast, the actor focuses on the environment, which leads to situational attributions.

Motivational biases refer to systematic mistakes that derive from our efforts to satisfy our own personal needs, such as our desire for self-esteem, power, or prestige. Simply put, motivational biases serve the function of making us *feel better* (usually about ourselves), even if they do so at the expense of distorting, obscuring, or falsifying reality.

One of our most powerful psychological drives is our need for control. Without a sense of personal control over our lives, the world would seem unsafe, threatening, and dangerous. How do we attempt to achieve control? One very important way is by seeking to explain events around us—that is, by assigning causal attributions (Kelley, 1967). We thus strive to understand our world so that it will become more predictable and, therefore, controllable.

Are we motivated to prefer one type of causal attribution over another? It would appear so. From early childhood, we are socialized (particularly in Western cultures) to believe that people can control their destiny and are the masters of their fate. Society, then, generally condones dispositional attributions, while it discourages situational attributions.

Why? It is extremely unsettling to believe that people are at the mercy of unpredictable, haphazard, or random events that lie beyond their control. We would prefer, instead, to believe that people must have power over their fate. After all, if we assume that other people have control over *their* outcomes, it reassures us that we, too, can control *our* outcomes. Thus, it makes us feel better to assign dispositional, rather than situational, attributions.

So strong, in fact, is our need to believe in a dispositional (internal) locus of control, that we frequently fool ourselves into overestimating the degree of control that we actually do have, while underestimating the impact of external factors that lie beyond our control. Put another way, we simply don't have as much control over people and events as we'd like to believe that we do. Nevertheless, making dispositional attributions provides us with an *illusion* of control. We are prone, therefore, to exaggerate our perceptions of controllability.

One very unfortunate consequence of this motivational bias is that people who are harmed by forces that are truly out of their control may be held more responsible for their circumstances than they should be. In other words, our illusion of control may lead us to blame people for the bad things that happen to them.

Why does this occur? Melvin Lerner (1970) theorized that we have great difficulty accepting the unfairness and injustices of life. Further, we have a strong need to believe that we live in a "just world," a world in which good is rewarded and bad is punished. This belief leads us to conclude that people get

what they deserve, and deserve what they get. In a just world those who succeed must merit their success; likewise, those who suffer must deserve their
suffering.

Instances of "just world" attributions abound:

>*"Rape victims must have behaved seductively."*
>*"Battered spouses must have had it coming to them."*
>*"People who get cancer must have brought it on themselves."*
>*"Victims of persecution must be guilty of something, or they wouldn't be persecuted."*
>*"What goes around, comes around."*
>*"Sooner or later, your karma will catch up with you."*

Or, taken to its illogical extreme, in the vernacular of so-called "New Age"
metaphysics, every human being is completely responsible for everything that
happens to them, because "we all create and manifest our own reality." From
this point of view, even a baby born with AIDS is seen as fully responsible for
choosing that reality.

What compels people to make such attributions? Once again, in all likelihood, to preserve their illusion of control. Simply put, it is psychologically
more comforting to blame others for the disasters that befall them, rather than
face the cold reality that we live in an unjust world, a world in which such
events can happen at random. After all, if negative events are uncontrollable,
they could just as easily happen to *us*. By contrast, if the world is just, then presumably we can avoid catastrophe by behaving properly. In other words, by
assigning dispositional attributions, we hope to experience a greater sense of
control over our destiny.

Research shows that blaming people for accidents, for example, makes the
events seem more predictable and hence avoidable by the self. Further, the
more severe the consequences of the accident, the greater the blame we are
likely to assign. In an experiment conducted by Elaine Walster (1966), subjects
listened to one of several versions of a story, all of which began with a car that
had been parked on a hill, and then accidentally rolled down. In one version,
the car struck a tree, resulting in minimal damage. In another version, the car
missed the tree, but struck another vehicle, damaging its bumper. In a third
version, the car rolled into a shop, seriously injuring the shopkeeper and a
small child. Subjects were then asked to ascribe blame based on the facts provided.

Walster found that greater blame was assigned according to the seriousness
of the accidents. Thus, when the damage was minimal, subjects did not find
the car's owner to be particularly blameworthy; however, when people were
seriously injured, subjects believed that the owner was more responsible (for
example, for not having had his brakes checked recently) and therefore ought
to be punished. Walster concluded that subjects appeared to judge guilt not
just on the act itself, but on the severity of the consequences of the act.[3] Here
again, it appears that, in an effort to satisfy our needs for feeling less threat-

ened by the world around us, we have a motivational bias to assign dispositional attributions.

What can we conclude about the Fundamental Attribution Error? This simple but powerful principle probably is the single most important lesson of twentieth-century social psychology. Keep this in mind whenever you attempt to explain someone's behavior: *Never underestimate the power of the situation.*

Glossary Terms

The following terms (or variations) are defined in the Glossary:

Actor–Observer Bias	external
ascribe	external attribution
attitude	fact
attribution	Fundamental Attribution Error
behavior	internal
belief	internal attribution
bias	introvert
causal	judgment
causality	mental
cause	mental illness
clinical	motivational bias
cognitive	perception
cognitive bias	personality
consequence	personality trait
determinant	prediction
dilemma	psychological
disorder	psychology
disposition	random
event	social
experience	stimulus
explanation	thinking

Notes

[1] For a series of research studies that empirically demonstrate the Fundamental Attribution Error, see Jones and Harris (1967), Napolitan and Goethals (1979), and Ross, Amabile, and Steinmetz (1977).

[2] See Storms (1973) for experimental evidence supporting the perceptual salience explanation of the Actor–Observer Bias.

[3] Similarly, the Swiss psychologist Jean Piaget (1948) found that children assign blame primarily on the severity of an event's consequences.

Chapter **16**

XVI. The Intervention–Causation Fallacy: The Cure Doesn't Prove the Cause

> *Although traditional psychotherapy has insisted that therapeutic practices have to be based on findings of etiology, it is possible that certain factors might cause neuroses during early childhood and that entirely different factors might relieve neuroses during adulthood.*
> —EDITH WEISSKOPF-JOELSON*

> *Treatability [is] not a legitimate criterion of illness.*
> —THOMAS SZASZ**

Our ability to *modify* an event does not, *per se*, prove what originally *caused* the event. In other words, we cannot necessarily determine an event's cause solely on the basis of its response to a particular intervention. As such, the solution to a problem does not inherently point to its etiology. To believe otherwise would be to fall prey to the *Intervention–Causation Fallacy*. To take a very obvious example, we may be able to surgically remove a kidney stone, but our capacity to do so does not, in any way, explain what originally caused the creation and development of the kidney stone.

In the field of mental health, the most prominent incarnation of this error in thinking is the *Treatment–Etiology Fallacy*. This refers to arriving at the erroneous conclusion that a positive response to a medical treatment inherently proves that there was a medical cause. Counterintuitive as it may seem, a

*Quoted in Viktor E. Frankl's *Man's Search for Meaning*, 1959
**Insanity, 1987

favorable response to medication is *not* proof of disease. Nevertheless, if a psychotropic drug, for instance, is successful in alleviating the symptoms of a diagnosed mental disorder, many people wrongly conclude that the disorder therefore must have been caused by—or in fact *is*—a biological illness.

Let's explore these notions more fully by means of the following hypothetical scenarios. In the first example, imagine that you are practically crawling out of your skin with anxiety about an upcoming exam. In a state of near panic, you bolt to your medicine cabinet where you store your prescription of "mother's little helper" (i.e., Valium) for just such occasions. Within minutes after ingesting the precious yellow pill, lo and behold, your anxiety has vanished. What caused your anxiety to cease? Obviously, the Valium. But what caused your anxiety to occur in the first place? Can we, solely on the basis of its positive response to a prescription medication, attribute the etiology of your anxiety as being due to a biological illness? Of course not.

As another example, let's say that by the end of an exceptionally stressful day, you've developed a splitting headache. Once you've downed a couple of aspirin, however, your headache is history. Now, what cured the headache? The aspirin. But as for determining the initial cause of your headache, what are we to conclude? That you were suffering from a medical condition due to a "lack of aspirin?" Preposterous, right?

Let's examine one more scenario. Suppose that we observe someone with a diagnosis of schizophrenia who displays signs of auditory hallucinations, paranoid delusions, and bizarre affect. After we give him several doses of a powerful antipsychotic drug, his hallucinations diminish, his delusions abate, and his affect stabilizes. Did the medication reduce his symptoms? Yes. But can we take this favorable response to medication as incontrovertible proof that schizophrenia is, therefore, a biological disease? Using the same line of logic as in the above two examples, the answer is *no*.

This is not to argue that emotional or mental disorders don't have biological *correlates*. It would be shocking if they didn't. In fact, I would argue that *all* thoughts, feelings, perceptions, and experiences—both "normal" and "abnormal"—are reflected or mapped, in some form, in some configuration, in the human body (see Metathought III, Multiple Levels of Description). But remember, a *correlate* is not the same thing as a *cause* (see Metathought X, Correlation Does Not Prove Causation), and biological *differences* are not, *per se,* equivalent to biological *pathology* (see Metathought III, Multiple Levels of Description). Further, even if we were to hypothesize that all mental disorders are, in fact, rooted in biological pathology, don't make the mistake of assuming that their favorable response to medication provides the evidence. Again, a positive response to medical treatment is not proof of medical disease.

To underscore this last point, imagine a scenario in which you receive regular injections of an extremely valuable medication that virtually eliminates all signs and symptoms of anxiety, depression, and emotional distress. Assume further that, immediately upon receiving your dosage, you invariably and instantaneously feel significantly better, irrespective of your psychological status prior to the treatment. Last, suppose you discover that the precious medication is, in fact, an opioid analgesic by the chemical name of diacetyl morphine (better known as *heroin*).

On the basis of this information, what conclusions can you draw? That you are suffering from some kind of medical problem because the prescribed treatment always "improves" your status? That you, in fact, must have a "dis-ease," because after receiving your medicine you consistently experience less "dis-ease?" That your response to the treatment provides insight into the etiology of your pre-existing "condition?" That your medical condition is attributable to a "chemical imbalance"—namely, a deficiency of heroin in your bloodstream?

In closing, it is important to keep in mind that, although the solution to a problem does not *necessarily* provide proof of its cause, there certainly are instances where a successful intervention *can,* in itself, determine such cause. Take, for example, a situation where filling your empty tank with gasoline serves to answer the question of why your car wouldn't start. Here, the intervention clearly would establish the cause of the problem.

The following exercise is intended, therefore, to provide you with some practice at identifying the relationship—or lack thereof—between interventions (solutions) and etiology (causes).

First, briefly describe three instances in which the cause of a problem *can* be determined directly from its solution (in other words, when a successful intervention *does* inherently provide proof of etiology).

1. _____
   _____
   _____
   _____

2. _____
   _____
   _____
   _____

3. _____
   _____
   _____
   _____

Next, describe three instances in which the cause of a problem *cannot* be determined directly from its solution (that is, when a successful intervention *does not* inherently provide proof of etiology).

1._____

_____

_____

_____

2._____

_____

_____

_____

3._____

_____

_____

_____

Glossary Terms

The following terms (or variations) are defined in the Glossary:

affect	hypothetical
attribution	i.e.
belief	insight
causation	Intervention–Causation Fallacy
cause	logic
correlate	mental disorder
counterintuitive	normal
criterion	pathological
delusion	*per se*
diagnosis	perception
disease	prescription
disorder	psychological
emotion	psychotic
erroneous	psychotropic
etiology	response
event	symptom
experience	thinking
explanation	treatment
fallacy	Treatment–Etiology Fallacy

XVII. The Consequence–Intentionality Fallacy: The Effect Doesn't Prove the Intent

*Never attribute to malice that which
is adequately explained by stupidity.*
—ARTHUR BLOCH*

Nonintentionality is one of the criteria of mental illness.
—THOMAS SZASZ**

How do we go about determining the intent of someone's behavior? Quite commonly, we base our explanation solely on the *result* of the behavior. That is, we assume that the consequences of the behavior directly reflect the person's intent. And in many cases, this is likely to be an accurate assessment. However, the effect of someone's behavior does not, *per se, prove* the intent of the behavior. In other words, intentionality cannot be proven solely by consequences.

As a vivid illustration, let us examine one of the most puzzling and disturbing occurrences in the entire realm of human behavior: self-mutilation. The deliberate self-infliction of bloody wounds, typically by means of a razor, knife

*Murphy's Law, Book Two, 1980
**Insanity, 1987

or needle, is, unfortunately, not an infrequent event in psychiatric inpatient hospital settings. And as you might well imagine, the reactions of those who witness such behavior (staff and patients alike) range from shock, horror, disgust, and outrage to sympathy, compassion, and pity, to terror, panic, and frantic helplessness. In a word, self-mutilation invariably stirs up lots of *attention*.

Thus, the *consequences* of the behavior are crystal clear. But how do we explain why the behavior occurred in the first place? Can we rely on the effects of the patient's behavior on others to infer that gaining attention was, therefore, her primary goal? In other words, does the effect prove the intent? Although seeking the attention of others is one very tempting (and certainly plausible) explanation, before we jump to this conclusion let us consider some other possible reasons that might motivate self-mutilating behavior.[1]

1. *Self-punishment:* "I am so evil, I *deserve* to be hurt."
2. *Sensory stimulation:* "I'd rather feel *something*—even pain—than nothing, emptiness, or numbness."
3. *Confirmation of life:* "I feel dead inside. Seeing my own blood reassures me that I do have something inside of me."
4. *Reification of emotion:* "My emotional pain is confusing because it isn't tangible. By cutting myself and seeing my blood, it makes my pain somehow seem more *real*."
5. *Catharsis:* "I just want to get the pain that's inside, outside. I'm trying to relieve this horrible pressure that's built up inside of me."
6. *Revenge against pain:* "It's like my way of getting back at the pain."
7. *Displacement of anger:* "It's safer to hurt myself than the person I *really* want to hurt."
8. *Psychological control:* "My emotional pain is totally out of my control. At least when I cut myself, I get some control over how much pain I feel, where I feel it, and when I feel it."
9. *Suicide:* "I just want to end this pain—once and for all."

Even granting the possibility of these explanations, an observer would not necessarily be wrong in asserting that the patient was mutilating herself simply so that others would pay attention to her. The patient's intent may indeed have been principally (or even exclusively) to gain the attention of others. But the flaw in thinking occurs when the observer draws this conclusion *solely* on the basis of the consequences of the patient's behavior. In other words, the observer should not assume that the effect, in and of itself, proves the intent.

To take another example, let's evaluate the most prevalent of all the male sexual dysfunctions—premature ejaculation—as viewed from the psychoanalytic perspective. One of the most common consequences of premature ejaculation is that the man's partner is left feeling unsatisfied, frustrated, and angry because she has been deprived of a pleasurable sexual experience. But do her reactions reflect the man's intent, conscious or otherwise? Psychoanalytic theory would have us believe so.

Psychoanalytic theorists maintain that premature ejaculation is a neurotic symptom of deeper psychopathology (see Kaplan, 1974). Specifically, Freudian theory contends that premature ejaculators harbor unconscious feelings of sadistic hatred toward women. Premature ejaculation thus serves the unconscious functions of degrading and defiling the man's partner (symbolically, his mother), while also depriving her of pleasure. On the basis of this theory, psychoanalytic treatment attempts to uncover and resolve the patient's unconscious Oedipal conflicts and sadistic orientation toward women, which supposedly then results in an automatic improvement in his sexual functioning. The treatment sessions are conducted two to five times a week, over a period of several years, and employ the standard psychoanalytic techniques of free association, dream interpretation, and analysis of transference.

How valid are these theoretical assumptions and therapeutic procedures? Simply put, not very. In point of fact, decades of research have failed to support the Freudian tenet that the primary cause of premature ejaculation is unconscious hostility toward women. Further, there is no empirical evidence of any systematic correlation between premature ejaculation and either specific sexual conflicts or other forms of psychopathology. Moreover, clinical outcome research shows that psychoanalysis, as a method of treatment, is virtually worthless for premature ejaculation.

On what basis, then, did psychoanalysts develop their theories and reach their conclusions? It would appear that they might have fallen prey to a misattribution of causation by confusing consequences with intentionality; that is, they seem to have erroneously concluded that the *effects* of premature ejaculation prove its *cause*.

I am not arguing that unconscious hostility never contributes to the occurrence of premature ejaculation. Rather, as with the case of self-mutilating behavior, I am pointing out that consequences do not *necessarily* prove intentionality. In other words, intent cannot be determined solely by the effect.

What, then, are some alternative explanations for premature ejaculation? First, it may be due to faulty learning patterns (for example, stressful conditions during the young man's initial sexual encounters). Second, it may be a consequence of the man's hypersensitivity to erotic sensation. Third, it may be the result of the man's excessive concern over his partner's response (i.e., "performance anxiety"). Fourth, according to systems theory it may be a manifestation of a couple's maladaptive interpersonal dynamics. Fifth, it may be due to the man's failure to perceive preorgastic sensations which are necessary to bring the reflex function under control. Sixth, although rarely the case, it may be caused by certain medical conditions (such as local disease of the posterior urethra, multiple sclerosis, or other degenerative neurological disorders). Clearly, premature ejaculation is a complex phenomenon that, in all likelihood, involves a combination of both multiple causation as well as multiple pathways of causation (see Metathoughts XII and XIV, respectively).

The case of suicide is yet another instance where people frequently are quick to explain the intent of someone's behavior on the basis of the effects of the behavior. What are the consequences when a person takes his or her own life? The impact on others is, almost invariably, profound. They usually are left to struggle with intense feelings of hurt, guilt, sorrow, shame, remorse, or even animosity and resentment.

What motivates people to kill themselves? It is a common belief (held by many therapists and the general population alike) that suicide is, in essence, an act of anger and hostility, directed not just toward oneself, but toward others as well. On what grounds do people base this assumption? Here again, probably on the *consequences* of the act. The feelings evoked in others by suicide are so striking that it may seem as though the person *must* have intended to cause them. However, consequences do not prove intentionality. If, for example, somebody's suicide were to leave others feeling hurt or guilty, it would be a mistake to conclude that this was, therefore, the person's primary motive. People commit suicide for many reasons, of which "getting back" at others is but one.

In fact, as preposterous as it may seem, even the suicidal act itself is not necessarily proof of suicidal intent. Consider the tragically ironic scenario of a person who may be attempting to communicate a "cry for help" to others by means of a dramatic suicidal gesture, but who miscalculates the lethality of her method. The hapless individual may inadvertently succeed in committing suicide by, for instance, underestimating a fatal dosage of sleeping pills. Thus, even a suicidal outcome does not, *per se*, prove suicidal intent.

As a final illustration of this Metathought, let us examine the consequences and possible motives of so-called passive-aggressive behavior. What does this term mean? In clinical psychology it refers to a person's indirect expression of anger or hostility through seemingly innocuous or innocent behavior. For instance, the individual may display passive and negativistic resistance to the demands of others in the form of procrastination, dawdling, lateness, stubbornness, inefficiency, or "forgetfulness."

In its extreme form, it temporarily achieved the status of a full-blown mental disorder, classified in the *Diagnostic and Statistical Manual of Mental Disorders* (American Psychiatric Association, 1987) as Passive Aggressive Personality Disorder.[2] According to the DSM, "The name of this disorder is *based on the assumption* [emphasis added] that such people are passively expressing covert aggression" (p. 356). How does an observer make this assumption? By inferring the person's intent. And on what grounds is this intent inferred? Of course, almost invariably by the *consequences* of the person's behavior. Thus, the attribution of passive-aggressiveness is gauged primarily by the reactions of others who feel upset, frustrated, or angered by the person's seemingly innocent (yet "covertly hostile") actions. Consider these scenarios:

The employee who frequently misplaces his work orders
The housewife who repeatedly forgets to hang up clean bath towels

The student who consistently comes late to class
The therapy patient who habitually reschedules his appointments
The supervisor who routinely mispronounces her employee's name
The husband who forgets his wife's birthday present at work
The teenager who loses the family's house keys
The young woman who yawns throughout a dinner date
The executive who is "too busy" to return phone calls
The person who asks for advice, but politely rejects all suggestions.

All of these situations (and countless more) are ripe for attributions (or, perhaps more accurately, *accusations*) of passive-aggressive intent, which frequently assume some variant of the following exchange:

Person A: "Your behavior upset me. Therefore, you must have *intended* to upset me."

Person B: "But I didn't do it deliberately!"

Person A: "Then you must have *unconsciously* intended to upset me!"

As you can see, this is "checkmate," leaving Person B in the unenviable position of being completely powerless to disprove Person A's virtually invincible indictment.

What is the lesson to be learned here? We cannot safely infer other people's intentions (conscious or unconscious) solely on the basis of the consequences of their behavior. How can we overcome the problem of the Consequence–Intentionality Fallacy? One antidote is to force yourself to think about other plausible causes of the behavior, in addition to the one suggested directly by its consequences. (This process may be seen as analogous to exploring multiple pathways of causation; see Metathought XIV.) In other words, when attempting to understand or explain why someone behaved in a particular way, *consider alternative intents.*

To give you some practice in applying this antidote, let's analyze the following scenarios. For each event, first state the likely consequence of the behavior in question. Then, identify as many alternative intents as you can that could also plausibly account for the behavior.

1. *A spouse who has an extramarital affair*
Primary Consequence:

_____

Alternative Intents:

_____

_____

_____

_____

_____

2. *Parents who decline to financially support their adult son*
Primary Consequence:

_____

Alternative Intents:

_____

_____

_____

_____

_____

3. *A teenager who runs away from home*
Primary Consequence:

_____

Alternative Intents:

_____

_____

_____

_____

_____

Glossary Terms

The following terms (or variations) are defined in the Glossary:

analogous
antidote
assumption
attribution
behavior
belief
category
causation
cause
clinical
conscious
consequence
Consequence–Intentionality Fallacy
correlation
criteria
Diagnostic and Statistical Manual
   of Mental Disorders (DSM)

disease
disorder
displacement
DSM
dynamics
dysfunction
effect
emotion
empirical
erroneous
evaluation
event
existence
experience
explanation
fallacy
i.e.

infer
intentionality
interpersonal
interpretation
mental illness
motive
neurotic
per se
personality disorder
phenomenon
psychoanalysis
psychological
psychology

psychopathology
reification
resistance
response
sensory
symptom
theoretical
theory
thinking
transference
treatment
unconscious
vivid

Notes

[1] I collected this set of explanations over a period of several years at an inpatient psychiatric treatment center where I worked as the clinical supervisor. These quotes were taken virtually verbatim from the patients themselves, as well as from the team of psychiatrists, psychologists, and counselors at the weekly treatment planning conferences.

[2] I say temporarily because, in the most recent edition of the DSM (American Psychiatric Association, 1994), Passive Aggressive Personality Disorder was voted out of existence as a formal diagnostic category.

XVIII. The "If I Feel It, It Must Be True" Fallacy: The Truth Hurts; But So Do Lies

My mother loves me.
I feel good.
I feel good because she loves me.

I am good because I feel good
I feel good because I am good
My mother loves me because I am good.

My mother does not love me.
I feel bad.
I feel bad because she does not love me
I am bad because I feel bad
I feel bad because I am bad
I am bad because she does not love me
She does not love me because I am bad.
—*R. D. LAING**

An Englishman thinks he is moral
when he is only uncomfortable.
—*GEORGE BERNARD SHAW***

I never give them hell. I just tell the
truth, and they think it's hell.
—*HARRY S TRUMAN****

*Knots, 1970
**1856–1950, Man and Superman
***1884–1972, cited in William Safire, *Safire's Political Dictionary,* from The *New International Dictionary of Quotations,* Miner & Rawson, 1994

We rely on our feelings for many purposes, the most fundamental of which involves determining whether we like something or not. Although specific emotions (such as anger, sadness, happiness, or fear) vary tremendously in terms of their individual and unique characteristics, they all, to some degree, reveal the extent to which something *pleases* or *displeases* us. Our feelings thereby serve as the basis on which we formulate our subjective evaluations of events around us.

How do we come to know what we are feeling? Put another way, by what means do we identify our emotions? Simply stated, primarily by an awareness of our *somatic* or *physiological sensations*. Remember that emotions, like all psychological phenomena, are rooted in biochemistry and are therefore "mapped" in various physiological configurations (see Metathought III, Multiple Levels of Description). We thus learn to link particular visceral sensations to specific emotional states.

In general, when our somatic condition is comprised of comfortable or pleasurable sensations, we experience "feeling good"; in contrast, when it involves uncomfortable or unpleasurable sensations, we experience "feeling bad." In this way, our physiological status along the comfort–discomfort continuum functions as a barometer to help us ascertain our overall feelings.

As noted above, our feelings tell us whether or not an event is pleasing. But how do we determine whether or not the event is *true*? In many cases, we rely principally on our subjective perceptions of the event. Do you see a problem here?

The fact is, our experience of emotional comfort or discomfort is not a valid gauge for differentiating what is true from what is false. In other words, how we *feel* about an event is not proof of its *veracity*. Hence, what feels good isn't necessarily correct, and what feels bad isn't necessarily incorrect. Conversely, what feels bad isn't necessarily correct, and what feels good isn't necessarily incorrect.

TABLE 18-1   Interactions of Feelings and Events

Subjective Feelings	Veracity of Event	Descriptive Summary of Condition
Comfort +	True +	
Discomfort–	False –	
1. +	+	congruence between comfort and truth; receiving accurate and pleasing evaluations
2. +	–	living in a fantasy world, "in denial" of distressing facts; incongruent feelings
3. –	+	facing a painful truth; "unjustifiable defensiveness"
4. –	–	stung by a false accusation; "justifiable defensiveness"

Stated in a different way, feelings and truth are not intrinsically correlated; in fact, they are conceptually independent of (that is, *orthogonal* to) each other. As such, subjective feelings of comfort may be prompted by a pleasing truth as well as by a pleasing falsehood. Similarly, feelings of emotional discomfort may be due to a displeasing truth as well as a displeasing falsehood.

By treating subjective feelings (comfort versus discomfort) and the veracity of an event (true versus false) as two independent variables, I have summarized in Table 18-1 the four combinations to which they give rise, namely: comfortable truths, comfortable falsehoods, uncomfortable truths, and uncomfortable falsehoods.[1]

Comfortable Truths

This condition, represented in Row 1 of Table 18-1, involves pleasurable feelings that are a consequence of factual events, truthful assertions, or accurate observations. You may, for instance, experience pride, satisfaction, self-esteem, or self-respect when you solve a difficult problem, achieve a desired goal, or fulfill your own personal standards and expectations.

These situations also include feeling good about accurate evaluations, assessments, or appraisals from others. This may take the form of recognition, praise, or even constructive criticism from your teacher, coach, employer, or therapist. Similarly, it may entail receiving honest and valid feedback from a trusted family member, friend, or colleague. In sum, these are conditions in which there exists a state of congruence between the veracity of an event and one's experience of emotional comfort.

Comfortable Falsehoods

This condition, represented in Row 2, involves feeling emotionally comfortable in regard to statements, events, or beliefs that are *not* true. In other words, in these situations the acceptance of false or invalid information results in pleasurable feelings.

As an example, your best friend may succeed at alleviating your emotional distress by reassuring you of something that you *wish* were true, but *know* to be false (for instance, that your doomed romantic relationship still has a chance of working out). Thus, even in the face of irrefutable evidence to the contrary, convincing yourself that your friend is right permits you to experience a sense of comfort. The problem, of course, is that just because your friend's prediction makes you *feel better* doesn't make it any more *accurate*. In other words, a falsehood—even a pleasing falsehood—is still a falsehood.

Similarly, your psychotherapist may provide you with feedback, observations, or interpretations that make you feel good, but are entirely *inaccurate*. He might, for instance, persuade you to take credit for events over which you, in reality, have absolutely no control. The fact that his erroneous attributions leave you feeling emotionally contented demonstrates, once again, that what feels good isn't necessarily true.

In order to experience pleasurable feelings in the face of potentially unpleasurable facts, these situations typically require a certain degree of distortion, falsification, or invalidation of reality. Specifically, they frequently entail the concomitant use of two Freudian ego defense mechanisms: *denial* and *fantasy* (A. Freud, 1936). In utilizing denial, the individual reduces his or her emotional discomfort by refusing to accept—or even perceive—a psychologically painful reality. Fantasy, by contrast, involves the creation of an imaginary and less threatening reality in which the individual seeks gratification in fictitious events, activities, or achievements.

Like the proverbial ostrich whose response to danger is to bury its head in the sand, people too may cope with emotionally threatening situations by burying their perceptions in the sands of denial, thereby blocking out any reminders of their actual circumstances. They may then *imagine* a reality that provides them with the illusion of safety, control, and comfort. As an illustration of how denial and fantasy can operate in tandem, a person who is faced with the calamity of having just been diagnosed with a terminal disease may cope with this information first by denying its presence and then escaping into a fantasy world in which the disease ceases to exist. We may resort to this same coping strategy in response to a wide range of disturbing events: denying the fact that you've been dumped by someone you love while fantasizing that they desperately beg you to take them back; denying your chronic problems with alcohol while fantasizing about being able to control its use; denying the reality of your dire financial straits while fantasizing about how you're going to spend your imminent lottery jackpot.

When taken to its most extreme form, this condition reaches psychotic proportions in which the individual exhibits gross impairments in reality testing. Here, people are virtually severed from the real world, living instead in a fantasy world of their own creation. Further, in an ironic twist, their expressed state of "emotional comfort" is likely to be interpreted by others as a manifestation of their *disease,* to which a host of psychopathological descriptors can be readily attached: mood-incongruent delusions, manic denial, hysterical denial, and pathological reaction formation, to name but a few. In these cases, their belief system permits them to feel emotionally comfortable, but at an enormous cost: loss of touch with reality.

Uncomfortable Truths

This condition, represented in Row 3, involves feelings of emotional discomfort that are a function of upsetting but true or factual events. Although these situations differ tremendously in terms of their specific manifestations, the common thread that links them together is the process of recognizing, acknowledging, trying to reconcile, or otherwise coming to terms with various forms of "painful reality," "painful truth," or "painful fact."

For example, you may be facing the painful realization that you have been betrayed by a trusted friend. Or that certain people in your life are never going to change. Or that your marriage is all but over. Or that you really do have a drug problem. Or that someone dear to you has a terminal illness. Or that your career is doomed. Or that you have no financial security in your old age. Or that you will never accomplish what you always wanted to. Or that your hopes, plans, and dreams have amounted to naught. Or that you just aren't as [fill in the blank] as you thought you were.

In the context of psychotherapy, this condition manifests itself when clients are confronted with potentially painful truths about themselves, to which they commonly respond with resistance or defensiveness (see discussion of "defensiveness" below). This occurs, for instance, when the therapist provides clinical observations, feedback, or interpretations which reveal particularly upsetting or disturbing aspects of the client's personality. For example, the therapist may be entirely correct in interpreting her client's dreams as revealing an unconscious hatred toward his parents. Despite the fact that this interpretation is valid (or, more accurately, *because* it is valid), the client is therefore prone to feel threatened, defensive, and to respond by denying, rejecting, or "resisting" the interpretation, all in the effort to avoid accepting this painful truth. In these cases, "the truth hurts."

Uncomfortable Falsehoods

This condition, represented in Row 4, involves feeling uncomfortable in the face of untrue assertions or false accusations. Here, one's state of emotional discomfort is a consequence of having been *wrongfully* accused, for instance, of committing unethical behaviors or of harboring immoral desires. Some specific examples would include a student being wrongfully accused of cheating on an exam; an employer of sexual harassment against an employee; a landlord of racial discrimination against a tenant; a son of intentionally harming his sister; a spouse of being unfaithful to his or her mate; a father of having molested his daughter; or a psychotherapy patient of being resistant to treatment.

One very common outcome of this process may be conceptualized as *justifiable defensiveness,* in which a person's "defensive" response is, in fact, an act of self-protection against a false charge or untrue accusation. This phenomenon can be differentiated from its theoretical polar opposite (see Metathought VI), namely *unjustifiable defensiveness,* which involves a defensive response to a *true* accusation (Row 3 above); in other words, the person is reacting defensively because "the truth hurts." By contrast, in the case of justifiable defensiveness the person is reacting defensively because "the lie hurts." Clearly, then, when it comes to understanding or interpreting displays of defensiveness, we should exercise great caution. Specifically, for example, if someone's comments provoke you to respond defensively, don't assume—based solely on your feelings of discomfort—that their observations must therefore be true.[2] Stated more generally, emotional discomfort is not, in itself, proof of veracity.

As an illustration of this phenomenon, try the following simple exercise. First, think of a person in your life whom you especially dislike, despise, or who, for whatever reason, just "rubs you the wrong way." More precisely, select someone around whom you feel particularly uneasy, anxious, offended, or in some way threatened.

Now take out a piece of paper and write down all of that person's personality traits, characteristics, and mannerisms that cause you to feel the way you do. In other words, make a list of all the adjectives you find to be loathsome, odious, abhorrent, repugnant, or otherwise aversive. Be completely candid and honest, and try to identify as many specific descriptors as you can.

[Note: In order for this exercise to achieve maximum impact, please complete the instructions above before you continue reading this section!]

Let's briefly examine the purpose and rationale underlying this exercise, which I routinely utilize in my graduate psychology classes to demonstrate Carl G. Jung's personality theory. According to Jung (1943/1953), each of us has parts of our own personality that are so repulsive, threatening, or frightening to us that we refuse to acknowledge their very existence. Because they are denied expression in our conscious self-identity, they coalesce into an unconscious and relatively autonomous "splinter personality," which Jung termed the *shadow* archetype.

Thus, the shadow is the "dark side" of our personality and is comprised of everything we hate or fear about ourselves. Moreover, instead of recognizing the shadow as being a part of us, we unconsciously project these "disowned" characteristics onto other people. Thus, Jung theorized, when we feel extreme aversion toward another person, we probably are responding to those very attributes that we despise and reject in ourselves.

The purpose of this exercise now should be apparent: from a Jungian perspective, it is intended to introduce you to your own shadow.

Okay, once you've completed your list, let's proceed to the next step. To the left of each descriptor, write out any one of the following phrases:

"I'm afraid that I am . . .";
"I'm afraid of the part of me that is . . .";
"I despise the part of my personality that is . . ."; or
"I hate the fact that, deep down, I am so . . ."

For example, if your list were to include the adjectives *stupid, aggressive, dependent,* and *insecure,* you would modify it as follows:

"I'm afraid that I am *stupid.*"
"I'm afraid of the part of me that is *aggressive.*"
"I despise the part of my personality that is *dependent.*"
"I hate the fact that, deep down, I am so *insecure.*"

Now, slowly and deliberately read the sentences *aloud*. Pay attention to your feelings as you hear yourself recite each statement. Although your reactions probably will vary from one "confession" to the next, on the whole you are very likely to experience a distinct and pervading sense of *discomfort*.

But what does this *mean*? And what does it *prove*? From one perspective, your feelings of discomfort could be interpreted as providing evidence which confirms the validity of Jung's shadow theory. After all (a Jungian might argue), these statements wouldn't be making you squirm unless they were "triggering" aspects of yourself that already exist and that, deep down, you know to be true. Further, the more discomfort you experience, the more likely it is that you have hit upon a series of "painful truths." Right?

Not necessarily. Recognizing a painful truth, by definition, involves feelings of discomfort. *But so does experiencing the sting of a false accusation!* In essence, painful truths *and* false accusations *both* produce uncomfortable feelings (see Metathought XIV, Multiple Pathways of Causation). Obviously, then, we cannot reliably differentiate true versus false statements solely on the basis of the feelings that ensue.

In a broader clinical context, this conundrum rears its ambiguous head whenever psychotherapists attempt to gauge the accuracy of their interpretations by their clients' concomitant emotional reactions (or lack thereof). In all such cases, therapists must remain cognizant of the fact that while an interpretation may be disturbing to the client because it is true, it also may be disturbing because it is *false*.

The task is especially problematic for traditional psychoanalysts, who routinely interpret the meaning of their patients' cognitions and behaviors (with particular emphasis on free associations, transferences, dreams, fantasies, defense mechanisms, resistances, and parapraxes or "Freudian slips"). Let's say, for instance, that an analyst interprets his female patient's career choice of a business executive as evidence of her repressed "penis envy." This interpretation, naturally, prompts her to feel extremely uncomfortable, if not outright hostile. Of course, the analyst is then likely to view her "defensiveness" and "resistance" to his interpretation as further evidence of its veracity. And the more vehemently she protests, the more convinced he may become that he has, in fact, exhumed a painful truth. But how can he be certain that she is not responding, instead, to a false (and rather demeaning) accusation? The fact of the matter is, in the absence of any corroborating evidence, *he cannot*.

To take another example, an analyst may interpret his patient's dream of plowing a field as symbolic of an unconscious wish to engage in sexual intercourse with his mother. On the one hand, the analyst's interpretation may be entirely accurate, which would (understandably) produce feelings of discomfort in the patient. Conversely, however, the interpretation may be completely *false*, which *also* could give rise to essentially the same emotional response.

To summarize, feelings of discomfort may be the result of a painful truth *as well as* a false accusation. Thus, hearing an interpretation which makes you feel uncomfortable does not, in itself, prove that the interpretation is *correct* or *incorrect;* in fact, the *only* thing it proves with any degree of certainty is that it makes you feel *uncomfortable!*

As a final illustration, let's briefly touch on what has been, and continues to be, one of the most controversial, protracted, and impassioned debates in the field of psychology, namely, the validity of repressed traumatic memories of childhood sexual abuse.[3] One area of particular contention concerns the degree to which human memory can be counted on as an accurate and trustworthy record or representation of our life experiences. Specifically, can we unconsciously forget (i.e., "repress") the occurrence of certain traumatic events, and then, at a later time, accurately recover these buried memories? By contrast, can we "remember" events that did not, in fact, ever actually occur? And if so, how can we distinguish between such "true memories" (actual events that have been *retrieved* or *recovered*) and "false memories" (illusory events that have been *constructed* or *created*)?

These questions are especially critical for individuals who are seeking to discover the truth about their past by attempting to "unearth" repressed memories. Unfortunately, their hunt is impeded (and their goal is all the more elusive) by virtue of the fact that both types of memory (authentic and manufactured) can seem equally "real."[4] Nevertheless, in the hopes of retrieving buried memories, people have turned to a diverse array of methods, techniques, and procedures, including individual psychotherapy; self-help workbooks, workshops, and seminars; participation in incest survivor support groups; traveling to childhood homes; hypnosis; guided imaging and visualization; age regression; and even sodium amytal (so-called truth serum) interviews.

How trustworthy are these methods? In two words, *not very.* Despite all the rhetoric and theorizing, pronouncements and declarations, claims and counterclaims, the stark reality is that *we do not yet have the tools to reliably distinguish true memories from false ones* (Loftus, 1993). Further, although the techniques we currently have at our disposal may indeed "lift the lid" of repression by unlocking authentic distant memories, they also might induce the manufacture of illusory memories. It is, therefore, most unfortunate that these methods not only may fail to accurately recover true memories, but, ironically, also can actually foster the creation of honestly believed but false traumatic memories!

These facts notwithstanding, many well-intentioned individuals continue to place their faith (not to mention their time, energy, and money) in such methods. On what basis do people gauge their veracity? As you probably have already anticipated, primarily (and sometimes exclusively) by the *feelings* they arouse. Specifically, in attempting to determine whether or not they were victims of childhood sexual abuse, the mere fact that a particular technique (such as hypnotically induced age regression) leaves them feeling uneasy or uncomfortable may lead them to conclude that the traumatic event, therefore, must *actually* have occurred. In other words, a state of emotional discomfort is seen as sufficient "proof" of abuse, even in the total absence of any specific memories or other corroborating evidence.

Regrettably, this fallacious line of reasoning and subsequent conclusion is frequently and actively encouraged by suggestions from popular writings, and, even worse, from some psychotherapists. For instance, in *The Courage to Heal* (Bass & Davis, 1988), which is often referred to as "the bible of incest survivors," the authors state, "If you are unable to remember any specific instances [of abuse]...but still have a *feeling* that something abusive happened to you, *it probably did*" (p. 21, italics added). Clearly, in light of the present discussion, this bit of advice stands out as being remarkably ill-informed, unsubstantiated, and potentially harmful.

The following exercise will serve to illustrate the danger in relying solely on one's feelings to make such a determination. Picture yourself as an infant, less than a year old, lying in a crib in your childhood bedroom. Now, try to imagine, as vividly and in as much detail as possible, one of your parents coming into your room late one night and sexually molesting you.

Invariably, just picturing this extremely disturbing scene is bound to arouse in you at least some feelings of discomfort, perhaps confusion, helplessness, fear, anger, nausea, pain, or other forms of distress. But obviously it would be a grave mistake to conclude that this traumatic event must *actually* have happened, based *solely* on your feelings of discomfort when imagining this unsettling scenario.[5] Clearly, the lesson to be learned here is not to misinterpret your emotional discomfort—no matter how distressed you might feel—with the likelihood that any given event is true.

To summarize this Metathought, feelings alone are neither an accurate nor trustworthy guide to the truth. Be careful, therefore, not to confuse your state of emotional comfort or discomfort with what is correct or incorrect. Further, do not rely on your emotions as the sole barometer for distinguishing what is true from what is false. Remember that how you feel is *one* source of data—and in many cases an *important* source of data—but it is not the *only* or *definitive* source of data. As a consequence, exercise caution in how you interpret the meaning of your emotional responses, keeping in mind that the only real certainty is *what* you are feeling, not necessarily what it "*proves.*"

Glossary Terms

The following terms (or variations) are defined in the Glossary:

ambiguous	clinical
attribution	cognition
behavior	conscious
belief	consequence
cause	continuous variable
chronic	correlate

critical	personality
data	personality trait
delusion	phenomenon
denial	prediction
description	projection
diagnosis	psychoanalysis
dichotomous variable	psychological
disease	psychology
ego defense mechanism	psychopathology
emotion	psychotherapy
erroneous	psychotic
evaluation	reaction formation
event	reasoning
existence	reliability
expectation	repression
experience	resistance
fact	response
fallacious	shadow archetype
fallacy	somatic
fantasy	subjective
i.e.	subsequent
independent variable	theoretical
intentionality	theory
interpretation	transference
intuition	treatment
mood	truth
observation	unconscious
orthogonal	validity
parapraxis	variable
pathological	veracity
perception	vividness

Notes

[1] Note that although the two variables included in this table are, in fact, continuous phenomena, for the purpose of conceptual simplicity they are presented and discussed here as if they were dichotomous variables; see Metathought V, Differentiating Dichotomous and Continuous Variables.

[2] Put another way, when comparing these two types of defensiveness, be careful not to allow their similarities to obscure their differences (see Metathought VII, the Similarity–Uniqueness Paradox).

[3] For a sampling of the divergent points of view on this topic, I refer you to the following sources: Erdelyi & Goldberg, 1979; Holmes, 1990; Loftus & Ketcham, 1994.

[4] The same may be said of *intuition*, clinical or otherwise: When you have an intuitive hunch, remember that although the intuition is always *real*, it may or may not be *right*.

[5] I am, at the same time, not making an argument that such an event therefore definitely did *not* occur. Rather, to reiterate the primary theme of this Metathought, feelings *alone* are not sufficient proof of veracity.

XIX. The Spectacular Explanation Fallacy: Extraordinary Events Do Not Require Extraordinary Causes

There are more things in heaven and earth, Horatio,
Than are dreamt of in your philosophy.
—WILLIAM SHAKESPEARE*

Shit happens.
—ANONYMOUS

What happens when you experience an extraordinary event? If you are like most people, your first inclination probably is to search for some extraordinary cause to explain the event. Let's take an example. Imagine that you were to flip a coin 100 times and, to your utter astonishment, the coin turns up heads 100 times in a row. Assuming that the coin had not been tampered with, this would truly be an extraordinary event. But was there necessarily an extraordinary *cause*? Not unless you consider the ordinary laws of probability extraordinary.

Allow me to explain. When a coin is flipped, what is the probability that it will turn up heads? The answer, of course, is one out of two, or fifty-fifty. Now, what is the probability of getting heads the very *next* time you flip the coin? Exactly the same as it was the first time: fifty-fifty. Why? Coins don't have memories. Since a coin cannot remember the results of the previous flip, it starts from scratch every time. In other words, each coin flip is independent

Hamlet, Act I, Scene 5

of (that is, completely and totally uninfluenced by) the preceding one. Thus, the fifty-fifty probability remains constant with every flip of the coin, whether it's the second, third, or hundredth time in a row that it turns up heads.

This same principle holds true for all games of pure chance, from slot machines and wheels of fortune to roulette and dice. Of course, streaks do occur, as any gambler would testify. But streaks are to be expected by chance alone, and do not require extraordinary causes (lucky rabbit's feet, superstitious chants, behavioral rituals, or the presence of an attractive stranger notwithstanding) to account for their occurrence. In other words, extraordinary events, such as unusual winning or losing streaks, can be due to very ordinary causes.

As an exercise, let's consider some less mundane examples. In the spaces provided below, give your best estimates as to the approximate frequency of each event in question.

1. Have you ever had the uncanny experience of listening to the radio, when you are startled to hear the very song that you had just been thinking of? _____
    If so, approximately how many times over the past month? _____
    The past year? _____
    In the course of your entire lifetime? _____

2. Have you ever received an unexpected telephone call from someone whose memory had just crossed your mind? _____
    If so, approximately how many times over the past month? _____
    The past year? _____
    Your entire lifetime? _____

3. Have you ever had a dream that coincided with, or even predicted, an event that actually occurred? _____
    If so, approximately how many times over the past month? _____
    The past year? _____
    Your entire lifetime? _____

Before you complete the second part of this exercise, let's examine some rather intriguing attempts to account for these unusual phenomena. One explanation was offered by the illustrious and controversial Swiss psychiatrist and personality theorist, Carl G. Jung. In essence, Jung's (1952/1969) extremely complex theory proposed that, in addition to direct causation, there exists another order in the universe, *synchronicity*, which involves an acausal yet meaningful relationship between two events, as mediated by the collective unconscious. Another explanation, set forth by parapsychologists (i.e., those who study events that are "beyond the normal"), postulates the existence of *extrasensory perception* (ESP) and various manifestations thereof, including telepathy, precognition, and clairvoyance.

But are extraordinary explanations of this kind necessary to account for such events? Could these unusual phenomena be due to nothing more than statistical coincidence, that is, pure chance? Ponder this alternative explanation while answering the following questions:

4.a. Have you ever been thinking of a song that *didn't* then appear on the radio? _____
>   If so, approximately how many times over the past month? _____
>   The past year? _____
>   In the course of your entire lifetime? _____

4.b. Have you ever heard a song on the radio that you *hadn't* just been thinking of? _____
>   If so, approximately how many times over the past month? _____
>   The past year? _____
>   Your entire lifetime? _____

5.a. Have you ever been thinking of someone who *didn't* subsequently call you on the telephone? _____
>   If so, approximately how many times over the past month? _____
>   The past year? _____
>   Your entire lifetime? _____

5.b. Has someone ever called you on the phone whom you *hadn't* just been thinking about? _____
>   If so, approximately how many times over the past month? _____
>   The past year? _____
>   Your entire lifetime? _____

6.a. Have you ever dreamt about an event that *didn't* actually occur? _____
>   If so, approximately how many times over the past month? _____
>   The past year? _____
>   Your entire lifetime? _____

6.b. Have any events ever occurred that you *hadn't* previously dreamt about? _____
>   If so, approximately how many over the past month? _____
>   The past year? _____
>   Your entire lifetime? _____

Now, in comparing your responses to the second part of this exercise with those of the first part, do you notice a not-so-subtle trend? What conclusions might you draw? Clearly, the occasions in questions (4), (5), and (6) are so commonplace that actually attempting to count them would prove to be a nearly impossible task. This stands in stark contrast to the relatively rare instances of "synchronistic" and "parapsychological" phenomena suggested in questions (1) through (3).

In fact, when we stop to consider the fact that literally billions of events occur in our lives every day, it would be shocking if there *weren't* any "uncanny coincidences"! Once again, we see that, by pure chance, exceptional events must occasionally be expected. Put another way, it is normal for some events to appear abnormal.

The age-old debate on the genetic transmission of psychological and behavioral phenomena provides fertile ground for yet another illustration of this Metathought. Have you ever wondered if one's personality traits, behavior patterns, or even specific attitudes and preferences can be inherited? Many publicized reports of identical twins seem to support this notion.

Consider the extraordinary case of "the Jim twins" (see Holden, 1980a, 1980b; Tellegen et al., 1988). Jim Springer and Jim Lewis were identical (monozygotic) twins who, after being separated at infancy, were reunited thirty-nine years later. Despite the fact that they had been raised in completely different environments, the similarities between the two brothers were truly startling. After having married and divorced women named Linda, both men married women named Betty. One had a son named James Allan; the other, James Alan. Both named their dogs "Troy." Both had worked as sheriff's deputies. Both chain-smoked Salem cigarettes and chewed their fingernails to the nub. Both drove Chevrolets and liked to race stock cars. Both had carpentry workshops in their basements and constructed white circular benches around trees in their yard.

Now, what is responsible for these remarkable similarities? Can such specific personality and behavioral characteristics be inherited? Are deeply-embedded genetic codes capable of exerting such astonishing outcomes?

Perhaps. But before we jump to this rather tempting conclusion, consider the similarities of the following two women (reported by the Associated Press on May 2, 1983): Both were named Patricia Ann Campbell. Both were born on March 13, 1941. Both had fathers named Robert. Both worked as bookkeepers. Both studied cosmetology and enjoyed oil painting as a hobby. Both had two children of the same age. Both married military men, within 11 days of each other. And these two women had *no genetic relationship* to each other.

How is this possible? Let us turn, once again, to the not-so-extraordinary laws of probability. Take any two strangers of the same sex and age, drawn at random from the telephone book. Ask them to spend hours and hours comparing their lives, from the broadest of descriptors to the most minute of details: their personality characteristics; their personal attitudes, beliefs, values, and goals; their vocational, educational, relationship, and sexual experiences; their behavioral habits and mannerisms; their family lineage; their interests, hobbies, and travels; their childhood heroes, tastes in food, and preferences in books, movies, and music.

If you ask enough questions, what are you likely to find? No doubt, an impressive array of "remarkable coincidences"![1]

In the realm of clinical psychology, consider any extraordinary (that is, "out of the ordinary") cases of human behavior, from delusions, hallucinations, catatonia, multiple personality, bestiality, or necrophilia to stunning acts of courage, bravery, and altruism, or remarkable instances of raw talent, artistic creativity, or intellectual genius. In these examples, and many more, we are prone to assume that aberrant behavior must be the product of aberrant causes. In fact, the more bizarre the behavior (such as cannibalistic serial murders), the more likely we are to search for bizarre causes (such as ritualistic Satanic cult abuse) or even to create bizarre theories (such as demonic possession) to account for it.

Yet, as Sigmund Freud pointed out many years ago (1900/1953), there is no need to assume that the principles underlying abnormal behavior are qualitatively different than those that govern normal, common, or "healthy" behavior. This Metathought would well be worth keeping in mind whenever you are confronted with instances of human behavior that are unusual, rare, or spectacular. Remember: *extraordinary events do not require extraordinary causes*. With all due respect to Hamlet's sage advise to Horatio, there are more things dreamt of in our philosophy than actually exist in heaven and earth.

Glossary Terms

The following terms (or variations) are defined in the Glossary:

acausal	fallacy
assumption	i.e.
attitude	normal
behavior	parapsychology
belief	personality
causation	personality trait
cause	phenomena
chance	probability
clinical	psychological
delusion	psychology
et al.	random
event	Spectacular Explanation Fallacy
existence	subsequent
expectation	synchronicity
experience	theory
explanation	thinking
fact	unconscious

Notes

[1] Along these lines, I refer you to the compelling research conducted by Robert Plomin and Denise Daniels (1987), who concluded that, despite our commonly held assumptions to the contrary, two children in the same family are, on average, as different from each other as are pairs of children selected randomly from the population.

P a r t **Four**

*Investigating
Phenomena*

Chapter **20**

XX. Deductive and Inductive Reasoning: Two Methods of Inference

> *All men are mortal.*
> *Socrates is a man.*
> *Therefore Socrates is mortal.*
> *—ARISTOTLE**

> *Assuming that persons lie and that mental*
> *patients and psychiatrists are persons, we*
> *should expect them to lie also. Indeed they do.*
> *—THOMAS SZASZ***

> *The temptation to form premature theories upon*
> *insufficient data is the bane of our profession.*
> *—SHERLOCK HOLMES****

Thinking tasks involve different forms of reasoning. Two of the most important methods are *deductive* and *inductive* reasoning. Whenever we draw an inference from a general premise to a specific conclusion, we are engaging in deductive thinking. In contrast, whenever we draw an inference from specific instances to a general conclusion, we are utilizing inductive thinking.[1]

---

*384–322 B.C.
**Insanity, 1987
***In Arthur Conan Doyle's *The Valley of Fear*, 1914

Deductive Reasoning

In deductive reasoning (also known as *theory-driven* or *top-down* cognitive processing), we begin with general or universal assumptions that we know (or believe) to be true. We then use these assumptions to arrive at particular conclusions. If the assumptions we begin with are indeed true, and if our logic is valid, then our conclusions must be true. To take a rather mundane example, we know as a general rule that all dogs have four legs. We are therefore justified in concluding that Rex, a specific dog we do not know, has four legs.

Scientists use deductive thinking when testing theories. To describe this process (known more formally as the *hypothetico-deductive method of scientific investigation*) step-by-step: We begin with a proposed explanation for understanding observable phenomena (i.e., a theory), from which we derive specific predictions (i.e., hypotheses). We then collect and quantify the relevant observations (i.e., data). If the data match the predictions, we conclude that our theory has empirical support.

Let us take, as an interesting illustration of the deductive process, the earliest empirical research on Leon Festinger's (1957) theory of cognitive dissonance. The theory maintains that whenever we hold two inconsistent or contradictory attitudes (cognitions), we experience an aversive drive state (dissonance) which impels us to reduce our discomfort by altering our behavior or our attitudes. Given this theory, we might make the specific prediction that when people perform an unpleasant behavior for minimal external rewards, they will experience a high degree of cognitive dissonance; as a consequence, they will alter their attitudes toward their behavior in a more favorable direction.

This hypothesis was, in fact, tested experimentally in 1959 by social psychologists Festinger and J. Merrill Carlsmith. The investigators asked research subjects to perform a series of dull, boring, and tedious tasks (that consisted of packing spools and turning pegs for about an hour). The subjects then were coaxed to convince other students (who were really a part of the experiment) that the tasks actually were fun, interesting, exciting, and enjoyable. For their assistance, some of the subjects were paid $20 (remember, this was 1959!); other subjects received only $1. All subjects were subsequently asked about their *true* attitudes toward performing the tasks.

Based on cognitive dissonance theory, which subjects do you think reported *enjoying* the experiment more, those who were paid $20 or those paid $1? As was originally hypothesized, those subjects who received *less money* ($1) rated the tasks *more favorably.* Why? They experienced more dissonance than did the $20 subjects; as a result, they felt compelled to *justify* their behavior by altering their attitudes toward the tasks. Festinger's theory of cognitive dissonance thereby received its first noteworthy empirical support. In this example, it is clear how deductive thinking guided the researchers from general assumptions to specific conclusions.

What are some common mistakes that we are prone to commit in our use of deductive reasoning? The first type of error involves utilizing valid logic, but beginning with an erroneous premise. For the sake of debate, let's consider the belief that mental illness is equivalent to physical illness. Under the assumption that this premise is true, it would logically follow that an individual with a mental illness should be diagnosed and receive medical treatment as a patient under the direction of a physician. However, if this premise is invalid (as has been argued by Thomas Szasz, 1960, 1987), the conclusion is suspect and surely must be reconsidered.

In the second type of error, one's initial assumptions are valid, but the subsequent logic is flawed. Such is the case in instances of tautologous or circular reasoning (see Metathought IV). For example, "People who are pessimistic expect the worst; therefore, people who expect the worst are pessimistic." Another variety of faulty logic is illustrated in the following parody of Aristotle's now famous syllogism:

> *All men are mortal.*
> *Socrates is a man.*
> *Therefore all men are Socrates.*

Inductive Reasoning

In inductive reasoning (also known as *data-driven* or *bottom-up* cognitive processing), we begin with particular observations and then generalize to broader principles. As a simple exercise, consider the following series of numbers: "2,4,6,..." Now, which number do you believe should be next? Why? What is the principle that underlies this series? Our use of inductive reasoning would lead us to conclude that the next number is 8, based on a pattern consisting of a sequence of even numbers.

To take another example, suppose you notice that whenever you think about taking classroom exams, you experience heart palpitations, difficulty breathing, dizziness, sweaty palms, dry mouth, nausea, hot flashes, diarrhea, a sensation of choking, and a fear of dying. You thus might conclude, by induction, that you have some test anxiety.

Scientists use inductive thinking when creating or building theories. Initially, the scientist collects enough data that a pattern begins to emerge. From this pattern, he or she induces the underlying principle that appears to account for the pattern. In this way, the scientist formulates an explanation (that is, a theory) on the basis of specific observations. For example, physicists, in their attempt to identify and understand a large number of physical phenomena in the universe, have inductively created theoretical constructs such as "force," "gravitation," and "energy."

In like fashion, we use induction when we create psychological constructs (such as the mind, personality, motivation, and intelligence). Consider, as an illustration, the following scenario: You observe that certain people in the world tend to evaluate their attributes and abilities in very positive terms; they describe themselves as worthy and competent, and they report feeling confidence in and respect for themselves. They also seem not to worry excessively about things that might go wrong for them; they easily "bounce back" from failure and frustration, and they aren't easily threatened by criticism. You might then think to yourself, "This constellation of characteristics appears to set these people apart from other people. How shall we refer to this common theme? What shall we call it? How about *self-esteem*?" Note that self-esteem was not "discovered" as an observable or concrete entity (see Metathought II, the Reification Error). Rather, it was a perceiver-created invention, arrived at inductively, to help us account for and better understand our observations.

What are some of the potential pitfalls associated with inductive reasoning? One of the most pervasive errors involves jumping hastily to a conclusion on the basis of an insufficient or unrepresentative sampling of data. For example, when a client is observed under the highly structured, artificial, and time-limited constraints of a first psychotherapy session, the therapist may erroneously *overgeneralize* from this behavior and thereby arrive at an incorrect clinical diagnosis.

How else might we go wrong? In a number of ways, many of which are presented and examined at length in other sections of this book. These include our tendencies:

>to draw upon data from our memory solely because it is vivid or salient (Metathought XXVIII, the Availability Bias);

>to ignore important statistical information, such as sample size and prior probability (Metathought XXVII, the Representativeness Bias);

>to selectively seek out observations that are consistent with our prior beliefs (Metathought XXIV, the Confirmation Bias);

>to ignore or reject observations that are inconsistent with our beliefs (Metathought XXV, the Belief Perseverance Effect);

>to oversimplify and artificially distort continuous phenomena by conceptualizing them as dichotomous (Metathought V, Dichotomous and Continuous Variables);

>to misinterpret correlation and causation (Metathought X, Correlation Does Not Prove Causation);

>to confuse deductive and inductive thinking, and the circumstances under which each is appropriate.[2]

As an exercise in recognizing errors in deductive and inductive reasoning, consider the potential pitfalls that have been identified and described thus far.

Then, select three specific errors and provide an original example of each. For instance:

Error: Potential flaw in deductive reasoning due to an invalid premise.
Example: Gaps in memories of childhood are always due to some kind of significant sexual, emotional, or physical trauma. My client can't remember much of his childhood. Therefore, he must have been traumatized as a child.

Error: Potential flaw in inductive reasoning due to overgeneralizing from an unrepresentative sample.
Example: Every designer I've ever met is homosexual. Therefore, my design instructor, whom I've not yet met, has got to be homosexual.

Ready to try some on your own?

Error: _____
Example: _____
_____
_____

Error: _____
Example: _____
_____
_____

Error: _____
Example: _____
_____
_____

Solutions and Applications

Let's briefly enumerate some solutions for these various problems. First, learn to differentiate between deduction and induction, recognizing that different types of problems call for different reasoning strategies. Second, make your selection based on the nature and goal of the particular question, task, or situation. Third, with respect to deductive reasoning, be sure that your initial assumptions are correct and that your logic is sound. Fourth, when utilizing inductive reasoning, in addition to the specific solutions discussed in each of the chapters cited above, be especially careful not to hastily overgeneralize from unrepresentative, inadequate, or otherwise biased observations.

Note that some situations call for *both* deductive and inductive strategies. In arriving at a differential clinical diagnosis, for example, the psychotherapist uses both types of reasoning. Suppose that a person comes to see you, a therapist, for a clinical intake interview. She complains that, for the past six months, she has been feeling sad, hopeless, and worthless. She reports further that she has no energy, poor appetite, difficulties in concentrating, and thoughts of death. Using your powers of inductive reasoning, you put these pieces together and conclude that she has some kind of mood disorder.

But what type? Could it be a bipolar (i.e., manic-depressive) disorder? You would use the process of deduction to test this hypothesis. So, you ask her, "Have you ever experienced any periods of time when you've had exceptionally high energy, very little need for sleep, racing thoughts, a euphoric mood, and been extremely talkative and easily distractible?" She replies, "No, I haven't." With this hypothesis disconfirmed, you then tentatively conclude that she probably is suffering from a unipolar depressive disorder.

Of course, this depiction of the clinical diagnostic process is, of necessity, overly simplistic. However, it does serve to illustrate how deductive and inductive strategies can, and do complement each other in the real-world setting of clinical psychology.

Glossary Terms

The following terms (or variations) are defined in the Glossary:

assumption	empirical
attitude	erroneous
attribution	evaluation
behavior	experience
belief	experiment
bias	explanation
causation	external
clinical	hypothesis
cognition	i.e.
concrete	induction
consequence	inductive reasoning
construct	inference
continuous variable	logic
correlation	mental illness
data	mind
deduction	mood
deductive reasoning	motivation
description	observation
diagnosis	personality
dichotomous variable	phenomena
differential diagnosis	physical
disorder	prediction

premise
probability
psychological
psychology
psychotherapy
quantify
reasoning
representativeness
scientific

social
subsequent
tautologous reasoning
theoretical
theory
thinking
treatment
universal
vivid

Notes

[1] For philosophical perspectives on deductive and inductive reasoning, I refer you to the writings of Aristotle, Francis Bacon, Galileo Galilei, John Stuart Mill, and David Hume.

[2] A comprehensive discussion of errors and biases in deductive and inductive reasoning may be found in *The Teaching of Thinking* (Nickerson, Perkins, & Smith, 1985).

XXI. *Reactivity: To Observe Is to Disturb*

Search not a wound too deep lest thou make a new one.
—*ANONYMOUS**

The scientific method is based on tampering with what would be happening if we were doing nothing to it.
—*R. D. LAING***

One could not find the location of any one subatomic particle because any measurement, necessarily with light, affected the result.
—*WERNER KARL HEISENBERG****

Reactivity is a phenomenon in which the conduct of research affects the very entity that is being studied. The problem of reactivity exists to some extent in practically all fields, but is particularly acute in the social sciences.[1] Specifically, whenever people are aware that they are being studied, they are likely to alter (either consciously or unconsciously) their responses. Thus, the investigation of normal human activity is impeded, ironically, by the investigator himself. The dilemma is profoundly consequential: How can we possibly know what people are "really" like if, by observing them, we cause them to change?

Whether utilizing survey or experimental research methods, and whether conducting research in the field or in the laboratory, social scientists find themselves constantly plagued by the effects of reactivity.[2] When we wish to study people's attitudes or opinions, for example, our most commonly used

*Quoted in Barber, *The Book of 1000 Proverbs*, 1876/1971
**The Facts of Life*, 1976
***1901–1967, German physicist

research method is to ask them questions about a particular topic. Unfortunately, however, such questions may be highly reactive by stimulating the respondents to think about the topic in a new way, or even by instigating them to formulate an opinion when they previously had none. Yet how can we know if an attitude or opinion exists at all until it has in some way been elicited?

Reactivity is especially problematic in the conduct of psychological laboratory research. Almost without exception, the moment that subjects enter the laboratory setting, they quickly and automatically develop expectations, hunches, or hypotheses about the purpose of the experiment and how they may be expected to behave. Suppose, for example, that a researcher is interested in studying whether self-disclosing statements by one person will elicit self-disclosures in another person. Because the subjects are aware of being observed, they may be prompted to behave in ways that they believe to be socially desirable (perhaps by being more self-disclosing). Thus, whether subjects are cooperative or uncooperative, trusting or suspicious, sociable or inhibited, submissive or defiant, the experimenter will be unable to measure their "natural" behavior, thereby compromising the validity of her observations.

As a consequence, reactivity limits the extent to which investigators can confidently generalize, apply, or relate their findings to other populations and settings. In the parlance of social scientists, reactivity is a threat to the study's *external validity* (see Campbell & Stanley, 1963). Two specific forms of this threat are the *reactive effect of testing* (when subjects' receptivity to the experimental treatment is altered by preceding observations or testing) and the *reactive effects of experimental arrangements* (when the artificiality of the research setting itself causes subjects in the experiment to respond differently to the treatment than would people in nonexperimental settings). Thus, whenever external validity or generalizability are issues of concern, problems related to reactivity always must be considered.

Reactivity is sometimes referred to as the *Hawthorne Effect,* deriving its name from a classic study conducted at the Hawthorne Plant of the Western Electric Company in Chicago (see Roethlisberger & Dickson, 1939). The researchers were interested in studying some of the factors, such as rest periods and quitting times, that might affect employees' work performance. Much to their surprise (and initial confusion), the researchers achieved positive results no matter what they did. Even when employees' rest periods were *eliminated* or when *later* quitting times were instituted, the result was still an increase in work output. The researchers concluded that a reactive effect had occurred; that is, the workers' morale (and therefore their productivity) had been boosted simply because somebody was paying attention to them. In effect, the researchers' very presence altered worker productivity.

The ubiquity of reactivity cannot be overemphasized. In the clinical context, it occurs, to some degree, whenever we attempt to diagnose a patient by conducting an intake interview, assess personality by asking people what they see in blots of ink, measure intelligence by administering standardized IQ tests, gauge someone's level of stress by taking their blood pressure, explore unconscious processes by instructing a person to "free associate," examine a family's communication patterns by observing them in therapy, evaluate a clinical trainee by observing how she conducts group therapy sessions, or study human sexual responses in the laboratory by attaching physiological measuring devices to research subjects' genitalia.

More broadly defined, reactivity is evident throughout our daily lives, influencing everything, from how we respond to public opinion polls to our behavior on job interviews and first dates. The impact of reactivity is particularly salient in the context of media broadcasting. Consider, for instance, news interviews with "people on the street"; the presence of television cameras in courtroom trials; media coverage of meetings, demonstrations, or riots; and various "reality programs," such as those that capture law enforcement activity on videotape. In all of these cases, and countless more, remember that simply measuring something can change it.

As an exercise, select three situations (either from the examples above or of your own choosing) in which you consider the issue of reactivity to be especially problematic. Then, for each situation, describe specifically how reactivity might influence the outcome. Last, offer your suggestions for reducing the problem (see below for some suggestions).

Situation 1: _____

Effects of Reactivity: _____

_____

_____

_____

Solution(s): _____

_____

_____

Situation 2: _____

Effects of Reactivity: _____

_____

_____

_____

Solution(s): _____

_____

_____

Situation 3: _____

Effects of Reactivity: _____

_____

_____

_____

Solution(s): _____

_____

_____

Because one of the most common criticisms of the social sciences is that we frequently alter the behavior that we seek to study, it is crucial that we not only remain constantly vigilant as to the presence of reactivity, but that we also make every effort to minimize its impact. How can this be accomplished? For all practical purposes, if people are not aware of being studied, reactivity ceases to be a problem. This fact has prompted social scientists to devise a wide variety of innovative *unobtrusive* or *nonreactive* techniques: clandestine observation (using, for example, hidden cameras, tape recorders, or one-way mirrors), indirect measures (such as the erosion of carpeting to measure foot traffic), and document analysis (also known as "archival research," such as the inspection of academic or personnel files). Clearly, the decision to utilize such unobtrusive measures has its drawbacks, not the least of which involves complex ethical and legal issues, particularly the invasion of privacy. But, of course, as with all matters, every decision is a trade-off (see Metathought XXX).

Glossary Terms

The following terms (or variations) are defined in the Glossary:

acute	effect
affect	ethics
attitude	evaluation
behavior	expectation
belief	experiment
cause	external validity
clinical	fact
concept	generalizability
consequence	measure
continuous variable	normal
decision	observation
diagnosis	opinion
dichotomous variable	personality
dilemma	phenomenon

psychological
reactive effect of testing
reactive effects of experimental arrangements
reactivity
response
science

social
treatment
ubiquitous
unconscious
validity

Notes

[1] Of historical note, the concept of reactivity is related to the *uncertainty principle*, first stated mathematically by the German physicist, Werner Heisenberg. The uncertainty principle maintains that, in the domain of quantum mechanics, the mere act of observation affects what one is observing. Specifically, it is impossible to determine, with absolute certainty, the exact position and momentum of any one subatomic particle because the measuring device itself affects the particle's position and momentum.

[2] Bear in mind that reactivity typically is a continuous, rather than dichotomous, variable (see Metathought V). As such, it usually is more a question of its relative magnitude or degree, rather than its absolute presence or absence.

XXII. The Self-Fulfilling Prophecy: When Expectations Create Reality

> Respect a man, and he will do the more.
> —ANONYMOUS*

> LIZA: You see, really and truly, apart from the things anyone can pick up . . ., the difference between a lady and a flower girl is not how she behaves, but how she's treated. I shall always be a flower girl to Professor Higgins, because he always treats me as a flower girl, and always will; but I know I can be a lady to you, because you always treat me as a lady, and always will.
> —GEORGE BERNARD SHAW**

The attitudes and beliefs that we hold toward other people can, with or without our intent, actually produce the very behaviors that we expect to find. In other words, a perceiver's assumptions about another person may lead that person to adopt those expected attributes. This phenomenon is known as the *Self-Fulfilling Prophecy.*

In what is probably the most famous (and still very controversial) study of the self-fulfilling prophecy, Robert Rosenthal and Lenore Jacobson (1968) informed teachers at a San Francisco elementary school that, on the basis of a reliable psychological test, some of the pupils in their classroom would show dramatic spurts in academic performance during the upcoming school year. In

*Quoted in Barber, *The Book of 1000 Proverbs*, 1876/1971
**1856–1950, from *Pygmalion*, 1913

reality, there was no such test, and the children designated as "intellectual bloomers" were chosen *at random*. Nevertheless, when the children's performance was assessed several months later, those students who had been earmarked as "bloomers" did, indeed, show an improvement in their schoolwork; even more remarkably, their IQ scores had increased! The teachers thus unwittingly *created* the very behaviors that they *expected*.[1]

In another fascinating illustration of the self-fulfilling prophecy, student experimenters were told that some of their laboratory rats were "maze-bright," while others were "maze-dull" (Rosenthal & Fode, 1963). The experimenters subsequently found that the "bright" rats actually learned a standard maze faster than did the "dull" rats, this despite the fact that the rats had been *randomly* designated as "bright" or "dull" and did not differ initially with respect to their maze-learning ability. Apparently, the students' prior expectations must have caused them to handle the two groups of rats differently, which in turn affected the animals' behavior. Here again, we see that entirely false beliefs can generate their own reality.

The self-fulfilling prophecy has been demonstrated with a diverse array of both positive and negative perceiver expectancies,[2] including hostility (Snyder & Swann, 1978), extraversion (see Snyder, 1984), gender stereotypes (Skrypnek & Snyder, 1982), racial stereotypes (Word, Zanna, & Cooper, 1974), and even stereotypes concerning physical attractiveness (Snyder, Tanke, & Berscheid, 1977). These studies underscore how prejudice of any kind can set in motion a self-perpetuating and ever-escalating vicious cycle of adverse repercussions (see Metathought XI, Bi-Directional Causation), in which the self-fulfilling prophecy serves to influence not only how the prejudiced person behaves toward the victim, but also how the victim may then behave in a way that confirms the person's initial prejudices.

In the examples we have considered thus far, the perceivers were aware of their own expectations; that is, their expectations were conscious. Can self-fulfilling prophecies occur also as a consequence of expectations, attitudes, or beliefs that are, for the most part, out of awareness or *unconscious*?

Some theorists think so. Melanie Klein (1946), for example, introduced the term *projective identification* to describe the unconscious splitting of one's own unacceptable (that is, *ego-dystonic*) attributes, and the projection of these attributes onto another person. The perceiver then relates to the other person in terms of these disowned attributes—for example, with fear, dread, disgust, or rage—and, in so doing, elicits the other's behavior along these lines (see Horwitz, 1983).

Similarly, R. D. Laing (1969) used the term *induction* to denote unconscious components of the self-fulfilling prophecy. As an illustration, a husband may unconsciously "induce" his wife to embody his projection of his own mother. As noted by Laing, "It is not sufficient to say that my wife introjects my mother, if by projection, I have manoeuvred her into such a position that she actually begins to act, and even to feel, like her" (pp. 119–120).

It must be emphasized that not only are we seldom aware of the extent to which our expectations can influence others' behavior, but moreover we probably are even less aware of how others' expectations are capable of influencing *our* behavior. It is thus important to remember that our actions are shaped not only by our own attitudes, but also by the expectations of those with whom we interact. Put another way, we are continually cultivating the construction of each other's social realities.

Given the ubiquity of the self-fulfilling prophecy, we would do well to consider its potential impact in all of our social interactions. In the clinical setting, for instance, what do you suppose might occur if a therapist expects his or her new client to be cooperative? Resistant? Emotionally fragile? Seductive? Paranoid? Borderline?

In like manner, what if a client expects his or her therapist to be empathic? Critical? Accepting? Devious? Intimidating? Insincere? Gentle? Rejecting? The therapist and client can ultimately end up creating a reciprocally-reinforcing projection system that supports their respective initial expectations, much of which may be occurring entirely outside of their direct awareness.

As an exercise, select three scenarios—either hypothetical or factual—involving the self-fulfilling prophecy. In making your selections, consider a variety of

> >topics (e.g., stereotyping, prejudice, clinical assessment and diagnosis, child rearing, impression management, creativity, athletic competition, sexual performance);
> >settings (e.g., classroom, therapy, workplace, religious, military, laboratory, courtroom);
> >relationships (e.g., professional, familial, romantic, platonic);
> >units of analysis involving broad societal or governmental policies, programs, and laws (e.g., welfare, unemployment, affirmative action, desegregation, immigration, mandatory retirement, competency to stand trial, insanity defense).

Then, for each scenario, present your thoughts as to how Person A's expectations might influence his or her behavior toward Person B. (As a hint, you may wish to peruse Metathoughts XXIII and XXIV, the Assimilation Bias and the Confirmation Bias, respectively).

Last, discuss how Person A's actions could cause Person B to behave in accordance with Person A's prior expectations. In other words, identify some of the specific factors or events that you believe are capable of transforming Person A's initial expectations into the reality of Person B's subsequent attitudes and behavior.

Scenario 1: _____

_____

Effects of Person A's expectations on his or her behavior toward Person B:

_____

_____

_____

Effects of Person A's behavior on Person B's subsequent actions:

_____

_____

_____

_____

Scenario 2:_____

Effects of Person A's expectations on his or her behavior toward Person B:

_____

_____

_____

Effects of Person A's behavior on Person B's subsequent actions:

_____

_____

_____

_____

Scenario 3:_____

Effects of Person A's expectations on his or her behavior toward Person B:

_____

_____

_____

Effects of Person A's behavior on Person B's subsequent actions:

_____

_____

_____

_____

Glossary Terms

The following terms (or variations) are defined in the Glossary:

assumption	attribution
attitude	behavior

belief
cause
clinical
consequence
denote
e.g.
ego-dystonic
event
expectation
extraversion
fact
hypothetical
induction
intent
phenomenon

projection
projective identification
psychological
random
reciprocal
reinforcement
reliability
resistance
Self-Fulfilling Prophecy
social
stereotype
subsequent
ubiquitous
unconscious

Notes

[1] Interestingly, the self-fulfilling prophecy has also been demonstrated in *students'* expectations of their *teachers* (see Feldman & Prohaska, 1979; Feldman & Theiss, 1982; Jamieson, Lydon, Stewart, & Zanna, 1984).

[2] See Darley and Fazio (1980) for an excellent and comprehensive review of research on the self-fulfilling prophecy.

Chapter **23**

XXIII. The Assimilation Bias: Viewing the World through Schema-Colored Glasses

Two-thirds of what we see is behind our eyes.
—CHINESE PROVERB

To the man who wants to use a hammer badly, a lot of things look like nails that need hammering.
—MARK TWAIN*

Rules govern the whole social field. Unless we can "see through" the rules, we only see through them.
—R. D. LAING**

One of the most fundamental and pervasive of all human psychological activities is the propensity to categorize. People appear to possess an innate drive to classify, organize, systematize, group, subgroup, type, subtype, or otherwise structure the world around them.

We categorize everything from people, objects, places, and events to concepts, experiences, feelings, and memories. The phenomenon is omnipresent, the breadth is enormous, and almost nothing is immune: sex and race; plants and animals; words and numbers; books and records; occupations and hobbies; religious denominations and political affiliations; anatomical structures and geographic territories; subatomic particles and celestial constellations; time and space.

*1835–1910
***The Politics of the Family,* 1969

In the field of psychology we have created taxonomies of personality traits, types, and characteristics; intellectual, interpersonal, and emotional functioning; mental disorders; theoretical orientations; methods of research; approaches to psychotherapy; communication styles; ego defense mechanisms; and stages of psychosexual, psychosocial, cognitive, and moral development, to list but a few.

We can conceptualize all such categories (yet another category!) as mental representations, or *schemas*.[1] A schema is a cognitive structure that organizes our knowledge, beliefs, and past experiences, thereby providing a framework for understanding new events and future experiences (see Cantor & Mischel, 1979; Fiske & Taylor, 1984; Levy, Kaler, & Schall, 1988; Piaget, 1952; Sears, Peplau, & Taylor, 1991). Put another way, schemas (or *schemata*) are general expectations or preconceptions about a wide range of phenomena. In the social domain, these include perceptual sets about yourself, about particular people whom you know, and even about people whom you do not know, based on their sex, race, nationality, occupation, social role, or any other characteristic. In fact, we may view stereotypes as equivalent to group schemas (Hamilton, 1979, 1981).

What function do schemas serve? First and foremost, they enable us to process the plethora of stimuli we continually encounter in a relatively rapid, efficient, and effortless manner. In other words, schemata reduce our cognitive processing load. Whenever we are faced with new information, we quickly and automatically compare it to our preexisting schemas, which greatly simplifies the task of organizing and understanding our experiences.

What happens when we come across information that is discrepant from our preconceptions? Put another way, what do we do when there is a clash between the data and our schemas? The Swiss psychologist Jean Piaget (1954, 1970) identified two complementary processes that we utilize in such situations: *accommodation* and *assimilation*. According to Piaget, both of these responses are integral components of cognitive development and constitute the means by which we adapt to our environment and construct our reality.

Accommodation refers to the process wherein we modify our schema to fit the data. In other words, we change our preexisting beliefs so that they make room for (that is, "accommodate") new information. Assimilation, by contrast, means to modify the data to fit our schema. Here, we incorporate new information into our preexisting beliefs, even if it means changing or distorting the information itself.

The conduct of scientific investigation involves the processes of both assimilation and accommodation. Specifically, scientists use their preconceived theories to help them make sense out of an overwhelming array of seemingly disjointed, frequently bewildering, sometimes incoherent, and all-too-often ambiguous events. In other words, they assimilate observed phenomena into their conceptual schemas. And so long as the data and the theory "fit" each other, assimilation effectively and successfully serves its purpose. Suppose, however, that a particular observation disconfirms or contradicts the scientist's expectations; that is to say, the new datum does not fit the old theory. Now what? In the pursuit of knowledge, good scientists put aside their pride, their stubbornness, and their egos, and they alter their theory to accommodate the facts.[2]

But do people in general make appropriate use of assimilation and accommodation? The answer, by and large, is *no*. Considerable research shows us time and time again that discrepancies between data and schemas typically are resolved more in the direction of assimilation than accommodation. In other words, we are more likely to make the data fit the schema, rather than the other way around.

Before we explore some specific illustrations and applications of this Metathought, let's take a step back and evaluate the advantages and disadvantages inherent in schematic processing. How do schemas both help and hinder our thinking process?

On the plus side of the ledger, the advantages of schematic processing are significant and well-documented (see Fiske & Taylor, 1984). In addition to the benefits discussed above, schemas help us to perceive, recognize, and remember new information; to retrieve from memory old information; to fill in gaps in our knowledge; to draw inferences; to make interpretations; and to prepare for the future by providing us with experience-based expectations (Cantor & Mischel, 1977; Taylor & Crocker, 1981).

Of course, benefits are always accompanied by costs, and schematic processing is no exception to this principle (see Metathought XXX, Every Decision Is a Trade-Off). Our use of schemas entails a host of predictable and systematic mistakes and biases in thinking. First, schemas are, by their very nature, abstractions and simplifications of reality; as a consequence, they tend to foster incomplete, inaccurate, and sometimes naive generalizations that fail to take into account the complexity of real-world phenomena. Further, because schematic processing occurs automatically and relatively unconsciously, it is very resistant to change, even when it is fraught with errors.

With respect to this Metathought, schemas bias the perception, processing, and interpretation of information in the direction of confirming our expectations; conversely, we tend to overlook, misconstrue, or even reject valid information when it is not consistent with our schemas. In a word, a fundamental and pervasive liability of schematic processing can be seen as a problem of *assimilation*.

This bias manifests itself in a wide variety of forms and contexts, the most important of which are listed here (along with references to pertinent Metathoughts). Specifically, we are more likely

>to notice information that is consistent, rather than inconsistent, with our schemas (the Availability Bias);

>to rely excessively on vivid but not necessarily appropriate information (the Availability Bias);

>to interpret ambiguous, irrelevant, or even contradictory information as fitting our schemas (the Belief Perseverance Effect);

>to selectively search for information that corroborates our schemas (the Confirmation Bias);

>to recall or misinterpret information about past events so that it validates our schemas (the Hindsight Bias);

>to draw inaccurate inferences and erroneous conclusions (Correlation Does Not Prove Causation, errors in Deductive and Inductive Reasoning); and

>to unwittingly elicit the very events that we expect to find (the Self-Fulfilling Prophecy).

We also are prone

>to distort our perception, coding, and storage of new information;

>to fill in gaps in our knowledge with schema-consistent but erroneous information; and

>to engage in and perpetuate stereotyping (all of which directly involve the Assimilation Bias).

In sum, schemas bias our perceptions of reality to make them consistent with what we already believe. As such, the Assimilation Bias represents a significant obstacle to clear thinking and effective problem-solving. In viewing the world through "schema-colored glasses," we subject virtually all incoming information to varying degrees of distortion, misinterpretation, and invalidation.

Scores of research studies have concluded that schemas greatly influence what we perceive and the manner in which we perceive it (see, for example, Bruner & Potter, 1964; Reason & Mycielska, 1982; Vokey & Read, 1985). To take one example, the impact of the Assimilation Bias on schematic processing was demonstrated in a classic experiment by the eminent social psychologist Harold H. Kelley. The experiment (known as the "warm–cold" study) was conducted in 1950 at MIT and used undergraduate students as research subjects. All the students were informed that they would be attending the lecture of a guest speaker and were provided with some brief background information about him.

Half of the subjects were told that the speaker was twenty-nine years old, married, and that people considered him "a rather cold person, industrious, critical, practical, and determined." The rest of the subjects were given the same information, with one exception: They were told that he was considered to be "a rather warm person, industrious, critical, practical, and determined." Thus, the *only difference* between the two groups of subjects was that half were informed that the visitor was cold, and the other half were told that he was warm.

Kelley had selected the warm versus cold dimension based on prior research carried out by one of the pioneers of modern social psychology, Solomon Asch (1946). In his study, Asch found that *warm–cold* is a significant "central trait" in terms of its impact on the impressions we form of other people. Kelley hypothesized therefore that this one-word difference would create substantial expectancy and perceptual differences between the two groups.

Both groups of students subsequently saw the *same speaker* presenting the *same lecture,* and both groups spent the entire class period with him. Yet, their impressions of him were, as Kelley had predicted, powerfully affected by the one-word difference. Each group interpreted the speaker's behavior based on their "knowledge" of him as either warm or cold. Specifically, the subjects who were told that the speaker was warm had significantly more positive impressions of him than those who were told that he was cold. In essence, the subjects had filtered (i.e., assimilated) the speaker's behavior through their respective schemas, and, as a consequence, arrived at strikingly different impressions of him. As was elegantly demonstrated in this experiment, the impact of a single expectancy variable on our perceptions can be profound. The underlying principle here again becomes manifest: More than believing what we see, we tend to see what we believe.

As an illustration of the Assimilation Bias in the clinical setting, consider how a therapist's beliefs and expectations may predispose him to "see" psychopathology wherever he looks. Suppose you were to ask a therapist to explain the meaning of behaviors that clients might exhibit on arriving for their scheduled therapy session. Let's imagine further that this therapist happens to view the world through a densely filtered schema of psychopathology. He thus calmly, cooly, and confidently offers you the following interpretations:

> *If the patient arrives early for his appointment, then he's anxious. If he arrives late, then he's hostile. And if he's on time, then he's compulsive.*

This witticism about psychoanalysis dates back to the 1930s. Although originally intended as a joke, it may have been more prophetic than anyone at that time could have anticipated, for it is not just a humorous illustration of the Assimilation Bias, but is also a revealing and sobering parable that alerts us to the dangers inherent in maintaining schemas that allow—and even encourage—virtually any human behavior to be subsumed under one or another of pathological categories.

Let's examine another clinical application of schematic processing. Psychotherapists typically align themselves with, and work from a foundation of, some clinical frame of reference known as a "theoretical orientation." A theoretical orientation is, in essence, the clinician's schema for identifying, mapping, and understanding the behavior of his or her clients. As such, these schemata are, of course, subject to the same biases in assimilation discussed above. In this way, the therapist would be inclined to perceive, interpret, and explain clients' symptoms principally (or perhaps even exclusively) in terms of his or her own theoretical orientation, sometimes irrespective of its actual relevance or suitability.

We shall designate this phenomenon the *Clinical Orientation Assimilation Bias* (COAB), which, by definition, may predispose therapists to systematically overlook, discount, or reject alternative perspectives and ways of understanding their clients. We can further delineate specific subcategories of the COAB, several of which are identified below. Also indicated are the factors that, in extreme forms of the COAB, are held exclusively accountable for producing the problems of every client:

The *Biomedical Assimilation Bias*
  –neurochemical imbalances and disease processes;
The *Psychodynamic Assimilation Bias*
  –unconscious motivations and conflicts;
The *Psychosocial Assimilation Bias*
  –situational and environmental stimuli;
The *Cognitive–Behavioral Assimilation Bias*
  –faulty belief systems and maladaptive learning;
The *Humanistic–Existential Assimilation Bias*
  –incongruent perceptions and loss of meaning in life;
The *Family Systems Assimilation Bias*
  –dysfunctional family relationships;
The *Substance Abuse Assimilation Bias*
  –an addictive personality;
The *New-Age Metaphysical Assimilation Bias*
  –unlearned lessons from "past lives."

The following exercise will give you some practice at viewing the same event through the lenses of different clinical orientations. Suppose that you are a therapist and a client comes to see you with the complaint of feeling "very unhappy." Select one of the clinical orientations listed above (or from any other source) and write a few statements that, from that perspective, attempt to explain and to solve the client's presenting problem.

Here is an example:

Clinical Orientation: Cognitive-Behavioral Therapy
Explanation and Solution: The client's unhappiness probably is due to his or her unreasonable expectations and self-defeating behaviors. Therefore, the appropriate

treatment would consist of challenging these faulty beliefs and rewarding more adaptive behavioral responses.

Ready to try one on your own?

Clinical Orientation: _____

Explanation and Solution: _____

_____

_____

_____

_____

Now, "switch lenses" by approaching the same problem from a different orientation.

Clinical Orientation: _____

Explanation and Solution: _____

_____

_____

_____

_____

Do the same with another orientation.

Clinical Orientation: _____

Explanation and Solution: _____

_____

_____

_____

_____

Diagnostic Labels as Schematic Filters: The Assimilation of Psychopathology

Nowhere is this Metathought more vividly illustrated than in David L. Rosenhan's (1973) renowned study that dramatically demonstrated the biasing power of diagnostic labeling. In the study, eight researchers (including Rosenhan), posing as "pseudopatients," gained voluntary admission into psychiatric hospitals in six different states. The pseudopatients complained of "hearing voices" that said "empty," "hollow," and "thud." Other than presenting this complaint (and giving false names and occupations), the pseudopatients truthfully answered all questions asked of them. All eight pseudopatients were diagnosed as psychotic, seven of them as suffering from schizophrenia.

The pseudopatients entered the hospitals with the knowledge that it was up to them to get themselves discharged, essentially by convincing the staff they were "sane." On admission to the hospital ward, the pseudopatients immediately ceased simulating any signs of mental disturbance, and thereafter behaved on the ward as they "normally" behaved.

Rosenhan and his pseudopatient–colleagues found that their relatively healthy behavior in the ward did not serve to invalidate, nullify, or revoke their diagnoses; as a matter of fact, once they were designated as abnormal, all of their other behaviors and characteristics were profoundly colored by the diagnostic labels. Specifically, the hospital staff molded their observations of the pseudopatients into a portrait consistent with "mental illness." For example, many of the pseudopatients' quite normal life histories, when viewed in a psychopathological context, appeared somehow aberrant: "[The patient manifests]. . . ambivalence in close relationships, which begins in early childhood" (see Metathought IX, the Barnum Effect).

The diagnostic labels were so powerful, in fact, that ordinary human activity on the part of the pseudopatients was perceived as a manifestation of their psychopathology. For example, after observing a pseudopatient–researcher taking notes, one nurse commented in her daily report, "Patient engages in writing behavior," thereby pathologizing an ostensibly mundane human activity. In another instance, a psychiatrist observed some patients sitting outside the hospital cafeteria half an hour before lunchtime. The psychiatrist explained to a group of residents that such behavior on the part of the patients was "characteristic of the oral-acquisitive nature of the syndrome." (Rosenhan points out that it appeared not to occur to the psychiatrist that, in a psychiatric hospital, there are very few events to look forward to, with the exception of eating.)

In spite of their appearance of sanity, not one of the pseudopatients was ever detected.[3] None of the pseudopatients was discharged in less than a week. The average length of hospitalization was nineteen days; the longest stay was fifty-two days. When the pseudopatients were released, it was not because they were discovered to be sane fakers; rather, they typically were discharged with a diagnosis of "Schizophrenia, in remission." Clearly, as emphasized by Rosenhan, "a psychiatric label has a life and an influence of its own."

Are there any ways in which we can guard against the adverse effects of the Assimilation Bias? First, make it a point never to underestimate the extent to which your prior beliefs, knowledge, and expectancies (that is, your schemata) can affect your current experience, impressions, and perceptions. Second, try to become as conscious as possible of the schemata that are most important to you. Remember that awareness of schemata greatly increases your ability to modify them. Third, experiment with temporarily lowering (or even removing) your "perceptual filters" and "schema-colored glasses" by attempting to understand, as fully as possible, someone else's subjective (phenomenological) perceptions and experience. Fourth, learn to differentiate your use of assimilation versus accommodation, particularly when you are faced with a discrepancy between your beliefs (schemas) and the information (data). Further, attempt to identify those specific situations in which you are more likely to engage in assimilation. Last, prod yourself to accommodate when, out of habit, reflex, or just sheer laziness, you typically would be inclined automatically to assimilate. By striving to enhance your cognitive flexibility, you will decrease the likelihood of falling prey to "hardening of the categories."

Glossary Terms

The following terms (or variations) are defined in the Glossary:

abstract	experiment
accommodation	explanation
affect	fact
ambiguous	family therapy
assimilation	generalization
Assimilation Bias	humanistic therapy
Availability Bias	i.e.
behavior	inference
belief	interpersonal
bias	interpretation
category	knowledge
clinical	mental
Clinical Orientation Assimilation	mental illness
Bias (COAB)	motivation
cognition	normal
cognitive–behavioral therapy	observation
concept	pathological
conscious	perception
consequence	personality
construct	personality trait
critical	phenomenology
data	phenomenon
diagnosis	preconception
dimension	psychoanalysis
disease	psychodynamic therapy
disorder	psychological
dysfunction	psychology
effect	psychotherapy
ego defense mechanism	psychotic
emotion	reification
erroneous	response
evaluation	schema
event	scientific
existential therapy	social
expectation	stereotype
experience	stimulus

subjective
subsequent
symptom
syndrome
taxonomy
theoretical

theory
thinking
trait
unconscious
variable
vividness

Notes

[1] The word *schema* is derived from the Greek word for "form," thus referring to the overall form or outline of our knowledge about any given concept or stimulus. Bear in mind, of course, that the concept of a schema is just that, a theoretical construct. Thus, be careful not to reify schemas by treating them as if they were tangible objects (see Metathought II, the Reification Error).

[2] Keep in mind that the operative word here is *good* scientists, lest we fail to take heed of Hans Eysenck's not-so-subtle admonition that "Scientists ... are just as ordinary, pig-headed, and unreasonable as anybody else, and their unusually high intelligence only makes their prejudices all the more dangerous because it enables them to cover these up with an unusually glib and smooth flow of high-sounding talk" (1957, p. 108).

[3] Interestingly, however, it was quite common for the *real* patients to recognize the pseudopatients' sanity. For example, one patient remarked, "You're not crazy. You're a journalist, or a professor. You're checking up on the hospital."

XXIV. The Confirmation Bias: Ye Shall Find Only What Ye Shall Seek

What the analyst shows interest in, the kinds of questions he asks, the kind of data he chooses to react to or ignore, and the interpretations he makes, all exert a subtle but significant suggestive impact upon the patient to bring forth certain kinds of data in preference to others.
—JUDD MARMOR*

If you look hard enough for what doesn't exist, eventually it may appear.
—ANONYMOUS

The psychiatrist's eagerness to find mental illness wherever he looks is matched only by his reluctance to define mental illness.
—THOMAS SZASZ**

Whether we are conducting formal scientific research investigations or simply attempting to solve everyday problems, we are faced with a host of obstacles and pitfalls that can impede our pursuit of valid and trustworthy results. One particularly problematic area involves the manner in which we go about gathering evidence to answer our questions.

In order to evaluate the veracity of our assumptions, expectations, and beliefs, we ultimately must subject them to some kind of empirical test by

*Quoted in Hans J. Eysenck's *Decline and Fall of the Freudian Empire,* 1985
**Insanity,* 1987

weighing them against the evidence. If our beliefs are supported by the data, we become that much more confident of their accuracy. If, by contrast, the data are disconfirming, we need to revise (or perhaps even abandon) our original beliefs.

But before we are in a position to *weigh* the evidence, we first must *collect* the evidence. Ideally, our search should be conducted in a manner that is impartial, fair, and free of prejudices or biases. Unfortunately, however, the ways in which we actually procure such information frequently are far from unbiased. Specifically, we tend to selectively gather information that is consistent with our prior expectations. That is, we more eagerly search for evidence that will confirm our beliefs, while we are less likely to seek out evidence that might refute them. Our proclivity to gather information in this slanted fashion is called the *Confirmation Bias*. We may, for instance, unintentionally ask "leading questions" that serve to verify our initial beliefs. Because social information often is ambiguous and subject to numerous interpretations, it is not difficult to amass evidence that inevitably ends up supporting our expectations.

The Confirmation Bias has been examined in a diverse array of research settings (Klayman & Ha, 1987; Skov & Sherman, 1986; Wason, 1960), all of which demonstrate how people employ strategies for eliciting information from others that preferentially support their initial beliefs (see Higgins & Bargh, 1987, for a review). In one such study (Snyder & Swann, 1978), college students were instructed to conduct individual interviews with other students to ascertain the presence of certain personality traits. Half of the subjects were told that their goal was to determine if the interviewee was an extravert (i.e., outgoing, sociable, and gregarious); the goal for the other half was to determine if the interviewee was an introvert (i.e., shy, reserved, and timid). All subjects then were presented with a list of questions that assessed extraversion and introversion, from which they were instructed to select questions to ask the interviewee.

Results of the study showed that subjects who were asked to find out if the interviewee was an extravert preferentially chose extraversion questions (e.g., "What would you do if you wanted to liven things up at a party?"), whereas those who were told to determine if the interviewee was an introvert selected introversion questions (e.g., "What factors make it really hard for you to open up to people?"). As a consequence, simply by answering the questions asked of them, the interviewees revealed those aspects of themselves that corroborated the particular goal of the interviewer. Thus, those who were tested for extraversion actually appeared more extraverted; likewise, those who were tested for introversion appeared more introverted. In essence, interviewers "found" the very personality traits for which they had been probing, *solely on the basis of the questions they had chosen to ask*.[1]

In the context of psychotherapy, the Confirmation Bias can lead therapists to selectively elicit clinical information that affirms their initial diagnostic impressions or expectations. As an example, suppose you are informed by a colleague that your new therapy patient, whom you have not yet met, is an alcoholic. Based on your academic training, clinical experience, and knowledge of the research literature on alcohol abuse, you begin to form an image of him as a person who is likely to

>under-report how much he drinks;

>hide his drinking habit from others;

>sometimes drink secretly;

>socialize with people who also drink;

>have hangovers;

>experience memory blackouts;

>suffer periods of depression;

>have bouts of insomnia;

>display mood lability;

>experience family conflicts;

>manifest problems at his place of employment, such as lateness, absenteeism, or low productivity; and

>to be generally dishonest in admitting to the extent of his problems.

So, in your initial therapy session you ask him a wide range of questions about his drinking habits ("How much do you drink?" "How often do you drink?" "With whom do you drink?" "Do other people know how much you drink?" "Have you ever had occasion to drink alone?"); you explore his history of substance use ("Have you ever had hangovers?"); you query him about any lapses in his memory ("Have you ever forgotten events that happened to you the night before?"); you investigate his experiences with depression and disturbances in his sleeping habits ("Do you sometimes feel very sad?" "Do you ever have problems falling or staying asleep?"); you assess for the presence of mood lability ("Do you ever find that your moods sometimes change very quickly?"); you probe into his marital conflicts ("Do you have arguments with your wife?"); you inquire about any irresponsible behavior he might display at work ("Do you ever have problems getting to work on time?"); and you search for indications of dishonesty ("Do you sometimes not tell the truth to others?").

You are not surprised one iota, of course, to find that all of his responses confirm your beliefs about him as a closet drinker who is in denial about his chemical dependence problem, but who, nevertheless, fits the profile of an "alcoholic personality." After working with him for several weeks, however, you slowly come to the disconcerting realization that, in fact, he doesn't have a drinking problem at all!

Once you've gotten over the initial shock and have overcome your own inevitable resistance to accepting this new conclusion (see Metathought XXV, the Belief Perseverance Effect), you probably would attempt to ascertain what went wrong. Did your patient or your colleague deliberately deceive you by providing you with false information? Let's assume not. More likely, you deceived *yourself* by selectively seeking information that supported your prior expectation. In retrospect, (see Metathought XXVI, the Hindsight Bias), it now strikes you as glaringly obvious that *many* people who are *not* alcoholic

>are reluctant to disclose fully their alcohol usage to others;
>drink at parties or by themselves;
>have endured hangovers;
>experience occasional lapses in memory;
>suffer through periods of depression or insomnia;
>display mood swings;
>argue with their wives;
>are sometimes irresponsible at their place of employment;
>and are less than totally honest in their dealings with others.

But because of the context and manner in which you queried your patient about these events, he provided you with all the evidence you needed to corroborate your prior belief about him as an alcoholic. In other words, due to the Confirmation Bias, you unintentionally guided him down the path of affirming your preconceived conclusion.

In the same manner, a therapist may erroneously "verify" the presence of a multitude of other specific clinical problems, ranging from depression, anxiety, impulsivity, paranoia, and dependency to eating disorders, sexual disorders, personality disorders, or even repressed incidents of childhood sexual abuse.[2]

As an exercise in learning to identify and to remedy the Confirmation Bias, select a particular psychological problem, either from the list above, or one of your own choosing. Now, imagine that you, as a clinician, are assigned the task of conducting an initial intake interview with a client about whom you know nothing, except for his or her "admitting diagnosis" (which, for purposes of this exercise, is the problem you have just selected).

Next, construct a list of *leading questions* that, by their very nature, are virtually certain to confirm the diagnosis. For instance, if the admitting diagnosis happens to be paranoia, some of your questions might include: "Do you ever feel suspicious of other people's motives?" "Do you believe that other people talk about you when you are not present?" or "Have others sometimes behaved toward you in a way that is threatening or demeaning?" (Additional suggestions appear in Appendix 2.)

"_____?"
"_____?"
"_____?"
"_____?"
"_____?"
"_____?"
"_____?"
"_____?"
"_____?"
"_____?"

How, then, shall we address the problem of overcoming the Confirmation Bias? The antidote lies in adopting a strategy of eliciting information that is deliberately *not consistent* with our prior expectations. Specifically, your task is to generate a series of questions that could, in principle, refute, disconfirm, or invalidate the admitting diagnosis. To continue with the example of paranoia, sample questions could be: "What evidence or proof do you have that other people have intended to harm you?" "On a scale from one to ten, how sensitive to criticism are you?" or "How frequently do your suspicions about others usually turn out to be true?" (Other suggestions are presented in Appendix 2.)

"_____?"
"_____?"
"_____?"
"_____?"
"_____?"
"_____?"
"_____?"
"_____?"
"_____?"
"_____?"

The Confirmatory Bias of Theoretical Orientations

The impact of the Confirmation Bias can be both insidious and pervasive, guided in large measure by the therapist's own personal and professional convictions, values, and beliefs. Specifically, for instance, therapists tend to ask questions, probe for information, and direct the focus of treatment based on their respective theoretical orientation. As a consequence, clients are apt to provide evidence that supports their therapist's particular school of thought, thereby "confirming" the validity of their approach. In this way

>Freudians search for and therefore are more likely to "find" unconscious infantile sexual conflicts;

>Jungians find unreconciled psychological opposites and nonintegrated archetypes;

>Adlerians find strivings for superiority that compensate for perceived inferiority;

>Eriksonians find deficient ego strength arising from inadequate resolution of psychosocial crises;

>Rankians find separation anxiety;

>Kleinians find sadistic rage toward one's mother;

>Sullivanians find unhealthy interpersonal relationships;

>Kohutians find narcissistic injuries;

>Horneyites find alienation from one's real self;

>Humanists find incongruent self-perceptions and hindered actualization tendencies;

>Existentialists find struggles for meaning in life and ontological insecurity;

>Gestaltists find restricted awareness and incomplete gestalts;

>Behaviorists find maladaptive learning patterns;

>Classical Behaviorists find disruptive conditioned associations;

>Social Learning therapists find faulty role modeling;

>Cognitive therapists find irrational belief systems;

>Family therapists find dysfunctional family systems;

>Bowenian family therapists find low levels of differentiation;

>Communications family therapists find ineffective communication patterns;

>Strategic family therapists find interpersonal power struggles;

>Psychodynamic family therapists find unconsciously motivated repetition compulsions; and

>Structural family therapists find maladaptive boundaries, roles, and coalitions.

To summarize, the Confirmation Bias can profoundly influence the overall focus, direction, and course of psychotherapy. In particular, therapists are inclined to selectively probe for information and to ask leading questions that serve to verify their preconceived theoretical convictions; in short, they are likely to find only what they seek.

The Confirmatory Bias of Projective Psychological Testing

As a final illustration of the Confirmation Bias, let's examine one of the most controversial topics in psychology: projective personality testing. To provide a brief background, projective tests refer to a variety of psychological assessment techniques, all of which involve exposing the examinee to a relatively unstructured or ambiguous stimulus and then soliciting his or her perceptions. The rationale underlying the use of projective tests is known as the projective hypothesis (Frank, 1939), which in essence proposes that when people are presented with an ambiguous stimulus, they will respond by automatically assigning or imposing (that is, "projecting") structure, organization, or meaning onto the stimulus, thereby revealing their psychological dynamics (such as their attitudes, beliefs, fantasies, conflicts, needs, expectations, fears, and so on), both conscious and unconscious.

The most well-known projective tests are the Rorschach Inkblot Test, the Thematic Apperception Test (TAT), the House-Tree-Person (HTP) Projective Drawing Test, and various versions of sentence completion tests (for example, the Curtis Completion Form). Criticisms of projective tests are numerous and well documented (see Anastasi, 1988), but for our purposes we shall focus on just one, namely, the problem of Confirmation Bias.

In most settings, clinicians employ projective tests as one component of a full psychological assessment battery, which typically includes a diverse array of methods and techniques (such as a structured interview, behavioral observations, standardized personality questionnaires, and measures of cognitive functioning). The clinician then analyzes and integrates the data from these sources, usually with the goal of arriving at a diagnosis and treatment plan.

What role, then, do projective tests play in this process? Although they may serve several functions, one purpose in particular is to confirm the clinician's diagnostic impressions. (Do you see any potential problems here?)

Let's examine one hypothetical scenario. Suppose that, based on the results of other components of an assessment battery, a clinician tentatively concludes that the examinee (Mr. X) has "aggressive tendencies." To confirm this provisional diagnosis, she decides to utilize the Rorschach Inkblot Test. Following standard procedure, for each of the ten inkblots she asks Mr. X, "What might this be?" and then scrupulously jots down verbatim his responses, some of which include: "Two animals are fighting there . . . It looks like a bullet smashing through something . . . It looks like a piece of denim that's being torn . . . Two people arguing about something . . . Two insects are trying to knock down this post . . . Their mouths are open like they're gonna bite something . . . The part in the center is getting blown up."[3]

Now, what specific evidence does the clinician look for to support her diagnosis? According to John Exner (1993), the world's leading authority on the Rorschach, aggressive tendencies are manifested in responses which involve actions such as fighting, breaking, tearing, stalking, exploding, or looking angry. Thus, Mr. X's responses clearly confirm the clinician's initial diagnosis. She therefore concludes that, "Mr. X exhibits evidence of aggressive tendencies, which appear to constitute a significant component of his psychological dynamics."

But now let's suppose, by contrast, that Mr. X had *not* provided *any* responses of this kind. Would this disconfirm the clinician's diagnosis? Not necessarily. She could just as easily conclude that, "Mr. X appears to be resisting, denying, or covering up his aggressive tendencies, which are likely to be buried just beneath the surface of his nonaggressive veneer." Thus, even the complete *absence* of "aggressive" responses can confirm her "aggressive" diagnosis!

Finally, what if the examinee were to manifest a "typical" number of aggressive responses on the Rorschach? The clinician still may confidently conclude that, "Mr. X appears to be only partly successful in his attempts at controlling his aggressive tendencies." Once again, her diagnosis has been validated. In short, no matter what Mr. X does or does not actually perceive, his responses may be interpreted as confirming the clinician's diagnostic expectations.

How is this possible? Remember that projective tests involve stimuli that are ambiguous not only for the examinee, but for the clinician as well. As a consequence, they permit *both* persons to project their respective psychological perceptions. In other words, an ambiguous stimulus, just like the proverbial knife, "cuts both ways." Thus, irrespective of what the examinee happens to perceive in the stimuli, the Confirmation Bias can lead the clinician to selectively perceive evidence that corroborates her initial beliefs. (In this respect, keep in mind that projective tests can reveal as much about the examiner as they do about the examinee.)

Taken to its extreme, virtually any diagnosis can be "confirmed" with the use (or, more accurately, the *misuse*) of projective tests. Moreover, the intrinsic nature of these tests all but ensures that the clinician's diagnosis won't (and frequently *can't*) be directly disconfirmed. This is due to the fact that the results of projective tests can be open to a variety of interpretations. Thus, even if genuinely disconfirming evidence were to exist somewhere amongst the examinee's responses to inkblots, pictures, drawings, or incomplete sentences, we currently have no reliable way of identifying them and ruling out alternative or conflicting explanations. All told, it is ironic indeed that the very purpose for which these tests frequently are utilized (that is, to confirm a diagnosis) is the one that they are least capable of achieving and least likely of providing valid results.

How can we guard against the Confirmation Bias? First and foremost, by being aware that we are prone to be biased collectors of evidence. Specifically, never forget that the questions we ask may lead us selectively to arrive only at those answers that corroborate our initial beliefs. As a consequence, make it a point to actively seek out evidence that *could*, in principle, *refute* your preconceptions. In this way, you will help to ensure that a conclusion will not have been reached before the search has even begun.

Glossary Terms

The following terms (or variations) are defined in the Glossary:

ambiguous	interpersonal
antidote	interpretation
assumption	intrapsychic
attitude	introversion
behavior	knowledge
behavior theory	measure
belief	mental illness
bias	mood
clinical	motive
cognitive	observation
cognitive therapy	ontological
cognitive–behavioral therapy	perception
Confirmation Bias	personality
conscious	personality disorder
consequence	personality trait
data	preconception
denial	projective hypothesis
diagnosis	projective test
disorder	psychodynamic therapy
dynamics	psychological
dysfunction	psychology
e.g.	psychotherapy
empirical	reliability
erroneous	repression
evaluation	resistance
event	response
existential therapy	scientific
expectation	social
experience	stimulus
explanation	subsequent
extraversion	theoretical
family therapy	treatment
Gestalt therapy	truth
humanistic therapy	unconscious
hypothetical	validity
i.e.	veracity

Notes

[1] In a noteworthy replication of this study, Fazio, Effrein, and Fallender (1981) reported that interviewees who had been asked the extraversion questions subsequently even perceived *themselves* as more outgoing than those who had been asked the introversion questions (see Metathought XXII, the Self-Fulfilling Prophecy).

[2] On this last point, I highly recommend *The Myth of Repressed Memory* (Loftus & Ketcham, 1994), which presents a superb examination of the alleged recovery of repressed memories.

[3] These examples of "aggressive" (AG) responses were taken directly from Exner's (1990) *Rorschach Workbook*.

XXV. The Belief Perseverance Effect: The Rat Is Always Right

The great tragedy of Science—the slaying of a beautiful hypothesis by an ugly fact.
—T. H. HUXLEY*

If the facts don't fit the theory, so much the worse for the facts.
—GEORG WILHELM FRIEDRICH HEGEL**

We are least open to precise knowledge concerning the things we are most vehement about.
—ERIC HOFFER***

In our attempts to understand the world around us and to navigate our way through life, we adopt a wide variety of beliefs, the content of which ranges from the mundane (e.g., the best brand of detergent, the most flattering hairstyle) to the profound (e.g., the meaning of life, the existence of God). One of the most significant characteristics of our beliefs is the degree to which we become personally invested in them. The attachment may be so strong, in fact, that our beliefs feel as if they are a vital and indispensable component of our very identity.

What happens, then, when our beliefs are challenged? Particularly those beliefs that we happen to *like*? Or those that we regard as *important*? Or those that we have come to accept as *truths*?

*1825–1895, *Collected Essays,* 1959
**1770–1831
***1902–1983, *The Passionate State of Mind,* 1954

If we were to respond to such challenges in a purely rational manner, we would simply detach our personal feelings from the dispute, evaluate the substance of the challenge as objectively and dispassionately as possible, and then, if appropriate, modify our beliefs accordingly. We would, in other words, accommodate the new information by modifying our preexisting schemas (see Metathought XXIII, the Assimilation Bias).

But we are not always so rational. In fact, sometimes we are not rational at all. Specifically, when our beliefs are being challenged, we are prone to feel that *we personally* are being challenged. When our beliefs are criticized, we feel criticized. When our beliefs are attacked, we feel attacked. Our first impulse, therefore, typically is to *protect* our beliefs, as if to protect ourselves. As such, we tend to cling to our beliefs, sometimes even in the face of contrary evidence. This bias in thinking is called the *Belief Perseverance Effect* (sometimes also referred to as the Belief Perseverance Phenomenon; see Lord, Ross, & Lepper, 1979).

When we engage in belief perseverance, we usually respond to such challenges by discounting, denying, or simply ignoring any information that runs counter to our beliefs. That is, we treat potentially disconfirming evidence as if it didn't even exist. For instance, suppose a friend of yours believes that eating a meal late at night causes more weight gain than eating the same meal earlier in the day. So, you carefully explain to her the results of widely accepted scientific research demonstrating that weight gain is not related, *per se,* to the time of day at which food is ingested. She then pauses for a moment, apparently mulling it over, and replies, "Oh, I see what you mean. But, you know what? I *still* think that it causes more weight gain at night." Her position is, of course, tantamount to maintaining that, "If the facts don't support my theory, the facts must be wrong."

The Belief Perseverance Effect was demonstrated empirically in a study by Charles Lord and his associates (1979). The researchers began by selecting two groups of college students, one in favor of capital punishment and the other opposed to it. The subjects then were shown the results of two purportedly new research studies, one that supported the efficacy of capital punishment as a deterrent to crime, and one that refuted its efficacy. Thus, each group was presented with the identical body of mixed evidence. How did they respond? Subjects in *both* groups were favorably impressed with the study that supported their own prior beliefs, while they discounted the study that contradicted them. The researchers concluded that showing the two opposing groups an identical body of mixed evidence failed to narrow their disagreement; as a matter of fact, it actually *increased* it.

Our beliefs can be so intractable, in fact, that they stubbornly persevere even when we acknowledge that the evidence supporting them is erroneous. This phenomenon was evidenced in a research study in which subjects were administered a personality test that purportedly showed them to be especially "socially sensitive" (Ross, Lepper, & Hubbard, 1975). Subjects were subsequently informed that the test actually was *fake,* and therefore provided invalid results. Even with this knowledge, however, subjects *still persisted* in believing that they were socially sensitive. Other studies have corroborated the general conclusion that it requires much more compelling evidence to *change* our beliefs than it did to *create* them in the first place (Ross & Lepper, 1980).[1]

Can we engage in belief perseverance without rejecting contradictory information? What if we are not able, or even choose not, to discount, deny, or ignore potentially disconfirming evidence? Is there any way that we can continue to cling to our cherished beliefs and still emerge victorious?

The answer, as you probably have already anticipated, is yes. Like the martial arts expert who masterfully redirects and transforms his opponent's force to his own advantage, in a brilliant feat of logical contortionism, we simply find a way to bend, twist, or reframe the information so that it actually *supports* our original belief.

The following parable will illustrate how people can reinterpret contradictory and potentially disconfirming data to support their preexisting beliefs.

> *A woman walks into a psychiatrist's office, complaining that she's a zombie. The psychiatrist, trying his best to convince her otherwise, says, "You're walking and talking, aren't you?" "Zombies walk and talk," replies the patient. "Well, you're breathing, too." "Yes, but zombies breathe." "Okay, what don't zombies do? Do they bleed?" "No, of course not," says the patient, condescendingly. The doctor replies, "Good. Then I'm going to stick this needle into your arm and we'll see if your belief is right or wrong." So, he plunges the needle into the woman's arm, and, of course, blood starts to trickle out of the wound. The woman is stunned. In utter dismay, she slowly turns to the psychiatrist and says, "I guess I was wrong . . . Zombies do bleed."*

Another illustration of how the Belief Perseverance Effect can lead to the negation and gross distortion of disconfirming evidence to support one's original beliefs comes from the autobiography of Carl G. Jung, *Memories, Dreams, Reflections* (1961). In describing his early experiences as an apprentice in a psychiatric clinic, Jung recalled:

> . . . *I had to be most circumspect about treating my schizophrenic patients, or I would have been accused of woolgathering. Schizophrenia was considered incurable. If one did achieve some improvement with a case of schizophrenia, the answer was that* it had not been real schizophrenia *(p. 128; emphasis added).*

Let us now turn to a sampling of variations on this very robust theme. In particular, note how the participants in these brief scenarios are able to support their positions by employing a creative assortment of flaws in thinking, including tautologous logic (Metathought IV), misattributions of intentionality based on consequences (Metathought XVII), confusing feelings with truth (Metathought XVIII), and errors in deductive and inductive reasoning (Metathought XX).[2]

Wife People who love someone should just *know* what they need.

Husband I do love you—I just don't know what you need.

Wife Then, you must not *really* love me. Because if you *did*, then you'd know.

Confidant Man I'm telling you, she is really attracted to me.

Unconvinced Friend But she totally ignores you.

Confidant Man Well, that proves it! She wouldn't be making such an active effort to ignore me if she weren't, deep down, really attracted to me.

Student Trainee My patient possesses the deeply ingrained characterological traits of Dependent Personality Disorder.

Clinical Colleague But she conducts her life in a fashion that is self-reliant, independent, and autonomous.

Student Trainee Obviously, that's just her way of engaging in the ego defense mechanism of overcompensation, which she utilizes to deny the fact that she's really got Dependent Personality Disorder.

Freudian Psychoanalyst All women have unconsciously repressed penis envy.

Female Student I'm a woman, and I don't wish to have a penis.

Freudian Psychoanalyst See what I mean? That just shows how deeply repressed in the unconscious your penis envy is.[3]

Worried Person They're plotting against me! They're plotting against me!

Doubter Now, hold on. Do you have any *evidence* that they're plotting against you?

Worried Person No, but I *feel* that they are, therefore they *must* be.

Sociopolitical Theorist Jews control the media.

Skeptic But the vast majority of people who head the networks and newspapers aren't Jewish.

Sociopolitical Theorist Exactly my point. All that proves is how *clever* they are in creating the appearance that they don't have any power. They have *so much* control that they've been able to dupe you into believing that they don't have *any* control.

Crusader All atheists, deep down, are profoundly depressed due to a lack of faith in God.

Nonbeliever But I'm an atheist, and I'm not depressed.

Crusader Then you can't really be an atheist.

Female Group Therapy Member All men really want is sex.

Male Group Therapy Member I'm a man, and that's not all *I* want.

Female Group Therapy Member Well, then either you're lying to me, or you're lying to yourself, or you're not *really* a man.

As an exercise in further examining the various manifestations of belief perseverance, try completing a few more of these scenarios on your own.

Person A You're planning on betraying me. I just *know* it.

Person B But I've treated you with nothing but honesty, respect, loyalty, and unconditional love.

Person A _____

_____ .

Person A You can't love anybody else unless you first love yourself.

Person B Well, I don't really love myself all that much, but I do love my child.

Person A _____

_____ .

Person A People who are frightened of intimacy were abused as children.

Person B But my boyfriend, who is very frightened of intimacy, wasn't abused as a child.

Person A _____

_____ .

Person A You've got a real problem with your anger issues.

Person B But I don't feel particularly angry, I don't have violent thoughts, and I almost never lose my temper.

Person A _____

_____ .

Person A You're attracted to your wife because she unconsciously reminds you of your mother, toward whom you have an unresolved Oedipal conflict with highly repressed incestuous sexual desires.

Person B But my wife is nothing like my mother.

Person A _____

_____ .

Person A The defendant is insane.

Person B But he claims to be completely responsible for his actions.

Person A _____

_____ .

As for antidotes to the Belief Perseverance Effect, there appear to be two useful strategies. The first one involves becoming more aware of our own cognitive processes. Specifically, we should remind ourselves (and others as well) to think carefully about how we evaluate evidence and to closely monitor our biases as we formulate conclusions (Fiske & Taylor, 1984). For instance, if you are a strong adherent of a particular method of psychotherapy, you should caution yourself against the tendency to exaggerate the evidence in favor of your own point of view while discounting evidence that supports the efficacy of other types of therapy.

Another method for reducing the impact of belief perseverance is to actively *counterargue* your preexisting beliefs (Anderson, 1982). In other words, ask yourself in what ways your beliefs might be wrong. Similarly, you can encourage others to explain why their beliefs might be wrong. One specific technique of doing so is to *consider the opposite* (see Metathought VI). Research shows that when people are instructed to consider the possibility that the opposite of their beliefs might be true, they are less likely to fall victim to belief perseverance (Lord, Lepper, & Preston, 1984).

For instance, if you are of the belief that the only effective way to ameliorate emotional distress is by exploring one's unconscious dynamics (such as unresolved early childhood trauma), consider the opposite: Namely, ask yourself in what ways one might be able to reduce emotional distress by focusing on one's *conscious* processes (for example, current goals or choices in life). Similarly, if it is your belief that significant changes in behavior can occur only by modifying one's *internal attitudes,* ask yourself how behavior might also be changed by modifying one's *external situations.*

To conclude, make an effort to keep an open mind to different, alternative, and (especially) challenging points of view. Unless you actively guard against the tendency to cling stubbornly to your beliefs in the face of disconfirming evidence, you may find that you will have unknowingly painted yourself into a corner where your only recourse and last line of defense will be to whimper woefully, *"Please* don't confuse me with the facts!"

Never forget that, in the final analysis, "the rat is always right." What is the meaning of this Metathought's cryptic subtitle and admonition? As a thought experiment, imagine that you have developed a magnificent theory concerning the behavior of rats in your laboratory maze. From your theory, you derive a specific hypothesis (that is, a prediction) that rats will always turn right in the maze. Now, let's say that you run thousands, even millions, of trials of rats in your maze. And, time after time, you are delighted to observe that, *without exception,* the rats do, in fact, turn right. Then late one night, to your astonishment (not to mention horror), one rat actually has the audacity to turn *left*! *Now* what do you do? Obviously, something's got to give. But what? The theory or the rat? Let me give you a hint: The rat wasn't wrong. In fact, in this context, the rat is *never* wrong. All it takes is *one* disconfirming piece of evidence, one ugly fact, and an entire theory can topple. In short, it's time to revise your theory to account for this new (albeit very unwelcome) bit of truth. If not, the theory ultimately will die on the vine. In sum, belief perseverance notwithstanding, *the rat is always right.*

Glossary Terms

The following terms (or variations) are defined in the Glossary:

accommodation	hypothesis
antidote	inductive reasoning
attitude	intentionality
behavior	internal
belief	knowledge
Belief Perseverance Effect	logic
bias	objective
cause	personality
clinical	personality disorder
conscious	phenomenon
consequence	prediction
data	psychotherapy
deductive reasoning	rational
disorder	reasoning
dynamics	reframe
e.g.	repression
effect	schema
efficacy	scientific
ego defense mechanism	skepticism
empirical	subsequent
erroneous	tautologous reasoning
evaluation	theory
existence	trait
external	truth
fact	unconscious

Notes

[1] For further experimental studies on belief perseverance, see Anderson, Lepper, and Ross (1980) and Lepper, Ross, and Lau (1986).

[2] These examples were drawn directly from my own experiences in a variety of settings, including classrooms, therapy sessions, clinical case conferences, and media broadcasts.

[3] For a comprehensive discussion of how belief perseverance appears to have been related to the development and current status of Freudian theory, I recommend Hans Eysenck's, *Decline and Fall of the Freudian Empire* (1985).

Chapter 26

XXVI. The Hindsight Bias: Predicting a Winner after the Race Is Finished

Life is lived forwards, but understood backwards.
—SØREN KIERKEGAARD*

Anything seems commonplace, once explained.
—DR. WATSON**

*A first-rate theory predicts; a second-rate theory forbids;
and a third-rate theory explains after the event.*
—ALEKSANDER ISAAKOVICH KITAIGORODSKII

The *Hindsight Bias*, also known as the *I-knew-it-all-along phenomenon* (see Fischoff, 1975), refers to our tendency to believe that we would have foreseen how something turned out, after learning the outcome. In retrospect, events appear to us as obvious, predictable, or even unavoidable and inevitable. In other words, we tend to overestimate or exaggerate what we could have anticipated. It is one thing to explain after the fact why a particular horse won the race; it is quite another matter to predict beforehand which horse will win. Postdiction is easy; prediction is difficult.

In a classic example of the Hindsight Bias, the proverbial "Monday morning quarterback" can tell you, with astonishing confidence and precision, what his opponent was planning, what his team should have foreseen, and

*1813–1855
**In Arthur Conan Doyle's *Sherlock Holmes*

what could have been done to win the game—but, of course, all in retrospect. You may have experienced the Hindsight Bias yourself when reading a detective novel or seeing a mystery movie. Once the solution has been revealed, it seems glaringly obvious. Again, hindsight is always 20/20.

The Hindsight Bias is particularly problematic for "psychohistorians" who perform "psychological autopsies" on famous personalities (see Runyan, 1981) and for clinical psychologists who write retrospective case studies on their clients. In both instances, the investigator begins by already knowing what there is to "predict" (that is, how the person actually turned out). With this knowledge in hand, the investigator can proffer extensive and detailed after-the-fact (*post hoc*) explanations that, of course, confirm his theory and carry almost no risk of being disproven. Thus, irrespective of the writer's theoretical orientation, hindsight virtually guarantees a valid and infallible "explanation."

As an illustration of the Hindsight Bias, consider the following scenario. Suppose that, as you are browsing through the newspaper, you spot an interesting obituary about a great humanitarian, a man who dedicated his life to helping the downtrodden and the needy. He donated millions of dollars to charitable organizations, he provided food and shelter to the homeless, and he built schools, libraries, and hospitals for underprivileged children. You read further that his own childhood was exceptionally traumatic. He grew up in abject poverty, he witnessed the brutal murder of his father, and he watched helplessly as his mother slowly and painfully succumbed to cancer. Why did this man become such an altruist? It would be easy (perhaps even obvious) to explain his accomplishments in terms of his attempts to overcome or to compensate for the events of his childhood, by giving to others all of the things that he wished had been given to him.

Now, imagine the same scenario, but with one crucial difference: Suppose that, instead of becoming a humanitarian, he ended up becoming a serial killer, a man who was responsible for abducting, molesting, and murdering over a dozen elderly widows. How might we explain this outcome? Suddenly, the same past events (namely, his childhood poverty, his father's murder, and his mother's protracted and fatal illness) take on a completely different meaning. In fact, the very factors that in the first scenario ostensibly created an altruist, in the second scenario produced a psychopath. The outcome of his life now can "obviously" be explained in terms of his repressed rage, displaced aggression, and symbolic revenge... thanks to the Hindsight Bias.

The Hindsight Bias has been demonstrated empirically in numerous research studies (e.g., Fischoff, 1975, 1982; Fischoff & Beyth, 1975; Slovic & Fischhoff, 1977; Wood, 1979), all of which confirm that events seem far less obvious and predictable beforehand than in hindsight, and that knowing a result makes it seem inevitable. For example, when people are informed of the outcome of a historical event or a psychological experiment, it appears to be less surprising to them than it is to people who are asked to guess the outcome.

In this context, let's examine Stanley Milgram's (1963, 1974) experiments on obedience to authority, which are perhaps the most famous and controversial studies ever conducted in the field of psychology. To summarize briefly his basic experimental design, Milgram led the research subjects (all of them adult males) to believe that they were participating in an investigation on the effects of punishment on learning. As part of the experiment, the subjects were instructed to administer painful electric shocks to another subject every time he gave a wrong answer. (In fact, no real shocks were given, and the "other subject" actually was an accomplice[1] of the experimenter.) As the experiment progressed, the experimenter ordered the subjects to deliver more and more intense levels of shock. The accomplice, meanwhile, protested vehemently and screamed in agony. When the shocks seemed to reach fatal levels, the accomplice stopped responding entirely. Milgram's primary (dependent) variable of interest was the magnitude of shock that each subject would administer. The astonishing results were that nearly two-thirds of the subjects were fully obedient to the experimenter's orders, delivering the maximum "fatal" level of 450 volts.

Milgram subsequently performed a number of variations on this experiment, one of which entailed the use of female subjects. What effect do you think the sex of the subjects might have had on their degree of obedience? In the space below, indicate your best guess as to the outcome, *before reading any further.*

_____

_____

_____

_____

_____

As it turned out, the female subjects were substantially *more* obedient than were their male counterparts, with over 90% of them delivering the maximum shock level. Now, as an exercise, briefly offer your explanation for the underlying cause(s) of this result. In light of your prior prediction, how "obvious" or "unsurprising" does the outcome seem to you?

_____

_____

_____

_____

_____

Did you theorize that the female subjects were more obedient than male subjects because women in our culture are socialized to be more compliant toward authority figures? If so, you were mistaken, but not for the reason you might think. Actually, I must confess that I was less than honest in presenting to you the true results of this experiment, which did not turn out the way I indicated. In point of fact, the female subjects were significantly *less* obedient than were the male subjects, with most of them refusing to administer even the minimal levels of painful shock. Now that you know the actual results, how might you explain the cause(s)? Does the outcome now seem more obvious?

_____

_____

_____

_____

_____

Did you postulate that women tend to be less aggressive and more empathic than men; therefore, their resistance to shocking an innocent victim would be higher? Well, I hate to tell you this, but…that's right, I gave you false results again. (Please understand that I engaged in this bit of benign deception with the sole intention of allowing you to experience firsthand just how the Hindsight Bias can operate.)

By the way, the *real* outcome of the experiment revealed that the rate of obedience for women was virtually *identical* to that of men. (Honest.) How would you explain *this* result? Does it now seem somehow more obvious?

_____

_____

_____

_____

_____

This exercise is similar to a common method of studying the Hindsight Bias, which consists of presenting purported research findings, which are opposite and contradictory, to two groups of subjects. For example, one group may be informed that scientific research supports the belief that "out of sight is out of mind," whereas the other group is told that scientific research supports the belief that "absence makes the heart grow fonder." As it turns out, people in *both* groups find whichever result they were given as unsurprising "common sense." Of course, the results appear to be common sense only in hindsight.

Thus, the problem with many "common sense" explanations is not that they are wrong, but that we tend to use them only *after* we already know the outcome. In other words, they *describe* or *justify* much better than they *predict* or *explain*. As the example above shows us, we can find a proverb to make nearly any result seem like common sense. Because so many outcomes in life are possible, we have proverbs (many of them contradictory) to account for any occasion. As the following table illustrates, you can always find a commonsensical proverb to "explain" why an event turned out the way it did, no matter *what* the outcome.

TABLE 26-1   Which Proverb in Each Pair Is "Only Common Sense"?[2]

"Out of sight is out of mind." (Arthur Hugh Clough)	"No evil can happen to a good man." (Plato)
"Absence makes the heart grow fonder." (Sextus Aurelius)	"Nice guys finish last." (Leo Durocher)
"Haste makes waste." (John Heywood)	"Let your conscience be your guide." (Alexander Pope)
"He who hesitates is lost." (Anonymous)	"Conscience doth make cowards of us all." (William Shakespeare)
"'Tis better to have loved and lost than never to have loved at all." (Samuel Butler)	"Honesty is the best policy." (English proverb)
"A taste of honey is worse than none at all." (Anonymous)	"Tell the truth and get your head bashed in." (Hungarian proverb)
"Birds of a feather flock together." (Anonymous)	"If at first you don't succeed, try, try again." (William Edward Hickson)
"Opposites attract." (Anonymous)	"It's no use beating a dead horse." (Anonymous)
"You're never too old to learn." (Anonymous)	"It's not whether you win or lose but how you played the game." (Grantland Rice)
"You can't teach an old dog new tricks." (Anonymous)	"Winning isn't everything—it's the only thing." (Vincent Lombardi)
"No man is an island." (John Donne)	"There is no proverb that is not true." (Cervantes)
"Every man is an island." (Thomas Wolfe)	"General notions are generally wrong." (Lady Mary Wortley Montague)
"Opportunity knocks but once." (Anonymous)	
"Look before you leap." (Samuel Butler)	

The Hindsight Bias thus sheds light on one of the most prevalent criticisms of the entire field of psychology, namely, that it is "only common sense" expressed in more sophisticated terms and technical language. Specifically, some people view psychological research as trivial because it merely documents the obvious.[3] But just how obvious, *really*, are the results of psychological research? Remember that we typically learn of such studies only *after the fact*. When viewed in hindsight, how could they, in the vast majority of cases, appear as anything else *but* obvious and inevitable?

Is there an antidote to the Hindsight Bias? Slovic and Fischoff (1977) apparently found one. Subjects in their investigation were informed of the results of a number of experiments. Some of the subjects were then asked, "Had the study worked out the other way, how would you explain it?" These subjects saw the actual results as much less inevitable than did those subjects who had not been instructed to imagine the opposite result.

The conclusion? The Hindsight Bias can deceive you into believing that you know more than you actually do; however, one way to reduce its effect is to imagine how you might explain a result that is *different* from the one that actually occurred.

Glossary Terms

The following terms (or variations) are defined in the Glossary:

antidote	knowledge
belief	phenomenon
bias	postdiction
clinical	*post hoc*
dependent variable	prediction
description	psychological
e.g.	psychology
effect	repression
event	resistance
experience	scientific
explanation	social
fact	subsequent
Hindsight Bias	theoretical
intent	theory

Notes

[1] In the parlance of social researchers, an experimental accomplice is also referred to as a *confederate*.

[2] Unfortunately, I was not able to verify (or in some cases even locate) the original sources for a number of these quotations. Which reminds me of another quotation that seems apropos: "The most valuable quotation will be the one for which you cannot determine the source. The source for an unattributed quota-tion will appear in the most hostile review of your work." (Fortunately, I *do* have the reference for this quote: Arthur Bloch, *Murphy's Law, Book Two*, 1980).

[3] In his excellent textbook, David Myers (1995) effectively applies critical thinking principles to examine this phenomenon, as well as other contemporary issues facing the field of psychology.

P a r t *Five*

Other Biases and Fallacies in Thinking

XXVII. The Representativeness Bias: Fits and Misfits of Categorization

*We all know we are unique individuals, but we tend
to see others as representative of groups.*
—DEBORAH TANNEN*

*If my theory of relativity is proven successful,
Germany will claim me as a German and France
will declare that I am a citizen of the world. Should
my theory prove untrue, France will say that I am
a German and Germany will declare that I am a Jew.*
—ALBERT EINSTEIN**

*If it walks like a duck, and quacks like a duck,
then it just may be a duck.*
—WALTER REUTHER***

In everyday life, we are frequently called upon to make rapid judgments in circumstances that do not lend themselves to thoroughness or accuracy. Consider the following scenarios:

>At a job interview, you have a limited amount of time to figure out how
to create the right impression.

*Quoted in Santrock, 1995
**Address, at the Sorbonne, quoted in *The Pocket Book of Quotations*, Davidoff, 1952
***1907–1970, attributed by William Safire, *Safire's Political Dictionary;* cited in *The New International Dictionary of Quotations*, Miner & Rawson, 1994

171

>After receiving an urgent telephone call, you might have to decide on the best way to break some bad news to a close friend.

>During a committee meeting, you may be required to expeditiously narrow down a large pool of candidates who are applying for a limited number of positions.

>In a therapy setting, you might be assigned the task of quickly conducting an intake interview and determining a clinical diagnosis.

An ideal strategy for making decisions in these situations (and countless others like them) would involve the opportunity to conduct a comprehensive and systematic analysis of the problem, collect relevant data, test various hypotheses, draw appropriate inferences, thoroughly evaluate the pluses and minuses of all possible outcomes, and arrive at the optimum conclusions before having to take final action.

Well, so much for the ideal. For obvious reasons, such a strategy is impractical in most real-life circumstances. We do not have the time, information, or resources (not to mention incentive) that would enable us to solve most problems in this manner.

How, then, *do* we proceed to make decisions in the face of varying degrees of uncertainty? Cognitive psychologists Amos Tversky and Daniel Kahneman (1974) theorized that people use a variety of mental shortcuts, rules of thumb, or *heuristics* that reduce complex and time-consuming tasks to more simple, manageable, practical, and efficient problem-solving strategies. We all have a repertoire of such shortcuts, which we tend to use automatically, without necessarily considering their accuracy or validity in each situation.

Unfortunately, these rules of thumb are double-edged swords. On the one hand, they permit highly efficient information processing and rapid solutions to the problem. In other words, they help us to make quick "seat-of-the-pants" decisions. However, they do so at the expense of thoroughness and precision. In essence, we trade off accuracy for speed (see Metathought XXX, Every Decision Is a Trade-Off). Thus, the price we pay for their efficiency can be bad or wrong judgments. Nevertheless, despite their drawbacks, heuristics are an extremely useful collection of strategies that greatly facilitate rapid information processing in the multitude of decisions—both large and small—we make every day.

Tversky and Kahneman (1973, 1982) identified a number of such shortcuts, including the *representativeness* heuristic and the *availability* heuristic (see Metathought XXVIII).[1] According to Tversky and Kahneman, representativeness is the most basic cognitive heuristic. Essentially, it involves judging the likelihood that something belongs to (that is, "represents") a particular category. Stated slightly more formally, representativeness is a method of estimating the probability that Instance *A* is a member of Category *B*.

We use the representativeness heuristic to identify phenomena in our environment by automatically and intuitively comparing the phenomenon (be it a person, object, event, or ideology) to our mental representation, *prototype*, or *schema* of the relevant category. In so doing, we are attempting to ascertain if there is a "match" on the basis of whether the phenomenon's features are similar to the essential features of the category. If there is a match, we conclude that we have successfully identified the phenomenon; if not, we continue our cognitive search.

One of our most common uses of the representativeness heuristic involves judging whether a person belongs to a specific group based on how similar he or she is to typical members of that group. As an exercise, consider the following personality sketch (from Tversky & Kahneman, 1974): "Steve is very shy and withdrawn, invariably helpful, but with little interest in people, or in the world of reality. A meek and tidy soul, he has a need for order and structure, and a passion for detail."

Now, if you were asked to guess Steve's occupation, which of the following would you select: farmer, trapeze artist, librarian, salvage driver, or surgeon? (Indicate your answer by circling the appropriate job title.)

Approximately how long did it take you to reach your decision? _____

On what basis did you arrive at this conclusion? What method or rationale (if any) did you employ?_____

_____

_____

_____

_____

_____

Before we discuss your response, let's examine an "optimal" approach to solving this problem. With no constraints placed on your time or resources, you could (although I'm not quite sure why you'd ever *want* to) systematically calculate the statistical probabilities that Steve is a member of each occupation. In so doing, you would need to acquire, organize, and analyze extensive data on the comparative frequencies of job membership as well as the correlations between these occupations and particular personality characteristics.

Needless to say, such an endeavor would be thoroughly impractical and unquestionably not worth the costs involved. Fortunately, the representativeness heuristic provides a relatively quick, simple, and painless alternative.

Back to the exercise. If you are like most research participants, you reached your decision very quickly with the use of the representativeness heuristic. Specifically, you were likely to have surmised that Steve is a librarian. Why? Because the description of his personality (Instance *A*) most closely resembles the characteristics stereotypically associated with librarians (Category *B*).

Consider a few more illustrations. The representativeness heuristic could, in like manner, lead you to conclude that Jill (*A*) is an actress because she behaves like your stereotype of an actress (*B*). Or that Jack (*A*) belongs to a fraternity because he looks like your prototypical fraternity member (*B*). Or that Barbara (*A*) is a therapist because her demeanor is similar to your schema of a therapist (*B*). Or that Joe (*A*) is an alcoholic because his appearance matches your conception of an alcoholic (*B*).

In addition to identifying people, we also use the representativeness heuristic for identifying objects (model of automobile, flavor of food, style of art), events (recreational, romantic, dangerous), ideologies (religious, philosophical, political), or even as a means of assigning causal explanations to actions (random, unintentional, malevolent). As you can readily see, this simple act is fundamental to all subsequent inferences and behaviors: Before any other cognitive task can be addressed, we must first answer the question, "What is it?"

As an exercise in identifying and exploring the nature and content of your own cognitive schemata, select three social categories (e.g., sex, race, ethnicity, occupation, religion, political affiliation, and so on) for which you happen to have fairly well-defined attitudes, beliefs, or impressions. Now, describe in detail the specific content (i.e., your personal perceptions) of each schema. Next, try to determine the schema's etiology (origin) and development. Last, try to recall (or imagine) an occasion where you came across an instance that clearly was inconsistent with (i.e., did not "fit") your schema. How did (might) you respond? What happened (might happen) to the schema itself?

Social Schema 1: _____

Content: _____

_____

_____

_____

Etiology and development:_____

_____

_____

_____

Your response to schema-inconsistent event: _____

_____

_____

_____

Social Schema 2: _____

Content: _____

_____

_____

_____

Etiology and development: _____

_____

_____

_____

Your response to schema-inconsistent event: _____

_____

_____

_____

Social Schema 3: _____

Content: _____

_____

_____

_____

Etiology and development: _____

_____

_____

_____

Your response to schema-inconsistent event: _____

_____

_____

_____

Systematic Sources of Error

Although in most instances the representativeness heuristic yields quick and relatively accurate results, it sometimes produces systematic errors in information processing. We shall refer to this effect as the *Representativeness Bias*. There are numerous factors that can cause the Representativeness Bias (see Metathought XIV, Multiple Pathways of Causation), the most significant of which are enumerated and discussed below. Fortunately, most of them can be ameliorated by becoming sensitive to their presence and taking appropriate corrective measures (see Fiske and Taylor [1984] for a comprehensive discussion).

1. Our use of representativeness gives rise to faulty judgments when our initial prototypes are inaccurate, biased, or incomplete. In these instances, we are attempting to classify phenomena by comparing them to invalid schemata. To continue with the examples described above, ask yourself just how accurate are your prototypes of librarians, actresses, fraternity members, therapists, alcoholics, or any other group of people. To the extent that any given stereotype is erroneous (as they all, to some degree, are), the result could be a mistake in judgment. In the same way, if a therapist compares a client's presenting symptoms (*A*) to his or her inaccurate clinical schemata (*B*), a misdiagnosis is all but inevitable.

2. Other critical sources of error leading to the Representativeness Bias are due to the failure to take into account relevant statistical information, such as *base rates, sample size,* and *chance probability.* First, we tend to underuse or even ignore base-rate information (that is, data pertaining to the actual frequency of events in a particular group). Instead, we are prone to reach decisions primarily on the basis of how well any given phenomenon *resembles* our own subjective conceptions of the category. Referring back to the previous example, suppose you discover that Steve lives in a small, rural town where most of the residents are chicken farmers. Clearly, your judgment that he is a librarian should be modified by these facts. Unfortunately, however, such vital base-rate information often is overlooked or disregarded when we rely principally on the similarities we believe to exist, for instance, between personality characteristics and group membership.[2] As a consequence, in comparing instances (*A*) to categories (*B*), we run the risk of allowing perceived similarities to obscure genuine differences (see Metathought VII, the Similarity–Uniqueness Paradox). In other words, we tend to overvalue similarities while undervaluing the actual distribution of likelihood.

3. The Representativeness Bias can also result from our insensitivity to the effects of sample size. Research has shown us, time and time again, that estimates that are derived from large samples are more reliable than estimates derived from small samples. Nevertheless, when forming judgments, we typically do not take this principle into account. As a consequence, despite the fact that data collected from small samples cannot be counted on as trustworthy predictors of a population's characteristics, we are prone to commit the error of overgeneralizing from too small a sample. To illustrate this concept mathematically, even though 7 out of 10 looks like better odds than 60 out of 100, the more reliable indicator is the 60 out of 100.

4. Our misconceptions about what "chance events" ought to look like can also produce the Representativeness Bias. In particular, when we are confronted with an exceptionally rare or extraordinary event (for instance, an unusual winning or losing streak, uncanny coincidence, or bizarre behavior), we might be tempted to conclude that it was due to an extraordinary cause. Yet, as discussed in the Spectacular Explanation Fallacy (Metathought XIX), chance alone predicts the occasional occurrence of extraordinary events. Thus, it would be an error to conclude that an unusual phenomenon (*A*) is *necessarily* indicative of anything other than statistical probability (*B*).

5. Last, consider how your own *motivational biases,* personal wishes, or desires for something to fit (or not fit) a particular category may bias your perceptions and subsequent judgments. Thus, even though there may be a match between an instance and a category, if you don't want it to exist, you would be less likely to perceive it. Similarly, if you do want there to be a match, you would be more inclined to "see" one, whether or not it actually exists (see Metathought XXIII, the Assimilation Bias).

For example, let's say that you have a client in your psychotherapy practice of whom you are especially fond (or, in the vernacular of clinical psychology, toward whom you have developed a *"positive countertransference"*). You may, as a consequence, have a tendency to inadvertently minimize, or even overlook, the severity of her psychological problems. In such an instance, when faced with the question of determining her clinical diagnosis, your use of the representativeness heuristic could result in a significant (and potentially costly) mistake. In particular, by relying primarily on your own idiosyncratic impressions (rather than a structured, systematic assessment of specific diagnostic criteria), you run the risk of unintentionally allowing your positive feelings toward your client to distort, obstruct, or otherwise bias your clinical perceptions and judgment. Thus, you may fail to see, for instance, that her symptoms match the criteria for a diagnosis of schizophrenia. In this way, the Representativeness Bias yields a *"false negative"* diagnostic error (that is, not perceiving a problem that actually does exist).

Your personal, motivational biases can also produce the opposite outcome. Suppose that you have a client whom you especially *dislike* (aka *"negative countertransference"*). Even on a good day, you find her to be nothing short of irritating, obnoxious, belligerent, and just plain rude. Here, you may be prompted to come up with a diagnostic label that best explains away her odious demeanor (and thereby also reduce your own sense of frustration). Needless to say, your clinical perceptions and judgment in this process are liable to be adversely distorted by your negative feelings toward her. Thus, you may quickly, easily, (and perhaps unconsciously) see a match between your client's behavior and a diagnosis of, let's say, Borderline Personality Disorder, irrespective of whether or not she actually meets the clinical criteria. In scenarios of this type, the Representativeness Bias produces a *"false positive"* diagnostic error (that is, perceiving a problem that does not actually exist).

Before concluding this Metathought, one final point deserves mention. Despite all of the problems, pitfalls, and liabilities associated with the use of cognitive heuristics, we persist in relying on them as an integral component of our decision-making processes. Why? One of the main reasons is that, on the whole, they provide us with more right answers than wrong ones. Moreover, even in those circumstances where they are incorrect, the results typically are inconsequential.

One significant exception, however, can occur in relation to our usage of prototype categories about particular groups of people, based on, for example, their race, sex, culture, nationality, religion, or even clinical diagnosis. When viewed in this context, such group-related schemata are equivalent to stereotypes. Thus, when heuristics such as representativeness are utilized with respect to these categories, extreme caution is advised. As history has repeatedly demonstrated, stereotyping can have far-reaching and potentially harmful social consequences, not the least of which include prejudice, bigotry, and discrimination . . . outcomes that are far from inconsequential.

Glossary Terms

The following terms (or variations) are defined in the Glossary:

attitude
availability heuristic
base rate
behavior
belief
bias
category
causal
cause
chance
clinical
cognitive
concept
consequence
correlation
countertransference
criteria
critical
data
decision
description
diagnosis
disorder
e.g.
effect
erroneous
etiology
evaluation
event
explanation
fact

heuristic
i.e.
ideology
intuition
judgment
mental
motivational bias
negative countertransference
perception
personality
personality disorder
phenomenon
positive countertransference
probability
psychological
psychology
psychotherapy
random
reliability
Representativeness Bias
representativeness heuristic
schema
social
Spectacular Explanation Fallacy
stereotype
subjective
subsequent
symptom
unconscious
validity

Notes

[1] It should be noted that these are not the only heuristics that people employ in reaching decisions under conditions of uncertainty. Others include the *simulation* heuristic (Kahneman & Tversky, 1982) and the *anchoring and adjustment* heuristic (Tversky & Kahneman, 1974). In addition, the social perceiver also utilizes idiosyncratic heuristics that apply to the individual's particular life circumstances (see Fiske & Taylor, 1984).

[2] For the results of a study that investigated people's perceptions of the relationships between personality characteristics and occupational role schemata, see Levy, Kaler, and Schall (1988).

Chapter 28

XXVIII. The Availability Bias: The Persuasive Power of Vivid Events

One picture is worth a thousand words.
—ANONYMOUS

When a dog bites a man, that is not news.
But when a man bites a dog, that is news.
—JOHN B. BOGART*

For we must make no mistake about ourselves:
we are as much automaton as mind.
—BLAISE PASCAL**

As a means of introducing this Metathought, try to give your best estimates for the following questions:

1. What are the odds of sustaining a fatal accident traveling by car as compared to traveling by commercial airplane?

2. What percentage of deaths in the United States each year are caused by accidents and what percentage by cardiovascular diseases (such as heart attacks and strokes)?

3. What are the relative frequencies of deaths annually due to tornados, versus accidents, versus asthma?

---

*1845–1921, quoted in Frank M. O'Brien, *The Story of the Sun;* cited in *The New International Dictionary of Quotations,* Miner & Rawson, 1994
**1623–1662, *Pensées:* 821

4. Which is more frequent in English, words that start with the letter *k,* or words that have *k* as their third letter?

5. What is the prevalence of persons who either are, or ever have been, in psychotherapy?

6. What are the rates of psychopathology (such as depression, anxiety, or substance abuse) in the general population?

7. How common is the use of the insanity defense in courtroom trials?

Setting aside for the moment the actual answers to these questions, consider the cognitive processes you utilized reaching your conclusions. How, specifically, did you go about arriving at your estimates for each question? Did you notice any similarity in the mental strategies you employed?

If you are like most people in this way, your estimates probably were determined primarily on the basis of how *easily* or *quickly* specific instances of each question came to mind. And what types of incidents are more likely to stand out in memory? In general, events that create the most powerful impressions are those that are particularly vivid, dramatic, important, personally relevant, or otherwise salient to us. We are also prone to more quickly think of instances that are simply easy to imagine.

Unfortunately, however, the problem in relying on the ease with which events can be retrieved from memory for determining their likelihood is that our perceptions cannot necessarily be counted on as an accurate reflection of reality. Specifically, this strategy leads us to *overestimate* their actual occurrence, frequency, or distribution in the world.

Did you inadvertently succumb to this bias in answering any of the questions posed above? Let's examine each one in turn.

1. Few events are more disturbing than the graphic sights and sounds of a catastrophic airplane crash. Even a mere glimpse of these horrific images on the eleven o'clock news is likely to stamp in our minds a potent and indelible impression. Such tragic accidents, therefore, become easily accessible and readily available in our memory. As a consequence, many people erroneously jump to the conclusion that they are at greater risk when traveling by commercial airplane than by car. Yet, mile for mile, Americans are nearly *100 times* more likely to die in an automobile accident than in a commercial plane accident (Greenwald, 1986).

2. Despite the fact that cardiovascular diseases cause *ten times* as many deaths as accidents (50% versus 5%), most people overestimate the relative frequency of accidents. Why? Because accidents, compared to more common causes of death, are so much more startling, vivid, and therefore, memorable (see Slovic, Fischoff, & Lichtenstein, 1976).

3. When people are asked to estimate the frequency of deaths from a number of causes, they typically overestimate the rare and sensational instances (for example, deaths due to accidents or tornados), while underestimating the less dramatic but more frequent instances (for instance, deaths due to asthma). In point of fact, however, asthma causes *sixteen times* more deaths than accidents and about *twenty times* more deaths than tornados (see Slovic, 1987).

4. Most people choose the *k*-initial words, despite the fact that *k* is three times more likely to appear as the third letter. Why? According to Tversky and Kahneman (1974), it is *easier* to retrieve words from memory by their initial letter than by their third one, the consequence of which is a biased estimate of their frequency.

5. In responding to this question, your thoughts probably turned automatically to the number of people you personally know who are, or who have been, psychotherapy clients. Now, if you happen to be a mental health professional, a graduate student in psychology, an undergraduate psychology major, or even someone who is "psychologically-minded," the chances are that you know quite a few people who have, at some point, been in therapy. Further, you also are more likely to *notice* and *remember* instances of such persons. Conversely, if your area of study, practice, or interest is essentially unrelated to psychology, you are less likely to know (or perhaps be aware of) many people who are in therapy. Either way, you would be prone to arrive at a biased judgment (*overestimation* in the former case, *underestimation* in the latter case), based on the relative ease (or difficulty) with which instances of persons in therapy come to mind.

6. Your strategy for estimating the frequency of different forms of psychopathology also was very likely to have been a function of specific examples that, for various reasons, happened to stand out in your memory. In addition to direct knowledge of individuals from your personal and professional relationships who exhibit psychological problems, what other sources of information influenced your judgment? Did you consider the omnipresent and virtually inescapable barrage of psychological phenomena in the popular media? Take a few moments to reflect on the potential power of feature films; news broadcasts; television talk shows; radio call-in programs; disease-of-the-week, made-for-TV movies; documentaries; docudramas; newspaper and magazine articles; televised courtroom trials; and self-help books, not to mention advertising in the form of public service announcements; television and radio commercials; and billboards and print ads, to name but a few.

Because the media's very existence is, to a large extent, predicated on grabbing and holding our attention, instances of psychopathology typically are presented in a manner that ranges from the dramatic and engrossing, to the rare and unusual, to the sensationalistic and shocking: in a word, *memorable*. All of this leads us to overestimate its frequency in the general population. For the same reasons, we almost certainly would underestimate the incidence of "nonpathological," "normal," or "healthy" (whatever that might be) instances of human behavior—none of which is particularly newsworthy, entertaining, or otherwise useful for the vast majority of media purposes.

7. Popular opinion notwithstanding, the insanity defense—"not guilty by reason of insanity"—is utilized very infrequently. Over time, it has been invoked in less than 2 percent of courtroom cases (Fersch, 1980), in fewer than 1 out of 400 homicide trials, and even more rarely in nonhomicide trials (Rosenhan & Seligman, 1995). Further, it has been successful in many fewer cases than that (Rosenhan & Seligman, 1995). Why then, do people typically overestimate the extent to which the insanity defense is employed? This misconception is attributable primarily to the notoriety surrounding high-visibility cases in which it has been exposed to widespread public scrutiny. Certainly one of the most notorious cases in point was the trial of John W. Hinckley, Jr., who, on June 21, 1982, was found to be not guilty by reason of insanity in his attempted assassination of former President Ronald Reagan. Here again we see how vivid, although rare, events can exert a disproportionate influence on our estimates of their actual frequency.

You will recall from our discussion of the Representativeness Bias (Metathought XXVII) that, because we are limited in our capacity to process complex information, we utilize mental shortcuts or *heuristics* to simplify the world and thereby reach expedient solutions. In other words, we tend to focus on rapid and efficient, rather than slow and accurate, understanding.

The specific cognitive strategy demonstrated in the above examples has been termed the *availability heuristic* (Tversky & Kahneman, 1973) because it refers to the process of drawing on instances that are easily accessible or "available" from our memory. This heuristic helps us to answer questions concerning the frequency ("How many are there?"), incidence ("How often does something happen?"), or likelihood ("What are the odds that something will occur?") of particular events.

If examples are readily available in memory, we tend to assume that such events occur rather frequently. For instance, if you have no trouble bringing to mind examples of *X*, you are likely to judge that it is common. By contrast, if it takes you awhile to think of examples of *X*, you are prone to conclude that it is uncommon. In sum, when an event has easily retrieved instances, it will seem more numerous than will an equally frequent category that has less easily retrieved instances.

As is the case with the representativeness heuristic, very little cognitive work is needed to utilize the availability heuristic. Further, under a great many circumstances, the availability heuristic provides us with accurate and dependable estimates. After all, if examples easily come to mind, it usually is because there are many of them.

Unfortunately, however, there are a number of biasing factors that can affect the availability of events in our memory without altering their actual occurrence. Problems arise when this strategy is used, for instance, to estimate the frequency or likelihood of rare, though highly vivid, events as compared to those that are more typical, commonplace, or mundane in nature. When our use of the availability heuristic results in systematic errors in making such judgments, we may refer to this as the *Availability Bias.*

Perhaps the single most important factor underlying the Availability Bias is our propensity to underuse, discount, or even ignore, relevant base-rate information (that is, data about the actual frequency of events in a particular group) and other abstract statistical facts in favor of more salient and concrete, but usually less reliable, anecdotal evidence. As a consequence, personal testimonials, graphic case studies, dramatic stories, colorful tales, intriguing narratives, eye-catching illustrations, vibrant images, extraordinary occurrences, and bizarre events all are liable to slant, skew, or otherwise distort our judgments.

To cite one example, Borgida and Nisbett (1977) found that when students were faced with the task of forming impressions of a potential classroom instructor, they were more influenced by a few personal testimonies than by a comprehensive statistical summary of many students' ratings of the teacher. In the study, subjects (students) were informed that the average rating by 112 students for a Learning and Memory course was between "very good" and "excellent." Subsequently, some subjects also heard two or three students from the course express their feelings directly ("I thought the course was too simplistic..."). Now, statistically speaking, the subjects should simply have combined these few additional personal testimonies with the much larger data pool, the net effect of which would have been virtually inconsequential. Such was not, however, the case. In fact, the very small number of student testimonials actually had *more impact* on subjects' perceptions than the statistically summarized ratings of a substantially larger group of students. As this study so clearly demonstrates, a mere dollop of vivid information is capable of completely eclipsing and overshadowing more reliable but less "personal" statistical data.

Another significant problem related to the Availability Bias concerns our proclivity to *overgeneralize* from a few vivid examples, or sometimes even just a single vivid instance. This error in inductive reasoning (see Metathought XX) is responsible, at least in part, for the phenomenon of *stereotyping.*

In general, how do we formulate our beliefs about particular groups of people, whether racial, cultural, national, religious, political, occupational, or any other category? We typically base our impressions on observations of specific members of the group. But *which* members? By and large, our attention is drawn to the most conspicuous, prominent, or salient individuals. We then are prone to overgeneralize from these few extreme examples to the group as a whole, the result of which is a role schema (see Metathought XXIII, the Assimilation Bias) or stereotype. In this way, the Availability Bias leads us to perpetuate vivid but false beliefs about the characteristics of a wide variety of groups in our society.

Fortunately, there are a number of strategies you can employ to mitigate against the Availability Bias. First, whenever you are faced with the task of estimating the frequency or likelihood of an event, be careful not to rely on the ease or speed with which relevant examples come to mind. Instead, make a conscious effort to seek out and utilize base-rate information or other pertinent statistical data in reaching your conclusions. Suppose, for instance, that you are attempting to determine the prevalence of various types of psychopathology in the general population (as in question (6) above). In this case, a wise course of action would be to consult well-designed epidemiological research studies,[1] which are unquestionably more reliable sources of information than one's own "top of the head" impressions.

Second, take anecdotal evidence not with a grain but with several large shakers of salt. Although personal testimonies and dramatic case studies may be very persuasive, remember that they are not inherently trustworthy indicators of fact. Further, clinicians should exercise extreme caution when evaluating the results of any psychological assessment techniques that are highly reliant on the observer's subjective impressions and interpretations (such as the House-Tree-Person or other projective drawing tests), in contrast to tests that are empirically validated on appropriate research populations.

Third, resist the temptation to overgeneralize from a limited selection of instances or events. Don't forget that the best basis for generalizing is not from the exceptional, though vivid, cases one finds at the extremes, but rather from a representative sample of cases.

In conclusion, we tend to be more persuaded by an ounce of anecdotal evidence than by a pound of reliable statistics. Although vivid and dramatic events can make for appetizing fiction, they are ultimately unsatisfying to those with a taste for reality.

Glossary Terms

The following terms (or variations) are defined in the Glossary:

abstract	data
affect	disease
attribution	effect
Availability Bias	empirical
availability heuristic	erroneous
base rate	evaluation
behavior	event
belief	existence
bias	fact
category	heuristic
cause	inductive reasoning
cognitive	interpretation
concrete	judgment
conscious	knowledge
consequence	mental

mind	psychotherapy
normal	reliability
observation	Representativeness Bias
opinion	representativeness heuristic
perception	schema
phenomenon	stereotype
projective test	subjective
psychological	subsequent
psychology	vivid

Notes

[1] Examples of such research would include the comprehensive investigations of Myers and associates (1984), Robins and associates (1984), and Regier and associates (1988).

Chapter **29**

XXIX. The Insight Fallacy: To Understand Something Isn't Necessarily to Change It

It is naive to expect that, by telling people what we think we see they are doing, we will enable them to stop doing it.
—*R. D. LAING**

Recollection without affect almost invariably produces no result.
—*JOSEF BREUER AND SIGMUND FREUD***

One of our most prevalent and enduring societal myths is that once we can *understand* a problem, it will automatically *solve* the problem. In other words, people have a tendency to assume that insight alone invariably produces useful change.

Why is this an invalid assumption? Let us take, as a rather obvious example, the problem of removing kidney stones. We may understand perfectly well how kidney stones are created. And this knowledge might be very useful in helping us to design interventions that prevent the formation of kidney stones. But the knowledge itself doesn't inherently solve the problem of kidney stone removal; unfortunately, all the insight in the world can't dissolve or extract a kidney stone!

Within the field of psychology, nowhere is the Insight Fallacy more apparent than in psychotherapy. Many persons—therapists, clients, and the public

*The Politics of the Family, 1969
**Studies on Hysteria, 1895

alike—cling to the alluring yet unproven belief that by understanding a psychological problem, it will somehow spontaneously resolve itself: "If I can only figure it out, then I'll feel better and it will go away."

As an illustration, suppose that you are a client in psychotherapy. And after undergoing month after year after decade of intensive analysis, taking batteries of psychological tests, interpreting your unconscious dynamics, recognizing your recurring life themes and patterns, correlating your current situation with your past situations, seeing the connection between your parents' behavior and your behavior, attending dozens of weekend self-growth workshops, reading innumerable self-help books and magazine articles, you finally turn to your therapist and say something akin to:

"Doc, I entered therapy because I felt so abandoned/abused/abusive/acrophobic/addictive/aggressive/agitated/agoraphobic/alexithymic/alienated/alone/ambivalent/angry/anxious/apathetic/avoidant/bashful/betrayed/bitter/borderline/bored/catatonic/claustrophobic/codependent/compulsive/competitive/confused/crazy/critical/cruel/dangerous/defensive/delusional/dependent/depersonalized/depressed/deprived/desperate/detached/devastated/discontented/discouraged/disillusioned/disordered/disorganized/disoriented/dissatisfied/dissociated/distressed/disturbed/dumb/dysfunctional/emotional/emotionless/empty/enmeshed/evil/explosive/fake/fearful/frightened/furious/grandiose/guarded/guilty/helpless/hostile/histrionic/hopeless/hydrophobic/hypermanic/hypersomnic/hypochondriacal/hypomanic/hyposomnic/impatient/impulsive/inadequate/incompetent/indecisive/indifferent/immature/inferior/insecure/insomnic/irritable/isolated/jealous/judgmental/lonely/lost/maladjusted/malcontented/manic/manipulative/masochistic/miserable/misunderstood/narcissistic/needy/nervous/neurotic/numb/obsessive/odd/overcontrolled/overresponsible/oversensitive/oversocialized/pained/panicky/paranoid/passive/passive–aggressive/pessimistic/phobic/phony/powerless/pressured/psychotic/rebellious/rejected/repressed/revengeful/sad/sadistic/screwed-up/selfish/shy/split-off/stressed/stubborn/stuck/stupid/suicidal/suspicious/tense/terrified/tormented/tortured/toxic/trapped/troubled/unattractive/uncontrolled/undersocialized/unfeeling/unhappy/unlovable/unloved/unreal/unstable/unsuccessful/victimized/weird/worried/xenophobic/yearning/zoophobic.

And now I can honestly say that I truly understand *why* I feel so abandoned/.../zoophobic.

But, Doc, the problem is that I *still feel* abandoned/.../zoophobic. And I still don't know what to *do* about it."

In presenting this hypothetical (and obviously exaggerated) vignette, I certainly am not suggesting that explanations are worthless; or, as others have concluded, that insight is "the booby prize of life." In fact, I would like to underscore the value of insight in psychotherapy by enumerating three of its most useful attributes.

Benefits of Insight

First, gaining insight into the causes of a problem can, in itself, provide us with a source of relief or comfort simply by stripping away the mystique that frequently shrouds unexplained phenomena. Once we discover a rational basis or explanation for the occurrence of a problem, it is likely to feel more manageable; thus, *insight empowers by demystifying.*

Second, insight can be a critical first step toward adopting specific problem-solving strategies. If the causes of a problem can be identified, we may be in a better position to select a particular course of action to alleviate the situation. To take an example, consider a person who enters psychotherapy because she is plagued by chronic and unremitting depression. No matter what she's tried, she's been completely unable to break free of her intransigent misery. In the course of therapy, however, she gains the insight that her depression is due primarily to unresolved (and heretofore unrecognized) grief over the numerous losses—both literal and symbolic—that she has experienced in her life. Armed with this knowledge, the therapist may then design and implement specific therapeutic techniques that help her to adaptively and appropriately mourn these losses, thereby lifting her shroud of depression.

Third, insight can function as the "psychological glue" that consolidates and integrates one's thoughts, feelings, behavior, and experiences into a meaningful new whole, thereby resulting in more stable and long-lasting change. Once the person is able to explain, understand, or otherwise make sense of himself and his situation, this knowledge becomes internalized and therefore more enduring. As a consequence, the client is better able to translate (or generalize) the gains he has achieved in therapy into his future relationships and life challenges. In this context, insight can serve as a vital final step in the therapy process.

Limitations and Drawbacks of Insight

These advantages notwithstanding, problems can arise when people fail to recognize the *limits* of what insight is able to provide. Specifically, a number of clinical orientations (such as Freudian psychoanalysis and other psychodynamic approaches) have come under heavy fire for their fundamental belief that intellectual insight is a *sine qua non* (that is, an essential and indispensable ingredient) of successful therapy. Critics not only question the validity of this underlying assumption, they also point to the absence of clear empirical evidence that insight is, in fact, a necessary component of therapeutic effectiveness (see Corey, 1991).

As a consequence, numerous alternative orientations have emerged that discount (or even dismiss outright) the role of insight in clinical practice, some of which include: behavior therapies (systematic desensitization, progressive relaxation, biofeedback, flooding, aversive conditioning); strategic and structural family therapies; experiential psychotherapies (Gestalt therapy, psychodrama, movement therapy, art therapy, music therapy); and hypnotherapy—none of which relies fundamentally on achieving insights or understanding to produce significant and effective change.

Moreover, some people have gone so far as to argue that emphasizing insight can be *counterproductive*, even *detrimental*, to therapeutic progress. They maintain that extensive searching for cognitive insight allows both clients and therapists to avoid feeling unpleasant (yet essential) emotions, and instead to hide behind the comfort and apparent safety of logic, reason, and rationality. Unfortunately, then, it actually may hinder clients' progress by encouraging them to make excessive use of the ego defense mechanisms of *intellectualization, rationalization,* and *isolation of affect* (see A. Freud, 1936). Although this outcome may succeed in temporarily blocking out their anxiety, it does so at the expense of cutting themselves off further from their feelings, as well as falsifying, distorting, or denying reality. Taken to its extreme, seeking insight becomes an empty exercise in intellectual futility, which can exacerbate the client's problems by isolating them into the "neck-up" region of emotional dissociation. Thus, winning the battle of insight may, ironically, contribute to losing the war of genuine therapeutic success.

To summarize, insight can be a useful, even indispensable, tool to solve problems and to alleviate human suffering. However, we must continually remember to recognize the *limits* of insight, and therefore seek to explore additional avenues of change. For certain people, with certain problems, in certain situations, insight may be sufficient or necessary. For others, it may be sufficient *and* necessary. But for some, it is neither.

Exercises: Exploring the Limits of Insight

These exercises are intended to help you identify and examine the limits of insight. The following list encompasses a wide range of problems. In responding to the exercises, you may draw on this list or supply your own original examples. (Note that these groupings are purely for convenience and for purposes of this exercise.)

—*emotional problems* (depression, anxiety, guilt, anger, jealousy, loneliness, irritability, panic)

—*psychological problems* (phobias, insomnia, paranoia, sexual dysfunctions, hypochondriasis, schizophrenia, repressed traumatic memories)

—*behavioral problems* (delinquency, criminality, child abuse, spousal abuse, sexual abuse, violence, self-mutilation, suicidality)

—*compulsion problems* (drinking, drugs, gambling, shopping, overeating, working, studying, exercising)

—*interpersonal problems* (arguments, mistrust, dependence, miscommunication, rebelliousness, victimization)

—*medical problems* (flu, infections, headaches, bone fractures, allergies, hypertension, ulcers, AIDS, cancer)

1. a. Identify and describe some problems from your own life experience for which gaining insight into their causes directly served to solve the problems.

_____

_____

_____

_____

_____

1. b. What do these types of problems have in common?

_____

_____

_____

_____

_____

2. a. Identify and describe some problems from your own life experience for which gaining insight into their causes did *not* directly serve to solve the problems.

_____

_____

_____

_____

_____

2. b. What do these types of problems have in common?

_____

_____

_____

_____

_____

3. What *differences* do you see in the types of problems you have identified in Question (1) as compared to Question (2)?

_____

_____

_____

_____

_____

4. Can you think of instances or conditions for which insight is *sufficient* (that is, insight alone can solve the problem)?

_____

_____

_____

_____

_____

5. Can you think of instances or conditions for which insight is *not sufficient* (that is, insight alone cannot solve the problem)?

_____

_____

_____

_____

_____

6. Can you think of instances or conditions for which insight is *necessary* (that is, the problem cannot be solved without insight into its causes)?

_____

_____

_____

_____

_____

7. Can you think of instances or conditions for which insight is *not necessary* (that is, the problem can be solved without insight into its causes)?

_____

_____

_____

_____

Glossary Terms

The following terms (or variations) are defined in the Glossary:

affect	insight
assumption	Insight Fallacy
attribution	intellectualization
behavior	interpersonal
behavior therapy	interpretation
belief	isolation of affect
cause	knowledge
chronic	logic
clinical	myth
cognitive	phenomena
consequence	psychoanalysis
correlate	psychodynamic therapy
critical	psychological
dysfunction	psychology
emotion	psychotherapy
empirical	rational
experience	rationalization
explanation	reasoning
fact	repression
fallacy	unconscious
family therapy	validity
Gestalt therapy	value
hypothetical	vignette

P a r t **Six**

Conclusions

C h a p t e r **30**

XXX. *Every Decision Is a Trade-Off: Take Stock of Pluses and Minuses*

> *In order for something to become clean,*
> *something else must become dirty.*
> *—ARTHUR BLOCH**

> *Eternal vigilance is the price of liberty.*
> *—WENDELL PHILLIPS***

> DRUMMOND: *Gentlemen, progress has never been a bargain. You've*
> *got to pay for it. Sometimes I think there's a man behind a counter*
> *who says, "All right, you can have a telephone; but you'll have to give*
> *up privacy, the charm of distance. Madam, you may vote; but at a*
> *price; you lose the right to retreat behind a powder-puff or*
> *a petticoat. Mister, you may conquer the air; but the birds will*
> *lose their wonder, and the clouds will smell of gasoline!"*
> *—JEROME LAWRENCE and ROBERT E. LEE****

Every decision, activity, or event involves some kind of a trade-off. For each of our choices, the outcome has both pluses and minuses: For everything that we get, we give something up; for everything that we give up, we get something in return. You never get something for nothing, or nothing for something. When making a decision, therefore, it is wise to take stock of the advantages and the disadvantages—the benefits and the costs—of *all* your alternatives.

**Murphy's Law, Book Two*, 1980
**From the speech *Public Opinion* in 1852; cited in *The Pocket Book of Quotations*, Davidoff, 1952
***Inherit the Wind, 1955

197

After weighing them out, you will be in a much better position to decide your course of action.

Remember that whatever choice you make leaves all others behind. Even something so simple as choosing to make a left turn, for example, entails forfeiting your choice to turn right. If you go to sleep, you give up staying awake. If you listen to music, you give up silence. Put another way, you *can* have your cake *and* eat it too, but if you do, then you *can't* have either one alone.

Should you have that extra scoop of ice cream? Should you buy a new coat? Should you take the day off from work? Should you start an exercise regimen? Should you stop smoking? Should you end a painful romantic relationship? Should you enter psychotherapy? Should you terminate psychotherapy? Should you go to graduate school? Should you change careers? Should you move to a new city? Should you get married? Should you have children? Should you retire from your job? Some decisions may be easy, some may be difficult, but they *all* involve making trade-offs.

"To Diagnose or Not to Diagnose?"

A vivid illustration of this Metathought is provided by the perennially heated debate in the mental health field over the practice of classifying, labeling, or diagnosing people with psychological problems. Here we see, once again, that taking a stand on *either* side of the issue entails both costs and benefits.

Arguments for the Use of Diagnostic Categories

1. By serving as the language currency of the mental health profession, diagnostic categories enable us to *communicate* more effectively with one another (Spitzer, 1975).

2. Diagnostic classifications permit clinicians and investigators to conduct controlled *research* into the causes and outcomes of mental disorders (American Psychiatric Association, 1987).

3. Diagnoses can guide the type and course of clinical *treatment* (Spitzer & Wilson, 1975). For example, in the case of a diagnosed phobia, systematic desensitization is a likely treatment of choice. For Bipolar ("manic-depressive") Disorder, lithium carbonate typically is indicated. For Major Depressive Disorder, a combination of cognitive psychotherapy and antidepressant medication might be most effective.

4. Diagnostic classifications help to *bring order out of chaos,* in that we are better able to organize phenomena in the world by naming them. In the course of a typical clinical intake interview, for example, the therapist is inundated with an overwhelming quantity and diverse array of information, much of which can be summarized and systematized with the use of clinical diagnoses.

5. Using diagnostic categories *sharpens our skills of perception* by bringing into focus what we might otherwise have overlooked. The mere act of naming something makes it stand out more distinctly from its context; thus, by having specific terms for different phenomena, we can more effectively discriminate among them.[1] As an illustration, consider the fact that Eskimos have over a dozen words for identifying and differentiating various types of snow (Carroll, 1956). Similarly, the Yiddish language contains a plethora of terms that refer to many types of fools, nerds, and jerks (Rosten, 1968).[2] Analogously, our use of specific diagnostic terms may help us better recognize different types of mental disorders.

6. Our use of diagnostic categories provides us with greater *scientific objectivity* and a concomitant reduction in our reliance on vague and subjective impressions, perceptions, and interpretations.

7. Diagnoses can serve as a reminder for clinicians to maintain a *professional distance* from their patients.

8. In order to provide *financial reimbursement,* most insurance carriers and managed care organizations require clinicians to submit formal clinical diagnoses of their patients.

Arguments against the Use of Diagnostic Categories

1. The use of diagnostic categories *depersonalizes* and *dehumanizes* the person to whom the label is attached (Rosenhan, 1973). Put another way, such labeling promotes "I–It" rather than "I–Thou" interpersonal relationships (Buber, 1958).

2. Despite claims to the contrary, psychiatric diagnoses are *unscientific* or *pseudoscientific.* Specifically, they frequently are statistically unreliable (Rosenhan, 1973), and they appear to be more a reflection of societal or political mores, creeds, and values than they are of objective fact. Szasz (1960, 1987), in fact, goes so far as to view diagnoses essentially as psychiatrists' "Index of Prohibited Behaviors." As noted by R. D. Laing (1975), the use of diagnostic labeling in many cases tells us much more about the person assigning the label than about the person who is being labeled.[3]

3. Once someone has received a diagnostic label, we tend to view that individual in a significantly different manner (Farina, 1982; Rosenhan, 1973). In particular, the labels create *biased preconceptions* that pathologize our subsequent perceptions and interpretations of the person's behavior (see Metathought XXIII, the Assimilation Bias).

4. Diagnostic categories are *stigmatizing labels,* which, once attached to people, follow them around for the rest of their lives and adversely influence others (relatives, friends, employers, government agencies) with whom they come into contact (see Link, Cullen, Frank, & Wozniak, 1987; Page, 1977).

5. A diagnostic label can become analogous to the proverbial *procrustean bed,* within which the client is metaphorically stretched to fit into the category.

6. Psychiatric diagnoses can result in a *self-fulfilling prophecy* (Metathought XXIII) in that they may actually elicit the very behaviors they are attempting to describe.

7. Diagnostic categories foster the use of *false dichotomies* (Metathought V) in our conceptualizations of people's behavior.

8. The use of psychiatric diagnoses encourages treating people as *helpless patients,* rather than as responsible human beings (Szasz, 1974).

"To Metathink or Not to Metathink?"

As a final illustration of this Metathought, let us turn to an evaluation of this book's principal content: the Metathoughts themselves. In a sense, the Metathoughts may be seen as cognitive schemas. As such, they provide the same benefits—and, of course, are subject to the same liabilities—inherent in all schematic processing (see discussion in Metathought XXII).

More specifically, in terms of their advantages, they

>significantly reduce or eliminate a wide variety of systematic biases, errors, and mistakes in thinking;

>improve the clarity of thinking and the accuracy of solutions;

>open pathways to new perspectives and alternative points of view;

>promote and facilitate innovative and creative approaches to problem-solving;

>serve as a foundation for identifying other as-yet-unidentified cognitive errors (that is, new Metathoughts), as well as their antidotes.

As for their disadvantages, their use

>requires more time and effort (particularly at first);

>involves greater complexity at the cost of simplicity;

>is likely to result in increased ambiguity;

>can leave you feeling frustrated or confused;

>may be impractical or inappropriate in some situations.

In sum, like all other choices, the acceptance or rejection of the ideas in this book entails costs and benefits. Thus, once you have made the effort to study, understand, and apply these Metathoughts in your life, take stock of their pluses and minuses. Once having weighed them, you will be able to make an informed choice as to your course of action. Either way, ultimately the decision is yours.

Exercise: Evaluating Trade-Offs

Read through the following hypothetical questions and select three that are of particular interest or relevance to you. Then, for each question list all of the "pluses" and "minuses" that you can think of (use additional paper if necessary). After taking stock of the pros and cons, see in which direction your decision is leaning.

Should you decide
—To go on a diet?
—To repair your broken television set?
—To purchase a motorcycle?
—To drink alcohol?
—To use drugs?
—To stay out late?
—To get a dog?
—To buy insurance?
—To cheat on your taxes?
—To accept financial assistance from your parents?
—To use deception as part of your research investigation?
—To conduct your research study in the laboratory or in the field?
—To have regular medical check ups?
—To always tell the truth in your relationships?
—To engage in unprotected sex?

Question 1 _____

Pluses   Minuses

Conclusion _____

Question 2 _____

Pluses   Minuses

Conclusion _____

Question 3 _____

Pluses   Minuses

Conclusion

Glossary Terms

The following terms (or variations) are defined in the Glossary:

ambiguous   interpretation
analogous   mental
antidote   metaphor
behavior   objective
bias   perception
category   phenomena
clinical   preconception
cognitive   procrustean bed
cognitive–behavioral therapy psychological
concept   psychotherapy
decision   reliability
diagnosis   schema
dichotomous variable   Self-Fulfilling Prophecy
disorder   subjective
evaluation   subsequent
event   thinking
fact   treatment
hypothetical   truth
hypothesis   vivid
interpersonal

Notes

[1] This may be seen as an extension of Whorf's (1956) hypothesis of linguistic relativity, which states in essence that language influences thought. Thus, for example, because different cultures have different languages, they have different ways of thinking about the world.

[2] As noted by Arthur Naiman, author of *Every Goy's Guide to Common Jewish Expressions* (1981), "Yiddish has more words for this concept than any other ten languages put together." A sampling from this veritable cornucopia of descriptors includes: *kuni lemmel, narr, nayfish, nebbish, nudnik, putz, schmuck, shlemiel, shlimazl, shlump, shmageggie, shmendrik, shmo, shnook, yutz,* and *zhlub.*

[3] For a satirical perspective on this theme, I refer you to my essay on "Pervasive Labeling Disorder" (Levy, 1992), which appears in Appendix 1.

Epilogue

Concluding Meta-Metathoughts

A conclusion is the place where you got tired of thinking.
—ARTHUR BLOCH*

Throughout this book I have sought to abide by the educational tenet that knowledge is sterile and meaningless without application. For each Metathought principle, therefore, I have cited practical applications in the form of "real-world" examples, illustrations, anecdotes, clinical vignettes, and contemporary social problems and issues.

This final chapter presents some closing thoughts about the Metathoughts (or "meta-Metathoughts"), focusing primarily on the application of this book as a whole to the differing needs of psychology students, teachers, clinicians, and researchers. Before we begin, however, please take note of the following brief but important caveat:

> *The applicability and usefulness of the Metathoughts are limited only by the creativity, imagination, and resourcefulness of the user. The following recommendations, then, should be seen as a starting point, not the last word. Your own individual contributions will be the key ingredients that can infuse the contents of this book with unique characteristics and new life.*

As an analogy, think of the Metathoughts as a collection of specialized tools for working on a diverse array of problems. When faced with a new task, one of your initial steps, naturally, would be to select the right tool (or tools)

**Murphy's Law, Book Two, 1980*

for the job. An effective method of accomplishing this goal is to systematically sort through your inventory of Metathoughts, retaining the ones that apply to the problem at hand and setting aside those that don't. Obviously, the greater your familiarity, experience, and practice in working with these tools, the more proficient you will become, both in minimizing your expenditure of time and energy, and maximizing the accuracy, quality, and utility of your results.

Tools of Critical Thinking also may be seen as a pragmatic reference guide— not meant for rote memorization or rigid adherence—but rather for "trouble-shooting" errors, biases, and pitfalls in thinking. As such, you may wish to keep this book alongside your other useful references (dictionary, thesaurus, writing manual), all within reach for quick and easy access.

Because different Metathoughts are pertinent to various circumstances, your time would be well spent on a brief review of this book whenever you find yourself facing a new task or a change in the subject of your work. Examples would include studying a new topic in school, teaching a different course, or evaluating the outcome of a research investigation.

More generally, you might find it beneficial to periodically peruse the book's contents as a means of refreshing, refining, or "tuning up" your critical thinking skills. (The Summary and Antidote Table is especially useful for this purpose.) This practice will enhance your ability both to identify and to solve problems in thinking.

With respect specifically to psychology, the Metathoughts encompass a broad spectrum of perspectives, topics, and units of analysis: from philosophical to scientific, theoretical to empirical, conceptual to applied, descriptive to explanatory, normal to pathological, individual to interpersonal, biochemical to social, nomothetic to idiographic, historical to contemporary, legal to moral.

They are intended to assist you, for instance, in your efforts to describe, define, and differentiate psychological phenomena, to identify the strengths and weaknesses in various schools of psychological thought, to evaluate the usefulness of psychological theories, to recognize and improve on errors and biases in our cognitive processes, and to open up new avenues of exploration and insight. Thus, they may be employed to critically evaluate everything from sophisticated, empirically based research studies published in scientific and scholarly journals to the latest claims, trends, and topics touted in the self-help literature or reported in the popular media.

In addition to these general guidelines, the remainder of this chapter focuses on how *Tools of Critical Thinking* can be utilized to address the particular needs of five specific groups: psychology students, psychology classroom instructors, psychotherapists, psychological researchers, and students and instructors in other fields of study. What follows, then, is a compendium of suggestions, ideas, and recommendations for applying *Tools of Critical Thinking* to various people, in various contexts, and for various purposes.

To the Psychology Student:

You will find that ideas in this book are applicable throughout your schooling, from your first undergraduate introductory psychology course all the way to the final class of your doctoral degree. In a sense, the book will accompany your intellectual growth, with different Metathoughts emerging as especially relevant at various stages of your academic and professional development.

This book should be consulted whenever you seek a deeper and more comprehensive understanding of any issue or problem. In particular, the Metathoughts are ideally suited for any assignments in which you are instructed to "think critically" about a specific topic. You now have at your disposal the tools with which you can effectively review, evaluate, analyze, and critique books, journal articles, research studies, lectures, workshops, debates, or media presentations. Once you have your topic, peruse the Metathoughts, and select your tools. (Or your *weapons*, as the case may be.)

To the Psychology Classroom Instructor:

Tools of Critical Thinking can be utilized with great effectiveness as a supplementary text in a variety of both undergraduate and graduate psychology courses.[1] Of course, this book is ideal for any courses devoted specifically to critical thinking, problem-solving, or logic.

In the classroom context, the Metathoughts themselves can be used in a variety of ways. First, when beginning a new class, devote some time to presenting a didactic lecture on the Metathought principles that are relevant to the content of the course. Augment the examples from this book with those from your own and from your students' experiences. Inform students that, as the course progresses, you will be drawing on the Metathoughts to critically evaluate specific topics. Alert them, further, that you will be calling on them to do the same.

Second, demonstrate the process of critical thinking to your students by functioning as a role model. That is, don't just *tell* them how to think critically, but *show* them as well. Specifically, utilize the pedagogic technique of "thinking aloud," whereby one verbalizes every phase of problem-solving, step by step, from beginning to end. For instance, you would, speaking in the present tense, identify a problem, establish your goal, decide on a course of action, select the relevant Metathought(s) and provide your rationale for doing so, apply the Metathought to the problem, and reach your conclusion. Further, you could speculate what your conclusions might have been *without* applying any tools of critical thinking. This use of vicarious learning is both an extremely effective and efficient method of instruction, in that it places students in a minimal risk situation in which the process of critical thinking is simultaneously displayed and demystified. Further, it demonstrates vividly not only that critical thinking *can* be achieved, but also *how* it can be achieved.

Third, after having role-modeled this process, you can ask your students to follow suit. This technique provides direct experience and practice for students, allows for your immediate feedback, and increases their sense of competence and efficacy.

Fourth, design in-class and homework assignments that require students to apply tools of critical thinking. You might, for example, instruct them to write a paper in which they utilize the Metathoughts in their analysis of a relevant issue of their own choosing. Or you may elect to assign the topic yourself. Some examples, depending on the subject of the course, could include, "What are the problems in defining psychopathology?"; "How should we treat mental illness?"; "Is alcoholism a disease?"; "What accounts for psychological differences between men and women?"; "Why do people stereotype others?"; or any other real-world issues of concern. You might also have students use the Metathoughts in a critique of a published article (anything from a scientific journal to a "pop psych" magazine) or a media broadcast (such as radio psychology call-in programs or televised courtroom trials).

Fifth, utilize the Metathoughts yourself as part of your course preparations. They are especially useful for presentations that call for critical analyses of particularly complex or controversial topics.

To the Psychotherapist:

It is interesting to note that one of the most widely utilized and most effective approaches in modern clinical practice, cognitive therapy, is devoted primarily to identifying and correcting errors in the thought processes of clients in treatment. With meticulous precision, the clinician zeroes in on, confronts, and attempts to modify the client's erroneous assumptions, faulty belief systems, biased schemata, distorted perceptions, flawed logic, misattributions, overgeneralizations, and unfounded conclusions.

How ironic, then, that in many cases it is the *clinicians themselves* who unknowingly fall prey to these same errors. Yet very little, if any, attention is focused on teaching therapists how to examine and improve their own cognitive processes. To rectify this situation, it is vital that clinicians learn to regularly subject their own cognitions to the same kind of close scrutiny and appropriate modifications that are afforded to their clients.

The Metathoughts are a very useful means by which this critical goal can be achieved. For the student intern, as an example, clinical supervision and practicum courses would be excellent arenas in which to utilize these tools to address issues related to the therapist's own personal biases (countertransference) on an individual, case-by-case basis. For the professional clinician who is already in independent practice, this book can function as a vehicle of continuing education, to be intermittently studied and applied throughout one's career.

To the Psychological Researcher:

This book can be of tremendous use to you at every stage of your investigations, for a diverse array of purposes, and for virtually every type of research methodology: theoretical to empirical, basic to applied, descriptive to experimental, retrospective to prospective, and micro to macro levels of analysis.

The Metathoughts provide direct guidance in helping to ensure that your research is comprehensive, logically consistent, internally and externally valid, and accurately described. Further, they both alert you to and supply you with remedies to common research pitfalls; they assist you in exploring alternate hypotheses and perspectives; and they provide a path for creative solutions to difficult and complex problems.

In particular, they improve your ability to create and evaluate theories, test hypotheses, utilize deductive and inductive reasoning, select research topics, review background literature, conceptualize and measure psychological variables, collect and analyze data, understand statistical interactions, differentiate correlation and causation, examine and determine directions of causation, gauge probability, interpret results, generalize findings, and communicate conclusions. In addition, they help you to identify and ameliorate specific research problems pertaining to reactivity, expectancy effects, demand characteristics, and systematic biases in assimilation, belief perseverance, confirmation, and hindsight.

Note that all thirty Metathoughts have been grouped into conceptual categories, such as Explaining Phenomena, Investigating Phenomena, and Common Misattributions, each of which is relevant for different stages of conducting research. The intent of this thematic organization is to provide a framework that maximizes the likelihood that each and every set of issues will be addressed, explored, and resolved in a manner that is systematic and comprehensive.

Last, you can use the Metathoughts as a kind of "check list" to evaluate and critique the work of other researchers, as well as your own. In this way, you might identify, and hopefully rectify, potential weaknesses or flaws in your work *before* somebody else does.

To Students and Instructors in Other Fields of Study:

As I indicated in the Preface, although the examples I've presented are drawn almost entirely from psychology, the basic principles delineated and examined in this book are both flexible and robust enough to be readily applied to numerous other fields, such as education, law, philosophy, communication, medicine, business, economics, history, anthropology, sociology, political science, journalism, and even the arts. One need only adapt the book's basic framework to a new content area and then supply the relevant examples. In this way, *Metathoughts for Psychology* can be modified to become, for instance, *Metathoughts for Business, Metathoughts for Communication,* or *Metathoughts for Law.* In short, while the Metathoughts are relatively universal and constant, the applied topics are essentially interchangeable.

Final Meta-Metathoughts

Thomas Szasz once remarked, "I don't have the answer to every one of life's problems. I only know a stupid answer when I see one" (quoted in Miller, 1983). In like manner, the Metathoughts won't necessarily provide you with correct solutions to all of the questions that you will ask or that will be asked of you. Nevertheless, cultivating your skills of critical thinking certainly will, at the very least, enable you more easily and consistently to identify and discard "the stupid ones," thereby freeing your time, energy, and resources for more productive endeavors.

Of course, trade-offs are both inevitable and inescapable. In using these thought principles it is essential, therefore, to prepare yourself for their costs as well as their benefits. In particular, they can lead to conclusions that are more complex, intricate, ambiguous, and tentative than you ever bargained for. On the other hand, the more obstinately you search for simplistic, clear-cut answers to the innumerable problems in this world, the more likely you are to end up with nothing more than a bloodied head from having blindly and repeatedly bashed it against a wall.

Glossary Terms

The following terms (or variations) are defined in the Glossary:

ambiguous	critical thinking
analogy	data
assimilation	deductive reasoning
assumption	description
belief	didactic
bias	disease
category	efficacy
causation	empirical
clinical	erroneous
cognitive	evaluation
cognitive therapy	experience
cognitive–behavioral therapy	experiment
correlation	external validity
countertransference	idiographic
critical	inductive reasoning

Insight Fallacy
intent
interpersonal
interpretation
knowledge
logic
measure
mental illness
meta
nomothetic
normal
pedagogic
perception
phenomena
pragmatic
probability
psychological

psychology
psychotherapy
reactivity
reasoning
schema
scientific
social
theoretical
thinking
treatment
universal
utility
variable
vicarious
vignette
vividness

Notes

[1] Some courses for which this text is particularly appropriate include Introductory Psychology, Abnormal Psychology (Psychopathology), Research Methods and Design, Social Psychology, Theories and Methods of Psychotherapy, Theories of Personality, Clinical Psychology Practicum, Psychological Testing and Assessment, Multicultural Psychology, Law and Ethics in Psychology, and Seminars on Contemporary Problems and Issues in Psychology.

Metathoughts Summary and Antidote Table

I. The Evaluative Bias of Language

Summary

In describing phenomena, particularly social phenomena, the language that people use invariably reflects their own personal values, biases, likes, and dislikes. As a consequence, descriptions can reveal at least as much about the *observer* as they do about the *observed*.

Antidotes

1. Remember that descriptions, especially concerning personality, can never be truly objective, impartial, or neutral.
2. Acknowledge how your own personal values and biases influence the descriptive language that you use.
3. Avoid presenting your value judgments as objective reflections of truth.
4. Recognize how other people's use of language reveals their own values and biases.

II. The Reification Error

Summary

It is a mistake in reification to treat an abstract, hypothetical concept (*construct*) as if it were a tangible, concrete thing (*object*). Constructs, in contrast to objects, are not directly measurable or quantifiable. This principle is particularly relevant to the delineation and evaluation of Construct (Type C) Theories and Event (Type E) Theories.

Antidotes

1. Learn to differentiate between abstract constructs and physical objects.
2. In particular, don't make the mistake of treating a construct as if it were an object.
3. Remember that constructs are *created*, not "discovered."
4. Evaluate Event (Type E) Theories in terms of their *accuracy;* evaluate Construct (Type C) Theories in terms of their *utility.*

III. Multiple Levels of Description

Summary

The same phenomenon can be described at different levels of analysis. In particular, an event can be described both at a *physical* level and at a *conceptual* level. Because these levels occur *simultaneously,* they do not, strictly speaking, *cause* each other. Thus, "biological" and "psychological" are two different ways of describing the same simultaneous event. Further, every psychological event has a biological correlate, but not every biological event has a psychological correlate.

Antidotes

1. Remember that the same event can be described at different levels of analysis, the most basic of which are the *physical* and the *conceptual* levels.
2. When analyzing a phenomenon, first *identify* the various levels at which it can be described, then *select* the most appropriate level(s) of description for purposes of your analysis.
3. Be aware of how these levels relate to each other. In particular, because they occur *simultaneously,* their relationship is *not causal.* Thus, don't make the mistake of concluding that once you've located a biological *correlate* to a psychological event, you have therefore discovered its biological *cause.*
4. Moreover, don't equate biological *correlates* with biological *diseases;* remember that *differences* are not, *per se,* valid proof of *disease.*
5. Be extremely cautious when addressing the logically senseless question, "Is the person's problem physical *or* mental?"

IV. The Nominal Fallacy and Tautologous Reasoning

Summary

Naming a phenomenon does not, *per se, explain* the phenomenon. Nevertheless, we may fool ourselves into believing that, once we've invented a special label (such as a psychological diagnosis) for someone's behavior, we have therefore explained the behavior. The Nominal Fallacy typically involves tautologous reasoning, which is a circular pseudo-explanation that, despite its appearance, is essentially void of useful information.

Antidotes

1. Don't confuse a *name* with an *explanation.*
2. Remember that labeling any particular behavior (such as with a clinical diagnosis) does not automatically explain the behavior.
3. Learn to identify tautologous (circular) reasoning, and to extricate yourself from its web.
4. Remind yourself that, although tautologies may have the *appearance* of being logical, they are, in fact, an invalid method of reasoning, explanation, and proof.

V. Differentiating Dichotomous and Continuous Variables

Summary

Dichotomous phenomena can be classified into either of two, mutually exclusive *categories*. Continuous phenomena, in contrast, can be placed somewhere along a particular *dimension*, depending on their frequency or magnitude. Thus, dichotomous variables are a matter of classification (*quality*), whereas continuous variables are a matter of degree (*quantity*). The problem is that people have a tendency to dichotomize variables that, more accurately, should be conceptualized as continuous.

Antidotes

1. Learn to differentiate between variables that are dichotomous versus those that are continuous.
2. Avoid the tendency to "dichotomize" continuous phenomena.
3. Remember that most person-related phenomena (especially psychological constructs) lie along a continuum; thus, it is both artificial and inaccurate to group them into categories.

VI. Consider the Opposite

Summary

In order to understand any given phenomenon, its theoretical polar opposite should also be addressed and explored. To contrast a phenomenon with its opposite is to provide definition to both terms. Polar opposites depend on each other for their very conceptual existence; without one, its opposite ceases to exist.

Antidotes

1. When seeking to define or understand a phenomenon, take the time to consider and explore its theoretical polar opposite.
2. When you are working on a problem and find yourself stuck at a conceptual dead end, gain a new perspective on the issue by considering the opposite. Specifically, in addition to asking "What *is* it?" also pose the questions, "What *isn't* it?" and "What's its *opposite?*"

VII. The Similarity–Uniqueness Paradox

Summary

All phenomena are both *similar to* and *different from* each other, depending on the dimensions or sorting variables that have been selected for purposes of evaluation, comparison, and contrast. No phenomenon is *totally identical* or *totally unique* in relation to other phenomena. The degree of similarity or uniqueness revealed between any two events is a function of the *points of critical distinction* (PCD).

Antidotes

1. When comparing and contrasting any two phenomena ask yourself, "In what ways are they similar?" *and* "In what ways are they different?"
2. Before beginning your evaluation, ask yourself, "What is the *purpose* of this analysis? What am I trying to find out?" Asking these questions will help you to choose the most appropriate and relevant dimensions and sorting variables.
3. Carefully and judiciously select the dimensions on which you will evaluate various phenomena. Recognize that the dimensions you select will ultimately determine the degree of "similarity" or "uniqueness" displayed between the two phenomena.
4. Despite what may appear to be an overwhelming number of similarities between two events, always search for and take into account their differences; conversely, regardless of what may seem to be a total absence of commonalities between two events, search for and take into account their similarities.
5. Don't allow yourself to be swayed by individuals who maintain that, "These events are *exactly* the same," or "You can't compare these events because they have absolutely *nothing* in common."
6. Keep these principles in mind whenever you are asked any "compare-and-contrast" type questions.

VIII. The Naturalistic Fallacy

Summary

The frequency of an event does not inherently determine its moral value or worth. What is common, typical, or normal isn't necessarily good; what is uncommon, atypical, or abnormal isn't necessarily bad. Conversely, what is common isn't necessarily bad, and what is uncommon isn't necessarily good.

Antidotes

1. Don't make the mistake of equating statistical frequency with moral value. Thus, if most people do something, that does not intrinsically make it right; if most people do not, that does not therefore make it wrong. In like manner, if most people do something, that does not make it wrong; if they do not, that does not make it right.
2. Learn to differentiate *objective descriptions* from *subjective prescriptions*. Specifically, don't confuse one's *description* of what "is" or "isn't" with one's *prescription* of what "should" or "shouldn't" be.

IX. The Barnum Effect

Summary

Barnum statements are "one-size-fits-all" personality interpretations that are true of practically all human beings, but that don't provide distinctive information about a particular individual. Thus, the problem with Barnum statements isn't that they are *wrong;* rather, because they are so generic, universal, and elastic, they are essentially *useless.*

Antidotes

1. Learn to differentiate Barnum statements from person-specific descriptions and interpretations.
2. Be aware of the limited utility inherent in Barnum statements. Specifically, remember that, although Barnum statements have validity about people in general, they fail to reveal anything distinctive about a *particular* individual.
3. Whenever feasible and appropriate, make it a point to reduce the Barnum Effect by qualifying personality descriptions and interpretations in terms of their *magnitude* or *degree.*

X. Correlation Does Not Prove Causation

Summary

A *correlational* relationship between events does not prove that there is a *causal* relationship between them. Although a correlation enables us to make *predictions* from one variable to another, it does not provide an *explanation* as to *why* the events are associated. Further, it does not permit us to draw unequivocal conclusions as to the source or direction of causes and effects.

Antidotes

1. Remember that the presence of a correlation is not, in itself, proof of causation.
2. Keep in mind that correlations enable us to make *predictions* from one event to another; they do not, however, provide *explanations* as to *why* the events are related.
3. When a correlation is observed, consider all possible pathways and directions of causation. For example, if Event *A* and Event *B* are correlated, does *A* cause *B*? Does *B* cause *A*? Do *A* and *B* cause each other? Does *C* cause *A* and *B*?

XI. Bi-Directional Causation

Summary

In contrast to unidirectional causation, when Event *A* causes Event *B*, in bi-directional causation Event *A* and Event *B* are linked in a circular or *causal loop,* in which each is both a cause and an effect of the other. In such instances, the pathway of causation is a "two-way street."

Antidotes

1. Don't assume *a priori* that the causal link between two variables is a unidirectional "one-way street."
2. When investigating directions of causation, consider the possibility that the variables are linked in a *causal loop;* that is, each might be both a cause and an effect of the other.

3. Remember that in a case of bi-directional causation, which variable appears to be the "cause" and which variable appears to be the "effect" may depend entirely on the point at which you happen to enter the causal loop.

XII. Multiple Causation

Summary

Any given event can be, and typically is, the result of *numerous* causes. It is therefore invariably an oversimplification to assume that there is *only one determinant* of any phenomenon as complex as human behavior.

Antidotes

1. In attempting to explain why an event occurred, don't limit your search to *one* cause. Instead, explore *multiple* plausible causes, *all* of which may be responsible for producing the effect.
2. When faced with an *either/or* question, always consider the possibility that the answer might be *both/and*.

XIII. Degrees of Causation

Summary

In a case of multiple causation, the causal factors are likely to vary in the degree to which each of them is responsible for producing the effect. Not all causes are of the same importance, magnitude, or weight: Some causes are "more equal" than others.

Antidotes

1. In situations involving multiple causation, remember that causation usually is a matter of *degree*. Remind yourself that causal factors typically differ as to their relative weight; in other words, not all causes are equal.
2. Attempt to assess the proportion that each cause contributes to the outcome.
3. Make an active effort not to disregard, rule out, or dismiss automatically those causes with less apparent relative weight, one of which may be analogous to the proverbial straw that broke the camel's back.

XIV. Multiple Pathways of Causation

Summary

The same event may be produced by different, independent causal routes or pathways. In other words, different antecedent conditions can lead to the same outcome. Multiple Pathways may apply both to the *etiologies* of various problems, as well as to their *solutions*.

Antidotes

1. When attempting to explain a phenomenon, consider all possible pathways of causation that might be *independently sufficient* to produce the same effect. In other words, on the road to your destination, always be on the lookout for alternate routes.
2. Don't assume *a priori* that similar outcomes must be the product of similar causes.
3. Keep in mind the possibility that an event may involve *both* Multiple Causation *and* Multiple Pathways of Causation.

XV. The Fundamental Attribution Error

Summary

In arriving at causal attributions to explain people's behavior, we have a tendency to overestimate the impact of their internal personality traits ("dispositions") and to underestimate the impact of their environmental circumstances ("situations"). This attributional error appears to be due to both *cognitive biases* and *motivational biases*.

Antidotes

1. Don't underestimate the power of external, situational determinants of behavior.
2. Remember that, at any given time, how people behave depends *both* on what they bring to the situation ("who" they are), *as well as* the situation itself ("where" they are).
3. Keep in mind that this attributional error can become *reversed,* depending on the perceiver's point of view. Specifically, while people are prone to underestimate the impact of others' situations, they tend to *overestimate* the impact of their *own* situations.
4. Be sure to take into account both cognitive *and* motivational biases that are responsible for producing these attributional errors.

XVI. The Intervention–Causation Fallacy

Summary

Our capacity to *change* an event does not necessarily prove what originally *caused* the event. Thus, we cannot draw valid conclusions about an event's etiology solely on the basis of how it responds to various interventions. As applied to psychopathology, the *Treatment–Etiology Fallacy* refers to arriving at the erroneous deduction that a favorable response to medical *treatment* is, in itself, conclusive proof of medical *disease*.

Antidotes

1. Remember that the factors that initially *caused* a problem may be entirely unrelated to the factors that might *solve* the problem.

2. Don't make the mistake of assuming that successful *treatment* is, in itself, valid and sufficient proof of *etiology*. In short, the *cure* doesn't necessarily prove the *cause*.
3. With respect to psychopathology, as counter-intuitive as it may seem, a positive response to medical treatment is *not* proof of medical disease.

XVII. The Consequence–Intentionality Fallacy

Summary

We have a propensity to assume that the *effect* of people's behavior reflects the *intent* of their behavior. However, consequences alone are not sufficient proof of intentionality. That is, we cannot determine others' intentions solely by the effects of their actions.

Antidotes

1. When attempting to understand or explain what motivated someone's behavior, remember that their intent cannot be ascertained solely on the basis of the consequences of their actions. In other words, the *effect* does not, in itself, prove the *intent*.
2. Make an active effort to consider other plausible causes or pathways of behavior, in addition to the ones implied directly by its consequences; in short, *consider alternative intents*.

XVIII. The "If I Feel It, It Must Be True" Fallacy

Summary

One's experience of emotional comfort or discomfort is not necessarily a valid gauge for differentiating what is true from what is false. Thus, subjective feelings of comfort may be prompted by a pleasing truth as well as by a pleasing falsehood. Similarly, feelings of discomfort may be due to an unpleasant truth as well as an unpleasant falsehood. Yes, the truth hurts; but so do lies.

Antidotes

1. Don't assume that truth or falsity are necessarily correlated with one's subjective feelings of comfort or discomfort. Thus, be careful not to confuse the degree of comfort/discomfort you are experiencing with the degree of truth/falsity inherent in a given observation, situation, or conclusion.
2. Remember that psychological or emotional discomfort does not always signal the discovery of a "painful truth."
3. Do not rely on your emotions as the sole barometer for distinguishing truths from falsehoods. There may be certainty in *what* you are feeling, but not necessarily in what it *"proves."*

4. Remember that what feels good isn't necessarily true, and what feels bad isn't necessarily false. Conversely, what feels bad isn't necessarily true, and what feels good isn't necessarily false.

XIX. The Spectacular Explanation Fallacy

Summary

When attempting to understand extraordinary events, we have a tendency to search for extraordinary explanations. Further, the more unusual or bizarre the events, the more likely we are to seek out bizarre causes—or even to create bizarre theories—to account for them. However, we typically overlook the fact that very ordinary causes can produce very extraordinary effects. In fact, pure chance alone predicts the occasional occurrence of extraordinary events. Thus, it is very normal for some events to appear very abnormal.

Antidotes

1. Don't assume that extraordinary *events* necessarily require extraordinary *explanations*.
2. Keep in mind that *very ordinary causes* are capable of producing *very extraordinary effects*.
3. Remember that statistical laws of probability predict the occasional occurrence of extraordinary events.
4. Whenever you are confronted with instances of human behavior that are particularly unusual, rare, spectacular, or odd make a deliberate effort to consider ordinary, commonplace, or mundane causes and explanations.

XX. Deductive and Inductive Reasoning

Summary

Two primary forms of reasoning are *deduction* and *induction*. Deductive reasoning involves inferring specific conclusions based on a general premise. Inductive reasoning involves inferring a general conclusion based on specific instances. Errors in deductive reasoning typically are due to erroneous premises and faulty logic. Errors in inductive reasoning are usually the result of overgeneralizing from biased, insufficient, or inappropriate observations.

Antidotes

1. Learn to differentiate between deductive and inductive reasoning.
2. Recognize that different types of problems call for different reasoning strategies. Thus, make your selection based on the nature and goal of the particular question, task, or situation.

3. In using deductive reasoning, be sure that your initial assumptions are correct and that your logic is sound.
4. When utilizing inductive reasoning, be careful not to hastily overgeneralize from an unrepresentative, inadequate, or otherwise flawed initial data base.

XXI. Reactivity

Summary

Reactivity refers to the phenomenon in which the mere act of *observing* an event can, in itself, *change* the event. Reactivity is particularly problematic in the study of human activity, in that it impedes our ability to accurately ascertain people's "true" behavior. Reactivity thus limits the extent to which researchers can safely generalize their findings.

Antidotes

1. Remember that measuring something, to some degree, changes it. In a nutshell, "to observe is to disturb."
2. Be constantly vigilant as to the presence and potential impact of reactivity. In particular, when conducting research, always take into account the specific ways and the degree to which reactivity presents a threat to the validity of your investigation.
3. Recognize that, even if the effects of reactivity cannot be entirely eliminated, they can (and should) be reduced. Thus, whenever feasible, actively search for and utilize unobtrusive, nonreactive, or minimally reactive measures.

XXII. The Self-Fulfilling Prophecy

Summary

The assumptions, attitudes, and beliefs that we hold toward other people can, with or without our intent, actually *produce* the very behaviors that we *expect* to find. Similarly, *our own* behavior may inadvertently be shaped by other people's expectations of us. In sum, expectations can generate their own reality.

Antidotes

1. In all of your social interactions, remember that expectations can, in themselves, create their own reality.
2. Make a conscious effort to become aware of your own expectations and the ways in which they may lead you to induce those very behaviors in others.
3. Don't forget that *your own behavior* is not immune to the influence of the self-fulfilling prophecy. Specifically, keep in mind that your behavior can be shaped by other's expectations of you.

4. In conducting research, initiate safeguards to reduce the potential impact of expectancy effects. This may be accomplished by, for example, keeping the experimenters unaware of (i.e., "blind" to) the specific purpose, goals, or hypotheses of the study.

XXIII. The Assimilation Bias

Summary

A *schema* is a mental structure that organizes our preconceptions, thereby providing a framework for understanding new events and future experiences. *Accommodation* means to modify our schema to fit incoming data; *assimilation,* in contrast, means to fit incoming data into our schema. In general, we are more prone to assimilate than to accommodate, even if this entails altering or distorting the data. Thus, assimilation can profoundly bias our perceptions of reality.

Antidotes

1. Don't underestimate the extent to which your *prior* beliefs, knowledge, and expectations (schemata) can affect your *current* experience, impressions, and perceptions.
2. Try to become as aware as possible of schemata that are important to you; awareness of schemata increases your ability to modify them.
3. Experiment with temporarily lowering or altering your "perceptual filters" or "schema-colored glasses" by attempting to understand someone *else's* subjective (phenomenological) experience.
4. Learn to *differentiate* your use of *assimilation* versus *accommodation,* particularly when you are faced with a discrepancy between your beliefs (schemas) and the information (data). Beware of the general tendency to assimilate, rather to than accommodate.
5. *Prod yourself to accommodate* when, out of habit, reflex, or just sheer laziness, you would typically be inclined to automatically assimilate. Strive toward flexibility; guard against "hardening of the categories."

XXIV. The Confirmation Bias

Summary

The manner in which we seek answers to our questions frequently tends to be biased. Specifically, we more actively seek out information that will confirm our prior beliefs and expectations than information that might refute them. In short, we are prone to be biased collectors of evidence; as a consequence, we are more apt to find only what we seek.

Antidotes

1. Be aware that the ways in which you search for evidence, such as the questions that you ask, may lead you to arrive selectively only at those conclusions that corroborate your initial beliefs.
2. Make it a point to actively seek out evidence that could, in principle, disconfirm your prior expectations.

XXV. The Belief Perseverance Effect

Summary

We have a tendency to stubbornly cling to our beliefs, sometimes even in the face of disconfirming evidence. This is especially likely to occur when we feel personally invested in our beliefs. Thus, when these beliefs are challenged, we feel impelled to protect them, almost as if we were protecting ourselves. One consequence of this phenomenon is that it generally requires much more compelling evidence to *change* our beliefs than it did to *create* them in the first place.

Antidotes

1. Keep an open mind to different, and especially challenging, points of view.
2. Remind yourself (and others as well) to think carefully about how you evaluate evidence and to monitor your biases closely as you formulate your conclusions.
3. Make it a point to actively *counterargue* your preexisting beliefs. That is, ask yourself directly in what ways your beliefs might be wrong. One specific method of doing so is to *consider the opposite*.
4. When faced with a discrepancy between your beliefs and the facts, resist the natural tendency to assume that your beliefs are right and the facts must somehow be wrong.

XXVI. The Hindsight Bias

Summary

We tend to overestimate the extent to which events could have been anticipated, foreseen, or expected. In retrospect, outcomes appear to us as obvious, predictable, or even unavoidable; however, in reality, they are far less so beforehand. Because knowing a result makes it seem inevitable, hindsight creates an illusion of predictability. Postdiction is easy; prediction is difficult.

Antidotes

1. Remember that, in retrospect, nearly any outcome seems obvious.
2. Be careful not to overestimate what could have been predicted or foreseen. Although hindsight is 20/20, foresight frequently is shrouded in obscurity.
3. Recognize the limitations of after-the-fact "explanations" that, by their very nature, can't be disproven.
4. When attempting to understand an event, imagine how you might explain a result that is different from the one that actually occurred.

XXVII. The Representativeness Bias

Summary

In order to identify any given phenomenon (such as a person, object, event, or ideology), we automatically and intuitively compare the phenomenon to our mental representation, *prototype*, or *schema* of the relevant category. Although this cognitive shortcut (or *heuristic*) generally produces accurate results, errors can occur as a result of faulty prototypes, failure to take into account pertinent statistical data (such as base rates, sample size, and chance probability), or when motivational dynamics bias our search.

Antidotes

1. In situations when you are likely to utilize the representativeness heuristic, make a conscious effort to consider the possibility that the prototype in question might be inaccurate, biased, or incomplete.
2. Take into account relevant statistical information, such as base rates, samples sizes, and chance probability.
3. Beware of the natural tendency to overestimate the degree of similarity between phenomena and categories.
4. Recognize that your personal attitudes about phenomena and prototypes can bias your comparisons and subsequent judgments.

XXVIII. The Availability Bias

Summary

We utilize the *availability* heuristic whenever we attempt to assess the frequency or likelihood of an event on the basis of how quickly or easily instances come to mind. Thus, vivid examples, dramatic events, graphic case studies, and personal testimonies, in contrast to statistical information, are likely to exert a disproportionate impact on our judgments. In this way, anecdotes may be more persuasive than factual data.

Antidotes

1. When estimating the frequency or probability of an event, remind yourself not to reach a conclusion based solely on the ease or speed with which examples can be retrieved from your memory.
2. Whenever feasible, utilize base rates and other relevant statistical information.
3. Resist the temptation to generalize from a few, vivid anecdotal examples.

XXIX. The Insight Fallacy

Summary

Our ability to *understand* something does not necessarily enable us to *change* it. Specifically, insight into the cause of a problem does not invariably solve the problem. Moreover, an overemphasis on insight may be counterproductive or even detrimental. In sum, despite its virtues, insight may be the booby prize of life.

Antidotes

1. Recognize the *limits,* as well as the benefits, of what insight can provide.
2. Don't make the mistake of assuming that if you can *understand* a problem, then that will automatically *solve* the problem.
3. Keep in mind that, in some situations, insight is neither necessary nor sufficient for bringing about change.
4. Actively explore alternative methods of change that do not rely solely on insight.

XXX. Every Decision Is a Trade-Off

Summary

All events, activities, and outcomes are comprised of both pluses and minuses, advantages and disadvantages, upsides and downsides. Thus, every decision involves a trade-off of some kind. Although decisions vary in terms of their content, complexity, and importance, they all entail trade-offs. Of course, the costs and benefits in the "ledger" may not turn out to be equitably balanced, but they always exist and therefore should be identified, examined, and weighed in your decision-making process.

Antidotes

1. Come to terms with the reality that *any* decision you make will *always* involve a trade-off of some kind.
2. Before making a decision, *take stock* of the pluses and minuses of all your alternatives.
3. Weigh the trade-offs, and then act accordingly.

A Proposed Category for the Diagnostic and Statistical Manual of Mental Disorders (DSM): Pervasive Labeling Disorder[1]

The purpose of this essay is to propose a new diagnostic category for inclusion in the American Psychiatric Association's *Diagnostic and Statistical Manual of Mental Disorders,* better known as the DSM. As noted in a recent edition (American Psychiatric Association, 1987), the DSM should be viewed as "only one still frame in the ongoing process of attempting to better understand mental disorders." The category proposed here represents a significant contribution to the composition of the next still frame by focusing on one of the most ubiquitous, yet least recognized, of all mental disorders.

409.00 Pervasive Labeling Disorder

Diagnostic Features

The essential features of this mental disorder are: (1) an uncontrollable impulse, drive, or temptation to invent labels and to apply them to other people, (2) a repetitive pattern of trying to fit people into preconceived categories, (3) an increasing sense of fear or inadequacy before committing the act, (4) an experience of overwhelming triumph or relief at the time of committing the act.

Manifestations of the disorder appear in many situations, but are especially likely to occur when the person with Pervasive Labeling Disorder (PLD) feels uncomfortable around other people. The person then spontaneously assigns a label to others, thus viewing them as "types," rather than as human beings. Because the disorder serves to control other people and to keep them at a distance, it provides the person with the temporary illusion of both superiority and safety.

Associated Features

People with PLD frequently display marked signs of arrogance, smugness, grandiosity, and a sense of personal entitlement. They exhibit an especially condescending attitude toward others who do not share this mental disorder.

These persons derive immense pride from inventing seemingly incisive and articulate (yet ambiguous and indecipherable) pseudoscientific neologisms. When called on to explain the precise meaning of these newly created labels, however, they typically display peculiar speech characteristics and inappropriate communication patterns, including: catatonic silence; stammering and cluttering; verbal perseveration on the label, coupled with poverty of content of speech; and psychomotor agitation, such as engaging in beard-stroking, head-shaking, or eye-rolling behaviors.

Persons with PLD operate under the fallacious belief that, by having named something, they have therefore explained it (i.e., **Delusional Disorder, Nominal Type**). Research indicates that many persons with PLD are exceptionally adept at seeing in other people the flaws they cannot see in themselves.

Prevalence

PLD is widespread throughout all sectors of society, but many people have found a means to obtain reinforcement for this disorder in socially acceptable ways by becoming psychiatrists, psychoanalysts, psychologists, astrologists, Scientologists, evangelists, cult leaders, authors of self-help books, politicians, and interview guests on radio and television shows.

Specific Culture and Age Features

Despite its prevalence, the disorder typically is not recognized until the person has attained a position of social power.

Course

Recovery from PLD rarely occurs once the person's annual income exceeds six figures.

Complications

Because persons with chronic, intractable, and severe cases of PLD are incapable of achieving and maintaining any type of human bonding, they rarely have any real friends.

Predisposing Factors

Vulnerability to this disorder is directly correlated with the extent to which one has a fear of one's own feelings. When PLD is found in psychotherapists, it typically serves to mask their deeply hidden and nagging fears that they haven't the faintest idea as to how to actually help their patients.

Differential Diagnosis

Obsessive Compulsive Personality Disorder, Social Phobia, and **Delusional Disorder (Grandiose Type)** are related to, and therefore sometimes difficult to distinguish from, **Pervasive Labeling Disorder.** To ensure diagnostic validity, flipping a coin, tossing the *I Ching,* or utilizing the Eenie-Meenie-Meinie-Moe (EM³)method is recommended.

Subtypes and Specifiers

409.01 With Narcissistic Personality Features. This category should be used for the person with PLD whom you think has too much self-esteem.

409.02 With Codependent Personality Features. This category should be used for the person with PLD whom you think has too much empathy.

409.03 With Histrionic Personality Features. This category should be used for the person with PLD whom you think is too emotional.

409.04 With Schizoid Personality Features. This category should be used for the person with PLD whom you think is not emotional enough.

409.05 With Neurotic Personality Features. This category should be used for the person with PLD whom you think worries too much.

409.06 With Antisocial Personality Features. This category should be used for the person with PLD whom you think doesn't worry enough.

409.07 With Borderline Personality Features. This category should be used when the person with PLD is disliked intensely by others, especially unsuccessful psychotherapists.

409.08 With Adult-Child-of-Alcoholic Personality Features. This category should be used when the person with PLD came from parents who, in any way whatsoever, did not satisfy each and every one of his or her needs as a child.

409.09 With Resistant Personality Features. This category should be used when the person with PLD doesn't do what you want him or her to do.

409.10 With Cognitive Slippage Features. This category should be used for the person with PLD whom you can't understand, but don't want to admit it.

409.11 With Transference Features. This category should be used for psychotherapy patients with PLD who have any feelings whatsoever about their therapist.

409.12 With Countertransference Features. This category should be used for psychotherapists with PLD who have any feelings whatsoever about their patients.

Notes

[1] This article originally appeared in the *Journal of Humanistic Psychology* (Levy, 1992).

Appendix 2

Selected Answers to Chapter Exercises

I. The Evaluative Bias of Language

Suggested Responses from the Perspective of Person B:

obstacle—*challenge*
problem—*issue*
issue—*learning opportunity*
failure—*learning experience*

terrorist—*freedom fighter*
murder—*sacrifice*
handout—*subsidy*
conformity—*pro-solidarity*
hostage—*detainee*
brainwashed—*enlightened*

perversion—*alternative lifestyle*
slut—*promiscuous*
promiscuous—*sexually liberated*
idiot savant—*autistic savant*
retarded—*developmentally disabled*
developmentally disabled—*developmentally challenged*

anal retentive—*tidy*
egocentricity—*self-esteem*
thought disordered—*creative*
irresponsible—*spontaneous*
psychotic—*eccentric*
catatonic—*reserved*
codependent—*empathic*

rationalization—*rationale*
resistance—*autonomy*
defense mechanism—*coping strategy*

psychotherapy—*counseling*
therapy patient—*client*
psychiatric institution—*treatment center*

Dependent Personality Disorder—*loyal*
Avoidant Personality Disorder—*cautious*
Paranoid Personality Disorder—*vigilant*
Narcissistic Personality Disorder—*self-confident*
Histrionic Personality Disorder—*colorful*
Obsessive–Compulsive Personality Disorder—*meticulous*

II. The Reification Error

Answers to Chapter Exercise:

humor: (C)
laughter: (E)

tearfulness: (E)
sadness: (C)

smiling: (E)
happy: (C)

nervous: (C)
fidgety: (E)

restless: (E)
anxious: (C)

energy: (C)
activity: (E)

talkative: (E)
extraverted: (C)

quiet: (E)
introverted: (C)

personality type: (C)
blood type: (E)

muscular strength: (E)
ego strength: (C)

disordered psyche: (C)
disordered desk: (E)

housing complex: (E)
inferiority complex: (C)

drunkenness: (E)
alcoholism: (C)

heartburn: (E)
heartache: (C)

rotten egg: (E)
rotten attitude: (C)

sea sickness: (E)
love sickness: (C)

broken dream: (C)
broken nose: (E)

lost toothbrush: (E)
lost soul: (C)

healthy outlook: (C)
healthy spleen: (E)

free will: (C)
motionless: (E)
love: (C)
disorganized: (E)
heavy: (E)
self-concept: (C)
self-actualization: (C)
deviant: (E)
unseen: (E)
hepatitis: (E)
schizophrenia: (C)
repression: (C)
intuition: (C)
suicide: (E)

V. Differentiating Dichotomous and Continuous Variables

Answers to Exercise:

conscious–unconscious: (C)
feminine–masculine: (C)
gun fired–gun not fired: (D)
optimist–pessimist: (C)
married–single: (D)
present–absent: (D)
emotionally secure–emotionally insecure: (C)
published–not published: (D)
airborne–grounded: (D)
day–night: (C)
good mood–bad mood: (C)
licensed–unlicensed: (D)
honest–dishonest: (C)
morning person–evening person: (C)
neurotic–nonneurotic: (C)
mailed–unmailed: (D)

subjective–objective: (C)
alcoholic beverage–nonalcoholic beverage: (D)
successful basketball shot–unsuccessful shot: (D)
psychological trait–psychological state: (C)
tenured–untenured: (D)
"Type A" personality–"Type B" personality: (C)
guilty verdict–not guilty verdict: (D)
power on–power off: (D)
addicted–not addicted: (C)
therapeutic–nontherapeutic: (C)

XII. Multiple Causation

Suggested Answers to Exercise on the Multiple Causes of Overeating:

C_1 love the taste of food
C_2 severe hunger
C_3 extreme nervousness
C_4 "stuff down" unwanted feelings
C_5 fill internal void of loneliness
C_6 long-term habit pattern
C_7 learned response/positive reinforcement
C_8 parental role modeling
C_9 compensation for unfulfilled love
C_{10} poor impulse control
C_{11} avoidance of intimacy
C_{12} cannabis intoxication
C_{13} substitute for mother's love
C_{14} self-destructive displacement of anger
C_{15} struggle for exertion of control
C_{16} symbolic act of rebelliousness
C_{17} psychological regression to infancy
C_{18} fear of food unavailability
C_{19} attempt at self-nurturance
C_{20} low self-esteem
C_{21} fixation at oral stage
C_{22} sublimation of sex

$\rightarrow$ *E* (Overeating)

XIV. Multiple Pathways of Causation

Causal Pathways Pertaining to the Etiology of Anxiety:

>the ingestion of drugs (such as caffeine, cocaine, or amphetamines);

>withdrawal from drugs (such as alcohol, sedatives, or opiates);

>physical illness (such as hyperthyroidism, pheochromocytoma, or hypercortisolism);

>fear of actual external events (also known as "reality anxiety," such as an angry King Cobra that corners you in your tent);

>fear of anticipated external events (such as social rejection or disapproval);

>fear of losing control over your own potentially destructive impulses (also known as "neurotic anxiety," such as being overwhelmed by powerful sexual or aggressive drives);

>fear of your own self-judgment, self-criticism, or guilt (also known as "moral anxiety");

>prior learning (such as by classical conditioning, operant learning, or vicarious learning);

>ontological insecurity and fear of existential nothingness.

XXIV. The Confirmation Bias

Additional "Leading" Questions That Are Likely to Confirm a Diagnosis of Paranoia:

"Do you sometimes doubt the sincerity of other people's intentions?"

"Do you believe that people may say one thing to your face and something else behind your back?"

"If somebody unexpectedly goes out of their way to do something exceptionally nice for you, are you inclined to wonder about their motives?"

"When people make an exaggerated effort to reassure you, does that sometimes only serve to make you feel even more concerned or suspicious?"

"Have you ever found that co-workers, friends, or family members weren't as loyal to you as they had led you to believe?"

"Do you sometimes get the feeling that others may have the desire to hurt or demean you in some way?"

"Do you ever feel the need to be on guard to prevent others from manipulating, exploiting, or taking advantage of you?"

"Have other people ever tried to hold you back from succeeding?"

"Have you noticed others being jealous of your talents, skills, or achievements?"

"Have you ever felt betrayed by someone whom you trusted?"

"When someone insults or injures you, might you sometimes be inclined not to forgive and forget?"

"Have you noticed that other people often don't take responsibility for the harm that they inflict on others?"

"Do you find that you can sometimes be overly sensitive to criticism?"

"Do you ever experience feelings of tension, apprehension, or worry?"

Additional "Non-leading" Questions That May Disconfirm a Diagnosis of Paranoia:

"How often do your suspicions turn out to be confirmed by actual proof, evidence, or facts?"

"What are your reasons for mistrusting others?"

"How frequently have you, in fact, been betrayed by others?"

"Can you name some specific instances when your suspiciousness was warranted?"

"Are you in a position of power or authority that might tempt others to manipulate, exploit, or take advantage of you?"

"Why might others be jealous of you?"

"For what reasons might others begrudge your achievements?"

"What special or unique talents do you have that others might envy?"

"What specific reasons have you had for questioning the loyalty of co-workers, friends, or family members?"

"Do you have valid reason to be jealous of your spouse?"

"Has your spouse ever given you cause to doubt her/his word or question her/his loyalty?"

"Have others, whom you do trust, ever told you that your suspicions, fears, or concerns are excessive or unreasonable?"

"In general, to what degree would you say that you are wary of other people's motives?"

"Compared to most other people, how pronounced are your feelings of tension, apprehension, or worry?"

Glossary

Author's Note: I have written this glossary with three explicit goals in mind:

1. To provide you with an easily accessible reference source for learning the meanings of a wide range of important terms and concepts;
2. To maximize the book's conceptual, as well as stylistic, consistency and continuity;
3. To communicate to you my thoughts and ideas in the most efficient way possible. In light of the fact that so many terms in psychology are subject to multiple meanings and interpretations, I felt that it was particularly important to clarify my use of them.

Guide to the Glossary:

>*n* = noun

>*vb* = verb

>*adj* = adjective

>*pl* = plural

>*sg* = singular

>*syn* = synonym

>*cf.* ("compare with") points out other terms that are either opposite to or, in some cases, difficult to distinguish from, the term in question.

>"see" is used to refer you to additional terms that are conceptually related to the original term.

>Terms appearing in **bold typeface** (or variations) are cross-referenced in the Glossary.

>Last, to locate the exact placement of terms in the text itself, please refer to the Subject Index.

abnormal   That which deviates from what is typical, common, or statistically average; (*cf.* **normal**).

abstract   (*adj*) Considered apart from **physical existence** or tangible **events**; **theoretical** or **hypothetical**; (*cf.* **concrete**).

acausal   To occur in the absence of a proposed **explanation** or **cause**.

accommodation   A **cognitive** process by which people adapt to their environment by modifying their preexisting **beliefs** or **schemas** to incorporate new information and **experiences**; (*cf.* **assimilation**).

Actor–Observer Bias   An error in **attribution** by which a person **perceiving** his or her own **behavior** tends to overestimate the impact of situational factors (**i.e.,** to assign **external attributions**), but an observer overestimates the impact of that person's **dispositional** characteristics (**i.e.,** to assign **internal attributions**).

acute   Of or pertaining to any **disorder** characterized by a sudden onset, a sharp rise in severe **symptoms,** and relatively brief duration; (*cf.* **chronic**).

affect   1. (*n*) The **observable** expression of **subjectively experienced** feelings or **emotions.** 2. (*vb*) To **cause** an **effect.**

ambiguous   (*adj*) The characteristic of being vague, obscure, or open to more than one definition, meaning, or **interpretation.**

analogous   (*adj*) Similar, alike, or parallel in a way that permits the drawing of an **analogy.**

analogy   (*n*) A systematic comparison of one **phenomenon** to another, with the **inference** that if they are similar in some respects, they probably will be similar in others; a proposed relation, correspondence, or parallel; (see **metaphor**).

antecedent   That which precedes an **event,** occurrence, or condition, whose relationship may or may not involve **causality;** (*cf.* **subsequent**).

antidote   A remedy to prevent or counteract an adverse **effect;** (see **treatment**).

a posteriori   Derived by or based on **inductive reasoning, factual** evidence, **empirical** examination, direct **experimentation,** or **sensory experience,** rather than presupposed **assumptions, preconceptions,** or **deductive reasoning;** (*cf.* **a priori**).

a priori   Formed or conceived beforehand; a presupposed **assumption** derived by **deductive reasoning,** rather than from **factual** evidence, **empirical** examination, direct **experimentation,** or **sensory experience;** (*cf.* **a posteriori**).

ascribe   (*vb*) To **infer, attribute,** assign, or conjecture a **cause,** quality, or source.

assimilation   A **cognitive** process by which people adapt to their environment by modifying new information and **experiences** to fit into their preexisting **beliefs or** schemas; (*cf.* **accommodation**); (see **Assimilation Bias**).

Assimilation Bias   The propensity to resolve discrepancies between preexisting **schemas** and new information in the direction of **assimilation** rather than **accommodation,** even at the expense of distorting the information itself.

assumption   A statement, supposition, or **premise** that is accepted as **true** without prior proof or demonstration; (see **a priori**).

attitude   A relatively stable **cognitive–emotional–behavioral** predisposition to **respond** in a particular way to various **phenomena,** including people, objects, **events,** situations, issues, and ideas.

attribution   1. The process of determining or assigning **causation** to an **event,** usually a person's **behavior;** (see **internal attribution, external attribution, Fundamental Attribution Error**). 2. Using available information to draw an **inference, interpretation,** or reach an **explanation.** 3. **Ascribing** characteristics, features, or qualities.

Availability Bias   Any condition where the **availability heuristic** produces systematic errors in **thinking** or information processing, typically due to highly **vivid** although rare **events.**

availability heuristic   A **cognitive** strategy for quickly estimating the frequency, incidence, or **probability** of a given **event** based on the ease with which such instances are retrievable from memory; (see **heuristic, representativeness heuristic**).

Barnum Effect   A **phenomenon** describing people's willingness to accept uncritically the **validity** of **Barnum statements.**

Barnum statement   Any **generic,** "one-size-fits-all" **personality interpretation** about a particular individual that is true of practically all human beings; (see **Barnum Effect**).

base rate   **Data** pertaining to the **normal** frequency with which an **event,** such as a **disease** or **disorder,** occurs in a particular group or the general population.

behavior An **observable** action or **response** emitted by an organism.

behavior theory (behaviorism) A theoretical orientation in **psychology** that focuses on **observable, measurable behavior,** rather than **mental** processes, and stresses strict adherence to **empirical** evidence and the **scientific method.**

behavior therapy A group of approaches to **psychotherapy** founded on the **scientific** principles of **behaviorism,** learning **theory, reinforcement,** and classical and operant conditioning; (see **cognitive–behavioral therapy**).

belief A conviction held with confidence, trust, or faith that a particular **phenomenon** (person, thing, or idea) is **true** or real.

Belief Perseverance Effect The tendency to cling stubbornly to one's **beliefs,** even in the face of contradictory or disconfirming evidence.

bias A prejudicial inclination or predisposition that inhibits, deters, or prevents impartial **judgment;** (see **cognitive bias, motivational bias**).

bi-directional causation A mutual, **reciprocal** relationship between two **variables** wherein each is both a **cause** and an **effect** of the other; (*syn* **causal loop**); (*cf.* **uni-directional causation**).

bifurcate To divide into two parts or branches.

category A defined division in a system of classification, or **taxonomy,** in which **phenomena** sharing common attributes can be grouped.

causal (*adj*) Of or pertaining to **cause.**

causality (*syn* **causation**).

causal loop (*syn* **bi-directional causation**).

causation A situation in which a given **cause** produces an **effect;** a cause-and-effect relationship between **variables;** (*syn* **causality,** determinism); (see **bi-directional causation, uni-directional causation**).

cause 1. (*n*) A circumstance, action, or **event** that necessarily brings about a particular result; (*syn* **determinant**); (see **causa-**

tion). 2. (*vb*) To create or produce an **effect.**

cf. Compare with (from the Latin, *confer*).

chance 1. The occurrence of an **event** in the absence of a discernable, **observable,** or demonstrable **cause;** an apparently **random** outcome. 2. To happen without **intent** or design. 3. The likelihood or **probability** of an event.

chronic Of or pertaining to any **disorder** characterized by a slow onset and prolonged duration or frequent recurrence; (*cf.* **acute**).

clinical 1. Of or pertaining to the direct **observation,** study, and **treatment** of clients or patients. 2. Emotionally detached, impersonal, or **objective.**

Clinical Orientation Assimilation Bias (COAB) A psychotherapist's inclination to **perceive, interpret,** and **explain** clients' **symptoms** principally (or exclusively) in terms of his or her own **clinical schema** or **theoretical** orientation, irrespective of its actual relevance or suitability; (see **assimilation, Assimilation Bias**).

cognition 1. A general term referring to the **mental** activity of **thinking;** the **psychological** process by which people become aware and acquire **knowledge.** 2. A discrete piece of information; a thought; (*cf.* **emotion**).

cognitive Of or pertaining to **cognition.**

cognitive–behavioral therapy (CBT) An approach to **psychotherapy** in which the principles of **behaviorism** are applied both to the individual's **behaviors** and **cognitions;** (*cf.* **behavior therapy, cognitive therapy**).

cognitive bias Any systematic error in **attribution** that derives from limits that are inherent in people's **cognitive** abilities to process information; (*cf.* **motivational bias**); (see **Fundamental Attribution Error**).

cognitive therapy An approach to **psychotherapy** that focuses on the client's **thinking** processes, with emphasis on identifying and correcting faulty **belief**

systems, irrational **expectations,** distorted **perceptions,** rigid or **biased schemata,** flawed **logic, erroneous attributions,** overgeneralizations, and unfounded conclusions.

concept A general or **abstract** idea that combines several elements to form a **mental** impression, typically derived through the process of **induction.**

concrete (*adj*) The quality of being tangible, **physical, observable,** or directly **measurable;** consisting of mass or material substance; (*cf.* **abstract**).

conditioned response (CR) In classical conditioning, a learned **response** to a previously **neutral stimulus;** (see **unconditioned stimulus, unconditioned response, behaviorism**).

conditioned stimulus (CS) In classical conditioning, an originally neutral **stimulus** that, after paired association with an **unconditioned stimulus,** is effective in eliciting a **conditioned response;** (see **unconditioned response, behaviorism**).

Confirmation Bias The tendency, **intentional** or unintentional, to selectively search for and gather evidence that is consistent with, and therefore supports, one's **preconceptions,** prior **beliefs,** and **expectations.**

connotation (*n*) The implied or suggested meaning of a word, symbol, or **event;** (*cf.* **denotation**).

connote (*vb*) (*cf.* **denote**); (see **connotation**).

conscious 1. (*adj*) The **mental** state of being aware, attentive, or cognizant. 2. (*adj*) Having **intent** or **intentionality.** 3. (*n*) A **theoretical construct** referring to the part of the **mind** that is responsible for the organism's awareness; (*cf.* **unconscious**).

consciousness The state of being **conscious.**

consequence 1. The result, outcome, or **effect** of a given **cause.** 2. A conclusion derived through **logic.**

Consequence–Intentionality Fallacy The **erroneous belief** that the **effect** of a

person's **behavior,** in itself, proves the **intent** of the behavior.

construct (*n*) A **concept** that is **mentally** conceived or constructed by combining **sensory** impressions or **empirical data;** an **abstract, theoretical** model that is not directly **observable, measurable,** or testable; (*cf.* **event**).

Construct (Type C) Theory A type of **theory** whose proposed **explanation** cannot be directly **observed** or **measured;** thus, even under ideal conditions, a Type C Theory is never provable or refutable; (*cf.* **Event Theory**).

Contiguity–Causation Error The **erroneous** conclusion that a **causal** relationship exists between two **events** solely on the basis of **temporal contiguity;** (see **parataxic reasoning**).

continuous variable Any **variable** that lies along a dimension, range, or spectrum, rather than in a discrete **category,** that can theoretically take on an infinite number of **values** and is expressed in terms of quantity, magnitude, or degree; (*cf.* **dichotomous variable**).

correlate 1. (*n*) A **phenomenon** that accompanies, is associated with, or is related to another **phenomenon;** (*syn* **correlation**). 2. (*vb*) To establish a mutual or **reciprocal correlation** between two or more **variables.**

correlation A statistical **measure** of the degree to which **variables** are related to or associated with each other, whereby changes in one variable are systematically accompanied by changes in the other variable; (see **orthogonal**).

counterintuitive Running contrary to **expectation** or common sense.

countertransference A distorted **perception,** usually **unconscious,** on the part of the psychotherapist toward a client based on his or her prior relationship **experiences;** the perception may be favorable (**positive countertransference**) or unfavorable (**negative countertransference**); (*cf.* **transference**).

criteria (*pl*) (see **criterion**).

criterion (*sg*) 1. A standard by which an **evaluation, judgment, decision,** or classification can be attained. 2. An independent **external measure** against which a test can be **validated.**

critical 1. Characterized by careful, exact, and comprehensive **evaluation** and **judgment.** 2. The quality of being essential, vital, or integral; a point that is crucial or definitive. 3. A derogatory, disparaging, or fault-finding **attitude** or **behavior.**

critical thinking (*vb*) An active and systematic **cognitive** strategy to examine, **evaluate,** and understand **events,** solve problems, and make **decisions** on the basis of sound **reasoning** and **valid** evidence. More specifically, critical thinking involves: maintaining an **attitude** that is both open-minded and **skeptical;** recognizing the distinction between **facts** and **theories;** striving for factual accuracy and **logical** consistency; **objectively** gathering, weighing, and synthesizing information; forming reasonable **inferences, judgments,** and conclusions; identifying and questioning underlying **assumptions** and **beliefs;** discerning hidden or implicit **values; perceiving** similarities and differences between **phenomena;** understanding **causal** relationships; reducing logical flaws and personal **biases,** such as avoiding oversimplifications and overgeneralizations; developing a tolerance for uncertainty and **ambiguity;** exploring alternative perspectives and **explanations;** and searching for creative solutions; (see **metathinking**).

data (*pl*) A collection of **facts,** information, or **empirical** evidence; a body of **measurements** gathered in the conduct of research.

datum (*sg*) (see **data**).

decision The act of making a choice, **judgment,** or arriving at a solution; (*cf.* **evaluation**).

deduction A form of **reasoning** that involves drawing an **inference** from a general premise to a specific conclusion; (*cf.* **induction**).

deductive reasoning (*cf.* **inductive reasoning**); (see **deduction**).

defense mechanism (see **ego defense mechanism**).

delusion A false **belief** that is firmly maintained as **true,** despite obvious and incontrovertible evidence to the contrary; a diagnostic **criterion** for certain **psychotic disorders.**

denial An **ego defense mechanism** by which the individual reduces his or her **emotional** discomfort by **unconsciously** refusing to accept, or even **perceive,** a **psychologically** painful reality.

denotation (*n*) The literal or explicit meaning of a word, symbol, or **event;** (*cf.* **connotation**).

denote (*vb*) (*cf.* **connote**); (see **denotation**).

dependent variable 1. In an **experiment,** the **variable** whose **value** is determined or **caused** by the manipulation, **treatment,** or **independent variable;** (*syn* outcome, **measure, response**). 2. In nonexperimental settings, a test, **observation,** or measure.

description An **objective** report or account of observed **phenomena,** without **inference, interpretation, explanation,** or **value judgment;** (*syn* **descriptor**); (*cf.* **prediction, evaluation**).

descriptor (*syn* **description**).

determinant (*syn* **cause**).

diagnosis The process of determining, identifying, and classifying the nature of a specific **disorder** or **disease** on the basis of its signs and **symptoms;** (see **differential diagnosis**).

Diagnostic and Statistical Manual of Mental Disorders (**DSM**) The American Psychiatric Association's official system of classification for **psychological disorders;** (see **mental illness, psychopathology**).

dichotomous variable Any **variable** that can be placed into either of two discrete and mutually exclusive **categories;** (*cf.* **continuous variable**).

didactic Designed to impart information, teach, or instruct.

differential diagnosis The process of distinguishing between **diagnoses** on the basis of an individual's particular **symptoms** or complaints.

dilemma A predicament involving two or more mutually exclusive or incompatible alternatives that seemingly defies a satisfactory solution; a conflict comprised of opposing **values** or **motives.**

dimension A range, scope, or spectrum on which a **continuous variable** can be placed; the degree, magnitude, or extent of a particular **phenomenon;** (*cf.* **category, dichotomous variable**).

disease Strictly defined, an **abnormal** or **pathological somatic** condition, **disorder,** or illness involving serious impairment in **physical** functioning. By extension, defined **metaphorically** as any abnormal **psychological** condition involving serious impairment in functioning; (see **psychopathology, symptom, syndrome**).

disorder A **pathological** or psychologically distressing state of body or **mind;** (*cf.* **disease**); (see **psychopathology, symptom, syndrome**).

displacement An **ego defense mechanism** by which the individual redirects and discharges **repressed** aggressive or sexual impulses on substitutive objects or people that are **perceived** as less threatening or dangerous than those that originally aroused the conflict.

disposition An individual's relatively stable and enduring constellation of **psychological (personality)** and **physical** (biological) **traits** or characteristics; one's **internal** attributes (as opposed to **external** circumstances, situations, or **events**).

DSM (see **Diagnostic and Statistical Manual of Mental Disorders**).

dynamics 1. The action of **psychological** forces, mechanisms, or **motivations.** 2. Pertaining to change, or that which initiates change. 3. Underlying or **unconscious causes.**

dysfunction Impairment, disturbance, or disruption in **normal physical** or **psychological** functioning.

effect (*n*) The inevitable result, **consequence,** or outcome of a preceding **casual event;** (see **causation, internal validity**).

efficacy 1. A term in **clinical psychology** referring to the effectiveness or efficiency of **psychotherapy treatment.** 2. An individual's perceived ability to exert influence and control over his or her outcomes.

e.g. For example (from the Latin, *exempli gratia*).

ego defense mechanism A collection of self-protective **psychological** processes, usually **unconscious,** whose function is to reduce anxiety by denying, falsifying, or distorting reality.

ego-dystonic Referring to aspects of a person's own thoughts, feelings, or **behavior** that are **perceived** as unacceptable, undesirable, or inconsistent with the individual's self-concept; (*cf.* **ego-syntonic**).

ego-syntonic Referring to aspects of a person's own thoughts, feelings, or **behavior** that are perceived as acceptable, desirable, or consistent with the individual's self-concept; (*cf.* **ego-dystonic**).

emotion A strong **subjective** feeling state (such as anger, sadness, happiness, or fear), accompanied by **somatic** changes; (see **affect**).

empirical Based on **objective measurement,** naturalistic **observation,** direct **experience,** or **experimental** procedures, without explicit regard for any particular **theory** or philosophical orientation; capable of being verified or disproven by analyzing and testing evidence, **facts,** or other **quantified data;** (*cf.* **theoretical, hypothetical, abstract**).

erroneous To be false, mistaken, or wrong.

et al. And others (from the Latin, *et alia*).

ethics Moral principles or standards for human conduct in the pursuit of aims or goals; **prescriptions** for **behavior** based on personal or professional **values** (**e.g.,** good versus bad, moral versus immoral, acceptable versus unacceptable).

etiology The study of origins and **causes,** usually pertaining to **disease.**

evaluation The act of determining or appraising the relative worth, importance, or **value** of a person, object, **event,** or other **phenomenon;** the most fundamental **dimension** underlying **perception** and impression formation; (*cf.* **judgment, description, explanation, inference, interpretation**).

event An **observable, measurable,** or **empirical phenomenon;** any **physical** occurrence; (*cf.* **construct**).

Event (Type E) Theory A type of **theory** whose proposed **explanation** is, in principle, **measurable;** thus, given the proper circumstances, a Type E Theory is provable, and therefore refutable; (*cf.* **Construct Theory**).

existence A state of being; reality as presented in **experience;** (see **ontological**).

existentialism A philosophy centered on the analysis of **existence,** the nature of the human condition, and the search for meaning in life. Existentialism stresses **subjective phenomenology,** the active creation of **experience,** and the acceptance both of free will and personal responsibility in the individual's struggle to break free from the **causal** influences of biological and environmental determinism.

existential therapy A group of approaches to **psychotherapy,** founded on the philosophy of **existentialism** that focus on the uniqueness of each individual in the context of a here-and-now encounter. Emphasis is placed on those qualities that are distinctly human, such as the capacity for self-awareness, personal responsibility, and the freedom to determine one's own fate. **Treatment** goals typically include maximizing awareness, choices, authenticity, and personal growth.

expectation The anticipated outcome of a situation; (see **prediction, probability**).

experience 1. Any **event** through which one has lived. 2. **Observation,** participation, or learning derived from one's prior history or personal background that results in a state of enhanced **knowledge.** 3. The totality of one's immediate and **subjective perceptions,** current **phenomenological** awareness, or present **consciousness.**

experiment A **scientific** research method that enables the investigator to draw **valid** conclusions regarding **causal** relationships between various **phenomena.** More specifically, a procedure carried out under controlled conditions for the purpose of testing **hypotheses,** in which the investigator manipulates the **independent variable** (such as a **treatment**) while holding all other **variables** constant, thereby permitting him or her to assess its **effect** on the outcome **measure** or **dependent variable;** (see **internal validity, scientific method**).

explanation The process of making clear, accounting for, or providing the reasons for understanding various **phenomena;** (*cf.* **interpretation, evaluation, judgment, description, prediction**); (see **theory**).

external Situated or existing on the outside or exterior, usually of the body; (*cf.* **internal**).

external attribution Ascribing the **causes** of **behavior** to people's situational factors, such as their circumstances, surroundings, or environment; (*cf.* **internal attribution**); (see **Fundamental Attribution Error, Actor–Observer Bias**).

external validity The extent to which research findings in one setting can be safely related or generalized to other contexts, populations, or settings; (*syn* **generalizability, representativeness**); (*cf.* **internal validity**).

extraversion A fundamental **personality dimension** in which the individual is oriented toward, and derives gratification from, the **objective, external** world of people, things, and **events;** a general **psychological attitude** focusing on one's **social** and **physical** environment; (*cf.* **introversion**).

extravert An individual who displays characteristics of **extraversion.**

fact Information or **datum** presented as having **objectively** demonstrable **existence;** an **empirically** observed **event;** something that is actual or real.

fallacious A misleading or deceptive **inference** involving a **fallacy.**

fallacy A mistaken **belief** based on **erroneous reasoning,** faulty **logic,** or an invalid **inference,** the result of which is a conclusion that is seemingly true, but actually false.

family therapy A group of **interpersonal** approaches to **psychotherapy** founded on the principles of general systems **theory,** communications theory, and **psychodynamic** theory, which maintains that **behavior** can best be understood and changed in the context of a family system and that **symptoms** serve a function for the system.

fantasy As an **ego defense mechanism,** the **mental** process whereby the individual escapes from anxiety-provoking reality by seeking gratification in imaginary **events,** activities, or achievements.

Fundamental Attribution Error A **bias** in attempting to determine the **causes** of people's **behavior** which involves overestimating the influence of their **personality traits,** while underestimating the influence of their particular situations; that is, overutilizing **internal attributions** and underutilizing **external attributions;** (see **cognitive bias, motivational bias, Actor–Observer Bias**).

generalizability The extent to which findings in one setting can be safely applied, related, or extrapolated to other contexts, populations, or settings; (*syn* **external validity, representativeness**).

generalization 1. A **universal concept** arrived at by **inductive** examination of particular instances; an **inference,** drawn inductively, about a whole **category** based on **experience** with a limited component of that category. 2. In the context of **behavior theory,** the tendency for **stimuli** that are similar to the original **conditioned stimulus** to elicit similar **responses.**

generic 1. General; not specific. 2. Relating to, or characteristic of, all members of a particular group, class, or **category;** (see **ubiquitous, universal**).

Gestalt psychology The **scientific** study of human **perception.** A holistic, **phenomenological** approach that postulates that the **mind** actively and spontaneously seeks to organize, structure, or otherwise make sense out of **stimuli.** Because **behavior** is assumed to be a function of the individual's perceptions, the **critical** factor is seen as **subjective interpretation,** rather than "**objective**" reality. (From the German word *Gestalt,* which translates roughly as "shape" or "form," and is embodied in the Gestalt tenet that the perceived whole is greater than the sum of its parts.)

Gestalt therapy An approach to **psychotherapy** founded on the principles of **existentialism, Gestalt psychology,** and **phenomenological** field **theory,** that focuses on the **concepts** of unity, closure, and wholeness of the person. The primary **treatment** goal is broadened awareness, attained through the exploration and integration of **cognitive, emotional, sensory,** and motoric (muscular) functions.

heuristic 1. (*n*) A **mental** shortcut or rule-of-thumb strategy for problem solving that reduces complex information and time-consuming tasks to more simple, rapid, and efficient judgmental operations, particularly in reaching **decisions** under conditions of uncertainty; (see **availability heuristic, representativeness heuristic**). 2. (*adj*) Serving to stimulate **thinking,** learning, investigation, discovery, or problem-solving.

Hindsight Bias The tendency to overestimate or exaggerate what reasonably could have been anticipated or predicted, only after having learned the outcome; also known as the **I-knew-it-all-along phenomenon.**

Humanistic psychology Referred to as the "third force" in **psychology** (after **psychoanalysis** and **behaviorism**), Humanistic psychology emphasizes people's positive virtues and focuses on higher human **motives** and **values,** such as self-enhancement, self-actualization, and the potential for growth. Although in agreement with many of the major tenets of **existentialism** (such as **subjective phenomenology,** free will, and personal responsibility), a **critical** exception is Humanistic psychology's fundamental **belief** in the innate goodness of human beings. Humanistic theorists view the individual, at his or her core, as rational, trustworthy, and intrinsically motivated to make **decisions** in the direction of healthy functioning, which they define as more than simply the absence of **disease.**

humanistic therapy An approach to **psychotherapy** founded on the principles of **Humanistic psychology.** The therapy is client-centered and focuses on providing an atmosphere of genuineness, empathy, and unconditional positive regard so that the client's inherent actualizing **motives** may be permitted to emerge. Faith is placed in clients' ability ultimately to resolve their own problems. Maladjustment (**psychopathology**) is seen as arising primarily from obstructions to the client's intrinsic drive toward growth and an incongruence between what one wants to be (**i.e.,** "ideal self") and what one is (**i.e.,** "real self"); (*cf.* **existential therapy**).

hypothesis 1. A **predicted** relationship between **variables,** derived either from **observations** or a **theory,** that can be tested **empirically** to determine its accuracy. 2. A tentative statement, proposition, or **assumption** that expresses the relationship between **events,** for the purpose of investigation or argument. In contrast to theories, hypotheses do not seek an **explanation** of the underlying **causal** relationships between **variables;** (see **scientific method**).

hypothetical 1. Of or pertaining to a **hypothesis.** 2. **Abstract** or **theoretical.**

ideology A system of ideas or **beliefs,** usually at the core of any particular social,

political, religious, philosophic, or economic orientation.

idiographic 1. Of or pertaining to that which is individual, particular, or **concrete.** 2. An approach to research emphasizing those aspects of **personality** that are distinctive and unique to each person; (*cf.* **nomothetic**).

i.e. That is; that is to say (from the Latin, *id est*).

I-knew-it-all-along phenomenon (*syn* **Hindsight Bias**).

independent variable 1. In an **experiment,** the **variable** whose manipulation **causes** a change in the **value** of the outcome **measure, response,** or **dependent variable;** (*syn* experimental **treatment**). 2. In nonexperimental settings, any condition or factor that is related to a particular outcome.

induction 1. A form of **reasoning** that involves drawing an **inference** from specific instances to a general conclusion; (*cf.* **deduction**). 2. (*syn* **projective identification**).

inductive reasoning (*cf.* **deductive reasoning**); (see **induction**).

infer (see **inference**).

inference A conclusion derived implicitly or explicitly on the basis of prior premises, results, or other **data;** (see **deduction, induction**).

insight 1. A sudden and novel realization of a heretofore unknown explanation or solution to a problem. 2. Clinically, the extent of a client's awareness and understanding of his or her **psychological motives** and **dynamics.** 3. The result of **intuitive perception.**

Insight Fallacy The **erroneous belief** that understanding the **cause** of a problem will automatically solve the problem.

intellectualization An **ego defense mechanism** in which the individual analyzes a problem or conflict in remote, detached, **abstract,** or cerebral terms, while feelings and **emotions** are denied or ignored; (*cf.* **isolation of affect**).

intent (see **intentionality**).

intentionality A **mental** state involving a deliberate, willful, or **conscious** purpose, aim, or goal; volition; (*syn* **intent**).

internal Situated or existing on the inside or interior, usually of the body; (*cf.* **external**).

internal attribution **Ascribing** the **causes** of **behavior** to people's **dispositional** factors, such as their **personality traits**, characteristics, or **attitudes**; (*cf.* **external attribution**); (see **Fundamental Attribution Error, Actor–Observer Bias**).

internal validity In research, the extent to which a **cause** and **effect** relationship can be established between the **independent variable** and the **dependent variable**, free from contamination by extraneous or confounding **variables**; (*cf.* **external validity**).

interpersonal Of or relating to **social phenomena;** that which exists between individuals; (*cf.* **intrapsychic**).

interpretation 1. A meaningful **explanation** of a **phenomenon** based on one's pre-existing conceptual **schemas**, models, **theories**, or **beliefs**; (*cf.* **description, prediction, evaluation**). 2. In **psychoanalysis,** the act of **explaining** the significance of a client's dream symbols, free associations, **parapraxes, resistances,** or other **behaviors** to promote **insight** and understanding (**i.e.,** to make the **unconscious, conscious**).

Intervention–Causation Fallacy The mistaken **belief** that one's ability to modify an **event** inherently proves what originally **caused** the event; (see **Treatment–Etiology Fallacy**).

intrapsychic Existing or taking place within the **mind** or **psyche**; (*cf.* **interpersonal**).

introversion A fundamental **personality dimension** wherein the individual is oriented toward, and derives gratification from, the **subjective, internal** world of thoughts, **concepts,** and inner **experience;** a general **psychological attitude** focusing on one's **mental** processes; (*cf.* **extraversion**).

introvert An individual who displays characteristics of **introversion.**

intuition 1. Direct or immediate **knowledge** or **insight,** without **intentional** effort, **rational** thought, or **conscious judgment.** 2. **Perception** by means of the **unconscious;** a strong premonition or hunch in the absence of **objective empirical** evidence.

isolation of affect An **ego defense mechanism** in which the individual detaches, dissociates, or otherwise cuts off emotions from anxiety-arousing **events,** situations, or memories; (*cf.* **intellectualization**).

judge (*vb*) (see **judgment**).

judgment The act of forming an **opinion,** reaching a conclusion, or making a **decision** by comparing and **critically** evaluating two or more alternatives; (*cf.* **evaluation, inference, reasoning, interpretation**).

knowledge Awareness or **understanding** of specific information acquired by **experience** or study; the sum of what has been **perceived,** discovered, or learned.

linear 1. A direct and orderly sequence, pattern, or arrangement. 2. Of or relating to a straight line; (*cf.* **nonlinear**).

logic The study and process of the principles of **valid reasoning, inference,** and proof; (see **deduction, induction**).

measure/measurement 1. (*vb*) To ascertain, determine, or **evaluate** the quantity or magnitude of an entity by assigning a numeric **value** to a given **variable.** 2. (*n*) The **quantification** of a variable's **physical** properties, such as dimension, capacity, or amount. 3. (*n*) The comparison of an **observed phenomenon** or **event** with a standard scale. 4. (*n*) A test, scale, questionnaire, or other statistical device of quantification.

mental Pertaining to the **mind** or processes associated with the mind; (see **psychological**).

mental disorder (see **mental illness**).

mental illness 1. A term that is used traditionally to refer to a **clinical syndrome** characterized by significant distress, disability, and impairment in functioning, the violation of societal norms, and/or a markedly increased risk of suffering, over which the individual ostensibly has little or no control. 2. The metaphoric or alleged literal equivalent of **physical disease** or biological illness. 3. More broadly defined, any **disorder** or **dysfunction** of the **mind;** (see **psychopathology**).

meta   Transcending; used with the name of a discipline to designate a new but related discipline designed to deal **critically** with the original one; **e.g.**, metacommunication, metatheory, meta-analysis, **meta-thinking.**

metaphor   (*adj* metaphorical) A linguistic device or figure of speech whereby an **abstract concept** is expressed by means of **analogy** or symbolism.

metathinking   The act of **thinking** about thinking; engaging in a **critical** analysis and **evaluation** of the thinking process; (see **critical thinking**).

metathoughts   Literally, thoughts about thought; (see **metathinking, critical thinking**).

mind   A **construct** referring to the organized totality of one's **psychological** or **mental** processes, including but not limited to **conscious** awareness, **unconscious dynamics,** thoughts, **emotions,** memories, **perceptions,** and **motives;** (*syn* **psyche**).

mood   Predominant state of feeling or **emotion.**

motivation   (*syn* **motive**).

motivational bias   Any systematic error in **attribution** that derives from people's efforts to satisfy their own personal needs, such as the desire for self-esteem, power, or prestige; (*cf.* **cognitive bias**); (see **Fundamental Attribution Error**).

motive   An impetus, **stimulus,** or drive, either **internal** or **external,** that **causes** an individual to act.

myth   A widely accepted but false **belief.**

Naturalistic Fallacy   An error in **thinking** whereby the individual confuses or equates **objective descriptions** with **subjective** value judgments, in particular by defining what is morally good or bad solely in terms of what is statistically frequent or infrequent.

negative countertransference   (*cf.* **positive countertransference**); (see **countertransference, transference**).

negative transference   (*cf.* **positive transference**); (see **transference, countertransference**).

neurotic   A **generic** and somewhat dated term referring to any relatively benign but enduring and distressing **psychological** or **emotional disorders,** such as those characterized by extreme anxiety, preoccupation with things that might go wrong, obsessions, compulsions, phobias, **somatic symptoms,** or excessive use of **ego defense mechanisms.** By definition, neurotic conditions are less serious than **psychotic** disorders (**i.e.**, reality testing is intact) and the symptoms are recognized by the individual as unacceptable or **ego-dystonic.**

neutral   1. Free of personal or **subjective bias;** not favoring or allied with any particular perspective in a conflict or dispute; fair, impartial, or **objective.** 2. In the context of the **measurement** of **values, attitudes,** or **beliefs,** a middle region between the extremes of two polar opposites.

Nominal Fallacy   The mistaken **belief** that naming a **phenomenon,** in itself, **explains** the phenomenon. The Nominal Fallacy frequently involves the use of **tautologous reasoning.**

nomothetic   1. Pertaining to the formulation of general, **universal,** or **abstract** principles. 2. An approach to research that emphasizes those aspects of **personality** that are common to all persons; (*cf.* **idiographic**).

nonlinear   1. Absence of a direct and orderly sequence, pattern, or arrangement. 2. Not related or pertaining to a straight line; (*cf.* **linear**).

normal   That which does not deviate markedly from what is typical, common, or statistically average.

objective 1. (*adj*) Existing in **fact** or in **physical** reality, based on **concrete events** that are independent of an observer. 2. (*adj*) Accessible to **observation** and free of **subjective bias,** such as personal **beliefs, values, opinions,** or **interpretations;** (see **neutral**). 3. (*n*) A goal, purpose, or aim.

observation The act of purposive and **intentional** examination of an **event,** particularly with the goal of gathering and organizing **data;** noting and recording an occurrence by means of **empirical measurement.**

ontological Pertaining to **existence** and the nature of being.

opinion A tentatively held **belief** that typically is open to modification; a point of view that is stronger than an initial impression but less strong than **factual knowledge;** (see **attitude, judgment, decision**).

orthogonal Pertaining to **phenomena** that are independent, conceptually unrelated, or statistically uncorrelated; (see **correlation**).

paradox A seemingly contradictory statement or idea that may nevertheless be true; (see **paradoxical intention, paradoxical intervention**).

paradoxical intention (*syn* **paradoxical intervention**).

paradoxical intervention (*syn* **paradoxical intention**) A **psychotherapy** technique in which the client is encouraged or instructed to engage in, or even exaggerate, the very **behaviors** for which he or she is seeking **treatment.** The primary rationale for this technique is to undermine the client's **resistance** to change by rendering it useless.

parapraxis (*pl* parapraxes) Any apparent "mistake" in **behavior** that is allegedly due to **repressed, unconscious motives;** commonly referred to as a "Freudian slip."

parapsychology The study of paranormal **psychological phenomena,** that is, **events** that seemingly cannot be accounted for in terms of known **scien-**

tific principles or **theories;** examples include extrasensory perception (ESP), telepathy, psychokinesis, and clairvoyance.

parataxic reasoning A distortion of reality brought about by **inferring** a **causal** relationship between **events** that are actually independent or **orthogonal;** a kind of "magical thinking," frequently responsible for superstitious **behaviors,** in which **events** that occur close together in time are construed as causally linked; (see **Contiguity–Causation Error**).

pathological (*adj*) Strictly defined, that which pertains to an **abnormal somatic** or biological condition, **disease, disorder,** or illness involving serious impairment in **physical** functioning. By extension, defined **metaphorically** as pertaining to any abnormal **psychological** condition involving serious impairment in functioning; (see **psychopathology**).

pathology (*n*) (see **pathological**).

pedagogic Pertaining to the art, **science,** or profession of teaching.

perceive (*vb*) (see **perception**).

perception 1. An individual's **subjective** or **phenomenological** organization and **interpretation** of **sensory** information. 2. A **theoretical** intervening process or **variable** that links **physical stimuli** with the organism's unique **psychological** characteristics, such as past **experiences, schemas, beliefs, expectations, attitudes,** and **mood.** In this way, the meaning **ascribed** to an entity or **event** is determined by a synthesis of **stimulus** factors and organism factors.

per se By or in itself; as such; intrinsically.

personality An individual's unique pattern of **psychological** and **behavioral** characteristics that are relatively stable over time and across or within situations.

personality disorder A class of **psychological disorders** marked by enduring, inflexible, and maladaptive **personality traits** or characteristics that lead to persistent **subjective** distress or significant impairment in **social** functioning.

personality trait   A fundamental and relatively permanent **psychological disposition,** characteristic, or **dimension** that underlies **personality** and that, in **theory,** accounts for both the systematic consistency and variability in an individual's **behavior.**

phenomena   *(pl)* A broad term encompassing both **concrete events** and **abstract constructs;** *(sg* **phenomenon).**

phenomenon   *(sg)* (see **phenomena).**

phenomenology   *(adj* phenomenological) The **description** of one's immediate **subjective experience** and **perceptions** without analysis, **interpretation,** or **explanation.**   Phenomenology is based on awareness and exploring the **conscious** (as opposed to the **unconscious),** with a minimum focus on **objective events** or **external, physical** reality.

physical   The quality of being tangible, **concrete, observable,** or directly **measurable;** consisting of mass or material substance; *(cf.* **mental, abstract);** (see **somatic).**

point of critical distinction (PCD)   A **conceptual** boundary delineating one **phenomenon** from another, before which point they are similar, and after which they are different.

positive countertransference   *(cf.* **negative countertransference);** (see **countertransference, transference).**

positive transference   *(cf.* **negative transference);** (see **transference, countertransference).**

postdiction   A statement about an **event's** prior outcome, made **subsequent** to its actual occurrence; *(cf.* **prediction);** (see **description, explanation, Hindsight Bias).**

post hoc   1. After the fact; (Latin for "after this"). 2. A shortened form of *post hoc, ergo propter hoc* ("after this, therefore because of this"), referring to the **logical** error that because Event *B* follows Event *A,* then *B* must have been **caused** by *A;* (see **Contiguity–Causation Error).**

pragmatic   The quality of being practical or realistic; concerned with **concrete facts,** **events,** or results rather than **abstract** ideas, processes, or **theories.**

preconception   Any preexisting **belief, opinion, attitude, schema, theory,** frame of reference, or conclusion.

prediction   A forecast about the likelihood or **probability** of an **event's** outcome made prior to its actual occurrence; *(cf.* **postdiction; description, explanation);** (see **expectation, Hindsight Bias).**

premise   A proposition, supposition, or **assumption** on which an argument, **inference,** or conclusion is based; (see *a priori).*

prescription   A directive, order, endorsement, guideline, or injunction; any suggested or recommended course of action; *(cf.* **description, explanation).**

prima facie   At first sight, view, or appearance, before closer inspection; apparent or on the surface.

probability   1. The likelihood that an **event** will occur. 2. In mathematical terms, a numeric **value** that corresponds with the degree of certainty in one's statistical estimate or **prediction.**

procrustean (procrustean bed)   A **category, schema,** or pattern into which someone or something is arbitrarily forced, with no regard for individual differences or special circumstances.

projection   An **ego defense mechanism** by which the individual reduces anxiety by **attributing** his or her own unacceptable **(ego-dystonic)** desires, **beliefs, traits,** or conflicts to others.

projective hypothesis   An **assumption** underlying **projective tests** that proposes that when people are presented with an **ambiguous stimulus,** they will respond by automatically assigning or imposing **(i.e.,** "projecting") structure, organization, or meaning onto the stimulus, thereby revealing their **psychological dynamics,** both **conscious** and **unconscious.**

projective identification   An **ego defense** mechanism involving the **unconscious splitting** and **projection** of one's own unacceptable **(i.e., ego-dystonic)** attributes such that they elicit those very

behaviors in another person; (*syn* **induction**); (see **Self-Fulfilling Prophecy**).

projective test Any **psychological** assessment technique based on the **projective hypothesis** that involves exposing the examinee to a relatively unstructured or **ambiguous stimulus,** and then soliciting his or her **perceptions.** Examples include the Rorschach Inkblot Test, the Thematic Apperception Test (TAT), house-tree-person (HTP) projective drawing test, and sentence completion tests.

psyche Of or pertaining to the **mind.**

psychoanalysis 1. As originally proposed by Sigmund Freud, a **theory** of **personality** that emphasizes primarily **unconscious motivations** and **repressed** sexual and aggressive conflicts. 2. An approach to **psychotherapy treatment** based on psychoanalytic theory, utilizing the techniques of free association, dream **interpretation,** and the analysis of **transference, resistance, ego defense mechanisms,** and **parapraxes;** (*cf.* **psychodynamic theory, psychodynamic therapy**).

psychodynamic theory A relatively broad group of **personality theories,** which, despite their differences, share common emphases on **unconscious motivations,** the influence of childhood **experiences** on adult **thinking** and **behavior, intrapsychic** tensions and conflicts, **ego defense mechanisms,** and conceptualizing the **mind** in terms of exchanges and transformations of psychic energy. (**Psychoanalysis** is one specific subset of psychodynamic theory.)

psychodynamic therapy A group of approaches to **psychotherapy** founded on the principles of **psychodynamic theory.** Specific goals and techniques vary, but typically include **interpretations,** the "working through" of **resistance** and **transference,** and the attainment of **insight** and understanding; in short, to make the **unconscious, conscious;** (*cf.* **psychoanalysis**).

psychological Of or pertaining to any **mental** and **behavioral** processes, including

but not limited to thought, **emotion, attitude, perception,** memory, **motivation,** and intelligence.

psychological disorder (*syn* **psychopathology, mental disorder, mental illness**); (see **pathology, disease, dysfunction, symptom, syndrome, DSM**).

psychology The **scientific** study of **mental** and **behavioral** processes.

psychopathology 1. Any **psychological** or **emotional disorder;** (*syn* **mental disorder, mental illness**). 2. The **scientific** study of **psychological disorders.**

psychosis (*adj* **psychotic**) A severe **clinical syndrome** that broadly indicates gross impairment in reality testing.

psychotic (see **psychosis**).

psychotherapy The **treatment** of **mental** or **behavioral** problems by **psychological** methods. Commonly referred to as "therapy," particularly when modifiers are utilized to identify a specific **theoretical** orientation or **clinical** approach (**e.g., behavior therapy, cognitive therapy, cognitive–behavioral therapy, existential therapy, humanistic therapy, psychodynamic therapy, family therapy, Gestalt therapy**); (see **psychoanalysis, mental disorder, psychopathology**).

psychotropic (*adj*) Literally, **mind**-altering or **mood**-altering; usually as pertaining to medication; (*syn* psychoactive).

quantify To numerically express, determine, or **measure** the amount or quantity of an entity.

random The absence of any apparent or discernable order, direction, or purpose; occurring haphazardly or by **chance.**

rational (*adj*) Of or pertaining to **reasoning** and **logic,** rather than **emotion;** (*cf.* **rationalization**).

rationalization An **ego defense mechanism** involving the attempt to justify one's own **attitudes** or **behaviors** by making them appear to be reasonable, sensible, and **logical,** but which actually conceals, and is a pretext for, the true **motivation** of **unconscious** anxiety reduction; (*cf.* **rational**).

reaction formation An **ego defense mechanism** by which the individual copes with **repressed, ego-dystonic** wishes, impulses, or **attitudes** by **unconsciously** transforming them into their opposite, and therefore more acceptable, form.

reactive effect of testing A threat to a study's **external validity** wherein taking a pretest may modify research subjects' sensitivity to the subsequent **experimental treatment.**

reactive effects of experimental arrangements A threat to a study's **external validity** wherein the artificiality of the research setting, or the subjects' awareness that they are participating in a study, may significantly limit the extent to which a researcher may safely **generalize** the **effect** of the **experimental treatment** to people in nonexperimental settings.

reactivity A **phenomenon** wherein the conduct of research, in itself, affects the very entity that is being studied; the extent to which **measuring** something **causes** it to change.

reasoning The process of **thinking,** problem solving, or drawing **inferences** in a manner that is **rational,** logical, or coherent; (*cf.* **tautologous reasoning, parataxic reasoning**); (see **logic, deduction, induction**).

reciprocal (*adj*) 1. Of or pertaining to mutual influence, action, or exchange; (see **bi-directional causation**). 2. Inversely related; opposite.

reframing A **psychotherapy** technique involving a verbal redefinition of **dysfunctional** or undesirable **events** or **behaviors,** with the purpose of making them appear more positive, understandable, or controllable; (*syn* relabeling).

reification The act of treating an **abstract concept** or **theoretical construct** as if it were a **concrete event** or **physical** entity.

reify (*vb*) (see **reification**).

reinforcement The operation of strengthening the **probability** that a given

response will recur by the presentation of a rewarding **stimulus** or the removal of an aversive stimulus; (see **behaviorism**).

reliability (*adj* reliable) 1. The state of being dependable, trustworthy, or accurate. 2. An index of the extent to which a test or **measure** is consistent, either internally, over time, across observers, or between alternate forms; (*cf.* **validity**).

representativeness The extent to which findings in one setting can be safely related or generalized to other contexts, populations, or settings; (*syn* **external validity, generalizability**).

Representativeness Bias Any condition in which the **representativeness heuristic** produces systematic errors in **thinking** or information processing.

representativeness heuristic A **cognitive** strategy for quickly estimating the **probability** that a given instance is a member of a particular **category;** (see **heuristic, availability heuristic**).

repression An **ego defense mechanism** by which the individual reduces anxiety by **unconsciously** blocking out or forgetting particular thoughts, feelings, or memories, usually of a traumatic nature.

resistance 1. In **psychotherapy** (particularly **psychoanalysis**), the client's **unconscious** unwillingness to acknowledge or confront areas of **repressed** conflict. This may manifest itself in the form of unconscious opposition to, or deflection of, the therapist's probing questions or uncomfortable (but possibly accurate) **interpretations.** 2. The natural tendency of a living system (such as a family) to avoid, obstruct, or prevent changes (positive or negative) in its current homeostatic functioning, even if this involves the maintenance of distressing **symptoms** or the sabotage of **treatment.** 3. More broadly defined, an **interpersonal phenomenon** whereby one person declines or refuses to do what another person wants him or her to do; a **conscious,** willful, or deliberate act of defiance, disobedience, or rebelliousness.

response 1. A reaction to a **stimulus.** 2. Any **behavior,** whether overt or covert. 3. An answer or reply to a question; (see **dependent variable**).

schema (*pl* schemas, **schemata**) A **cognitive** structure or representation that organizes one's **knowledge, beliefs,** and past **experiences,** thereby providing a framework for understanding new **events** and future experiences; a general **expectation** or **preconception** about a wide range of **phenomena;** (see **stereotype**).

schemata (*pl*) (see **schema**).

science An organized and systematic body of **knowledge** and approach to the investigation of natural **phenomena,** as obtained and verified through the application of the **scientific method.** In contrast to philosophy, science requires that its procedures and conclusions satisfy the **criterion** of **empirical** proof.

scientific (*adj*) Of or pertaining to **science.**

scientific method A relatively standardized set of rules and procedures guiding the conduct of **science,** which rests on a foundation of **empirical** evidence and **valid reasoning.** Its essential features include: the use of known **facts, observations,** and **inductive reasoning** to construct **theories; deductive reasoning** to derive testable **hypotheses;** specific research methods (such as **experiments**) to collect **data;** statistical analyses to **evaluate** the results; sound **logic** to draw appropriate **inferences** and conclusions; and **critical thinking** principles to maximize **reliability, validity,** and usefulness.

Self-Fulfilling Prophecy A **phenomenon** whereby people's **attitudes, beliefs,** or **assumptions** about another person (or persons) can, with or without their **intent,** actually produce the very **behaviors** that they had initially **expected** to find.

semantic (*adj*) Of or pertaining to meaning, or the study of meaning, particularly as related to words and language.

sensory (*adj*) Of or pertaining to the five senses or to the neurological mechanisms involved in the process of sensation; (*cf.* **perception**).

shadow archetype Those components of people's own **personality** that are so repulsive, threatening, or frightening (**i.e., ego-dystonic**) to them that they refuse to acknowledge their existence and, instead, **unconsciously project** these disowned characteristics onto other individuals.

skepticism (*adj* skeptical) An **attitude** of suspended **judgment,** uncertainty, or doubt that reflects an unwillingness to accept any statement or **belief** as **truth** in the absence of **empirical** evidence or other **valid** proof; (see **critical thinking**).

social Of or relating to **interpersonal events** or relationships.

somatic (*adj.; n* soma) Of or pertaining to the body.

Spectacular Explanation Fallacy The **erroneous belief** that extraordinary **events** are necessarily due to extraordinary **causes.**

splitting An **ego defense mechanism** by which the individual attempts to resolve **unconscious** conflict by **bifurcating** ambivalent **attitudes** and feelings into good versus bad **categories,** thereby failing to integrate the positive and negative qualities of the self or others into a cohesive whole.

stereotype A simplistic, overgeneralized, and relatively rigid **preconception** about a particular **social category** or group of people; (*syn* role **schema**).

stimuli (*pl*) (see **stimulus**).

stimulus (*sg*) Any **physical** or **psychological event** that **causes** a **response;** an impetus that prompts an organism to action; (see **motive, reinforcement, conditioned stimulus, unconditioned stimulus**).

subjective Existing solely within the individual's **mind,** personal **perceptions,** or private, **internal experience,** and incapable of direct, **external** verification; (*cf.* **objective**); (see **phenomenology**).

subsequent That which ensues or follows an **event,** occurrence, or condition, whose relationship may or may not involve **causality;** (*cf.* **antecedent**).

symptom   1. A **phenomenon** regarded as an indicator or manifestation of a medical **disease, psychological disorder,** or other **pathological** condition.
2. **Subjective perception** of illness, typically reported by the affected individual, rather than observed by the examiner; (see **syndrome**).

synchronicity   (*n; adj* **synchronistic**) An extraordinary or uncanny coincidence to which the person involved **ascribes** unique and significant meaning; a link between two events that is connected through their **subjectively experienced** meaning to the individual and that ostensibly cannot be explained or accounted for by the principles of direct **causation.**

syndrome   A cluster of related signs and **symptoms** that collectively characterize or constitute a particular medical **disease, psychological disorder,** or other **pathological** condition.

tautological reasoning   (see **tautologous reasoning**).

tautologous reasoning   Circular **reasoning** in which one conclusion rests upon another, which in turn refers back to the first. Tautologies involve the needless repetition of an idea, statement, or word, wherein the **phenomenon** is true by virtue of its **logical** form alone; thus, a tautology can never be falsified; (*syn* **tautological reasoning**).

taxonomy   Any classification system of **abstract** or **concrete phenomena,** based on their similarities and differences; (see **category, point of critical distinction**).

temporal   Of or pertaining to time.

temporal contiguity   Referring to the occurrence of one **event** immediately after or immediately before another event; two events that occur side by side in time; (see **Contiguity–Causation Error, parataxic reasoning**).

theoretical   1. Of or pertaining to **theory.**
2. **Abstract or hypothetical.**

theory   1. A proposed **explanation** of observed **events;** (see **Event Theory, Construct Theory**). 2. A systematic statement that sets forth the apparent relationships and underlying principles that make a domain of observable **phenomena** and **empirical** findings meaningful. In contrast to **hypotheses** (which seek to make **predictions** between **variables**), theories seek to explain the **causal** relationships between variables; (see **scientific method**).

thinking   The **mental** process of producing ideas; exercising the powers of intellect, **reasoning, logic, judgment, conception,** memory, or **inference;** (*syn* **cognition**).

trait   Any relatively enduring **physical** or **psychological** characteristic, feature, or **disposition;** (see **personality trait**).

transference   A distorted **perception,** usually **unconscious,** on the part of the client toward a psychotherapist based on his or her prior relationship **experiences;** the perception may be favorable (**positive transference**) or unfavorable (**negative transference**); (*cf.* **countertransference**).

treatment   1. In the **clinical** context, any medical or **psychotherapy** procedure whose purpose is to alleviate or eliminate a particular **disorder, disease,** or other related problem; (see **antidote, prescription**). 2. In research, an **experimental** condition or type of **independent variable.** 3. More broadly defined, the specific manner in which an individual regards, handles, deals with, cares for, or otherwise behaves toward another person.

Treatment–Etiology Fallacy   The **erroneous belief** that a favorable **response** to medical **treatment** is, in itself, proof of medical **disease;** (see **Intervention–Causation Fallacy**).

truth   1. The property of any statement or **belief** that is in accordance with **fact,** accuracy, or reality; (*syn* **veracity**). 2. The quality of being honest, candid, or sincere.

ubiquitous   (*adj*) Any **phenomenon** that is common, widespread, or omnipresent.

ubiquity (*n*) (see **ubiquitous**).

unconditioned response (UCR) In classical conditioning, an innate or unlearned **response** to an **unconditioned stimulus;** (*cf.* **conditioned response**); (see **behaviorism**).

unconditioned stimulus (UCS) In classical conditioning, any **stimulus** that elicits an unlearned or **unconditioned response;** (*cf.* **conditioned stimulus**); (see **behaviorism**).

unconscious 1. (*adj*) The **mental** state of being unaware or lacking in awareness. 2. (*adj*) A loss of consciousness. 3. (*adj*) According to **cognitive theorists,** information processing that is automatic, rapid, and essentially unintentional and out of awareness. 4. (*n*) According to **psychodynamic theorists,** that part of the **psyche** that is largely unknown, irrational, and **repressed,** but that nevertheless exerts a significant influence on people's **motivations, attitudes, perceptions, emotions,** and **behavior;** (*cf.* **conscious**).

uni-directional causation A relationship between two **variables** wherein one is the **cause** and the other is the **effect;** (*cf.* **bi-directional causation**).

universal Of or pertaining to that which is global, general, extensive, or omnipresent; (see **ubiquitous, generic**).

utility The quality of being useful; having practical relevance, **value,** or worth for some particular purpose; (*syn* **pragmatic**).

validity (*n; adj* valid) 1. The quality of being meaningful, correct, or well-grounded. 2. An index of the extent to which a test actually **measures** what it purports to measure; (*cf.* **reliability**); (see **internal validity, external validity**).

value 1. A material object or **social** principle that is held in high regard or **perceived** as desirable, worthwhile, or useful. 2. A numerical quantity that is assigned or is determined by calculation or **measurement.**

variable (*n*) 1. A characteristic, property, or attribute that may assume any one of a set of different qualities or quantities. 2. That which is capable of changing or being changed; (see **continuous variable, dichotomous variable**).

veracity The quality of being true, correct, **factual,** or real; (*syn* **truth**); (*cf.* **erroneous**).

vicarious 1. That which is learned or **experienced** indirectly by one person through another person via **observation,** proxy, or modeling. 2. Pertaining to or functioning as a substitute or surrogate.

vignette A short, **descriptive** sketch, synopsis, or narrative.

vivid Any property of a **stimulus** that produces a strong, intense, and usually immediate impact on one's attention, senses, or **perceptions;** characteristic of **events** that are dramatic, graphic, salient, striking, or otherwise memorable.

viz. Namely (from the Latin, *videlicet*).

References

American Psychiatric Association. (1987). *Diagnostic and statistical manual of mental disorders* (3rd ed., rev.). Washington, DC: Author.

American Psychiatric Association. (1994). *Diagnostic and statistical manual of mental disorders* (4th ed.). Washington, DC: Author.

Anastasi, A. (1988). *Psychological testing* (6th ed.). New York: Macmillan.

Anderson, C. A. (1982). Inoculation and counter-explanation: Debiasing techniques in the perseverance of social theories. *Social Cognition, 1,* 126–139.

Anderson, C. A., Lepper, M. R., & Ross, L. (1980). Perseverance of social theories: The role of explanation in the persistence of discredited information. *Journal of Personality and Social Psychology, 39,* 1037–1049.

Andreason, N. J. C., & Canter, A. (1974). The creative writer: Psychiatric symptoms and family history. *Comprehensive Psychiatry, 15*(2), 123–131.

Andreason, N. J. C., & Powers, P. S. (1975). Creativity and psychosis: An examination of conceptual style. *Archives of General Psychiatry, 32,* 70–73.

Angeles, P. A. (1981). *Dictionary of philosophy.* New York: Harper & Row.

Asch, S. (1946). Forming impressions of personality. *Journal of Abnormal and Social Psychology, 41,* 258–290.

Barber, J. W. (1971). *The book of 1000 proverbs.* New York: American Heritage Press. (Original work published 1876)

Bartlett, J. (1968). *Familiar quotations* (14th ed.). Boston: Little, Brown.

Bass, E., & Davis, L. (1988). *The courage to heal.* New York: Harper & Row.

Baumrind, D. (1983). Rejoinder to Lewis's reinterpretation of parental firm control effects: Are authoritative families really harmonious? *Psychological Bulletin, 94,* 132–142.

Berscheid, E. (1982). Attraction and emotions in interpersonal relationships. In M. S. Clark & S. T. Fiske (Eds.), *Affect and cognition: The 17th Annual Carnegie Symposium on Cognition.* Hillsdale, NJ: Erlbaum.

Bertalanffy, L. von. (1968). *General systems theory: Foundation, development, applications.* New York: Braziller.

Bloch, A. (1980). *Murphy's Law, Book Two.* Los Angeles: Price/Stern/Sloan.

Borgida, E., & Nisbett, R. E. (1977). The differential impact of abstract vs. concrete information on decisions. *Journal of Applied Social Psychology, 7,* 258–271.

Breuer, J., & Freud, S. (1895). Studies on hysteria. In *The standard edition of the complete psychological works of Sigmund Freud* (Vol. 2). London: Hogarth Press, 1955.

Bruner, J. S., & Potter, M. C. (1964). Interference in visual recognition. *Science, 144,* 424–425.

Buber, M. (1958). *I and thou.* New York: Charles Scribner's Sons.

Buri, J. R., Louiselle, P. A., Misukanis, T. M., & Mueller, R. A. (1988). Effects of parental authoritarianism and authoritativeness on self-esteem. *Personality and Social Psychology Bulletin, 14,* 271–282.

Cacioppo, J. T., & Berntson, G. G. (1992). Social psychological contributions to the decade of the brain: Doctrine of multilevel analysis. *American Psychologist, 47*(8), 1019–1028.

Campbell, D. T., & Stanley, J. C. (1963). *Experimental and quasi-experimental designs for research.* Chicago: Rand McNally.

Cantor, N., & Mischel, W. (1977). Traits as prototypes: Effects on recognition memory. *Journal of Personality and Social Psychology, 35,* 38–48.

Cantor, N., & Mischel, W. (1979). Prototypes in person perception. In L. Berkowitz (Ed.), *Advances in experimental social psychology* (Vol. 12, pp. 3–52). New York: Academic Press.

Carroll, J. B. (Ed.). (1956). *Language, thought, and reality: Selected writings of Benjamin Lee Whorf.* New York: Wiley.

Carson, R. C. (in press). Aristotle, Galileo, and the *DSM* taxonomy: The case of schizophrenia. *Journal of Consulting and Clinical Psychology.*

Coopersmith, S. (1967). *The antecedents of self-esteem.* San Francisco: Freeman.

Corey, G. (1991). *Theory and practice of counseling and psychotherapy* (4th ed.). Pacific Grove, CA: Brooks/Cole Publishing.

Darley, J. M., & Fazio, R. H. (1980). Expectancy confirmation processes arising in the social interaction sequence. *American Psychologist, 35,* 867–881.

Davidoff, H. (1952). *The pocket book of quotations.* New York: Pocket Books.

Dickson, D. H., & Kelly, I. W. (1985). The "Barnum Effect" in personality assessment: A review of the literature. *Psychological Reports, 57,* 367–382.

Dukas, H., & Hoffman, B. (Eds.). (1979). *Albert Einstein: The human side.* Princeton, N.J.: Princeton University Press.

Ellis, A. (1984). Rational-emotive therapy. In R. Corsini (Ed.), *Current psychotherapies* (3rd ed., pp. 196–238). Itasca, IL: Peacock.

Ellis, A., & Bernard, M. E. (1985). What is rational-emotive therapy (RET)? In A. Ellis & M. E. Bernard (Eds.), *Clinical applications of rational-emotive therapy* (pp. 1–30). New York: Plenum Press.

Erdelyi, M. H., & Goldberg, B. (1979). Let's not sweep repression under the rug: Toward a cognitive psychology of repression. In J. F. Kihlstrom & F. J. Evans (Eds.), *Functional disorders of memory* (pp. 355–402). Hillsdale, NJ: Erlbaum.

Erikson, E. H. (1950). *Childhood and society.* New York: Norton.

Exner, J. E., Jr. (1990). *A Rorschach workbook for the comprehensive system* (3rd ed.). Asheville, NC: Rorschach Workshops.

Exner, J. E., Jr. (1993). *The Rorschach: A comprehensive system Volume 1: Basic foundations* (3rd ed.). New York: John Wiley & Sons.

Eysenck, H. J. (1957). *Sense and nonsense in psychology.* Harmondsworth, Middlesex, England: Pelican Books.

Eysenck, H. J. (1985). *Decline and fall of the Freudian empire.* London: Viking.

Farina, A. (1982). The stigma of mental disorders. In A. G. Miller (Ed.), *In the eye of the beholder.* New York: Praeger.

Fazio, R. H., Effrein, E. A., & Fallender, V. J. (1981). Self-perceptions following social interaction. *Journal of Personality and Social Psychology, 41,* 232–242.

Feldman, R. S., & Prohaska, T. (1979). The student as Pygmalion: Effect of student expectation on the teacher. *Journal of Educational Psychology, 71,* 485–493.

Feldman, R. S., & Theiss, A. J. (1982). The teacher and student as Pygmalions: Joint effects of teacher and student expectations. *Journal of Educational Psychology, 74,* 217–223.

Fersch, E. A. (1980). *Psychology and psychiatry in courts and corrections.* New York: Wiley.

Feshbach, S., & Weiner, B. (1986). *Personality* (2nd ed.). Lexington, MA: D. C. Heath.

Festinger, L. (1957). *A theory of cognitive dissonance.* Stanford: Stanford University Press.

Festinger, L., & Carlsmith, J. M. (1959). Cognitive consequences of forced compliance. *Journal of Abnormal and Social Psychology, 58,* 203–210.

Fischoff, B. (1975). Hindsight ≠ foresight: The effects of outcome knowledge on judgment under uncertainty. *Journal of Experimental Psychology: Human Perception and Performance, 1,* 288–299.

Fischoff, B. (1980). For those condemned to study the past: Reflections on historical judgment. In R. A. Shweder (Ed.), *New directions for methodology of social and behavioral science* (Vol. 4). San Francisco: Jossey-Bass.

Fischoff, B. (1982). For those condemned to study the past: Heuristics and biases in hindsight. In D. Kahneman, P. Slovic, & A. Tversky (Eds.), *Judgment under uncertainty: Heuristics and biases.* New York: Cambridge University Press.

Fischoff, B., & Beyth, R. (1975). "I knew it would happen"—Remembered probabilities of once future things. *Organizational Behavior and Human Performance, 13,* 1–16.

Fiske, S. T., & Taylor, S. E. (1984). *Social cognition.* Reading, MA: Addison-Wesley.

Forer, B. R. (1949). The fallacy of personal validation: A classroom demonstration of gullibility. *Journal of Abnormal and Social Psychology, 44,* 118–123.

Frank, L. K. (1939). Projective methods for the study of personality. *Journal of Psychology, 8,* 389–413.

Frankl, V. E. (1959). *Man's search for meaning: An introduction to logotherapy.* New York: Washington Square Press.

Freud, A. (1936). The ego and the mechanisms of defense. In *The writings of Anna Freud* (Vol. 2). New York: International Universities Press.

Freud, S. (1953). The interpretation of dreams. In J. Strachey (Ed. and Trans.), *The standard edition of the complete psychological works of Sigmund Freud* (Vol. 4–5, pp. 1–621). London: Hogarth Press. (Original work published 1900)

Freud, S. (1961). Civilization and its discontents. In J. Strachey (Ed. and Trans.), *The standard edition of the complete psychological works of Sigmund Freud* (Vol. 21, pp. 64–145). London: Hogarth Press. (Original work published 1930)

Freud, S. (1964). New introductory lectures. In J. Strachey (Ed. and Trans.), *The standard edition of the complete psychological works of Sigmund Freud* (Vol. 22, pp. 7–182). London: Hogarth Press. (Original work published 1933)

Greenwald, J. (1986, January 13). Is there cause for fear of flying? *Time,* pp. 39–40.

Haley, J. (1976). *Problem-solving therapy.* San Francisco, CA: Jossey-Bass.

Hamilton, D. L. (1979). A Cognitive–attributional analysis of stereotyping. In L. Berkowitz (Ed.), *Advances in experimental social psychology* (Vol. 12, pp. 53–81). New York: Academic Press.

Hamilton, D. L. (1981). *Cognitive processes in stereotyping and intergroup behavior.* Hillsdale, NJ: Erlbaum.

Heider, F. (1958). *The psychology of interpersonal relations.* New York: Wiley.

Higgins, E. T., & Bargh, J. A. (1987). Social cognition and social perception. *Annual Review of Psychology, 38,* 369–425.

Holden, C. (1980a). Identical twins reared apart. *Science, 207,* 1323–1325.

Holden, C. (1980b, November). Twins reunited. *Science, 80,* pp. 55–59.

Holmes, D. (1990). The evidence for repression: An examination of sixty years of research. In J. Singer (Ed.), *Repression and dissociation: Implications for personality, theory, psychopathology, and health* (pp. 85–102). Chicago: University of Chicago Press.

Horwitz, L. (1983). Projective identification in dyads and groups. *International Journal of Group Psychotherapy, 33,* 254–279.

Huesmann, L. R. (1982). Television violence and aggressive behavior. In D. Pearl & L. Bouthilet (Eds.), *Television and behavior: Ten years of scientific progress and implications for the 80's.* Washington, DC: U.S. Government Printing Office.

Huesmann, L. R., Lagerspetz, K., & Eron, L. D. (1983). Intervening variables in the television violence–aggression relation: Evidence from the two countries. *Developmental Psychology, 19,* 71–77.

Huxley, A. (1959). *Collected essays.* New York: Harper.

Jamieson, D. W., Lydon, J. E., Stewart, G., & Zanna, M. P. (1984). *Pygmalion revisited: New evidence for student expectancy effects in the classroom.* Paper presented at the meeting of the American Psychological Association.

Jamison, K. R. (1993). *Touched with fire: Manic-depressive illness and the artistic temperament.* New York: Free Press.

Jones, E. E., & Harris, V. A. (1967). The attribution of attitudes. *Journal of Experimental Social Psychology, 3,* 2–24.

Jones, E. E., & Nisbett, R. E. (1972). The actor and the observer: Divergent perceptions of the causes of behavior. In E. E. Jones et al. (Eds.), *Attribution: Perceiving the causes of behavior.* Morristown, NJ: General Learning Press.

Jung, C. G. (1953). Two essays on analytical psychology. In H. Read (Ed.) and F. C. Hull (Trans.), *The collected works of C. G. Jung* (Vol. 7, pp. 8–292). Princeton, NJ: Princeton University Press. (Original work published 1943)

Jung, C. G. (1959). Aion: Researches into the phenomenology of the self. In H. Read (Ed.) and F. C. Hull (Trans.), *The collected works of*

C. G. Jung (Vol. 9ii, pp. 3–269). Princeton, NJ: Princeton University Press. (Original work published 1951)

Jung, C. G. (1961). *Memories, dreams, reflections* (R. Winston & C. Winston, Trans.). New York: Random House.

Jung, C. G. (1969). Synchronicity: An acausal connecting principle. In H. Read (Ed.) and F. C. Hull (Trans.), *The collected works of C. G. Jung* (Vol. 8, pp. 421–519). Princeton, NJ: Princeton University Press. (Original work published 1952)

Jung, C. G. (1971). Psychological types. In H. Read (Ed.) and F. C. Hull (Trans.), *The collected works of C. G. Jung* (Vol. 6, pp. 3–555). Princeton, NJ: Princeton University Press. (Original work published 1921)

Kahneman, D., & Tversky, A. (1982). The simulation heuristic. In D. Kahneman, P. Slovic, & A. Tversky (Eds.), *Judgment under uncertainty: Heuristics and biases* (pp. 201–209). New York: Cambridge University Press.

Kaplan, H. S. (1974). *The new sex therapy: Active treatment of sexual dysfunctions.* New York: Brunner/Mazel.

Kelley, H. H. (1950). The warm-cold variable in first impressions of persons. *Journal of Personality, 18,* 431–439.

Kelley, H. H. (1967). Attribution theory in social psychology. In D. Levine (Ed.), *Nebraska Symposium of Motivation* (Vol. 15, pp. 192–240). Lincoln, NE: University of Nebraska Press.

Klayman, J., & Ha, Y-W. (1987). Confirmation, disconfirmation, and information in hypothesis testing. *Psychological Review, 94,* 211–228.

Klein, M. (1937). *The psycho-analysis of children* (2nd ed.). London: Hogarth.

Klein, M. (1946). Notes on some schizoid mechanisms. *International Journal of Psycho-Analysis, 33,* 433–438.

Kosko, B. (1993). *Fuzzy thinking: The new science of fuzzy logic.* New York: Hyperion.

Laing, R. D. (1967). *The politics of experience.* New York: Pantheon Books.

Laing, R. D. (1969). *The politics of the family and other essays.* New York: Pantheon Books.

Laing, R. D. (1970). *Knots.* New York: Random House.

Laing, R. D. (1975). In R. I. Evans (Producer) & R. Cozens (Director). *R. D. Laing's discussion with Richard Evans: Dilemma of mental illness* [Film]. University Park, PA: Penn State Audio-Visual Services.

Laing, R. D. (1976). *The facts of life: An essay in feelings, facts, and fantasy.* New York: Random House.

Lawrence, J., & Lee, R. E. (1955). *Inherit the wind.* New York: Random House.

Lepper, M. R., Ross, L., & Lau, R. R. (1986). Persistence of inaccurate beliefs about the self: Perseverance effects in the classroom. *Journal of Personality and Social Psychology, 50,* 482–491.

Lerner, M. J. (1970). The desire for justice and reactions to victims. In J. McCauley & L. Berkowitz (Eds.), *Altruism and helping behavior.* New York: Academic Press.

Levy, D. A. (1985). Optimism and pessimism: Relationships to circadian rhythms. *Psychological Reports, 57*(3), 1123–1126.

Levy, D. A. (1991, Spring). How to be a good psychotherapy patient. *Journal of Polymorphous Perversity, 8*(1), 17–19.

Levy, D. A. (1992). A proposed category for the diagnostic and statistical manual of mental disorders (DSM): Pervasive labeling disorder. *Journal of Humanistic Psychology, 32*(1), 121–125.

Levy, D. A. (1993, Spring). Psychometric infallibility realized: The one-size-fits-all psychological profile. *Journal of Polymorphous Perversity, 10*(1), 3–6.

Levy, D. A. (1994). Is the remedicalization of psychiatry good for the mental health field? No. In S. A. Kirk & S. D. Einbinder (Eds.), *Controversial issues in mental health* (pp. 160–176). Boston, MA: Allyn & Bacon.

Levy, D. A., & Erhardt, D. D. (1988). Stinks and instincts: An empirical investigation of Freud's excreta theory. *Journal of Irreproducible Results, 33*(5), 8–9.

Levy, D. A., Kaler, S. R., & Schall, M. (1988). An empirical investigation of role schemata: Occupations and personality characteristics. *Psychological Reports, 63,* 3–14.

Levy, D. A., & Nail, P. R. (1993). Contagion: A theoretical and empirical review and reconceptualization. *Genetic, Social, and General Psychology Monographs, 119*(2), 233–284.

Lewin, K. (1931). The conflict between Aristotelian and Galileian modes of thought in contemporary psychology. *Journal of General Psychology, 5,* 141–177.

Link, B. G., Cullen, F. T., Frank, J., & Wozniak, J. F. (1987). The social rejection of former mental patients: Understanding why labels matter. *American Journal of Sociology, 92,* 1461–1500.

Loftus, E. F. (1993). The reality of repressed memories. *American Psychologist, 48*(5), 518–537.

Loftus, E. & Ketcham, K. (1994). *The myth of repressed memory: False memories and allegations of sexual abuse.* New York: St. Martin's Griffin.

Lord, C. G., Lepper, M. R., & Preston, E. (1984). Considering the opposite: A corrective strategy for social judgment. *Journal of Personality and Social Psychology, 47,* 1231–1247.

Lord, C. G., Ross, L., & Lepper, M. (1979). Biased assimilation and attitude polarization: The effects of prior theories on subsequently considered evidence. *Journal of Personality and Social Psychology, 37,* 2098–2109.

Mahler, M. S., Pine, F., & Bergman, A. (1975). *The psychological birth of the human infant.* New York: Basic Books.

Mandler, G. (1975). *Mind and emotion.* New York: Wiley.

Maslow, A. (1970). *Motivation and personality* (2nd ed.). New York: Harper & Row.

McGuire, W. J., & Papageorgis, D. (1961). The relative efficacy of various types of prior belief defense in producing immunity against persuasion. *Journal of Abnormal and Social Psychology, 62,* 327–337.

Meehl, P. E. (1956). Wanted—A good cookbook. *American Psychologist, 11,* 262–272.

Meehl, P. E. (1973). Why I do not attend case conferences. In P. E. Meehl (Ed.), *Psychodiagnosis: Selected papers* (pp. 225–302). Minneapolis: University of Minnesota Press.

Milgram, S. (1963). Behavioral study of obedience. *Journal of Abnormal and Social Psychology, 67*(4), 371–378.

Milgram, S. (1974). *Obedience to authority.* New York: Harper & Row.

Miner, M., & Rawson, H. (1994). *The new international dictionary of quotations* (2nd ed.). New York: Signet.

Miller, J. (1983). *States of mind.* New York: Pantheon Books.

Myers, D. G. (1995). *Psychology* (4th ed.). New York: Worth Publishers.

Myers, J. K., Weissman, M. M., Tischler, G. L., Holzer, C. E., Leaf, P. J., Orvaschel, H., Anthony, J. C., Boyd, J. H., Burke, J. D., Kramer, M., & Stolzman, R. (1984). Six-month prevalence of psychiatric disorders in three communities: 1980 to 1982. *Archives of General Psychiatry, 41,* 959–967.

Naiman, A. (1981). *Every goy's guide to common Jewish expressions.* Boston, MA: Houghton Mifflin.

Napolitan, D. A., & Goethals, G. R. (1979). The attribution of friendliness. *Journal of Experimental Social Psychology, 15,* 105–113.

Nickerson, R. S., Perkins, D. N., & Smith, E. E. (1985). *The teaching of thinking.* Hillsdale, NJ: Erlbaum.

Page, S. (1977). Effects of the mental illness label in attempts to obtain accomodation. *Canadian Journal of Behavioral Science, 9,* 84–90.

Pascal, B. (1966). *Pensées.* (A. J. Krailsheimer, Trans.). Harmondsworth, Middlesex, England: Penguin Books.

Perls, F. S. (1969). *Gestalt therapy verbatim.* Lafayette, CA: Real People Press.

Piaget, J. (1948). *The moral judgment of the child.* New York: Free Press.

Piaget, J. (1952). *The origins of intelligence in children.* New York: International Universities Press.

Piaget, J. (1954). *The construction of reality in the child.* New York: Basic Books.

Piaget, J. (1970). Piaget's theory. In P. H. Mussen (Ed.), *Carmichael's manual of child psychology* (3rd ed., Vol. 1, pp. 773–847). New York: John Wiley.

Plomin, R., & Daniels, D. (1987). Why are children in the same family so different from one another? *Behavioral and Brain Sciences, 10,* 1–60.

Reason, J., & Mycielska, K. (1982). *Absent-minded? The psychology of mental lapses and everyday errors.* Englewood Cliffs, NJ: Prentice-Hall.

Regier, D. A., Boyd, J. H., Burke, J. D., Rae, D. S., Myers, J. K., Kramer, M., Robins, L. N., George, L. K., Karno, M., & Locke, B. Z. (1988). One-month prevalence of mental disorders in the United States. *Archives of General Psychiatry, 45,* 877–986.

Robins, L. N., Helzer, J. E., Weissman, M. M., Orvaschel, H., Gruenberg, E., Burke, J. D., & Regier, D. A. (1984). Lifetime prevalence of specific psychiatric disorders in three sites. *Archives of General Psychiatry, 41,* 949–958.

Roethlisberger, F. J., & Dickson, W. J. (1939). *Management and the worker.* Cambridge, MA: Harvard University Press.

Rosenhan, D. L. (1973). On being sane in insane places. *Science, 179,* 250–258.

Rosenhan, D. L., & Seligman, M. E. P. (1995). *Abnormal psychology* (3rd ed.). New York: Norton.

Rosenthal, R., & Fode, K. (1963). The effect of experimental bias on the performance of the albino rat. *Behavioral Science, 8,* 183–189.

Rosenthal, R., & Jacobson, L. (1968). *Pygmalion in the classroom: Teacher expectation and pupils' intellectual development.* New York: Holt, Rinehart, & Winston.

Ross, L. (1977). The intuitive psychologist and his shortcomings: Distortions in the attribution process. In L. Berkowitz (Ed.), *Advances in experimental social psychology* (Vol. 10). New York: Academic Press.

Ross, L. D., Amabile, T. M., & Steinmetz, J. L. (1977). Social roles, social control, and biases in social-perception processes. *Journal of Personality and Social Psychology, 35,* 485–494.

Ross, L. D., & Lepper, M. R. (1980). The perseverance of beliefs: Empirical and normative considerations. In R. A. Shweder (Ed.), *New directions for methodology of behavioral science: Fallible judgment in behavioral research.* San Francisco: Jossey-Bass.

Ross, L. D., Lepper, M. R., & Hubbard, M. (1975). Perseverance in self-perception and social perception: Biased attribution processes in the debriefing paradigm. *Journal of Personality and Social Psychology, 32,* 880–892.

Rosten, L. (1968). *The joys of Yiddish.* New York: Pocket Books.

Rowes, B. (1979). *The book of quotes.* New York: E. P. Dutton.

Runyan, W. M. (1981). Why did Van Gogh cut off his ear? The problem of alternative explanations in psychobiography. *Journal of Personality and Social Psychology, 40,* 1070–1077.

Ryle, G. (1949). *The concept of mind.* London: Hutchinson's University Library.

Santrock, J. W. (1995). *Life-span development.* Dubuque, IA: Wm. C. Brown Communications.

Sears, D. O., Peplau, L. A., & Taylor, S. E. (1991). *Social psychology* (7th ed.). Englewood Cliffs, NJ: Prentice-Hall.

Shaw, G. B. (1913). *Pygmalion: A romance in five acts.* New York: Random House.

Skov, R. B., & Sherman, S. J. (1986). Information-gathering processes: Diagnosticity, hypothesis-confirmatory strategies, and perceived hypothesis confirmation. *Journal of Experimental Social Psychology, 22,* 93–121.

Skrypnek, B. J., & Snyder, M. (1982). On the self-perpetuating nature of stereotypes about women and men. *Journal of Experimental Social Psychology, 18,* 277–291.

Slovic, P. (1987). Perception of risk. *Science, 236,* 280–285.

Slovic, P., & Fischhoff, B. (1977). On the psychology of experimental surprises. *Journal of Experimental Psychology: Human Perception and Performance, 3,* 544–551.

Slovic, P., Fischoff, B., & Lichtenstein, S. (1976). Cognitive processes and societal risk taking. In J. S. Carroll & J. W. Payne (Eds.), *Cognition and social behavior.* Hillsdale, NJ: Erlbaum.

Smith, M. B. (1978). Psychology and values. *Journal of Social Issues, 34,* 181–199.

Snyder, C. R., Shenkel, R. J., & Lowery, C. R. (1977). Acceptance of personality interpretations: The "Barnum Effect" and beyond. *Journal of Consulting and Clinical Psychology, 45*(1), 104–114.

Snyder, M. (1984). When belief becomes reality. In L. Berkowitz (Ed.), *Advances in Experimental Social Psychology* (Vol. 18). New York: Academic Press.

Snyder, M., & Swann, W. B., Jr. (1978). Behavioral confirmation in social interaction:

From social perception to social reality. *Journal of Experimental Social Psychology, 14,* 148–162.

Snyder, M., Tanke, E. D., & Berscheid, E. (1977). Social perception and interpersonal behavior: On the self-fulfilling nature of social stereotypes. *Journal of Personality and Social Psychology, 35,* 656–666.

Spitzer, R. L. (1975). On pseudoscience in science, logic in remission, and psychiatric diagnosis: A critique of Rosenhan's "On being sane in insane places." *Journal of Abnormal Psychology, 84,* 442–452.

Spitzer, R. L., & Wilson, P. T. (1975). Nosology and the official psychiatric nomenclature. In A. Freedman & H. Kaplan (Eds.), *Comprehensive textbook of psychiatry.* New York: Williams & Wilkins.

Storms, M. D. (1973). Videotape and the attribution process: Reversing actors' and observers' points of view. *Journal of Personality and Social Psychology, 27,* 165–175.

Sullivan, H. S. (1954). *The psychiatric interview.* New York: Norton.

Sullivan, H. S. (1956). *Clinical studies in psychiatry.* New York: Norton.

Sullivan, H. S. (1962). *Schizophrenia as a human process.* New York: Norton.

Szasz, T. S. (1960). The myth of mental illness. *American Psychologist, 15,* 113–118.

Szasz, T. S. (1974). *The myth of mental illness: Foundations of a theory of personal conduct* (rev. ed.). New York: Harper & Row.

Szasz, T. S. (1984). *The therapeutic state: Psychiatry in the mirror of current events.* Buffalo, NY: Prometheus Books.

Szasz, T. S. (1987). *Insanity: The idea and its consequences.* New York: Wiley.

Taylor, S. E., & Crocker, J. (1981). Schematic bases of social information processing. In E. T. Higgins, C. P. Herman, & M. P. Zanna (Eds.), *Social cognition: The Ontario Symposium* (Vol. 1, pp. 89–134). Hillsdale, NJ: Erlbaum.

Taylor, S. E., & Fiske, S. T. (1975). Point of view and perceptions of causality. *Journal of Personality and Social Psychology, 32,* 439–445.

Tellegen, A., Lykken, D. T., Bouchard, T. J., Jr., Wilcox, K. J., Segal, N. L., & Rich, S. (1988). Personality similarity in twins reared apart and together. *Journal of Personality and Social Psychology, 54,* 1031–1039.

Tversky, A., & Kahneman, D. (1973). Availability: A heuristic for judging frequency and probability. *Cognitive Psychology, 5,* 207–232.

Tversky, A., & Kahneman, D. (1974). Judgment under uncertainty: Heuristics and biases. *Science, 185,* 1124–1131.

Tversky, A., & Kahneman, D. (1982). Judgments of and by representativeness. In D. Kahneman, P. Slovic, & A. Tversky (Eds.), *Judgment under uncertainty: Heuristics and biases.* New York: Cambridge University Press.

Unger, R. K. (1983). Through the looking glass: No wonderland yet! (The reciprocal relationship between methodology and models of reality). *Psychology of Women Quarterly, 8,* 9–32.

Vokey, J. R., & Read, J. D. (1985). Subliminal messages: Between the devil and the media. *American Psychologist, 40,* 1231–1239.

Wakefield, J. C. (1992). The concept of mental disorder: On the boundary between biological facts and social values. *American Psychologist, 47*(3), 373–388.

Walster, E. (1966). Assignment of responsibility for an accident. *Journal of Personality and Social Psychology, 3,* 73–79.

Wason, P. C. (1960). On the failure to eliminate hypotheses in a conceptual task. *Quarterly Journal of Experimental Psychology, 12,* 129–140.

Weiner, B. (1980). A cognitive (attribution)–emotion–action model of motivated behavior: An analysis of judgment of helpgiving. *Journal of Personality and Social Psychology, 39,* 186–200.

Whorf, B. (1956). *Language, thought, and reality.* Cambridge, MA: MIT Press.

Wood, G. (1979). The knew-it-all-along effect. *Journal of Experimental Psychology: Human Perception and Performance, 4,* 345–353.

Word, C. H., Zanna, M. P., & Cooper, J. (1974). The nonverbal mediation of self-fulfilling prophecies in inter-racial interaction. *Journal of Experimental Social Psychology, 10,* 109–120.

Zajonc, R. B. (1980). Feeling and thinking: Preferences need no inferences. *American Psychologist, 35,* 151–175.

Name Index

Amabile, T. M., 89, 255
Anastasi, A., 152, 250
Anderson, C. A., 160, 161, 250
Andreason, N. J. C., 59, 250
Angeles, P. A., 64, 79, 250
Anthony, J. C., 254
Aristotle, 119, 121, 125
Asch, S., 140, 250
Aurelius, S., 166

Bacon, F., 125
Barber, J. W., 73, 126, 131, 250
Bargh, J. A., 147, 252
Barnum, P. T., 50, 54
Bartlett, J., 50, 250
Bass, E., 109, 250
Baumrind, D., 61, 250
Benedict, R., 47
Bergman, A., 25, 254
Bernard, M. E., 25, 251
Bernston, G. G., 18, 250
Berscheid, E., 66, 132, 250, 256
Bertalanffy, L. von, 79, 250
Beyth, R., 163, 251
Bloch, A., 19, 59, 94, 167, 197,
    203, 250
Bogart, J. B., 180
Bohr, N., 27
Bonaparte, N., 47
Borgida, E., 184, 250
Bouchard, T. J., Jr., 256
Boyd, J. H., 254, 255
Breuer, J., 69, 187, 250
Bruner, J. S., 139, 250
Buber, M., 47, 199, 250
Buri, J. R., 61, 250
Burke, J. D., 254, 255
Butler, S., 166

Cacioppo, J. T., 18, 250
Campbell, D. T., 127, 250
Canter, A., 59, 250
Cantor, N., 137, 138, 250
Carlsmith, J. M., 120, 251
Carroll, J. B., 199, 250
Carson, R. C., 26, 251
Cervantes, M., 166
Clough, A. H., 166
Cooper, J., 132, 256
Coopersmith, S., 61, 251
Corey, G., 189, 251
Crocker, J., 138, 256
Cullen, F. T., 199, 254

Daniels, D., 115, 254
Darley, J. M., 135, 251
Davidoff, H., 76, 171, 197, 251
Davis, L., 109, 250
de La Fontaine, J., 76

Descartes, R., vii
Dickson, D. H., 52, 251
Dickson, W. J., 127, 255
Diderot, D., 65
Disraeli, B., 65
Donne, J., 166
Doyle, A. C., 119, 162
Dukas, H., 13, 251
Durocher, L., 166

Edison, T. A., 73
Effrein, E. A., 154, 251
Einstein, A., 11–12, 13, 47, 171
Ellis, A., 25, 251
Emerson, R. W., 65
Erdelyi, M. H., 110, 251
Erhardt, D. D., 53, 253
Erikson, E. H., 48–49, 251
Eron, L. D., 66, 252
Exner, J. E., Jr., 152, 154, 251
Eysenck, H. J., 145, 146, 161, 251

Fallender, V. J., 154, 251
Farina, A., 199, 251
Fazio, R. H., 135, 154, 251
Feldman, R. S., 135, 251
Fersch, E. A., 183, 251
Feshbach, S., 69, 251
Festinger, L., 120, 251
Fischoff, B., 162, 163, 166, 181,
    251, 255
Fiske, S. T., 41, 86, 137, 138,
    160, 175, 179, 251, 256
Fitzgerald, E., 76
Fode, K., 132, 255
Forer, B. R., 51, 251
Frank, J., 199, 254
Frank, L. K., 152, 252
Frankl, V. E., 29, 90, 252
Freud, A., 28, 104, 190, 252
Freud, S., 8, 28, 69, 72, 115, 187,
    250, 252

Galilei, G., 125
George, L. K., 255
Goethals, G. R., 89, 254
Goldberg, B., 110, 251
Greenwald, J., 181, 252
Gruenberg, E., 255

Ha, Y-W., 147, 253
Haley, J., 29, 252
Hamilton, D. L., 137, 252
Harris, V. A., 89, 252
Hegel, G. W. F., 7, 155
Heider, F., 84, 86, 252
Heisenberg, W. K., 126, 130
Helzer, J. E., 255
Heraclitus, 28, 34

Heywood, J., 166
Hickson, W. E., 166
Higgins, E. T., 147, 252
Hinckley, J. W., Jr., 183
Hoffer, E., 155
Hoffman, B., 13, 251
Holden, C., 114, 252
Holmes, D., 110, 252
Holzer, C. E., 254
Horwitz, L., 132, 252
Hubbard, M., 157, 255
Huesmann, L. R., 60, 66, 252
Hume, D., 45, 125
Huxley, A., 23, 252
Huxley, T. H., 155

Jacobson, L., 131, 255
Jamieson, D. W., 135, 252
Jamison, K. R., 59, 252
Jefferson, T., 47
Jones, E. E., 86, 89, 252
Jung, C. G., 27, 28, 106–107, 112,
    157, 252–253

Kahneman, D., 172, 173, 179, 182,
    183, 253, 256
Kaler, S. R., 137, 179, 253
Kaplan, H. S., 96, 253
Karno, M., 255
Karr, A., 34
Kelley, H. H., 87, 139–140, 253
Kelly, I. W., 52, 251
Ketcham, K., 110, 154, 254
Kierkegaard, S., 162
Kitaigorodskii, A. I., 162
Klayman, J., 147, 253
Klein, M., 25, 132, 253
Kosko, B., 26, 253
Kramer, M., 254, 255

Lagerspetz, K., 66, 252
Laing, R. D., 7, 19, 45, 101, 126, 132,
    136, 187, 199, 253
Lau, R. R., 161, 253
Lawrence, J., 197, 253
Leaf, P. J., 254
Lee, R. E., 197, 253
Lepper, M., 156, 157, 160, 161, 250,
    253, 254, 255
Lerner, M. J., 87, 253
Levy, D. A., 18, 33, 43, 53, 55, 61,
    137, 179, 202, 226, 253
Lewin, K., 26, 254
Lichtenstien, S., 181, 255
Lincoln, A., 47
Link, B. G., 199, 254
Locke, B. Z., 255
Loftus, E. F., 108, 110, 154, 254
Lombardi, V., 166

257

Subject Index

Note: *In addition to the cited pages, refer to the Glossary for definitions of key terms and concepts.*

DR. LAWRENCE BALTER
with Anita Shreve

ILLUSTRATIONS BY MARIKA HAHN

POSEIDON PRESS   NEW YORK

Dr. Balter's Child Sense

Understanding and Handling the
Common Problems of Infancy
and Early Childhood

A Poseidon Press Book
Published by Pocket Books, A Division of Simon & Schuster, Inc.
Simon & Schuster Building
Rockefeller Center
1230 Avenue of the Americas
New York, New York 10020
POSEIDON PRESS is a registered trademark of Simon & Schuster, Inc.
Designed by Karolina Harris
Manufactured in the United States of America

1 3 5 7 9 10 8 6 4 2

Library of Congress Cataloging in Publication Data

Balter, Lawrence.
Dr. Balter's child sense.

1. Children—Care and hygiene.   2. Infants—Care and hygiene.
3. Parent and child.   4. Child rearing.
I. Shreve, Anita.   II. Balter, Lawrence.   Child sense.
III. Title.   IV. Title: Child sense.
V. Title: Doctor Balter's child sense.   [DNLM:
1. Child Care—popular works.   2. Child Rearing—popular works.
3. Infant Care—popular works.   4. Parent—Child Relations—
popular works.   WS 113 B197d]
RJ61.B217 1985   649'.1   84–26602
ISBN 0-671-49627-1

To Karen
—L.B.

To Katherine and John
—A.S.

Contents

CONTENTS

Part Two
I'm Me; You're You
Eighteen Months to Three Years

Part Three
I'll Be You; You Be Me
Three to Five Years

CONTENTS

Part Four
Special Family Considerations

CONTENTS

Preface

As a child psychologist and also as a professor who trains child and school psychologists, I have worked with many parents, teachers and children. Over the years, I've discovered that children's behavior is often baffling and, as a result, misunderstood by adults. This bafflement sometimes produces angry harangues and power struggles between parent and child. To alleviate some of this needless frustration, I have tried to help parents understand why their children behave the way they do.

Recently I have been addressing some of these issues on my radio programs and on television. Many parents who have called in with child-care questions have asked if I have a book that would help them solve the dozens of behavioral problems that their infants, toddlers and preschoolers present. This book is in answer to those requests. In the book, I present the information I have learned from clinical practice and research in such a way that it will be practical and useful in common everyday situations.

It's important to keep in mind that, as parents, we are involved in a relationship. We're trying in a compassionate way to help an immature human being enter into a partnership, even though that child is not an equal partner. My emphasis in this book is geared to understanding the basis of the child's behavior and selecting the one of the numerous approaches that will best suit the individual child and particular situation.

Toward that end, perhaps the most critical precept is putting yourself in the child's place. By doing so, certain other empathic responses will follow naturally, such as introducing change to the child in very small increments in order to reduce stress; explaining as much as possible to the child in language he can understand; listening to the child without criticizing or silencing him because we don't like what we hear; verbalizing for the child when his own thoughts or fears may be unutterable; and watching the child's play for clues as to what may be going on inside him.

Loving a child means that you care enough about him to respect his point of view, to be interested in wanting to protect him, and to be willing to sacrifice for him. It does not mean, however, that you should sacrifice yourself unconditionally. After the initial infant months, it is important to teach your child, gently and with enthusiasm, to love and also to give, so that he will learn to get pleasure out of cooperating with you. Reciprocity is important in any relationship.

Being a parent is tough. I am hard pressed to think of a more demanding, or more important, job. And many of the difficulties of parenting stem from the paradoxes inherent in child raising. Think of the paradox inherent in the conflict between our long-term and short-term goals. We want our children, in the long run, to be leaders, critical in their thinking, to have good judgment and a strong character. But in the short term, in our day-to-day life, we want children who will not talk back to us, who will sit quietly when bored, who will go to sleep when it is time to do so and who will not engage in enlightening "physics experiments," such as spilling milk all over the table. How do we get children to obey us today, and yet still become independent individuals?

Or think of the paradox inherent in some of our ways of disciplining our children. Parenthood means protecting and guiding children in such a way that we will enhance their self-esteem and help them develop a sense of dignity. But unfortunately, all too often, we use shame and humiliation as a means of guiding (or controlling) them—not to mention an appalling amount of physical violence in the form of spanking.

Growing up implies a gradual process of becoming an individual—a separate person with preferences, standards and a particular way of looking at the world. Scientists don't know exactly how much of this is due to heredity and how much to environment, but it is safe to assume that a fair amount is due to the child's home environment. And it is also safe to assume that we, as parents, can do something about that environment. Children spend many years of their lives dependent upon us because they are forced to be. During that time, they become like us. Yet at the same time, they are breaking away in a long gradual process of separation. This, too, is a difficult paradox for a parent to cope with.

The book is organized into three sections, according to three generally accepted stages of development between birth and five years of age: infancy (birth to eighteen months); toddlerhood (eighteen months to three years); and the preschool period (three to five years). The first section is entitled "We Are One," and refers to the close physical and emotional bond of the infant to his parents. The second section is entitled "I'm Me; You're You" and refers to the need on the part of the toddler to begin to separate himself from his parents. The third section is called "I'll Be You; You Be Me" and refers to the stage of development in childhood in which children experiment with role playing and begin to imitate, often comically, the adults around them. There is also a "Special Family Considerations" section which deals with issues such as divorce, sibling relationships, moving and other family matters.

Occasionally you will come across questions that various parents have asked. These questions relate to important issues in child development. My approach to each question is twofold: First, I try to help you understand the reasons why the child is behaving the way he is at the age he is; and, second, I try to offer practical step-by-step advice to help you and your child with a particular problem. Frequently I will ask you to consider in whose interests a particular child-rearing decision is being made. While it is occasionally fine to make a decision in one's own interests, rather than in the child's interests, it is important for the parent to realize what he or she is doing. Generally speaking, however, I will advocate on behalf of the child's interests—and I will ask you to see the situation from his point of view.

But even though I will frequently put an accent on the child's perspective, I do not believe that parents should relinquish their authority. True power comes from understanding others and being able to lead them in a healthy and positive direction. True leadership sometimes requires compromise and sometimes requires standing fast to firmly held principles. Knowing when to compromise and when to be firm is difficult. It is my hope that this book will make that decision making easier.

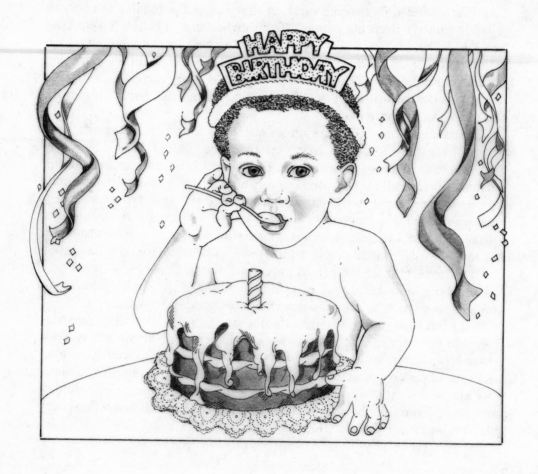

Part One

We Are One
Birth to Eighteen Months

Introduction

For years, parents and doctors alike thought of infants as very passive little creatures. The old school held that babies merely lay there like objects—you fed them, changed them, put them down for naps at prescheduled times, and that was it. Today, however, with more sophisticated research at our disposal, we know that newborns are capable of more activities and perceptions than anyone had previously thought possible. Whether or not this is also because mothers are given fewer narcotics during birth is uncertain, but what *is* certain is that we now understand babies to be more alert, and to see, hear and hold themselves better than anyone had thought they could. Babies who are healthy are active, not passive. They like stimulation, and they enjoy being in the world. The first eighteen months of a child's life is an extremely active period. A healthy child wants to grow. He wants to be involved.

Infants, however, are in a difficult position. Although a healthy child will want to grow and be involved in whatever is happening around him, he can't control very much. An infant can't yet manipulate his environment and is, in a sense, powerless. The baby *depends* on you to be his instrument in the world. A child wants to touch, see, taste and try many different experiences, but he can't unless you provide these experiences for him. One of the most important responsibilities a parent has during the first eighteen months of a child's life is to be *there* for the child—not just as a care giver in the old way of thinking, but also as a stimulator and a facilitator.

Much of this will come naturally. Even though you may be exhausted from getting up at all hours of the night to feed your child, although you may be frustrated and baffled by your infant's inexplicable bouts of colic or crying, and despite the fact that you are often dazed and bedazzled by your baby's constant demands, you will find yourself, as one mother recently put it, "falling in love." During a love affair, there is a loss of distance between you and the person you fall in love with, and the separation that naturally exists between two people begins to dissolve. You believe that the loved one is an extension of yourself, and you, in turn, are an extension of that person. So it happens with parents and their babies. Because you are so in love, you find yourself extending yourself to limits beyond those you thought possible. You stimulate and interact with your child simply because it's fun and you want to. In the truest sense, you and your baby are one.

The baby probably thinks you and she are one, too. Many child psychologists and early childhood specialists believe that infants don't experience themselves as separate and distinct from their mothers. On the contrary, they see themselves as being a part of their mother—a virtual extension of her. Only gradually, in successive moves away from her during this eighteen-month period, will the child begin to experience a feeling of separation.

The infant has been a fetus who has spent nine months inside the mother's body with no responsibilities. She didn't have to breathe, eat, excrete, listen to harsh sounds, or adjust to temperature changes. Suddenly she finds herself in a world with stimuli virtually bombarding her, and she needs to be comforted quickly. Parents sometimes wonder if their babies are being manipulative when they cry. I doubt that babies are very manipulative. They may cry because they want you to come to them. And then when you go to them, they smile. Does that mean they're being manipulative? Or if you go to a child who's shrieking from her crib and you find that by going in to her you comfort her, does that mean you've spoiled her? I don't think so. A child who is distressed wants to feel better. She needs you to be the one to make her feel better in one way or another. The baby is incapable of doing this for herself. Quickly comforting a child doesn't really seem to have much to do with the question of spoiling. The child has to catch up to the world. It may take months for her to feel truly comfortable in it. Who of us knows what discomforts a child goes through?

You may find you have an easier time of it if you are able to modify some of your expectations about what babies can and cannot do for themselves during this initial eighteen-month period. You may believe, for example, that babies should sleep through the night by the time they are three months old. Perhaps you have a friend whose baby slept through the night as soon as he was brought home from the hospital. Such expectations will only confuse you, however, because there is certainly no rule that says that every baby will sleep through the night—or that sleeping through the night should even be considered normal. Babies are born with different temperaments. Some are very reactive, some are placid. Some digest food better than others, some have faster reflexes. Some babies do come home from the hospital and are very cooperative and sleep through the night from day one. Many don't. Neither type of baby is doing anything wrong. As you become more familiar with your own baby and appreciate his or her uniqueness, then perhaps you will be able to lessen your confusion and frustration.

This isn't to say that you won't at times feel nearly overwhelmed. No one said having a baby was easy. Sometimes parents feel keenly disappointed because having a baby is not at all what they expected it to be. Our ideas about what it means to be a parent have evolved over many years—starting from when we were very young and our thoughts about such matters were not very discriminating. Our first idea of what it means to be a mother or a father comes from our perceptions about our own parents when we are very small, even as young as one-year-old. Although we grow older and are exposed to other ideas, those first perceptions don't go away. When you become a parent, those early ideas are reactivated. Now consider that when you were only a year old, a parent seemed like an all-knowing, all-powerful person. He or she had privileges, knew all the answers, seemed to be able to do what he or she wanted and could boss you around. Suddenly you are a parent, and you find yourself wondering why you don't feel all powerful and all knowing. You don't feel like a big boss with all the answers. Instead, most of the time you feel as if you have an awesome responsibility as well as a tremendous number of restrictions. You can hardly go anywhere at all.

These early ideas continue to roll around in the back of our minds and come to the fore as we experience our own infants. "Gee," we think to ourselves, "there's such a big gap between what I thought it would be like and what it really is like. I want to be The Mother [or The Father], but this baby isn't giving me any respect. This baby isn't cooperating. This baby is being totally unreasonable. I don't feel powerful at all. In fact, I feel as if I'm totally at the mercy of this child. This isn't the way I thought it was going to be at all."

There will be times when you would prefer to be doing something other than taking care of your child. After all, reading the same nursery rhyme book for the seventh time is boring. A *lot* of child care is boring. A good part of it is burdensome and just plain hard. This isn't to say that there aren't wonderful joyous moments, from which you derive a great deal of pleasure, but any job, day in and day out, can become tedious.

Perhaps you would like to have a bubble bath, read a magazine, make a favorite dish. But you can't, and you feel frustrated. You're responsible for somebody else who has to come first. Remind yourself, however, that it's perfectly normal to resent at times that very same little creature whom you love so much. It's not wrong of you to have these feelings. It's not wrong of you sometimes to want to strap your child in the infant seat, slam the door and take off for parts unknown. Just don't do it.

Many parents also experience a profound change in their own relationship. When a couple has a baby, the equation changes. They are now a family. Most couples do not really experience themselves as a family until they have children. And when the child comes, this feeling of family is at first exciting and brings with it a feeling of pride. But there are psychological adjustments that have to be made as well, for a child throws the original structure out of balance. Sometimes the parents find themselves competing with each other for the baby; occasionally the father may feel left out; often the parents are too tired to deal with one another's needs. More important, a great deal of the love that each spouse had for the other now seems to be going elsewhere—to the baby. "I remember feeling that my husband didn't love me anymore," said one new mother. "It just seemed as if all his love went from me to the baby in one fell swoop at a time when I felt that I should have been treated special, too. After all, I had just had a baby! I'd never done that before. I felt I needed a lot of support and care and attention. Instead, he seemed not even to notice I existed anymore."

This same feeling of neglect is also true for fathers. Men often feel that their wives are now totally absorbed in the new baby—ironically at a time when they, too, want to be reassured and attended to. One's early longings to be taken care of are reawakened along with the arrival of the baby. These feelings are normal and important—indeed, you have to have those feelings in order to give them to your baby—but they may make you feel deprived. Although you won't be able to act on these feelings very much—it simply isn't reasonable to expect to be mothered yourself during a time when so much mothering has to be given to the child—it is important to realize that you have these feelings, and to be able to express them. Certainly being able to talk about such feelings may make it easier to offer each other help. If you are aware of your needs and longings, your sense of disappointment may be softened and you will find yourself feeling less resentful. And a less resentful and disappointed parent is undoubtedly a happier and better parent.

By now it's common to say that the baby's personality is formed during the first several years of life, but it is true to a large extent. Certain basic attitudes toward life—such as a sense of confidence, self-assurance, competence, worthiness, optimism, and security—are more often than not learned from the parents. If your needs, as an infant, are taken care of properly, if you are made to feel a welcome person in the world, if you are comfortable in the knowledge that you won't be abandoned, if you feel that you are worth something, that you will succeed in your endeavors and that you are a good person, chances are these feelings will remain with you throughout your life. Such a gift is invaluable to a child.

1
Nurse or Housekeeper?

Many parents want to know, when they first bring the baby home from the hospital, if it is better to have a nurse or a housekeeper to help them during those first several weeks. There are four main options available to parents: the parents can share all the tasks between themselves with no outside help; a baby nurse can come to care for the infant; a housekeeper can come to do the housework; or a relative or close friend can come in during the day or in the evening to help you with either baby care or housekeeping, or both.

My feeling is that you should have help—but it should be someone who will help more with the housework than with the baby. (This is not true, of course, for women who for health reasons are unable to care for their babies. Some women who have Cesareans, for example, find it painful to move around the first couple of days after giving birth—but even in this case, the mother can take on as many of the baby care tasks as possible, by having someone bring the baby to her when necessary.)

I'm all in favor of letting someone else do the dishes, the cleaning and the shopping for you. After all, you're tired, you're getting up during the night, and you're experiencing the strain of a new and demanding situation. Get as much help as you can. But when it comes to holding the baby, walking the baby, feeding, changing and bathing the baby, the parents them-selves should do it. Not only is it better for your emotional bonding with the baby, but the more you care for the child, the more comfortable you will be-come about performing these tasks.

This doesn't mean that you have to start out absolutely green. Prior to giving birth, take a course in baby care. Many hospitals and clinics now offer short courses for parents in bathing, changing and nursing the baby.

If you have a relative or someone who has a lot of experience who can show you some baby-care tips, by all means watch and listen—but *don't* relinquish the parenting and nurturing itself to someone else. Let your mother, for example, show you how to do it—but *you* do it yourself. Some-times we ascribe to people who help us out qualities they don't really pos-sess. A new mother who allows her own mother to help her out may begin to think of her mother as a better parent than she herself is. It's a mistake to think that just because a person has had more experience in baby care, that she is a "better" parent. You should quickly take over the chores so that you can become the competent parent. Your mother may be more skilled than you in certain tasks, but you will learn them in no time. You're the one who has to develop an emotional bond with the child as well as con-fidence in yourself.

I am often saddened to hear of new parents who *have* relinquished the important baby-care tasks to others. One mother in particular dearly re-gretted having hired a baby nurse. "She took over from the first day, and was, I thought, very condescending when I tried to do anything for myself. I soon became very intimidated by her, and was actually afraid to do any-thing without asking her. I felt as if I wasn't the mother, and that I had given up my right to be a mother. It took me months to get over it. In fact, I never really gained any confidence in myself as a mother until I had my second child. This time I did not hire anyone else; I did it all myself and loved it."

2
Child Care

In the United States today, more than half of the mothers with young children go back to work full-time. Never before has the issue of good child care been so important, and an increasing number of women have been asking questions regarding surrogate care. What is the best kind of care for their child? Should they go back to work full-time or part-time? When can they safely go back to work? How many hours a day can they be away from their child without harming the child or the bond between mother and child?

These are all very important questions, and the answers are not yet fully known. There are, however, a number of options a working mother can choose from, and she should make these choices wisely.

There are several kinds of surrogate care available for the children of working mothers. If one can afford to do so, hiring a full-time housekeeper–baby-sitter or a live-in nanny is one possibility. Although this option is relatively expensive, it provides the baby with the kind of one-on-one child care that many psychologists, myself included, feel is best for infants. (If the live-in care giver is a relative, the cost will be considerably lower, but there may be other problems, such as jealousy and tension in family relations, to consider.)

An alternative to the housekeeper or live-in nanny is the family day-care mother. This is a neighborhood mother, with children of her own, who takes in, for a limited number of hours per day, the children of other working women. Family day-care mothers are more difficult to monitor than housekeepers, and your baby may be competing for attention with several others. Be sure to screen carefully potential care givers to make sure that they are prepared to care for your child in the manner you think best, and that they are willing to stimulate your child as well as feed, diaper and hold him. Unless you are convinced that your child will receive adequate attention, I would not rush into this type of arrangement.

Today, more and more mothers are choosing to send their infants to local day-care centers. These centers, which range in quality from the fast-food, profit-making institutional chains to small, intimate centers at which the staff-to-child ratio is very good and the staff is well trained, are often much less expensive than other forms of child care and have the added benefit of being fairly reliable. (Surrogate mothers and housekeepers can get sick or have to attend to their own families from time to time—or they can simply decide to quit.) Since there is such a wide variety in center day care, however, it will be necessary to make several visits to several centers to ascertain which is best for your child.

The issue of advisability of surrogate child care—and how much—is a controversial one. Some recent research has suggested that children raised in day-care centers tend to be more competent and more mature than home-based children of the same age in the size of their vocabulary, their ability to interact with an unfamiliar adult and in their play with a child they did not know. Other experts contend that it is not acceptable to leave a child of six months of age or younger in surrogate care for more than a few hours a day. Most research indicates that for the first several months, babies need lots of affection and attention. For the majority of their waking hours they must have ready access to someone who loves them. Other studies have put forth the idea that babies who are left in the care of surrogate parents, while their own parents go out to work full-time, have an anhedonic quality—a feeling of joylessness about them, an inability to experience pleasure. Still other experts maintain that there are no adverse effects on infants and young children from quality day care. Who is right?

My preference, for the first year of the child's life, is for the parents themselves to share the child care as best they can or to limit the surrogate care to only a few hours a day. Needless to say, not all women can arrange such a part-time schedule without jeopardizing their jobs and careers, and for those who cannot, I would choose a care-giving situation in which the infant will get as close to one-on-one care as possible, and one in which she will be adequately and affectionately stimulated, held, fed and played with. Observe carefully the manner in which the prospective care giver handles the babies in his or her care and make sure that he or she is flexible and amenable to your suggestions. Even though you will not be physically present for a certain number of hours in the day, you still have the responsibility for the care of your child during those hours—and that responsibility translates into finding her the best possible care.

Although there are still no hard data available to say definitively at what age and for how long a period of time an infant can optimally be left in someone else's care, many child development experts agree that three months seems to be a recommended time period for consistent care on the part of the mother so that the infant–mother attachment and bond can grow. The more one-on-one care a child can receive the better. As the infant moves into toddlerhood, he also needs a great deal of one-on-one care so that he doesn't get hurt. If this isn't possible, because of your work situation, then you should look for a setting that has the best adult–child ratio. You might also consider having your child participate in a small play-group experience so that he can engage in parallel play during toddlerhood while you are present.

꽃

I will be returning to work part-time in a few weeks. My son is six months old, and my tentative plan is to work two full days on

Tuesdays and Fridays. My thinking was that there would be two days when he could be with me between my work days. But I am uncertain whether or not this is a good idea. Would it be better to work two days together and get it over with?

Sometimes parents find that the day *after* they have left their child in another's care, the child is cranky. This is the child's way of expressing some of the upset he might feel at being left by his mother. For this reason, you may experience some of these same repercussions. If you are going to work on two days spaced far apart, you may then have two days of crankiness.

Despite the crankiness, however, I think you are doing the right thing— primarily because you will have two days between work days to help your son adjust to your absence. If your son does indeed become cranky after being left with a baby-sitter, for the next two days you will be *there* for him.

※

I am quite concerned about the child-care situation my daughter is in. She's fourteen months old now, and I have her with a neighborhood mother who has a boy of four years old. He is quite a nice little boy, but I'm beginning to wonder if my daughter is getting adequate attention. I suspect that the mother pays a lot more attention to her son than to my daughter, and even more attention to her housekeeping. (Her house is immaculate.) Also, on a couple of occasions, when I've gone to pick my daughter up early, I've noticed that the TV is on, even though no one seems to be watching it, and it certainly isn't a children's program. Should I remove my daughter from this situation?

I think there is adequate reason for alarm here. The setting of the child care is not really as important as the *attitude* of the care giver. In this case, the mother seems to be paying far more attention to her household chores than to the task of stimulating a fourteen-month-old baby. And I don't think a child of that age should have to compete with other children for attention. In a family day-care situation, one of the hazards is that the family day-care mother will almost naturally gravitate toward her own children at the expense of the client's children.

As for the television, I am very much against the concept of television watching for its own sake, and I certainly do not think a fourteen-month-old child can benefit from TV. I would think seriously about either talking to the family day-care mother (although one has very limited control over what another woman does in her own house), or searching out other surrogate care situations.

�233

I work as a dentist, and I employ a full-time, live-in nanny to care for my nine-month-old daughter. Recently I have become concerned about the attachment that Ellen is forming to the nanny. When we come home in the evening, my husband encourages Ellen to kiss Nanny good night and to give her a hug. This bothers me, since I am afraid that if Ellen becomes too attached to her, she will be seriously upset should the nanny ever leave for any reason. Perhaps I am just feeling jealous of Ellen's love for the nanny, but I think I am also genuinely concerned that she not get hurt.

I think you were more on target when you expressed feelings of jealousy about the intimacy between Ellen and the nanny than you were in your worries for the child's future. While it is natural for working mothers to feel anxious about being replaced in their child's affections, I think it is safe to say that Ellen knows, despite your fears, that you are her primary parent, even if you are not there with her as much as the nanny.

There is some evidence that babies, even newborns, can distinguish their mothers from all other people. And even though children who have spent all day with another care giver sometimes overlook Mom when she comes home (as is only natural if a child has spent all day "showing" accomplishments to another person), Mom shouldn't take this to mean that she has been replaced in the child's heart. She is still the primary person in her child's life.

Any attempts on your part to dilute the intimacy between the child and the nanny will be futile. A child forms a strong bond with someone who is a care giver full-time, someone who is fulfilling a child's primary needs during the day. Any normal person will develop an attachment to someone she is with every single day. Giving the nanny a kiss and a hug before bedtime is just an outward manifestation of this inner affection. Should you attempt and even succeed at curtailing this outward sign of attachment, you won't dilute the attachment itself. To try to get the child to stop showing affection will only confuse her.

You were also worried that the child would be deeply hurt if the nanny left one day. This is a natural concern and one that can be dealt with should the occasion arise. When the nanny leaves, the child may have a wrenching experience, but one can take a number of steps to help a child through this difficult time.

First, take a few days off from work if you can. Explain to the child, if she is at an age when you can verbally explain such things, that Nanny has had to leave. If you have had to dismiss Nanny, you needn't go into every gory detail. Rather, point out that the arrangement wasn't working out very well, and that you are finding someone else to help both you and your child. Tell her that someone will be coming to take care of her and that she won't be left alone. You will be meeting a lot of people and trying to pick out the best one for her.

If the nanny leaves for some other reason than the fact that you have discharged her—perhaps she is going back to school or to her own family, or she is retiring—you can encourage continuing contact. Perhaps the nanny could stay for a while and help you pick a replacement and even help train the new person so there will be some continuity. Or perhaps she can visit the child later, and, in turn, can be phoned or visited herself. In this way, Nanny doesn't simply vanish.

For older children, be cautious in what you say about the reason why the nanny is leaving. You don't want to convey to the child a sense of rejection. I know of one case in which the nanny left, saying, "It's time for me to move on. I only like caring for babies." After that, the child began to regress, clearly wishing to become a "baby" so that the nanny would stay.

Although having to replace a nanny is a difficult experience for a child, a lesson can be learned in the process. Mommy is always there. Other people are employees and may come and go, but Mom will always be there. To be sure, a nanny is more than just an impersonal employee, but nonetheless, she is paid to help Mom.

As the child gets older, she will become more conscious of who is in the family and who is not. When there are family gatherings, and cousins and aunts and uncles come around, it will be clear that Nanny is not a family member. Nanny will be seen to have another life somewhere else. As the child's concept of relationships grows, she will understand better where everybody fits.

My eighteen-month-old son has begun to focus all his attention on my purse rather than on me. He's clearly thrilled when I get home, but instead of running over to me, he cries for my purse. For the next fifteen minutes or so, that's all he's interested in—dumping out the contents and handling them. Eventually he turns his attention to his toys. Does he do this as a result of his anger at being left all day? How can I stop this behavior? Giving him the purse is inconvenient, because he scatters the contents all over the floor. He hides my keys and credit cards. So far I've simply been giving in to him. Should I give him a fake purse? Do you think that will satisfy him?

The child is focusing all his attention not on you but on something that belongs to you. In bypassing you and going directly to the object that belongs to you, he may be demonstrating some anger at having been left all day. Typically, children who are left all day show indifference and apathy to the mother when she comes home. Your child's behavior is one idiosyncratic way of dealing with the feelings he may have as a result of your being out of the house.

It certainly won't hurt to put together a fake purse, to keep the child from destroying or losing valuable items in a real purse. Better yet, try bringing home some surprises. Perhaps a small toy or a snack that the child would enjoy would distract him from his desire to have the purse and would act as a substitute.

If you suspect that the behavior stems from the child's angry feelings, you might try getting the child to express these feelings—even if it's a situation in which you do all the talking. You might say very casually, for example, "Gee, I bet you sometimes feel angry at Mommy for going off all day and leaving you." It may help the child simply to hear his own feelings expressed in words. Keep in mind, however, that it isn't necessary to rid the child of these feelings. The feelings are normal and healthy—it's expressing them that's important.

3
How Long Can I Keep the Baby in Our Room?

My daughter is four months old now, and I'm wondering if it's time to move her into her own room. Since birth, she has slept beside me in a bassinet. Not only is she getting a little big for the bassinet, but I've heard that babies should not stay in the parents' room for too long. Is this true? I find that although intellectually I think it's time for her to move, it's very difficult for me to face emotionally, which is why I've been putting it off for so long.

After the first several weeks following the baby's birth, and sometime before the age of six months, you can move the baby out of your room to a quiet peaceful place of her own (perhaps even her own room if you have one prepared at this point). Exactly *when* is largely a matter of personal preference.

I am in favor of moving the baby out as early as possible. For the first several weeks, you will want the baby nearby since you will be waking often during the night for feedings, and having the baby close to you is simply easier on everyone. But later you may discover that having the baby next to you disturbs your sleep (babies often wake for a few seconds and make noises loud enough to wake you, but then *they* drop right back off to sleep) and interferes with your privacy. More important, the longer you wait, the harder it will be for the baby to tolerate the move. While the baby is sleeping next to you, she is becoming accustomed to the sounds of your breathing and sleeping. Moving her to a quiet place may be more difficult for her when she is older. You don't want to wait so long that she begins to *depend* on your nearness in order to sleep well.

Many mothers have talked about how difficult it is for them to move their babies into a separate room. And it *is* a scary feeling. You wonder if your baby will be all right without you. But then when you think back on it, you realize that if she was all right every night in your room, the odds are she's going to be all right in her own room too. In many cases, it is often much harder for the parents to relinquish the child than for the child to give up being near the parents. Later the child will feel this separation more strongly.

Your goal is not to make the child independent, because an infant can't be independent. What you *are* trying to do is to avoid making the move more difficult for the baby. Certainly by the time the child is six months of age, she should be sleeping in her own room. If you wait much longer, you run the risk of overlapping with a stage of development that begins shortly after six months, during which the child is preoccupied with the idea of separation and may be excessively clingy. Moving a child out of your room at that point may be nearly intolerable for her.

When you move the child out of your room, your main consideration should be: Can you hear her easily? Mothers often develop an acute sense of hearing *for their babies only* and will awaken upon hearing even the tiniest cry from their own children. If, however, you live in a large house or apartment and are worried about being able to hear the baby, you might consider installing a relatively inexpensive intercom system that will allow you to monitor sounds in the baby's room while you are elsewhere in the house.

4

Scheduling Feeding Times

One of the most important things to keep in mind when considering putting your baby on a feeding schedule is the age of the infant. Certainly a very young baby should not be put on any kind of a rigid schedule. Newborns want and need to be fed much more often than older babies—in some cases even as often as every two to two and a half hours. And until the baby is quite a bit older, he should be fed whenever he wants.

Remember that a baby is growing. His need for food is automatic and natural. A child can hold only so much nutrition in his system at any given time, and will need to have that nutrition replenished often. Frequent feedings, therefore, are normal and necessary.

As the baby gets older, you will need to make a critical distinction between when the baby is crying from hunger and crying for some other reason. All too often, mothers use nursing as a pacifier when something else would work just as well. There will be times when a baby will wake up and won't necessarily be hungry. At these times, do not be tempted to automatically place a bottle or a breast into the baby's mouth just to calm him down. What may be required instead is simply walking around with the baby, letting him look at his environment, talking to him or even playing with him for a few minutes. Resist the temptation to feed the child because it's easier to do that than to spend time playing with him. Feeding a child whenever he cries may become a problem because the child may then associate the reduction of discomfort with having something in his mouth. Many of us know adults who overeat when they are tense. The origin of this behavior, some experts believe, lies in childhood—if we learn to associate tension alleviation with putting food into the mouth. Later this can translate into overeating, or worse, other habits such as smoking or drinking.

When babies reach the age of four or five months, they can go for longer time spans without eating. Check with your pediatrician about introducing solid foods at this time. By now, you will be pretty familiar with how long your own child can go without food, and you will probably have developed a schedule that accords with the child's needs. In most children, there is a natural evolution of the feeding process—many children can go for hours during the day without food, and then will sleep for periods of seven or eight hours during the night without needing nourishment.

So what's wrong with a rigid schedule? some parents ask me. The most important disadvantage is that a schedule doesn't really take into account the child's needs. How would it be if someone said to you, "Now you have to have juice and toast and a banana?" and you weren't ready for it. Or, on the other hand, what if someone told you, when you were dying for an apple, that you had to wait an hour. As adults, we are frequently forced to delay having something to eat until the appropriate time or place—but a baby isn't capable of this kind of self-control. For an infant, the delay can be terribly distressing.

5
Nursing

Is it possible to affect your child emotionally if you have problems breast-feeding? Because of my baby's jaundice at birth, she had to stay in the hospital four days longer than I. During that time, she was given bottles, and when she came home, we had tremendous difficulty readjusting her to the breast. I was very distraught, and I may have conveyed some of that concern to her.

Although I favor breast-feeding over bottle-feeding, that doesn't mean that if for one reason or another you are not able to nurse, or are not comfortable nursing, you shouldn't consider bottle-feeding. There can be numerous reasons why nursing may not go well. If it's a very strained and tense situation, it's probably better for you not to nurse.

Sometimes there are unforeseen circumstances that interrupt breast-feeding—an illness on the part of the mother, for example, that requires her to take medication that would be harmful to the baby, or an illness on the part of the baby, such as the situation above, which requires that she be separated from her mother long enough to interrupt nursing. During this time, the baby may get used to the bottle and "forget" the breast. Since nursing is an emotional as well as physical event for the mother, abandonment of nursing by the baby can cause painful feelings of inadequacy in the mother.

The best advice is to relax—nursing is a natural activity and the less self-conscious you are about it, the better. There are special classes and numerous books and pamphlets to help you prepare for nursing your child. Be sure that your pediatrician and the hospital staff are in favor of nursing. Sometimes an anti-breast-feeding attitude on the part of a hospital nurse or doctor can be the start of needless difficulties for a new mother. And if you should have to give up nursing altogether, you can certainly do a good job mothering and holding and comforting the baby with bottle-feeding.

�}

My three-month-old baby seems to have gotten into the habit of falling asleep at the breast. I don't know if this is a good idea or not. Will she always expect to fall asleep this way? Am I locked into a bad habit?

It's easy to see why one would get into the habit of having the baby fall asleep at the breast. It's very natural when she's eating for her to just nod off. Sometimes just the sucking alone will induce sleep. In early infancy, babies wake when they are hungry; when they are fed, they fall back to sleep. This early pattern becomes a convenient routine for you and your child. This parent was right, however, in worrying about what such a pattern might mean in the future. By anticipating the consequences of the decisions you make, you may avoid getting trapped into a habit that's hard to break.

A parent needn't worry about this problem for the first three months of infancy, but after that one should start thinking about how to change the pattern. It's not fair to you, and it's not fair to the baby. It's not fair to you because you don't want to have to be around every time the baby falls asleep. Nor do you want to be locked into a situation in which your baby has to have your nipple in her mouth in order to nod off. And it's not fair to the baby, because she ought to learn to fall asleep without that crutch. Not only should the child learn to do without your physical presence and without the nipple in her mouth, but she should also be encouraged to fall asleep lying down on a mattress. When you nurse a baby, you hold her in a certain way, perhaps cradled in your arms. For nursing, this is a warm and comforting position. If a child learns to fall asleep this way, it will be quite difficult for her to adjust to a prone position on a mattress.

One way of making the readjustments is to nurse your baby until she is about to fall asleep. But just before she begins to drift off—and you can usually tell because babies have characteristic ways of showing they are about to fall asleep—remove the breast from the baby's mouth. Lay the baby down in the crib or bassinet. She will probably wake up immediately and scream because she's used to falling asleep at the breast. When she wakes up, rub her back. If that doesn't seem to help, pick her up. If she's still upset, give her another drink. Again, just before she falls asleep, lay her down on her mattress and repeat the entire procedure. Do it as often as you need to—maybe five times an hour for the first night.

After several nights, the baby will get accustomed to being nursed and to having that one instant of being deprived of the nipple before falling asleep. In this way she will learn to fall asleep independently—without the nipple in her mouth and without being held.

All of this advice also holds true for bottle-fed babies. In fact, it's extremely important not to lay a baby down with her bottle. If the child is left unattended and the bottle drops out of her mouth, she not only experiences frustration at trying to reach the bottle, but also may develop gas pains with the intermittent sucking of the milk and air together. More important, milk accumulating in the mouth can cause "bottle-mouth syndrome"—a condition that dentists have recently realized is caused by bacteria growing extremely rapidly in the mouth, which results in tooth decay. Even the unerupted teeth of babies can be seriously damaged by allowing a child to fall asleep with milk in her mouth.

6

Weaning

When to wean is a personal decision. It's a cultural matter as well. Some people believe that it's desirable to keep a baby at the breast or on the bottle for many years—in some countries, it is commonplace for two- and three-year-olds to nurse. In our own culture, however, we have a variety of opinions. Some mothers wean their babies quite early. Others wait until their children are three or four years old. No one time is correct, and the decision should be based only on your own personal feelings about the matter, not on cultural conditioning or peer pressure.

Weaning is more than a baby's merely learning the mechanical task of going from the breast or bottle to the cup. It's an important step toward developing autonomy, independence and separateness. As a parent, you should be alert to signs of your child's desire to be weaned. Frequently they are missed. By seven or eight months, for example, some babies on the breast begin to turn their heads around while they are nursing. They want to look around, and you will find that you are struggling to keep them on the breast. The baby may keep pulling his head away from the breast, or, worse, may pull the nipple too. This will probably last for a period of about two or three weeks, and eventually you can win this battle, and the baby will go back to the breast. But is winning in the best interest of the child? If a child turns away from the nursing process, perhaps it's a good time to say to yourself, okay, let's cut down on this feeding technique.

When you do decide to wean, you should do it in gradual increments. Going "cold turkey" could be quite traumatic for both you and the baby. When you are very familiar with the child's schedule, select the easiest, most convenient feeding that you would like to eliminate from the baby's routine and skip it. If, for example, a baby is used to having a feeding when he wakes up, and another midmorning and another after lunch before his nap, try eliminating the midmorning feeding first. You needn't replace it with anything else. If the child is already on a cup, you could offer him a glass of juice. If the child gets cranky and cries and demands to be fed, simply say, "A little later you can nurse." The next feeding, scheduled after lunch, will be offered as usual.

Keep up this routine for two weeks. After the two-week period (or earlier if the baby adjusts rapidly and well), pick another convenient feeding to eliminate. You may find that the baby will suck a little longer at each feeding than he previously did, but that's okay. Most babies will adjust quite well to this gradual approach.

The most difficult feeding to eliminate will be the very last one of all. The final feeding is the most painful for some mothers to give up because it signals the end of an era. And don't underestimate the importance of this milestone. Many mothers go through a slight depression after giving up nursing and don't realize the reasons for it until later. Only in retrospect can they see that the last feeding marked the first major separation from their child.

For the child, the most difficult feeding to forgo may be the one just before bed. If the child is accustomed to falling asleep at the breast or with the bottle, it may be extremely difficult to get him to go to bed when the feeding is eliminated. For this reason, I would try at an early age to teach the child to fall asleep independent of the nursing. I have outlined in the preceding chapter a way this can be accomplished.

By the time the child is older—fourteen or fifteen months old—he is probably eating solid foods quite regularly as well as snacks, juices and other drinks from a cup. Some parents worry that when their children are weaned, they won't get enough milk. You don't have to be concerned. There are many foods that give children the same nutritional value as milk—cheese, yogurt and cottage cheese, for example. Check with your pediatrician if you think your baby isn't getting enough milk, and ask his advice as to good milk substitutes.

I have often been asked if it is a good idea to wean from the breast to the bottle, and then from the bottle to a cup. My answer is: Why bother with two weanings? If the child is old enough, it's far better to go straight from the breast to the cup and skip the bottle altogether. Introduce the cup by putting one mouthful of liquid into it at a time. In this way, the baby will be able to swallow the small mouthful without choking. It will also avoid a tremendous amount of mess. Be prepared for the baby to play with the cup. He'll turn it over or turn it upside down and drink from the wrong side. It's all part of his efforts to come to terms with this new object, and if a little liquid spills down his neck, don't discourage his play simply because it creates a mess. Not to allow a child this kind of exploration would be to refuse his attempts to establish independence. You'll also find that babies will probably suck on the rim of the cup. This is the child's way of shaping an old appropriate behavior to a new appropriate behavior. After the child has successfully negotiated the first mouthful, keep adding more mouthfuls, one at a time, until his thirst is satisfied. If he becomes frustrated or tired using the cup, reward his efforts by allowing him to finish off the meal with the familiar bottle.

For working mothers, the procedure will have to be a little different. Many working mothers will not have the luxury of weaning from breast to cup and will have to substitute relief bottles. This is not without its hazards, but it's a necessity. Both working mothers and nonworking mothers should introduce one relief bottle a day—either of your own milk or formula—to the child right from day one. You can never tell when you might have to be away from the child, and if the baby has never had a relief bottle, he may refuse to feed while the mother is gone. Most nursing mothers have discovered that if someone other than the mother (the father, for example) introduces the relief bottle, the transition will be easier. When the baby is with the mother, he is intensely reminded of the breast and may find it intolerable to accept a substitute. But if the father gives the bottle, the baby may accept it more readily. Many working mothers have found that they are able, after an adjustment period of a couple of weeks, to get the baby on a schedule on which he nurses from the breast in the morning and evening and takes relief bottles from a care giver during the day. Later, at about nine or ten months, the baby can then be weaned, for the daytime feedings, to a cup.

7
Self-Feeding

As a baby passes through the infant stage, he will want to do more and more things for himself. Encouraging this progression toward self-help is an important task for the parent, and one that should not be avoided because the results are often messy, frustrating or distasteful.

One of the most critical ways to help a child help himself is to allow him, at about five months, to begin to feed himself solid foods. Once a child is able to pick up pieces of food from a table or tray in front of him and get

41

them to his mouth, there's no reason why you can't give him small soft bits of vegetables and cooked fruit, or even bite-size pieces of bread or crackers. As long as the child is able to pick up the food in his hand and either gum it or properly chew it (if a couple of teeth have come in early), you should invite the child to do this—and you should also allow the experience to be fun.

Meals will now undoubtedly be extremely messy, and you may be alarmed that the child doesn't seem to be getting all the nutrients he needs. But right now, these are not the most important considerations. The task at hand is for him to learn to feed himself—and this will take time. Even if the child isn't getting all the foods you want him to have, resist the urge to overpower him and force him to eat what you put on a spoon. If you allow your child to feed himself, gradually he will let you feed him some of the time. This is particularly true if you can invent a game of letting him feed you, for example, followed by you feeding him. By the time the meal is over, the child will probably have eaten all the necessary foods. This is a delicate situation because some children become more dependent than they need to be if food is forced on them, and other children may flatly refuse to eat if they're not permitted to participate in the feeding process.

Sometimes parents miss the opportunity to help their children with self-help skills like self-feeding because it creates a big mess and because it seems as if it's play rather than the business of eating.

꙳

Recently my in-laws came to visit and were appalled by how my six-month-old daughter was taking her meals. I would put various foods on the tray of her highchair—peas, carrots, a glob of cottage cheese—and let her feed herself. The result was, of course, an incredible mess that they could barely tolerate. When my mother-in-law wasn't reaching for the napkin to wipe Amy's face, my father-in-law was holding forth on the importance of table manners. (At six months?) They were so distracted they could barely eat. I told them that this is how it was done these days, and that self-feeding was more important than table manners. I didn't convince anybody.

Regardless of the mess involved, it's important that a child experiment with self-feeding. And just because there's a mess at six months, that doesn't necessarily mean there will be one at eighteen months. We are sometimes afraid that if children don't start out performing a task the "right" way, they will learn bad habits. But it's foolhardy to think they're going to start out doing anything perfectly. After all *you* couldn't do anything perfectly in the beginning either.

If the mess bothers you, put newspapers on the floor under the child's feeding table or highchair. Then roll them up when your child has finished his meal. One mother I know opened up a large plastic garbage bag and fastened it to the sides and bottom of the highchair so that it would catch all the spills. After messy meals, the mother simply rolled up the garbage bag, disposed of it, and put out a new one.

For your child's sake, it's better to learn to live with the fact that the floor, the highchair, the child, the child's hair and even your own hair may be covered with food than to quash a child's early attempts at self-feeding. Some people are less than comfortable with that sort of sensuous primitive experience, and if you are one of them, do it within limits that you can tolerate. Gradually the child will become more coordinated and the mess will diminish.

Sometimes parents discourage self-feeding because they are afraid he will choke. They put off having the child eat solid foods for as long as they can and are often sorry later on, when they find that he no longer wants to feed himself. If a child becomes used to increasing numbers of bottles, he may lose the urge to try new and different foods. As soon as a child shows a willingness to taste something from your spoon, give him a little taste of it. He'll chew it and if he likes it, he may ask for more. Recently, new reports about choking have suggested that hot dogs, peanut butter, popcorn, biscuits, apple pieces, nuts and candy can cause a child to suffocate, although this does not occur frequently. More often than not, a child will cough up food and spit it out. You can, however, minimize choking problems by avoiding the foods mentioned as well as others that could potentially block the child's air passages.

One of the greatest obstacles to a child's learning the various forms of self-help is not a reluctance on the part of the child to experiment, but rather the fears and distastes of the parents. As best you can, try to overcome your aversions and uncomfortableness, and don't let your own fears interfere with the child's becoming more self-sufficient.

8
Sleep Problems

One of the most difficult aspects of new parenthood is getting enough sleep. In the very beginning, sleep is a very precious commodity indeed, as both mothers and fathers find themselves getting up at all hours of the night to feed and change the baby. Later, when routines are developed and the baby grows old enough to sleep for longer and longer periods of time, parents are able to get as many as five or six hours of sleep a night—which can seem like a luxury after having gotten only two or three hours of sleep at a stretch when the baby was first born. Not all babies, however, are so cooperative. Sleep disturbances—or what appear to be sleep disturbances— often occur during the first year of life and can throw even the most sanguine of parents into a tizzy.

My ten-month-old has always slept through the night—almost as soon as he was brought home from the hospital. Recently, however, he has started waking up several times during the night. When I go in to him, I find him standing up in his crib crying his head off. How can I get him to go back to sleep, and better yet, not to wake up at all?

A sudden change in a child's normal sleep patterns can signal that something new and interesting is happening in his life. Occasionally it is a specific event; more often than not it is a milestone that the child has reached, such as learning to stand for the first time, or learning to walk or to climb stairs. Accomplishing such a task can bring with it an almost frightening sense of independence. Although the child may be excited and even proud of his accomplishments, he is also a bit bewildered, too. What exactly does this mean? he wonders. His sense of contentment or complacency is disturbed, and this feeling of unease may surface in waking from sleep at inappropriate times.

What to do? Your main task as a parent is to reassure your child that he will be all right. When you hear your child crying in the night, and you walk into his room only to find him standing up, perhaps even "practicing" his new accomplishment, simply speak quietly to him and try to calm him down. Keep the atmosphere as sleepy as possible—the child may not really even be fully awake and may go back to sleep with little prodding—by talking in soothing tones and keeping the room dimly lit, if lit at all. Pat him on the back and return him to a prone position. He may stand right up again, in which case repeat the entire procedure.

Often when children first learn to stand up, or pull themselves up to a standing position, they do not yet know how to lower themselves down. When you hear crying in the night, it may be because the child hasn't figured out how to undo what he has just done. In this case, you may solve your problem quite easily by teaching your child how to let go and lie down again.

When the novelty of the new experience wears off, the child will probably return to his old routines again. Solving the problem may require only a few nights of reassurance or of helping him to practice his new skill during the day.

My daughter is just four months old, but she's got the entire household in a real state. She gets her days and nights mixed up. For the last couple of weeks, she's been waking up at one in the morning to play, and then going back to sleep at five A.M., and sleeping until about noon. When she's up, she's really up, and none of us can get much sleep. My husband and I take turns playing with her, but I have to be up at seven with a four-year-old, and my husband has to go to work in the mornings. Help!

Most babies sleep at least twelve hours in a twenty-four-hour period but not all at once. Some babies sleep for four-hour segments and then sleep for five or six hours during the night. Others sleep eight or nine hours at night and then take shorter naps during the day. This child, however, needs help getting oriented to the conventional day and night divisions. In such a case a parent has to actively manipulate the baby's schedule.

The goal is to get the baby to sleep her seven hours between midnight and seven, or perhaps eleven and six. To do this, you will have to clip off about twenty minutes or so at the end of the baby's long sleep the first day. The idea is that she will be tired twenty minutes earlier than usual and will fall asleep that much earlier for her next sleep. Try this for three or four days until that small goal is reached. After that, clip off another twenty minutes or half-hour and see if that also brings her schedule slightly more in line with what you would like. After another three or four days, clip off another twenty minutes, and so on, until your larger goal is reached.

Developing a bedtime ritual that is different from the nap-time ritual will also help steer a baby into a sleep–wake schedule that is convenient for you and your family. You might, for example, sing to the child, put her in special pajamas, read a "story" to the baby, or rub her back in a special way. It really doesn't matter what the ritual is, so long as it is repeated every evening, and so long as it occurs *only* at the beginning of the long night-time sleep.

Try not to use the crib to serve another purpose such as a place to play when you want to be free of the child or as a place for punishment. I've heard many parents say, "You were naughty, now you have to go into your crib." If this is done, the crib becomes associated with experiences other than sleep—and no wonder the child develops sleep-related problems!

It's also useful to remember from time to time that sleep cannot be legislated. You can put a child in her crib, but you cannot force her to go to sleep. Think for a minute how you would feel if someone walked over to you and said, "Okay, it's time for sleep. Here's a glass of milk." Then he walked you into the bathroom, brushed your teeth (if you had any), and placed you down on your bed. How would you feel if you weren't ready for sleep?

9
Crying

My baby is three months old. Recently I visited my mother with my new baby, and I was very conscious of wanting to be a good mother. While I was there, I put my daughter down for a nap, and she started crying. My mother said, "Let her cry." But my instincts told me to go to my daughter and to comfort her, that she wasn't going to go to sleep right then, and that she needed me. My mother, however, believes that to let a baby cry for a certain period of time will make the problem go away. In fact, she said that I would spoil my daughter if I kept going into her every time she cried. I felt very confused: Should I let my daughter cry it out when I put her to bed, or should I comfort her?

I would say unequivocally that one should not let a baby cry for more than a couple of minutes at a time. Put yourself in the baby's position. If you were unable, for whatever reason, to correct a situation you were in—a situation in which you felt thoroughly vulnerable—and the best you could do was to scream in the hope that something would happen to improve your condition, how would you feel if no one came to help you? Particularly if you knew that someone who could help you was in the next room and was choosing not to come to you? What would that do for your sense of well-being?

It seems to me that it's a torture not only for a parent to hear a baby scream, but it's also a torment for the baby. There is some wisdom in the idea that if you let the baby cry, eventually she will learn not to cry any more at nap time. But is that the best way to deal with your infant? To me, it seems like a heartless way to handle someone who can't do anything for herself. If you let a baby cry each night for a week, you might be effective in teaching her that crying doesn't help her much. And in one sense, you will have solved your problem. But what impact will that have had on the baby's sense of well-being? The times when you feel good—actually feel comfortable and physically secure—you feel good about yourself. When you feel poorly—when you are in discomfort—you define yourself as bad. I think this holds true for infants as well.

Stand up to those forces around you, even if it means saying "no" to Grandma. Simply say, when the occasion arises, "When you had *your* children, you did it your way. I'll take my chances and do it my way. If I'm wrong, I'll have to pay for it." But I don't think you will have to pay very dearly for it.

Some babies do seem to need to scream for four or five minutes before they fall asleep. This crying serves as a release of built-up tension. If you know that to be the case with your baby, then naturally you won't harm the child by letting her cry it out for a couple of minutes—assuming that she then falls asleep. But if the child is shrieking and howling, and it goes on for more than just a few minutes, then I wouldn't allow her to carry on like that. Nor would I make a habit of always permitting her to scream for four or five minutes before going in to pick her up. When a baby cries, a parent should go to her and take care of her.

When you know your baby better, her different cries will suggest different things to you. You will know, for example, if the cry means she's hungry or wet or tired or distressed in some other way. You will also be able to tell if the cry is just a moan or a whine and not something you need to take care of immediately.

❊

Sometimes it seems as if I can never put my daughter down without her crying. Very often, after supper until late into the evening, she just seems to cry and cry, and no matter how tired I get, or how fed up I am with walking and walking her all over the house, the minute I put her down, she starts in all over again.

Pediatricians sometimes refer to this inconsolable kind of crying as "colic." In most instances, this disturbance ceases at around three or four months of age. There is apparently little that can be done to prevent these crying bouts. Whether you suspect colic or not, don't blame the baby for crying. The child is simply doing what she needs to do in order to communicate her distress. Try to comfort the baby until she stops crying. I know that this is hard. And I can understand why, out of desperation, a parent would want to put a baby down and let her cry. But short of desperation, I feel that someone should walk the baby around or otherwise try to comfort her. If you consider the fact that a three-month-old cannot do very much for herself, and that you as a parent are solely responsible for the child's comfort, it may be easier to understand why you should do everything you can to ease your baby's distress.

Remind yourself from time to time that you are not doing something wrong. The fact that your baby is crying is not your fault. Nor do you have a defective baby. And perhaps most important of all, keep telling yourself that the crying will stop eventually. You may be very tired and miserable, but the hardships of parenthood come with the territory—and they *do end.*

The best tips for getting the baby to stop crying come from parents themselves—tips learned the hard way after weeks and sometimes months of trial and error. One frequent suggestion is to go on about your life and your chores holding your baby in a baby carrier—a sacklike device that fits snugly against your chest or back. In this way, your hands are freed for accomplishing chores, but the baby feels close to you and secure. Others have discovered that walking back and forth with the baby helps to soothe the child. Whether the monotonous rhythmical movement is what does the trick or not, walking definitely seems to make the baby feel better. Recently another mother suggested to me that when her daughter seemed to be crying for no apparent reason, she laid the child on her back and moved her legs around in a bicycling motion; the effort was successful, she thought, because uncomfortable gas inside the baby's abdomen was dislodged. Yet another mother said that putting the baby on a pillow over her knees, with the infant's abdomen down, was successful. The mother simply rocked her knees back and forth, and this seemed to be a miracle cure for ending bouts of crying. Sometimes sucking on a pacifier can work just as effectively. The sucking reflex is connected both to the digestive process as well as to an emotional sense of security and well-being. If you don't have a pacifier handy, or the child won't take a pacifier, you can offer the child your finger. Many a fretful baby has been calmed by sucking or gumming a parent's finger.

All of this assumes, of course, that you have thoroughly checked the baby out to see that she doesn't have any physical reason for her distress. Make sure that she doesn't have a fever, or is not suffering from a burning rash. And when you have satisfied yourself that the child is physically all right, then be ingenious. Perhaps a gentle massage on the shoulders and back will help; perhaps a drive in the car. No method is absolutely foolproof, however. Just when you think you've discovered the magic cure-all, the infant will confound you and begin crying all over again. But be persistent and keep trying. You may need a break. Perhaps a friend or your spouse can take over for a while while you take a walk, have a bath or take some refreshment. You don't need to martyr yourself to be a good parent.

10
Pacifiers

I would like to give our three-month-old baby a pacifier, but my husband hates them. He says they look as if you've plugged up your baby. But I think, in the long run, that a pacifier is better than having the child suck his thumb, because I've heard how difficult it is to get a child to give up the thumb-sucking. Can you help us on this one?

Sucking is a reflex that aids in a baby's survival. If a child is able to suck, he is able to feed and therefore grow and thrive. There is evidence that *in utero* some fetuses suck their thumbs. When a baby is first born, he must learn to coordinate both sucking and swallowing in order to take in nourishment. You may notice, for example, that the first time a baby nurses he spits out the milk, or his tongue forces the food out of his mouth. Later when the sucking and swallowing activities are coordinated, the baby can begin to nurse properly.

But sucking really takes on a life of its own beyond simply being an aid to feeding. Some babies have a stronger sucking drive than others and will suck on their thumbs or fingers or a piece of cloth—whatever is handy and whatever they can find. Children are very ingenious, and because the sucking drive is so strong, they will find something to suck on to soothe themselves.

You can help a child by introducing a pacifier, but don't give one to him

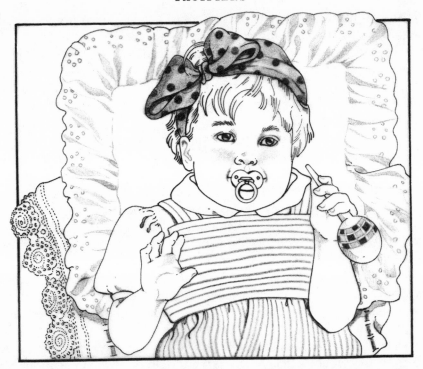

until he shows a desire to suck, yet is clearly not hungry. This is a very important distinction to make, and one that you should be alert to. For the first couple of months of the infant's life, you will be feeding on demand, and chances are that if the child makes a sucking motion with his lips, he is hungry. But later you will have to watch for signs of sucking and simultaneously rejecting the breast or the bottle. Try to avoid forcing the child to eat when he is really not hungry. Instead think about some of the options you have to calm the child down.

One of the options you have is a pacifier. Another is putting one of your own fingers into the baby's mouth and seeing if sucking on that will calm him down. Still another is helping the child to find his own thumb. If the baby takes to the pacifier—and not all babies do—I see no harm in letting him have it. In fact, some parents have found that if the baby has some digestive distress, sucking on a pacifier helps to ease the pain. Sucking works in tandem with the whole digestive process.

That doesn't mean that every time the baby shows distress you should whip out the pacifier. In the same way that you should avoid nursing the baby every time he cries or seems to be upset, so should you be careful not to abuse the pacifier simply because it mutes the child and is easier than taking an active role in comforting him. If you force a pacifier on a baby, he will eventually take it, calm himself down and probably fall asleep. But if he isn't making obvious sucking motions, then don't just insert the pacifier into the child's mouth to, as this father put it, "plug up" the child. Instead, walk him, talk or sing to him, and otherwise stimulate him. Calm the child by interacting with him.

Will you run into a problem somewhere down the road when you try to take the pacifier away from the child? Well, yes, you may—not always— but you may. But consider this: If the child has grown used to sucking his thumb, your problems may be bigger. You do have some control over a pacifier. But a child is literally attached to his thumb, and you can't take it away. Thumb-sucking cannot be stopped by the parent. The child has to decide to give up the thumb on his own. The pacifier, on the other hand, is something that at some point in the child's life you can gradually reduce the use of. The general consensus is that at about eighteen months, the baby's sucking drive begins to slacken off somewhat. Any time thereafter, you can begin to limit the amount of time the child is allowed to use the pacifier.

You wean a child from a pacifier in much the same way you wean a child from the breast—that is to say, gradually and in small increments. You may, for example, in the beginning, not allow the child to take the pacifier out of the house, or even out of his bed or crib. You may permit the child to use the pacifier only when falling asleep. In order to eliminate that use also, try holding back the pacifier for thirty seconds as the child falls asleep. Then give it to him. After a week of this, try delaying for as long as a minute. During this time, you might try some brainwashing as well: "I think pretty soon you will be able to fall asleep without the pacifier at all," you can say. Keep this tactic up for longer and longer periods, until the child no longer needs the pacifier to fall asleep. If, however, it doesn't work—if the child is clearly unhappy and upset without the pacifier, don't force it.

Dentists are not in total agreement as to the damage pacifiers do to the development of the teeth. But most believe that a child can suck on a pacifier or his thumb up until the age of three without any harm.

There *is* one hazard to using a pacifier, however. During the night, while they are asleep, babies often drop the pacifier out of their mouths and then wake up crying for it. You may find yourself having to get up ten times during the night to go into your baby and put the pacifier back into his mouth. In order to avoid this from the outset, remove the pacifier from the baby's mouth as soon as he has fallen asleep, if not the instant before he's drifted off. During the night the baby can suck on the roof of his mouth instead. In this way, the child may get accustomed to not having the pacifier in his mouth in order to fall asleep or to sleep throughout the night, and not having his sleep broken if it falls out.

11
Clinging

I have a ten-month-old daughter, and I think I'm going bananas because I can't even leave the room without her crawling after me, literally clinging to my leg. She's not interested in playing either by herself or with anyone else. Sometimes I even have to take her into the bathroom with me. Simple little things, like taking a shower, have become major problems in our house. Nothing is getting done. Sometimes I can't even cook dinner. Is there any way to encourage her to be more independent at this age?

I may be accused of being in favor of indulging a child, but I believe that this behavior is very normal at this age and, to the extent that you possibly can, you should allow the child to be as clingy as she wants to be.

Babies vary, of course, in the degree to which they become clingy, but almost all of them go through this stage. It helps to see this as a phase of development and, more important, as *temporary*.

Some children are relatively mild clingers—others will not let you out of their sight. Whatever the temperament of your child, go along with it as much as possible. Rather than pushing the child away and saying to yourself, "She's obviously spoiled and indulged and has to learn I can't be there for her every single minute," view her clinginess as a normal and important developmental need. It is best if this need is fully gratified. If your little girl is pushed away when she is in the throes of this clinginess, she's going to feel rejected and insecure. But if you allow her to hang onto you for a period of a month or two (which feels like a very long time and will be burdensome to you), she will be better able to end the clingy period on her own. In other words, if you let the child cling, she will then feel more confident about taking those first tentative steps away from you. She will know that she has a secure base to go back to. Pushing a child away, on the other hand, only intensifies her insecurity and may prolong the clingy period.

This doesn't mean that you have to be a prisoner to the needs of your child every single minute of every single day. What it does mean is that you simply have to take this stage of development into account. If you want your privacy, and you can provide a safe environment for your child— either a baby-sitter or someone else around to look after her—you can then go take a bath for ten minutes, *even if the child screams and carries on for those few minutes*. Although this attitude may seem cruel, it's not such a terrible thing to do. Likewise, if you have to go out shopping for an hour or two, and you have someone to take care of the child, don't hesitate to go out, even if the child is miserable for that time. Don't purposely, in order to teach her a lesson, go out for two hours every afternoon so that she will *learn* that she should get along without you. If you have to go out, go out— but not merely for the sake of leaving her and not to teach her a lesson.

Recently a mother told me that she was experiencing a similar clingy period with her daughter, and that she was able to get a few minutes breathing space this way: Periodically she would jump into the shower for a quick five-minute soak. Not only did this allow her a few minutes away from her daughter to gather her resources, but the shower blissfully muffled the cries of the child, who was, by the way, safely in the care of her father or a friend. The hot shower also had the added effect, she said, of releasing many of the tensions she was feeling as a cooped-up mom. "I got my act together and was able to emerge feeling refreshed and tolerant of another couple of hours of clinginess," she said.

This period can be very rough on a parent. It's difficult for anyone to be denied the freedom to move through life as one normally would. But it does help to try to understand why it is the child is behaving this way.

Developmental psychologists have noticed that around the age of nine months, children become very wary when strangers appear. You may notice that if a stranger walks over to the stroller and starts talking to your child, she will either turn around and put her face into the stroller or look up to see if you're behind her as you're supposed to be. If you are carrying her in your arms and a stranger appears, you will probably notice that she will turn around to face over your shoulder. It appears that the child is trying to blot out that stranger. Why?

This stranger reaction, which occurs around nine months, is a healthy sign. At this age, children are becoming a little more independent. They are beginning to feel, with this growing independence, a sense that their parents can be lost to them. They are more mobile, and they can crawl away from you—but these accomplishments make a child anxious that she will lose her parents. The sudden appearance of a stranger threatens, in the child's mind, the secure unit she has with her mother.

Psychologists have noticed an interesting phenomenon in the studies they have done with children of this age and their mothers. If you put a mother and a child in a room together, and the mother is seated, the child will, at some point, begin to crawl away from the mother. If the mother then gets up and moves—*even if the mother moves toward the child*—the child will become anxious and scurry back to the mother. The child does not want the mother to be a moving object. This threatens her sense of security. In other words, it's okay for the child to move away from the mother, but not at all okay for the mother to move—in any direction. When the mother no longer remains stationary, the child feels insecure, or adrift, in the world.

This feeling of needing a secure anchor is intensified as the child begins to go through the normal developmental stages of standing, taking the first step and toddling. Her new independence is somewhat frightening and you will find that she wants to hang on to you excessively. She will want to be the one to choose when to let go. And she will complain mightily should *you* decide to let go. After all, only very recently has she begun to absorb the awesome idea that you and she are not inseparable.

Paradoxically, the exaggerated attachment is related to the child's growing independence from you. As your daughter realizes that she can move away from you and perhaps even "lose" you, she will fluctuate between excessive clinging and gleeful exploration. The peek-a-boo game is so terrifically entertaining to children of this age precisely because it contains the elements of loss and recovery. Someone disappears and reappears. Mom is gone and then the two of you are reunited. This is a very important, indeed, crucial lesson for a child.

Keep in mind that this period is short-lived, and that it will end. While it seems like endless torment at the time, most parents, when they look back on this period, think of it as a very brief interlude in a whole long life.

※

My one-year-old daughter is excessively clingy and will not leave my side. If her father picks her up to play with her, she screams to come to Mommy. It's been going on for quite a while now, and my husband feels terrible. Although I try to explain the problem away by saying that most children are closer to their mothers, the bare fact is that every time it happens, he's hurt. I also don't know what steps to take to encourage her to go to him. Should I just go away for a couple of days? I really don't want this to continue. First of all, I'm going crazy from lack of relief. And second, my husband is miserable.

As we have just noted, children go through a phase of exaggerated attachment toward their mothers. For some children, this dependence can be very pronounced. For others, it's not. In this case, it sounds as if it's a bit on the extreme side.

Nobody really knows why one child is more dependent on the mother than another child. It would be almost too easy to suggest that there was a traumatic separation between mother and child in the first six or eight months of the child's life that caused it. And in most cases, this hasn't been so.

If the clinginess does indeed become unbearable, then you have to arrange to be out of the house for a couple of hours a couple of times a week. Not only will this give you a much needed break, but it will allow your child to develop a relationship with her father without your presence and without the constant reminder of her dependence on you. You shouldn't do this seven days a week just to teach the child a lesson—that's not the point. The point is to give yourself a break and possibly help your child, too.

Your husband may have to be prepared to put up with a lot of screaming the first time you do this. In fact, the child may scream so much that she throws up and then falls asleep in exhaustion. (Children often cry so much that they gag and then vomit. If this should happen, you have to nip this in the bud, because children can learn that this technique is a great way to get you to do whatever they want. Simply deal with the mess with dispatch and show no sign of concern or of being overwrought.) Even though the child may appear to be greatly distressed the first couple of times you try leaving her with her father, she eventually will adjust.

As for the father's feelings, keep reminding him that he shouldn't take this rejection personally and that it is fairly common for children to react in this way. Since, in this case, it's a daughter he's concerned about, there's a good chance that in the near future she's going to want to be "Daddy's girl" and all the problems will be solved.

12
Leaving the Child

Parents often ask me if it would be all right for them to leave their young children in the care of someone else so they can take a vacation together or go on a business trip. In order to answer the question, one has to take into consideration the age of the child, the duration of the trip and the kind of care the child will be receiving in the parents' absence.

Unless the father has been home and has been the full-time care giver of the child, it is probably the absence of the mother that is going to be most deeply felt. Most of the research on maternal deprivation, however, was done during the war years in Europe, when children were traumatically separated from their mothers due to wartime exigencies. The children were sent to foster homes and did not receive the best of care. But we are not talking today about such terrible situations. If the separation is brief, if the child is essentially healthy, has a good relationship with the parents, and has quality substitute care, then it's an entirely different story.

We know that children do go through certain reactions when they are separated from their parents. They may show mild despondency when the parents are gone, or crankiness or a generally low-key demeanor. Or they may be openly hostile and not very cooperative. When the parents come back, the child may, for a time, show indifference or apathy toward them. This indifference is probably a coping device. In essence the child is saying,

"Okay, I don't need you anyway." These feelings of indifference may alternate with demonstrations of excessive clinginess or heightened attachment to one parent or the other. This is the child's way of reassuring himself that you are not going to go away again and leave him. These episodes should be short-lived, however, and no one can document any research that says there are serious long-term consequences of having been briefly left at an early age by the parents. By brief, I mean up to a week or 10 days. Not a couple of months. In my estimation, even two weeks is a long time for a young child.

Many child development specialists maintain that a child under six months of age is not really aware enough to miss the mother. I tend to disagree. While the absence of the mother will not be as clearly felt as it would be at a later age, I think even a young infant is quite attached to and aware of the mother. Even when there are a number of children in the family, the mother still seems to be the major figure. If the mother is a working mother, and there is another primary care giver around, such as the father or a housekeeper, then the absence of that care giver will also show itself in the child's reactions.

Between six months and a year, children probably show stronger reactions to the absence of the mother, as they grow more aware of the mother and have gotten to know her better. And because between the ages of eight months and thirteen months, there's a very staunch and exaggerated clinginess anyway, a separation during this time is not advisable. If you leave a child during this period of his development, your absence will be quite upsetting to him. I cannot say with any certainty, however, that there will be any serious long-term consequences to leaving a child at this age—even though the child may react very strongly.

The arrangement you make for your child in your absence is the crucial factor. Make sure that a very specific schedule of your child's activities from the moment he wakes up to the moment he goes to sleep is written up for the care giver. If he is going to be upset because his mother is gone, at least let him have his normal routines. In the same vein, I would also make sure that the care giver knows all about your child's favorite foods and toys and games and that these are made readily available. Preferably, your child should remain at home. Again, if he has to learn to deal with the stress of not having his mother there, why add to it the stress of having to be in unfamiliar surroundings? It's also prudent to ask friends or neighbors who would normally drop in on you to stop by even in your absence so that your child experiences some continuity in his life.

Although we tend to think of goodbyes as being too painful for children to bear, it is very important to punctuate arrivals and departures. Do not be afraid to tell your child that you are leaving and that you will be back in a specified number of days. Take the child with you to the airport, let him see you get on the plane and see the plane take off. If a child is not allowed to experience goodbyes, he forms the opinion that people just drift and vanish and then reappear out of some murky place.

One mother suggested a good idea to ease the pain of the separation. Because she knew she would be away for a week, she made a basketful of presents—one for each day that she would be away. She wrapped them and told her child that he could open one present for each day that she was gone. Not only did this technique serve to help take the child's mind off his troubles, but it also helped him to count down the days until the mother's homecoming. I think you might also consider, if it's feasible, calling daily or sending cards to your child so that he has some sense of continuing contact.

If the care giver is not the father, or someone who is very much a part of the child's everyday life, it's very important to introduce this person weeks in advance of your departure. Be careful to stay with this new person while he or she is with your child. You don't want to give the child the impression that every time this person shows up, you leave. If that should happen, the child might become very overwrought when the time comes for you to actually leave for your trip.

If you can delay your trip until the child is fourteen or fifteen months of age, so much the better. By that time a child is a little more capable of understanding and doing things independently. And by the time the child is in the preschool ages, three to five, I think there is no harm whatever in taking a small trip. At that age, the child can readily express his needs, has other friends and playmates, and knows the difference between going and coming. In fact, such a trip can be a treat for a child of this age. If he goes to Grandma's for the duration, he can stay up later than he usually does and be indulged with ice cream and other goodies.

My general feeling is that you shouldn't leave a very young child for an extended period of time if you can help it. Whenever possible, take him along. Or, if you have to go away, start first with an overnight stay, and then possibly a weekend, to see how the child fares. If your child can experience your leaving him in small doses at first, he will be better able to tolerate a longer separation.

13
Baby-sitters

Many parents are concerned about when it is advisable to leave a young child with somebody else for an evening or a day out.

You can leave even an infant in someone else's care while you take in a movie or go out to dinner, *provided* that you feel very comfortable with the baby-sitter. Make sure it's a person who is experienced with infants and skilled enough to feed and change the child. If you are nursing your infant, you're not going to be able to go out for any great length of time anyway, and it will probably not be necessary for the baby-sitter to have to feed the child. But if you are not nursing, make sure the person is well trained in all the necessary skills.

A very young baby may be distressed to find someone else attending to him in your absence. He may cry for an hour, for example. This behavior is entirely normal. To offset this unpleasant surprise, I would advise having someone else—such as a relative or even a friend who has dropped over during the day—perform from time to time some of the routine child-rearing tasks so that the child will get used to having someone else care for him. If only one person always changes the child and gives him a bottle, he will become so used to this that the introduction of any new person will be upsetting. But if other people occasionally come into your home and say to the baby, "Come on, I'll give you a little drink from your bottle," or "*I'll* change you this time," the child will grow accustomed to having someone else occasionally *do* for him.

This isn't to say, however, that you should let everybody feed and change your child. Nor should the child be passed around from one strange pair of hands to another at a family gathering. Very young children become upset in this kind of a situation and often scream and carry on. Relatives may misinterpret this behavior as a sign that the child's spoiled or overindulged, but in fact, that's not the case at all. Simply put, too much handling is too much for a young child to handle. Instead, you want the child to learn to become comfortable with an *occasional* other person lending a helping hand, so that he will not be bowled over the first time you go out and leave him with a baby-sitter.

When the child is a bit older, he will be better able to tolerate being left with a baby-sitter—indeed, he may even have favorites among the baby-sitters and may look forward to the experience. You can tell the baby-sitter that she can indulge the child a bit—let the child stay up a little longer, for instance, or have a treat. Since it's a night out for you (and it's fine to want a vacation from your child), why not let your child have a vacation as well? Whatever it is that he perceives as a treat will add to the pleasant anticipation of having the baby-sitter come. If the child has to lose you for the night, at least he will have something to look forward to—to balance the scales.

The baby-sitter should be someone with whom the child is very familiar. Introduce your child to the baby-sitter long before the anticipated night out. Perhaps the baby-sitter could come over for an afternoon while you are with your child, and the three of you could be together for an hour or so. Let the baby-sitter become part of the child's cast of characters so that he won't be alarmed when a strange person comes to take care of him. Put yourself in the child's shoes for a moment. After all, you wouldn't want to spend the night in the care of a totally unfamiliar person either.

As children get older, they develop preferences, and they may dislike certain baby-sitters. If the child doesn't like a baby-sitter, regardless of whether there's a good reason or not (and there may be a good reason that you are not aware of), don't insist that the child stay with him or her. Find someone else. Your child may not like a particular person's looks or smell or demeanor. Why insist that the child stay with someone whom he doesn't enjoy being with?

14
Stimulation

Children are born with a variety of sensory and perceptual abilities that need appropriate stimulation in order to become perfected. To learn eye–hand coordination, fine motor control or to be able to track objects in space with their eyes, babies must be stimulated and must practice these new skills. Therefore, no matter what the age of the infant, it is important to provide your child with adequate stimulation. This excerpt from a new mother's diary shows that even at three months a baby is hungry for new experiences.

※

Dear Emily: Today you are three months old. Right now you are sitting on the bed in your infant seat with a pretty flannel dress on. When I went in to you, you were studying your hands. This last month has been a total joy for me as I have watched you take in the world around you. You smile a lot, suck your thumb and play with your hands as if they were a new toy you've just discovered. You like to bat at a musical star we hung from the ceiling and to look at a clown music box that Daddy got for you for Christmas. Sometimes we take trips in the car and you seem to like that a lot. In the evenings, we hold you and play with you and rock you in the rocking chair.

One of the main sources of stimulation comes from the parents themselves through the talking, humming or singing that they do with their baby. Even though your baby can't speak to you, it's very important that you talk to her. Several things can be accomplished by stimulating your child in this way, and although they are not necessarily supported by scientific fact, experience bears them out.

The human voice calms a baby, and there's no reason why you shouldn't talk to her as you are walking away from her. Although you are increasing the distance between you and your child by physically moving away from her, you can keep the connection alive simply by talking to her, telling her where you are going, and that you'll be right back. There's a distance, but there's a connection, too. This also works if the baby is in the next room and cries for you. If you can call into the baby and say, "I'll be there in a minute," the child is soothed by the sound of your voice and gradually learns that there is a connection between some utterance on your part and an action that will eventually help her.

Talking to a baby in a nice, calm reassuring manner also teaches her to attend to the human voice. Simply barking commands at a child won't help, but speaking whole sentences in an affectionate manner will encourage the child to want to listen to the human voice. She learns to take in an entire sentence or paragraph of words, at the same time increasing her attention span.

Babies can also learn at a very young age—as young as three or four months old—to identify objects in their environment by name, simply by having heard you call them by their names. One parent said that he had tested this with his four-month-old by asking the baby where his "pink mouse" was. The baby's eyes tracked over the entire room until his gaze rested on the toy mouse. When the baby gave a big grin at the moment he saw the "pink mouse," the father knew that the baby understood what he was saying.

Music is another kind of stimulation. Although you probably can't teach a child to love Beethoven by playing Beethoven constantly, you can both soothe and stimulate the child by the use of music. Emily's obvious attachment to her musical star and the clown music box that her father had bought for her indicates that she derived pleasure out of listening to them as well as playing with them.

Music and talking help to provide a kind of emotional and social stimulation and both are very important. These days, however, one of the major concerns of parents seems to be intellectual stimulation as well. While I'm not generally in favor of trying to produce little geniuses by showing them flashcards in infancy, I do believe children should be offered opportunities to do things that are not academic or schoollike but which are fun and from which they will derive information about the world around them. The young infant, for example, who spends most of her time lying down or propped in an infant seat should have access to objects that make noise, that she can reach and grasp and pull toward her. An older child might be entertained by playing with containers and learning that one fits neatly inside another. Libraries are full of pamphlets and books suggesting toys for infants and toddlers, and major toy companies have recently made a serious effort to test out the toys they offer. Make sure that the toys are age-appropriate, safe, nontoxic, colorfast and don't have tiny objects on them, like buttons, which can be pried off and put into little mouths. And, most important, do not use the toys or the music boxes or whatever object you've given the child as a baby-sitter. It won't do to simply hand the child a set of rings and hope for the best. Only by playing with the child and talking to him as you show him the new object, or as you both together listen to the new music box, will the child derive the maximum benefit from this type of stimulation.

Some parents have discovered that their children enjoy various kinds of physical stimulation as well, such as infant swimming, gymnastics programs and massage. But be wary of overstimulating your child. I would seriously caution against loud music or noises, roughhousing, passing the baby from person to person and bouncing the child on your knee. Some signs that your child may be overstimulated are crying, irritability, restlessness or crankiness—or the child may cope by being indifferent and apathetic.

15
Playpens

I recently bought a playpen for my six-month-old son, but he doesn't seem to want to spend any time in it. I'd like to be able to put him in it and have him amuse himself while I get my vacuuming done, or prepare dinner or whatever. Other children seem to like to play in their playpens but not my son. Can't I expect my child to spend any time in it at all?

Playpens are not the answer for each and every child. Just because someone has designed a piece of furniture for children, that doesn't mean that your child will want to conform to it. Some children are able to entertain themselves for long periods of time. Others don't want to be left alone for even a minute. In general, however, it's rare for a six-month-old child to be able to entertain himself for any length of time at all. And if he can, it will be a matter of minutes, not hours.

If you put a child in a playpen because you want to do something else, the chances are that the child will respond negatively to being thrust away from you in an unpleasant manner. The playpen won't feel like an inviting place to be. Rather, it will feel like a pen to hold him away from you, because you have more important priorities than the child. If, however, you introduce the playpen as an interesting, fun area in which the child can occupy himself with attractive toys, games, or stuffed animals, and in the beginning you are there with the child, then he may come to enjoy the playpen as a special area to play in. But if the playpen is used exclusively as a jail cell while you go about your chores, it will not seem attractive.

If your child never takes to the playpen, I wouldn't blame him. Some children simply never learn to like being confined in that way. A child who doesn't like a playpen in the house, however, might like it outside. Playpens are often useful in the backyard. If the weather is nice, your son or daughter can be secure and confined but still have the pleasure of looking at all the trees and birds and squirrels out of doors while you occupy yourself with other tasks. Be imaginative. Think of using the playpen in different places and for different reasons.

It's perfectly natural and healthy for a six-month-old to want to be in the company of his parent. In fact, it would be unnatural for him not to want to be in your company. A child certainly doesn't want to be alone. Not only is it more entertaining for a child to watch an adult go about his or her business, but it's important for the child to feel that he belongs to someone—that he's not alone and adrift in the world.

Occasionally mothers ask me: "Is it possible to harm a child by putting him in a playpen?" Some parents are adamantly opposed to the use of such devices for a child. If it is used poorly, as a jail cell, then, yes, harm can be done. Observe your child's reactions and use them as a barometer. If the child seems to be miserable, perhaps the playpen is not such a good idea. If the child appears to be enthralled with the objects and toys in the playpen, then the experience is probably a good one for him. But be wary of taking advantage of a mild-mannered, easygoing baby who might not complain very much if you put him in a playpen. For although the child doesn't protest, you might be depriving him of interesting and stimulating activities. Remember, too, that it's also important to carry a child around and have him look at new things, to introduce him to new sights and sounds.

Keep in mind that a playpen is a manufactured item. What in nature is similar? If you didn't have a playpen, what would you do with your child? You would probably put the child on your back or carry him close to you, as they do in many other countries. We manufacture playpens for the parents' benefit, but it's not a natural experience. Think of a playpen as an appliance to make your workload easier—but don't abuse it.

16
Too Much Attention?

My husband worries because our nanny gives our five-month-old daughter too much attention. He worries that she will be so used to all this care that she won't be able to entertain herself. How much attention is too much and how much is too little?

The question of how much attention is too much or too little varies with the age of the child. A child of five months can't do very much for herself, and to speak of giving too much attention to such a child is not really accurate.

While the long-term goal is for your child to learn how to entertain herself for certain periods of time, the parent has to begin this learning process by introducing self-entertaining activities in very small doses. It might be useful to begin by asking yourself this question: Can a five- or six-month-old actually entertain herself? I think the answer is no. At the very most, she can react to something you set up for her. The six-month-old might become interested in an object that she can manipulate but only if you have put it there for her. And at best, this interest will last for only a few moments. You can't expect much more than that.

If you think about it, a five-month-old infant is really terrifically handicapped. She can't walk around, she can't express herself verbally and she can't get to things she wants. Because you literally have to be her arms and legs and voice at times, it's almost impossible to give a child of this age too much attention. Keep in mind, however, that your long-term goal is to get her to develop interests. If you can set up an interesting playtime for your child and she becomes absorbed in this activity for a few moments, you've done your job. Build toward a time when she can do more on her own. But bear in mind that even preschool-age children don't like to sit in a room by themselves and do a task. They like to hear your voice and know you're around, and they like to check back with you from time to time. If they work on a picture, for example, they want to be able to show it to you.

In this case it would be useful for the parent to ask himself another question: What exactly would he expect a nanny to do while she is caring for a five-month-old? If the child is placed somewhere alone, she'll just cry. Putting her in a playpen with the expectation the child will find an interesting toy is not a reasonable alternative. Can she be put in her crib and left there? Looked at in this light, *not* paying nearly full-time attention to the child seems almost ludicrous. Gradually, as a child's attention span increases with age, you will find that she is able to do more and more things for herself, and that your constant attention is no longer necessary.

The only way a parent can pay too much attention to a child is if he anticipates the baby's needs before she expresses them. In that sense, you might make a mistake by paying too much "attention" to the child. Let the child squawk a little when she calls out for the bottle. Let her make a few sounds that indicate to you that she wants you to come over and pick her up. This doesn't mean that you should frustrate the child. Do the task quickly—but not before the request is made. Likewise, if the baby is taking a nap in the crib, wait until she stirs and begins to "ask" for you before you go in to her. Don't feel you have to sit there and wait for her to wake up so that she won't have any moments alone. Simply call to the child: "I'll be there in a minute." Even an experience such as this will help to teach her how to entertain herself for a brief period.

Some children awaken at night and play and gurgle for a while before calling out or falling off to sleep. This is a good opportunity for a child to get accustomed to entertaining himself. One parent complained that the baby's sounds were waking the other children, so she had to go in to him. Unfortunately he then shifted from occupying himself to wanting his mother's presence. There's always something!

17
Biting, Hitting and Hair Pulling

Many children between the ages of ten and fourteen months experiment with pulling your hair, biting or hitting. A parent's first reaction is usually to say, "No, don't do that. Let's be nice to Mommy." To some extent, the child can learn to respond to the words "be nice" by imitating what you show him to do. But beyond that, the words have no meaning to him. It's almost like telling a child to behave or to be good. What does that mean? A child of twelve or thirteen months can have no clear idea of exactly what these concepts mean.

"But," says the parent, "he knows that when I say to be nice, it means not to pull, to be gentle." That may be true. He thinks that your command to be nice is a game and that the words are a signal to act in a certain way for a moment. But that doesn't mean that the child can understand what it means to behave forever, or even for longer than he thinks the game is lasting. Nor does it mean that the child can "be nice" when the urge to bite or to pull or to hit is irresistible.

Pulling hair and taking a bite feel good to a child. Sometimes it's a release of pent-up energy or aggression, much in the same way a kitten will suddenly run up the side of a tree, or even your own leg. Your child doesn't know that biting you hurts you. Pulling and poking may get a rise out of you. You may yell "ouch," and you may get angry—but because your child can't empathize with you yet, he doesn't know what you're feeling.

Some parents have suggested biting the child back, so that the child will know how it feels. But while the child knows how it feels when you bite him, he can't yet make the connection between that feeling and how it feels when he bites you. As far as he's concerned, it hurts when you bite him, but it feels good (to him) when he bites you.

Because it feels good, he can't stop himself. A twelve-month-old child is incapable of resisting temptation. (Many adults are incapable of resisting temptation, too!) Because of this, you have to deal with the child on a level deeper than one of giving verbal commands. You have to appeal to something more primitive—you have to shake him up a bit. When the child bites you, put him down *immediately*, say "ouch" in an annoyed tone of voice (because it does hurt) and walk away from him. Don't slap the child, don't bite him, don't pull his hair in retaliation, but do walk away immediately. The child will be shocked and surprised that you left and will feel terribly rejected and cry.

Such a rejection may sound terrible. But if the child then tests you by crawling over to you and biting you again, you should do exactly the same thing. Look at your watch. If it's a one-year-old, give him thirty or forty seconds of the silent treatment. The child should feel rejected, and the rejection should be paired with that act. Everytime the act is repeated, reject him.

Don't use this tactic for everything, because it won't work; it will lose its potency. And remember that you must try this technique *immediately*. Sometimes parents miss a critical opportunity because the hair pulling took them by surprise, and instead of reacting with a rejection, they laughed instead. This merely will reinforce for the child that hair pulling and biting are games. It might be funny the first time, but it certainly won't be the twentieth.

Part Two

I'm Me; You're You
Eighteen Months
to Three Years

Introduction

The toddler stage is alternately referred to as the Terrible Twos or the Terrific Twos. Parents of toddlers will often say that this particular age was not only one of the most delightful they experienced, but also one of the hardest. For at the same time that the toddler is learning new skills at an incredibly rapid pace—walking, running, talking, playing games and charming the life out of you—he is also going through a maddeningly contrary period. The words terrible and terrific are really rather perfect to describe toddlers, for sometimes, even within minutes, life for the parent of a toddler can seesaw wildly between the two extremes.

There are many critical forces at work in children of this age, and frequently they are at odds with each other. These conflicts are largely responsible for the irrational behavior of the toddler—that behavior we have come to think of as "terrible": the constant "no," the contrariness, the whining, the crying and the temper tantrums.

One of the forces that dominates a toddler is his ability to move away from his parents physically. The stage is called toddlerhood, in fact, because that is precisely what the child can now do that he couldn't before—toddle away from you. This skill is thrilling for the child and for you too, but it is also a bit frightening for him. Once a child is physically able to move away from you, he suddenly fears that perhaps he is removing himself emotionally from you as well. He is taking one more step—this time a very critical step—in the long gradual process of separating from you.

The younger child, the infant, really doesn't see himself as being a different person from you. Only gradually, and with the development of new skills, does the concept become real for him. And, quite frankly, it's frightening for a two-year-old to move away emotionally—particularly since the two-year-old *knows* he really isn't ready to stand on his own two feet.

The urge to do so, however, is strong. The toddler tries hard to become a separate person, and many of the conflicts of this age stem from his fear that the distinctions between you and him might become blurred, yet at the same time he will not want to lose sight of you either. In other words, it is okay if *he* moves away—but not at all okay if *you* do.

As you will have noticed by now, if you have a two-year-old, one of the ways in which a child asserts his separateness is by being contrary. From the child's point of view, if he does things your way, or goes along with your ideas and suggestions—even if the offer is of something he dearly wants, such as an ice-cream cone—he risks losing the sense of where you end and he begins. A toddler will find it necessary to reject your ideas so that he can remind himself he is different from you. Consequently you will find that you're embroiled in fights with your child almost constantly.

Part of this urge to be contrary has to do with a new-found sense of power. Parents are often horrified to discover that their "sweet" little children enjoy inflicting pain on others. But the issue here is not simply one of cruelty—rather it's one of power. The toddler wants to be effectual in whatever way he can. If he can get a rise out of you, well and good. If he can make another child cry, he has power. Although toddlers can demonstrate sympathy and affection, they are also capable of doing whatever is within their power to get another person to react to them. Another child's crying is proof positive that the toddler matters.

Happily, this desire for power for its own sake is short-lived, and you needn't fear that you have a monster on your hands. This pleasure in his new-found power is really part of the toddler's development—the urge to grow up.

Most normal and healthy children have a strong desire to grow, to become more competent, to achieve things for themselves and to become more capable. Yet this desire to grow up is fraught with complications. At the same time they want to grow up, they discover that this means conforming. They fight conformity because they fear losing their individuality. These conflicts plague the toddler, and are often at the root of behavior that seems puzzling to parents.

There are several ways in which you can help yourself and your child through this difficult stage. As a parent, you should try to avoid direct confrontations as often as possible. Arguing with an irrational two-year-old is a losing proposition; you can't ever hope to win. The child keeps changing the rules. Sometimes children at this age become so negative it's ridiculous. No matter what you try to do, you can't make them happy. If possible, try to have a sense of humor about these predicaments. If you can't make your child laugh, perhaps a good joke about the current battle will at least make you smile and help you to keep your sanity.

Offering toddlers minor choices and alternatives may help relieve the monotony of the contrariness. Allow your child to practice decision making. These needn't be critical choices in your eyes, but for the toddler, they may be signs of his individuality and power.

Allow a child to blow off steam and have a tantrum. More to the point, don't take it personally when the child has a fit or picks a fight with you. Try to remind yourself of the larger issues at stake here. Rather than letting your frustrations and anger overwhelm you, try to redirect the child's attention to other activities. Plying him with distractions may divert his attention from the conflict at hand.

One of the hardest aspects of having a toddler is that it seems as though you can't progress in life. You can't get anything done because the child is always "in the way." Going to the supermarket, for example, can be a major battle. Your son doesn't want to go, he doesn't want to put his jacket on, he won't sit in the car seat, he won't sit in the shopping cart, he won't desist from knocking the groceries off the shelves. When you get home, you're exhausted; you feel as if you've just completed an obstacle course. Constantly running up against this little person who won't be cooperative about anything causes frustration and anger. And let's face it: It's very hard to cope with an irrational person—adult or child.

It's useful, however, when your own feelings of anger and frustration surface, to remember that this stage will pass, like all the others, and that the heart of the matter is that the child is doing something very natural and healthy and important for his development. Telling yourself this, even if you have to put yourself on automatic from time to time, can help you to tolerate the tantrums, the whining and the constant negative attitude.

You don't want to become *too* detached, however. You don't want to give the child the feeling he doesn't matter. Because *mattering* is what this stage is all about. Probably one of the hardest things for anyone to tolerate is not to be heard—literally and figuratively. You may find yourself saying from time to time, "He's just doing this to get my goat, to drive me crazy, to get a rise out of me." You're right. He is. And it's important for him to feel he is capable of doing that.

Some experts refer to this stage of development as the age of autonomy. Of course a toddler can't be autonomous since he isn't self-governing yet, but the drive to be self-governing is very potent. Your goal as a parent is to prepare the child for autonomy, and the way in which you handle this difficult stage is crucial. If you squelch the toddler, you risk stunting his emotional growth. A repressed toddler may well grow into a self-doubting, insecure child who may feel that he can't stand on his own two feet or tolerate being a separate person. This insecurity manifests itself in one of two ways. Either the older child, and later the adult, will feel an excessive need to be connected to someone else in order to define himself, or he may become overly defensive and unable to form an attachment to another person.

The goal for both you and your toddler is one of self-government. Granted, such self-government is a long way off, but these are the years when the groundwork is laid. Your task is to guide your child toward autonomy and to help him achieve for himself the firm belief that he is a separate individual, that he matters to those around him, and that he and his accomplishments are valuable.

18
The Ubiquitous No

It's inevitable that the toddler will go through a "no" stage. Some children go through this stage in a milder way than others, but no child will bypass it entirely. This "no" stage is a very significant and important part of a child's development. And to think you can break him of the habit is a mistake—not only because you can't (and believe me, you can't), but also because it's so critical to the child's growth. A deeper understanding of the meaning of such contrariness on the part of the child will make it easier for you to tolerate. And take heart: There *are* options you can fall back on when the child is in a negative frame of mind.

Let's try to understand why it is that the child feels compelled to say "no" so frequently during this stage. If you were to do an experiment during which you said "yes" from the first demand in the morning to every subsequent demand all day, at some point you would run into an argument with your child and get a "no." Even in your efforts to say yes to everything, you would be thwarted. There's a driven quality—a compulsion—to the child's desire to be contrary. You may notice, for example, that your child will say no to something you know he dearly wants—an ice-cream cone or a banana. Or you may notice that when you say, "Come on, let's put your jacket on now," the child will scream "no" even while cooperating and putting on the jacket. A mother once told me that her child woke up in the morning singing a little song: "No, no, no, no, no."

Why is the word "no" so important to the toddler? Why would an otherwise sane two-year-old pass up his favorite ice-cream cone? Some developmental psychologists say that children this age experience a need to exercise power and control over the parent, and that the "no" is really an emblem of a power struggle. Others feel that because toilet training coincides roughly with this period, that the "no" is really a battle of wills over toilet training. I tend to think the "no" is the result of a separate issue altogether. I don't think it's just that you're imposing your will, because you've always imposed your will. And I don't think it's simply a question of a power struggle for its own sake, although at times there may be an element of that.

More to the point, I believe that saying "no" all the time represents a healthy effort toward establishing one's sense of self. In a child's logic, he and you are essentially of one mind through infancy. (Remember that sense of "We are one"?) But now, at this stage, the child is beginning to establish a sense of separate selfhood. If he agrees with you and goes along with something you've said or offered him, there is no clear distinction between the two of you. And the one with the shakier, less established sense of separate self is therefore threatened. Guess who that is?

In order to maintain the newly gained sense of being a separate individual, the toddler says "no," and in so doing, establishes a distinction between the two of you. That's the crux of the issue—not the ice cream. The child is compelled to say the opposite of whatever you suggest. The actual offer is merely a vehicle for this conflict. The issue of separateness overrides whatever treat is being offered and is a much deeper concern. In a child's mind, he is saying, "I'm defining who I am. And who I am is threatened by my agreeing with you. If I agree with you, I'll get swallowed up in your being and in your ideas. Who am I? What happens to my sense of me?"

You may also notice at this stage that the toddler becomes obsessed with the idea of "me" and "mine." He is involved with the idea that his toys are "his," and he won't want to share. This, too, reflects the beginning of a sense of separateness. Personhood is really what is at issue here. To be possessive is a way of protecting boundaries as a separate individual.

Well and good. So what do you do about it? You can't keep a child from saying "no." No matter what you do, you will eventually hear it. But one piece of advice is not to use the word "no" very much with him in the months preceding toddlerhood. Starting at about a year of age, parents very often begin to use the word to excess. "*No*, don't touch. *No*, don't do that." In fact, some parents use only one monosyllabic demand: "*No*."

As early in the child's life as possible, I would talk in sentences. If the child picks up a knife, for example, tell the child that the knife is not a toy. There's a negative implied, but it's not just a "no." Other sentences you can say to a child who is doing something he shouldn't are: "Let's do something else now"; "Choose something that's not as dangerous." In so doing, you are making the child attend to words and helping him to think better. You are also providing him with a positive model to emulate later when the urge just to blurt out "no" to everything becomes very strong. If you're inclined to say "no" all the time to the child, that's what you are going to hear back when he goes through the "no" stage. To be sure, you will hear the word often enough, but if you don't use it much yourself, you won't hear it so frequently. You may get an argument back—but at least you won't hear "no, no, no," all the time.

If you can remind yourself that the particular issue of the moment is not critical and that it's really a battle for selfhood, some of those fights aren't going to get on your nerves quite so readily.

❧

What if you have to leave the house and you know it's cold outside, and you want the child to put on his jacket. But as soon as you show the jacket, the child begins to say "no." You have to get out of the house, and there isn't much room for negotiation. What do you do? Do you simply insist that he put on his jacket and leave it at that? Do you force him into it?

One technique that I have found effective is to slip the jacket on while talking about something else. Thus you will be avoiding a confrontation. The child might not mind putting on the jacket, but he might mind your telling him to. If there is a discussion, the child may feel compelled to say "no." But if there is no discussion, and if, in fact, you are talking about something else, you might get the jacket on without his even noticing. "Gee, won't it be fun to go to the playground?" you might say, or, "Remember those funny mittens that Rachel had on yesterday?" This doesn't always work, but it's worth trying.

My next suggestion is a bit more radical. If it's freezing outside, and the child doesn't want to put on his shoes or his jacket, let him run outside for a minute. Chances are he will hop right back in and slip on the shoes and the jacket. Letting a child live with the consequences of an irrational decision may work for you. I wouldn't always recommend this technique, but it's a possibility in certain circumstances.

One mother reported that a friend had taught her never to ask her daughter if she wanted to go outside but rather to present her daughter with two alternatives. In other words, the child wasn't offered a chance to decide if she was going to go outside but rather if she wanted to wear her blue jacket or her green sweatshirt. In this way, you are offering the child a choice—not an important one in your eyes—but one that she will perceive as important and will give her a sense of making a separate decision from you. Don't say, "Do you want to put the jacket on?" but rather, "Do *you* want to put the jacket on, or do you want *Mommy* to put the jacket on? Do you want to wear your *red* mittens or your *green* mittens?" Sometimes, of course, a child can be contrary about this, too. If you ask her if she wants the green or red mittens, she could very likely say "no," period.

Some battles don't pay to be fought every single day. Pick your fights. Some you will lose, but so what? This period of contrariness is finite. It may not seem so at the time, but it will end, and the child will become more cooperative. Once the sense of self has begun to strengthen, the battles will decrease in frequency and intensity.

19
Discipline

When most people hear the word discipline, they think first of punishment, and when they think of punishment, they think first of spanking the child. But discipline doesn't have to mean punishment, and punishment doesn't have to mean hitting. I think I should say right from the outset that I'm against hitting children.

Hitting a child conveys only one thing: that you are bigger than she is and that you can hurt her. Physical punishment is not effective—it doesn't work. Most parents who speak to me about spanking their children have said, "Oh, I've spanked Tommy, but he does it anyway." Which leads me to ask: So why do you spank him? If it doesn't work, why do it? The answer is simple. You do it because you are angry and when you are angry, you strike out. A child is an easy victim. She has no defenses. When you're frustrated, it gives you a certain amount of relief if you pound somebody—even a little shrimp. I can understand why someone would have the urge to strike out at a child; what I can't understand is trying to rationalize spanking as a philosophy of child rearing.

In fact, smacking a child is one of the worst things you can do to her. In effect, you are teaching a child that when she gets angry, she should lash out and hit. You notice that when your child is playing with someone else, and she gets angry, that she hits the other child. "I told you not to hit other children," you hear yourself saying. But if you've hit her, isn't that what you've taught her to do? Of course, children who have not been spanked may strike out when they are frustrated, too. Consider what happens when the child is angry with you, and kicks you or hits you. You immediately get furious. Hitting you is intolerable and cannot be allowed. Some parents will then turn around and hit the child for having hit them. Where does it all end?

If you constantly hit a child for "misbehaving," you give her a peculiar message about how to resolve conflict. What you are teaching her is that the best way to resolve conflict is to overwhelm the other person or to instill fear into her. Surely this is not the goal of any parent. If you want a child to be a critical thinker, to exercise good judgment and have opinions of her own, you cannot accomplish this by beating the child into submission.

There is one possible exception when spanking a child may be effective. And when I say *one,* I mean *one time only.* That is in situations that are potentially life threatening. If after having made a strenuous effort to supervise your toddler, for instance, when playing outside, and after having spoken repeatedly to him about not running out into the street, the child does endanger himself in some way, perhaps then, and only then, you could consider one swat on a very padded bottom to convey your disapproval. And you can do this one time only. It won't work if you do it more than once. The swat should be more for dramatic effect than to inflict pain.

If you continually smack a child, eventually it will lose whatever small effectiveness it has. Spanking a child one time when he is in danger of hurting himself has a certain shock value that can be effective. Overdoing this, however, will ruin that shock value. Older children, in fact, learn to steel themselves to being hit. They know it's part of the consequences of their actions—but it doesn't alter their behavior. A child who has learned to accept physical punishment in that way runs the risk of not developing a conscience. It is as though the infraction has a built-in price and once it is paid, another transgression is all right. Other children simply clench their fists and say to themselves, "You can't hurt me, you can't make me cry." But such an attitude can lead to all kinds of emotional maladjustments later on.

A lot of parents think that a good quick spanking clears the air. Whack, and the air is cleared. One good smack, one good shriek, problem's over and everyone can be friends again. I do think there may be rare occasions on which this type of attitude may be effective. But the problem is: When are those occasions? How can any parent be certain that one situation is better served with a quick spanking? In fact, what usually happens is that one spanking leads to another, and before you know it, the parent finds himself relying on spanking exclusively. Most of the time when parents smack a child, they are overwrought and not making very good judgments. They are reacting to their own frustrations and anger.

While I'm on the subject of undesirable discipline, I want to call your attention to a small group of familiar insidious forms of coercion. I am referring to the use of guilt inducement, shame and humiliation as means of controlling a child's behavior. We may think words cannot harm us, but to children they can be as painful as sticks and stones. "You're a pig." "That's disgusting." And sarcasm is terribly confusing to a small child. Consider a furious mother saying, "Well, thank you very much!" This only confuses a child because the words and feelings do not go together. "You make me sick," and "You're driving me crazy," are terribly destructive phrases and should be avoided. It is more useful to simply say, "That makes me angry," or "That annoys me," or "I would rather you stopped doing that." A mild scolding and a clear statement of your wishes convey your disapproval. Most children will try to avoid being scolded because they fear the loss of your acceptance. Of course, if there are constant criticisms, the child will become indifferent to mild admonishment.

So if you're not going to spank a child, how are you going to discipline her?

The word discipline actually stems from the root word "disciple." A disciple is someone who follows another out of respect and love. And isn't that really what your goal is? To get your child to follow your example out of respect and love? You want your child to pattern herself after you. You want her to share your values and preferences, and it's only through respect and love that you can accomplish that. A child will care about other people and their property only if she has the ability to empathize. A child will empathize with you out of love. But if you beat a child, she will never be able to develop that love and respect. Discipline should really be understood as helping a child to follow in your footsteps.

There are many alternatives to engaging in physical punishment. The goal of discipline is to help your child to develop self-discipline. This should be your goal, but remember that a toddler is not capable of self-government. A six- or seven-year-old child may be, to some extent, but not a two-year-old. So although you cannot expect self-discipline in a toddler, you can begin to prepare her for its development. Your role will be one of guiding and steering her, and of controlling her environment.

Let's look at some specific examples. Karen is tipping over a dish on the coffee table. If you say, "Karen, don't do that," chances are she's going to do it anyway, because she can't help herself. A toddler cannot look temptation in the eye and walk away from it. Your role then is to remove the dish, or to remove Karen from it, or to distract Karen from her desire by suggesting something else. If you get up and noisily walk away murmuring something about the apple in the kitchen or the record in the other room, Karen's curiosity will be piqued. She'll follow you without an invitation.

What about the child who is sitting at the table, looking you right in the eye and then delightedly tips her orange juice onto the floor? The answer is simple: Clean up the floor and take the juice away. You will accomplish nothing by spanking her or even by putting her in her room as a punishment. Removing her to her room may solve the problem momentarily since she won't have any juice to play with, but it won't help you tomorrow. The child in this case cannot *learn* not to tip over her juice yet. She's too young, and the temptation is too strong.

Let's say you're sitting out in the backyard with a neighbor and the neighbor's children. You notice that your daughter and the neighbor's son have started hitting each other. What do you do? Toddlers can't be expected to work out conflicts between themselves. Some parents say, "Well, let them fight it out and that will be the end of it." Unfortunately that won't work. Nor will punishing the child by spanking her for hitting another child. It's the parents' responsibility to intervene before the conflict gets to the point where the children are smacking each other. If it does get to that point, take your child aside immediately. You might say, "You made Billy cry, and that hurt him. He doesn't like to be treated that way." That may not work for the time being because the child hasn't developed empathy yet, but the ultimate goal is to appeal to the child's feelings. Sometimes separation is the only thing that will work. Even if you want to spend some time with your friend, it might be necessary to leave for the child's sake. Another possibility is to go somewhere else, like a park, where other children can help dilute the intensity and also serve as alternative playmates. In that way, you can still have your adult companionship.

※

We were all sitting around having dinner one night. Joshua, who was two, kept getting up on the table. His parents would tell him to get down, and next thing you knew, he was right back up on the table again. No matter how many times they told him to get down, he kept right at it.

Frustration can lead to aggression, regression and apathy. It can also lead to futile repetition, which means that you do the same thing over and over and over again, even though it doesn't help in any way. In order to solve the problem of Joshua climbing up onto the table, the parents have to help him and themselves break out of this pattern. Saying "don't" to Joshua doesn't do much because Joshua wants to be on that table.

The parents do, however, have a couple of choices. They're not pleasant choices, but there's no way to raise a toddler without a certain amount of self-sacrifice.

One method is for one parent to eat while the other walks outside with Joshua or reads a book to him. Another possibility is to put the child on your lap. "Come on Joshua, I'll hold you." It's a sacrifice. But when you have a toddler, you can't always have things the way you want them. You have to find a compromise. The trick is to find the best compromise. An active toddler needs to be occupied, and watching grown-ups eat and talk won't do it. To expect that the child will conform is the fatal error. Let's face it: A toddler has little sympathy for you and what you want.

Speaking of trying to eat a meal in peace, parents often ask me for some handy tips when taking their toddlers to restaurants. Taking a two-year-old to a restaurant can be a good idea—eventually he has to learn to be able to eat in one, and it can even be an enjoyable outing *under certain conditions*. But remember it is for the purpose of training the child. Do not expect perfect manners.

Find a restaurant that will tolerate a child. Fast-food restaurants do not tax a young child's patience and are often tolerant of little kids wandering around underfoot and of the mess they will inevitably leave. I know a set of parents who frequently took their three children to their favorite Chinese restaurant. The first thing the father did as he walked in the door, even before he looked at a menu, was to order appetizers. When the family sat down, they removed everything from the table—the silverware, the sugar bowl, the salt and pepper. Then they whipped out a package of crackers and some beverages they had brought from home. While they were looking at the menu, the appetizers arrived, and the children ate. While the parents were eating their meal, the children had their dessert. The parents ate quickly and expected ahead of time that there might be problems near the end of the meal. "I'm always prepared to lay down the cost of the meal and walk out if things get out of hand," said the father. The children had a brief experience at eating out, and learned to enjoy it more as they grew older.

Telling a child that if he doesn't "behave," he won't be allowed back into the restaurant won't work at all in this situation. A preschooler could perhaps understand that but not a two-year-old. As far as he's concerned, one event just flows into another. "Now we're in the restaurant, now Mom's screaming again, now we're in the car." He can't understand that if he doesn't behave, he won't be allowed to have the experience again.

Trips to the restaurant bathroom are interesting and exciting, and a learning experience for a child. We sometimes take things for granted. But for a child, it may be a novel experience, a real first. Why take that pleasure from him? "We do better when we don't expect the meal in a restaurant to be relaxing for us because it is not the intention," one mother said. I think she's right. You can pick another time for yourselves to dine out without the children.

Disciplining a child requires a great deal of self-discipline. It is one of the most difficult tasks of parenthood. So often the short-term goals and the long-term goals seem to run counter to one another. Try to remind yourself that just about everything requires practice and self-control. You have to allow for fooling around, mistakes, crankiness, impatience and more. If a child sees that the adults do not lose their cool, he will be more apt to calm down. Take solace in the fact that children change. They mature. They develop social skills, tolerate delays better and become more proficient in general. Toddlerhood is not forever.

20
Sharing

One of the greatest sources of upset and chagrin for parents of toddlers has to do with the issue of sharing toys. You take your loving, wonderful child out to the park, you go over to the sandbox, and he either grabs someone else's pail or another child grabs his shovel. A battle royal ensues.

Rule One: Never let young children fight. They're too young. And nothing is to be gained. As mentioned in the previous chapter, parents sometimes say, "Oh, let's just let them fight it out, and they'll learn not to do it." In all likelihood, they won't—and the situation is potentially dangerous. Someone could get poked in the eye or bashed on the head. Move in and separate them. Sharing is difficult at this age because toddlers can't conceptualize what's involved. Only recently has the toddler gotten a firm grasp on the concepts of *me* and *my* and *mine*. Toddlerhood is a definition-of-self stage: "Whatever I want is mine; whatever I have my hands on belongs to me." And of course the toddler wants everything. Two toddlers, therefore, can't share the same space very well.

Avoid the temptation to force your child to share his possessions. It touches too deeply on his sense of being. Since it is not mainly the material property in question, but also the notion of self-definition, forcing a child to share what is his can be experienced as a violation of his integrity and will affect his sense of well-being.

Sometimes parents inadvertently offer another child something that belongs to their son or daughter. I would not offer, or even worse, give away an article that is your child's. I prefer asking a child if he would like to lend it. Remember, at this age the idea of giving something away is impossible to grasp. One of the biggest difficulties for a child this age is understanding what you mean when you say, "Give it to Tommy just for a minute." If you take it away from Billy, how does it still belong to Billy? From the child's point of view, how can something belong to me and be mine if it is not in my possession? As adults, we know that we own something even if it is not in our possession; there are laws to protect ownership. But a child who thinks only concretely about things can't begin to understand how something can be *mine* if he gives it to someone else. Expect a strong protest when your child realizes the toy is not there for him to use. Often a forgotten object becomes a prized possession when you ask that it be donated to someone else. I would not force the issue.

Naturally you want your toddler to become a cooperative member of the community. This desire is threatened when you see him acting in a barbaric, selfish or greedy way. Toddlers actually exhibit two types of extreme behavior related to sharing. Some children will give up every toy they have as soon as they see another kid coming, because they can't tolerate the potential conflict. Others will grab everything in sight. Protect your child from both extremes. If your child is a grabber, expose him to other children and their toys on a limited basis, because he's going to find himself enmeshed in a number of conflicts and probably won't, for a period of time, be very popular. If your child is on the meek side, and gives up his toys too readily, I would step in and help him learn to negotiate with other children.

Teaching a child negotiating skills requires intervention on your part. Children can't just learn how to share without having a role model—and you have to be that role model. When you see a conflict over sharing brewing, step in and speak to the children. "Jennifer doesn't like it when you take her pail. Perhaps we can offer you something else. Would you like to play with Jennifer's wagon?"

Say that, but don't expect it to work. You can't hope that this lesson will solve the problem today or even tomorrow. What you're doing is planting seeds for the future so that later when your children are able to tolerate the idea of sharing, they will have some idea of the correct things to say and do.

You can also help teach a child about sharing by playing a game of exchange. The game works best if *you* introduce it because your child trusts you. He knows that you will give the toy back when the game is finished. The game is pretty simple but an important one for the child. Put a toy in his hand and one in yours. "Hand me that; I'll hand you this." "Now I'll give this back to you, and you give me that back." Through this game he will learn something about reciprocity, mutuality, exchange and trust—but it doesn't mean he'll then be able to go to the park and share his toys. Or want to. It just means that you're helping him with a concept. Someday in the future, if you protect and guide your child, serve as a model for negotiation skills for him, and play games of exchange, all of this will come together, and you will be rewarded by the sight of him lending his toys to other children in the sandbox.

21
Toilet Training

Toilet training your child can be one of the most difficult tasks of child rearing—and the one most fraught with emotional overtones. Poor handling of toilet training can cause a host of other problems later on, which may explain the anxiety many parents have about how to approach it.

As adults, we often take for granted the accomplishment of certain mechanical tasks. We expect a young child to be able to hop on and off a toilet without difficulty. But if that were all there was to toilet training, there would never be a question on the subject.

Even the simplest skill requires some practice. A more complex skill requires more practice. Can a pianist learn to play his instrument by sitting down once on a piano bench? Obviously not. He needs a period of time to practice. So too does a toddler need time to practice toilet training.

But practicing the physical skills is only half the battle. We tend to forget that there are many emotional issues that underlie the simplest of physical procedures. A child who is learning how to use the toilet is also practicing being more grown-up and taking on more responsibility. This is a serious step. A child has worn a diaper since he was born. That diaper has a special meaning to him. It's a comforter in some way; it's always been right next to him; it's been a constant companion, if you will. To be suddenly deprived of a constant companion can be very upsetting. This may sound absurd to a parent, but in some ways it's not unlike adult superstitions. We might, for instance, have a special pen that we take with us to a business meeting, or a special bracelet that we wear to an interview for good luck. Although we know, intellectually, that the bracelet is probably coincidental to doing well at the interview, emotionally we feel there's a cause and effect. So, too, with a child.

When a child is asked to put away his diaper, he wonders if he's going to have to give up being a child, too. Now we, as parents, know that it doesn't mean giving up childhood, but for a child such an action has a much more dramatic meaning. What's to be expected of me now? he wonders.

Parents often make the mistake of saying, "You're a big girl now." But who says a child wants to be a big girl? Isn't it a little too much for her? And what does it mean? We don't know what thoughts she may have on the subject. Does it mean she has to take on some other major responsibility? Will there be demand after demand after demand made upon her? Will she now be left on her own? For these reasons, pushing the concept of being a big boy or a big girl may not be a good strategy for all children. (As we shall see later, however, *some* children will respond to this.)

Besides the huge responsibility to grow up that toilet training implies, there is also the possibility of the training turning into a power struggle. The child may begin to feel that he's being coerced. He may feel he now has to give in to an outside authority over something that's very personal—control over his own body. It's not the same as saying to a child: "You can't have another piece of candy." This has something to do with his own body. As far as he's concerned, since he was born he's been able to do what he wanted with his body. Now he wonders why it is that his mother can dictate to him when and where he is supposed to urinate. This is no small matter for a child: A bit of precious autonomy is being robbed from him. Put yourself in his shoes. What if someone told you when to have a bowel movement, or that you had to hold on to it until you got to some predesignated place? The child senses that something has changed. Suddenly his freedom is in jeopardy.

Although these concerns may seem to a parent like making a big deal out of nothing, many things can go wrong with toilet training. Poor handling of toilet training (and by that I mean strict and punitive handling) is very unfortunate for children because it sometimes teaches them that what comes out of their bodies is bad. It can cause them to experience themselves and the products of their bodies as distasteful and clearly doesn't do much for their self-esteem. Children who've been handled poorly sometimes grow up with very deep conflicts about themselves. They experience their products as bad—and as adults this can translate into products such as ideas or feelings. Others can sometimes develop very strange ideas about themselves. They feel, for example, that they must become ultrafastidious adults.

One mother, concerned that toilet training wasn't progressing swimmingly, asked, "How can I get my two-year-old daughter to go in the potty? She appears to be very diaper-secure and very potty-scared. She'll say, 'I'm almost potty trained,' but when it comes to actually doing it, she's too frightened to perform."

The fact that this child was saying she was almost potty trained suggested that she wanted to please her mother. She understood that there was a goal in mind—otherwise she'd have said, "No. I don't want to." On the other hand, she's not ready to give in—perhaps for many of the reasons I mentioned earlier.

To help teach an insecure child such as this one to learn to use the toilet, try first, if she won't object too much, to put her on the toilet for just a minute at predetermined times during the day. Give her your watch, and ask her to observe the second hand complete a minute. In this way, she'll get accustomed to sitting on the toilet. If she does indeed do something, give her some mild form of praise. You needn't go overboard. Children get scared if you make a big fuss. And why bother? Everyone gets toilet trained at some point. If she doesn't do anything, tell her it's okay, and that maybe next time she will. Be very matter-of-fact. You're training her to do something for herself, and you don't want to get too involved. If it becomes a major struggle between the two of you, that's not a good idea. You should think of it as trying to help her achieve something for herself.

For a child who is feeling insecure about toilet training, your approach should be to help her feel more secure about herself in general and also about using the toilet. "See, you were able to sit on the toilet for a minute. We'll try it again later, and maybe you'll be able to do it for two minutes. When you're ready, I'm sure you'll be able to be potty trained like everybody else." Leave it at that.

Most children first communicate about potty training *after* the fact.

Don't jump to the conclusion that this means your child is ready for complete training. "Before" is a very different concept from "after." It takes more intellectual development to get it right. But the good news is that your child *is* telling you about it, which is the first step. Later she will be able to tell you before rather than after.

There are some things you can do to help a child with the concepts of before and after. You might try aiding her with the concept of serial ordering, that is, putting toys or objects in their correct order according to size. There are a number of children's toys, such as a cone with rings of different sizes and colors on it, that can help with this concept. Next you might try giving the child precise verbal instructions as to when certain tasks or activities can be done. "First we will get in the car, and after that, we will drive to the store." "Before we eat this cookie, we will finish the soup."

While we are on the subject of communicating ideas, I'd like to suggest that you provide your child with accurate words about the process of elimination. If you start early in your child's life, you will not feel uncomfortable using words like "urinate," "defecate," "bowel movement," and perhaps "b.m." when the time comes for toilet training. When we use figures of speech, idiosyncratic words, or baby talk we are conveying a sense of discomfort about the physiological functions. It is better to be accurate and precise and convey that there is no reason to be circumspect or ambiguous.

After you have had her on the toilet for brief predetermined periods, you may go through a stage when at odd times and in awkward places she says that she has to use the toilet. And then, to your chagrin, you find that she really doesn't have to after all. You might be tempted to lose your patience because it was inconvenient to take her to the bathroom in the restaurant, for instance. You might even insist that she do something. But this, if you think about it, is clearly counterproductive. How can you force someone to have a bowel movement?

Or you might be tempted to yell at her for saying she had to use the toilet, which, of course, is self-defeating. If you want her to tell you when she wants to use it, how can you yell at her when she does? It's a Catch-22. Instead, try to control yourself and see the request as a false alarm. Probably she thought she had to go. After all, she's just learning to identify the signs of having to urinate or defecate. She wanted to show you she was doing what was right. But when the time came to use the toilet, for whatever reason, she couldn't. Maybe she got too nervous; perhaps her muscles tightened up; maybe the urge passed.

Some parents have found it useful, if they know that their child usually urinates early in the morning, to keep clothes and a diaper off him for a while. Some children will not want to urinate or defecate on the floor. You can then take the child into the toilet without making a big fuss about it, and he can do what he has to there. If you do this once a day, you'll be started on your way. There's a risk in this tactic, however. Some children don't *mind* relieving themselves on the floor. But if this happens, don't yell at the child for what he did. Remember that you tried this as an experiment. Simply say, "Please don't do that here. People use the toilet when they have to do that."

Another gentle encouragement is to invite your child into the bathroom to have his bowel movement in his diaper. He'll be making another step toward doing it in the bathroom. Tell him to call you when he is finished. Change him standing up and deposit the contents in the toilet so that he can see you. Have him help you flush the toilet, and then dress him. Remind him that each time he has the urge to go, to do it in the bathroom.

Some children master both bladder control and anal sphincter control at about the same time. Overnight bowel control followed by daytime control is the usual sequence. For many children, however, bladder training is first. Overnight bladder control is usually the last to be achieved. These are only trends and should not be taken as rules to be obeyed. In general, children can begin to be trained at two and a half years of age. Girls tend to be a bit earlier than boys in this, however. If you feel that your child has the idea, is physically capable and can verbalize satisfactorily, then it is probably the right time to introduce the idea of toilet training. But don't hope for one-day results!

Some signs that your child may be ready to be toilet trained are that he signals to you fairly reliably that he needs to use the bathroom; he doesn't like the feeling of soiled diapers; he can go for a long period of time without urinating; he says he wants to try it; he shows interest and curiosity about the toilet; he likes to visit bathrooms; and he likes to watch animals or pets relieve themselves.

As we mentioned earlier, the idea of being a big boy or a big girl is frightening to many children. But *some* children can benefit from that kind of external motivation. If you sense this, you can invite your child to wear big-girl or big-boy underpants. Let him wear them for a couple of hours during the day. Walk him into the bathroom without much discussion and simply say, "I just want to help you so you don't wet your underpants today. You might have forgotten you're not wearing a diaper." But don't make a big fuss if he then soils the underpants. Remember, again, it was your idea!

Some signs that your child is not ready to be trained are that he seems to be oblivious to soiling himself; he shows no interest or curiosity in the entire process; he doesn't communicate about it after the fact; he doesn't seem to connect the urge to relieve himself with the act of going into the bathroom to do it; and he doesn't seem to grasp the connection between verbal symbols and action.

Most normal children have a strong urge to grow up. They want to master their environment and accomplish certain tasks. If you do not begin toilet training too early and you avoid turning it into a power struggle, your chances of having an easy time of it will be greatly enhanced.

※

My son is three and a half years old. He's had control of his bowel movements for over a year now. But he's still wetting his underpants daily. I try punishing him for ten minutes by saying he can't go outside to play. I don't want to put him back into diapers, but I really don't know what to do.

If such a situation arises, first have the child checked out thoroughly by your pediatrician, paying particular attention to his bladder and urethra. This doesn't mean there's anything necessarily physically wrong, but it's important to have him examined before we look for other explanations. When an older child wets his pants or his bed so often, we have to look first for neurological or physical disorders.

If your son checks out A-OK, then try to teach him to hold in his urine by playing this game. Start by saying, "Let's play a game. Let's see if you can hold it for thirty seconds. Here is a clock, and let's watch the second hand go around." After he has demonstrated that he can do that, praise him and then walk him into the bathroom so he can urinate in the toilet. The next time, extend the game to one minute. If he sees this activity as a game, it might not be so threatening to him. It gives him an opportunity to practice self-control.

I don't believe in punishing a child for wetting his pants. Do you really think he's doing something bad? Unless you think your son is wetting his underpants maliciously (which doesn't seem likely since it's been a daily habit for so long), the idea of punishment may not be very appropriate. It may be only that your son is a daydreamer, in which case it just never occurs to him to urinate in a toilet until it's too late. Or he may just get so excited playing outside with his friends that he doesn't want to leave to go to the bathroom.

Take a close look at what is going on in the child's personal and family life that might be causing him to have this problem. Perhaps there is a new baby, or you've been having marriage problems, or some other stressful situation exists. Your son may be showing his anger or fear by acting irresponsibly and babyish.

It's also important to find out how the child feels about his wetting. Does it disturb him or embarrass him in any way? If so, you can be a helper rather than a punisher by reassuring him that he'll be able to stay dry soon, and that you'll try to make it easier for him to accomplish this by reminding him (not nagging him) about going to the bathroom, and by rewarding him when he remembers on his own.

22

Temper Tantrums

There probably isn't a toddler around who hasn't embarrassed or alarmed her parents with a temper tantrum. One mother reported the dismay with which she watched her daughter have a temper tantrum in the middle of the supermarket. The little girl lay down on the floor and dragged herself along between the cornflakes and the apple juice as if she were doing an army crawl. "Mortifying," said the mother. "She seems to know when she's got me in an embarrassing position. What should I have done?"

A parent should start out with the premise that there's probably nothing you can do to stop your child from having temper tantrums. They seem to be inherent in the toddler. Let's consider why.

Children want everything most of the time. If you were to walk around wanting everything all day long, you would be terribly frustrated. The more unreasonable, greedy and self-centered you are, the more you will experience frustration. One of the problems with a toddler is that she doesn't know her limits. More to the point, she doesn't want to hear about limits. She wants what she wants right now. Because that isn't possible most of the time, toddlers feel more or less constantly frustrated. This may seem like a surprising and even a sad way to view children of this age, but it's true. A high level of frustration is a way of life.

Add to this the fact that toddlers have very little means of expressing their frustrations. A more verbal toddler might be able to tell you what she wants, and might even be able to give you an argument. Even so, you will almost certainly be able to out-argue her. For any toddler then, a certain amount of frustration is unavoidable.

In order to deal with this mounting frustration, a child will need to release the tension. And this is done in an obvious physical way. Even as an adult, you may feel the desire to stamp your feet, scream or even lash out at a person or an inanimate object. Certainly the toddler feels this too. Children scream, tear their hair out, bang their heads against the floor, arch their backs and flail their arms and legs.

From our point of view, such behavior is not always justified. But they behave this way because they sense they do not have any other options. For a toddler, there are few options anyway. They either have to have things their way, or they don't want anything at all. When thwarted, a temper tantrum may be the only option the child thinks she has.

Most children this age have temper tantrums. So the real question is: How do you, as a parent, handle such an event? There are two ways to deal with temper tantrums—one for outbursts in public places, one for tantrums in the home.

You're at a distinct disadvantage in a public place. Let's say you're in line at the bank, and your child is bored and frustrated. Keep in mind that the child cannot see that this boring activity has a beginning and an end and that in just a few minutes the wait will be over. Instead, she throws herself on the floor and begins to scream and carry on. What do you do?

Naturally you will be concerned about how you will look in other people's eyes, and you may be in an awkward situation if your hands are filled with packages or deposit slips and bankbooks. Nevertheless, you have to deal with the situation head-on. If there is no one else to help you, and you don't want to deal with the tantrum then and there, pick the child up and leave the bank. Do your banking later. If that's not an attractive option for you, ask someone to hold your place in line while you deal with your child.

Kneel down and envelop the child in your arms. Better yet, take the child over to a seat or a quiet corner of the bank. Hold the child firmly—not to crush her or punish her—but to restrain her, and then put yourself on *automatic*. Turn yourself into an automaton, so that your own anger won't interfere. Say in a monotone, over and over to the child: "You have to take it easy now. We're just going to be a little bit longer. We'll be finished in a little while. I don't want you to hurt yourself. I don't want you to hurt me. I'm just going to hold you until you calm down." Repeat that until the child quiets down. If that does not work, then the only thing to do is to leave with your child.

Although you cannot hope to stop temper tantrums altogether, it may be possible, on a given occasion, to *avert* a tantrum by giving in, compromising or distracting the child. Some parents don't really attend to what it is the child is asking for. Maybe your child would like to have a pencil and a deposit slip and sit down on the floor in the middle of the bank and pretend to be writing it out. So what? If you can't put her in a better spot, others will step around her. Most people will think it's cute anyway, and if you run into a few cranks, who cares? You will have done a constructive thing for your child. I always recommend bringing along some snacks— raisins, sliced fruits and vegetables or whatever. If you see a tantrum in the making, and can whip out an appealing box of raisins to occupy her while you finish your banking, sometimes you can avert an outburst.

This scenario is easier to handle at home. When the child has a tantrum, simply walk out of the room and let her finish. Don't make a big deal about it either. Just say, matter-of-factly, "When you finish the tantrum, we'll do something else." If the child is banging her head on a hard surface, and looks likely to harm herself, restrain her. Pick her up and put her in her room or on a carpeted surface. Frankly, most children are careful—unless they get very carried away. In fact, it's rather comical to watch the way a child will bang her head against the floor to get a rise out of you, stopping just short of really hurting herself, and then slyly look over at you to see if you're looking. It's not necessary to have a big hugging and kissing scene afterward. It's fine to acknowledge the end of the tantrum with a quick hug, but you needn't act overly solicitous or guilty about the tantrum. Some children, if exposed to angry and loving feelings simultaneously, sometimes grow up with confused ideas about the association between love and hate. You can ask if she's feeling better now, but limit it to that. One mother related that her daughter learned to tell her that her tantrums were over. "I all finished now, Mom," she would say. "I feelin' better now." A tantrum is an uncontrollable feeling that the child has to get off her chest—literally. When it's over, it's over, and it's best to be matter-of-fact about it.

⚹

What about when I lose my temper? Should I apologize to my daughter? Or is it a bad idea to say you're sorry to a toddler?

Sometimes parents lose their tempers, too. Let's say your daughter is being impossible—complaining about what to wear. "No, I want the pink dress. No, I want the green dress." And you find yourself saying, "If you don't put on this dress right now, I'm really going to be angry." Let's face it, parents lose control of their emotions, also.

In a case like this, it's okay to say you're sorry. Better than okay, it's a good idea. Most of us grew up with parents who never said they were sorry or wrong. But if you are wrong, why not admit it? Once in a while if there's a good reason—and I wouldn't make a habit of it—say you are sorry you got angry. Perhaps you could add, in language the child can understand, that you were feeling grumpy and cranky because she wouldn't make up her mind.

Recently there has been talk about the difference between telling a child that what she has done is naughty as opposed to telling her that she herself is naughty. "I love you, but I don't like what you did." While the intention is fine, such an abstraction really doesn't mean much to a toddler. A child that age really cannot see the subtle difference between what she did and who she is. If you tell a child that you're furious about something she's just done (and it's perfectly okay to use those words), she will feel that you are angry with her. And aren't you really? The truth of the matter is that you're mad at her—the perpetrator. "Yes, I was annoyed at you for doing that. I wish you wouldn't draw all over the walls." Isn't that more honest and direct?

Parents often ask me if it's harmful to yell at their children. No, not always. Children have to be able to see that you can express anger and survive it. If you feel angry but are in control of your anger, and you yell at a child, "I'm really mad at you. I want you to go to your room right *now!*" the child can tolerate that anger. It's also valuable for the child to see you angry with others. Perhaps you are annoyed at the gas station mechanic because he promised to have your car ready, and it's not. Say to your child, "You know, I'm really furious. What a nuisance. I'm going to call them up and

99

tell them what I think." This is a good demonstration of the constructive use of angry feelings.

"But what if my husband and I yell at each other in front of the child?" one mother asked. If the argument is a very serious one, it is probably best kept from the child. But if it's merely a disagreement over an issue, then it's okay (as long as the issue doesn't involve child rearing) for the child to hear you. But if you notice your child reacting badly to an argument you are having, pay attention to her fears. If she is cowering in the corner or biting her nails anxiously, say to her, "Mom and Dad still love each other. We just had a big fight because we were both feeling angry, but we're going to make up. We're not angry now. It's all over."

If the yelling is out of control or hysterical or if either one of you is beside yourself, this behavior will truly frighten the child, and for this reason, such uncontrollable feelings should be kept from her.

Incidentally, shouting commands at a toddler can often produce the opposite result of that which was desired. One research study demonstrated that if you suddenly scream to stop a child from an action, the child may well be stimulated to react by completing the intended act. She is not being defiant but is reacting in a physical way to an emotional stimulant.

Yelling and screaming are often part of a family's style of communicating. In general, subduing it a bit will probably prevent the children from feeling needless anxiety. But, by the same token, icy sardonic jibes from one parent to another can be just as damaging. There is no substitute for mutual respect and consideration.

23
Anger and Emotional Honesty

My daughter is two years and ten months old. I have begun to notice that she throws her baby doll around her room. She yells at the doll and sometimes says the same things that I yell at my daughter. I noticed that she whacked her doll a little while ago, yet I don't necessarily spank her much. But she also says creepy things like, "I'm going to twist your little head off." She seems to be really mad at this doll. Where does this violence come from?

Here's an example of a parent who feels afraid of her child's feelings. In this case, the feeling is one of rage. If you boil the episode down to its basic components, the child is throwing a doll around the room. So what? It's a doll. It's an inanimate object. The violence to the doll doesn't necessarily have any correlation to performing these acts, or wishing to, on a real person.

Anger is a feeling that many people have difficulty accepting. As civilized adults, we have learned not to go around killing and maiming others. We find the notion of one person hating another very undesirable. Little children, however, feel things very directly. They haven't yet learned to have "civilized" feelings. My guess is that the mother who had grown up to be a nice, decent person, who wouldn't harm a fly, became frightened when she heard her child's direct statements of anger in the form of violence. The child's anger triggered in the mother feelings she herself had suppressed in the interest of being civilized.

Every person has inside of him feelings of violence. Because parents sometimes equate feelings of violence with actual violent acts, they lie to their children about how their children are feeling. That lying confuses a child and makes her unaware of how she is really feeling at any given moment.

Suppose you say to a child, "Oh, don't say that. You don't wish that little Donald were really dead." Well, it may not be pleasant to hear, but perhaps the child really truly wishes that little Donald were dead. Remember that when a two-year-old says she wishes you were dead, she doesn't mean she wishes you were dead forever. In ten minutes she will want you to be alive and well and getting her a cookie. When a two-year-old says, "I wish you were dead," she is really saying, "I wish you would go away. I wish you would disintegrate. I wish you would vanish. I wish you would leave me alone." If you say to the child, "Oh, you don't really mean that," you're doing the child a disservice. You're teaching emotional dishonesty. Like it or not, the child really *does* wish you would be dead *for a little while*.

If you tell a child she really doesn't feel what she actually feels, how is she ever to know how she feels about anything? Later, as she grows older and gets a signal that she is feeling angry, she will immediately, without even realizing it, suppress that feeling and instead feel nervous and jittery.

101

She may then complain about an upset stomach or trembling hands or headaches. She'll feel anxious and nervous, but she won't know why unless someone helps her figure it out. When you bottle up or deny your anger, you feel something in its place: tension, nervousness, anxiety.

When a child demonstrates angry feelings, help her to identify them by labeling them for her. You might say to a child, "You seem to be pretty angry with the doll today. My goodness, what did she do to make you feel so angry?" Say this in a playful and gentle tone, but allow the child to express her anger. After several weeks of encouraging the child in this way, you may then introduce very gradually the idea of helping the dolly not to misbehave in some way other than twisting her head off.

Don't be tempted to squelch the child's anger in your own interests or because you think it is uncivilized and unattractive. It is *in* the child's interests to allow her to feel and label the anger and then to teach her other ways to deal with it. It's important to let the child know that she's furious and it's all right to feel that way. You may even teach her all the words that adults commonly use to express anger: anger, fury, disappointment, rage, disgust, irritation. Recognizing anger doesn't necessarily mean that a child will act on it—in fact, understanding anger helps a child *not* to act on it, but rather to express it verbally instead.

24
Whining

Whoever said child rearing was easy! Sometimes children do things that drive you right up the wall—and your primary concern becomes how to keep your own sanity. The Terrible and Terrific Twos are filled with such land mines—displays of inexplicable behavior that leave you limp. Whining is a perfect example.

Lately my daughter, two and a half, has begun to whine. I must say of all the things that she has ever done, I find this the most intolerable. It drives me crazy. I notice that she whines most when she's crossed and also when I pick her up from her six-hour day at the day-care center. A friend of mine said that she solved the problem by turning her head away when her son started to whine. She didn't get angry, nor did she give in to the whine. She ignored it. I've tried that, but it doesn't seem to work. Generally, Kate's been a very easy child to care for—an angel, really, until this. Help!

I believe that whining is unexpressed or muffled anger. Kate's mother was on to that herself when she noticed that Kate whined whenever she was crossed. Some children are very vociferous in their objections: They scream at you, yell at you or smack you. But other children have a more docile demeanor—not aggressive and not hostile. When they get angry, the anger is suppressed: It has a lid on it. The rage, therefore, comes out as a whine. That's why it drives you crazy. If Kate confronted her mother directly with rage, her mother would know what it was and how to handle it. But a whine is rage masquerading as something else. Because you can't respond directly to it, it's infuriating and confusing.

There are a couple of ways to approach this situation—behaviorally and psychodynamically. Turning your head away is a behavioral approach. The behavioral tradition in psychology suggests that parents not reward a certain kind of behavior. If the child does "X" and you turn away, you're not giving her a reward. There's nothing wrong with that approach, but behaviorism doesn't apply to every situation. Behavioral approaches are okay when appropriate, but it's important also to understand the meaning behind the behavior—not just to concentrate solely on correcting it.

Kate's mother could help her daughter by first telling Kate that she was whining. "I notice you're whining," she might say. "Is something bothering you?" Kate can't answer that; it's a rhetorical question. But the reason for asking it is to help Kate label what she's doing. Children don't reflect on what they're doing, but by labeling it, perhaps one day she'll hear herself whine.

Then Kate's mother could ask her if there were something that she wanted. Perhaps there wasn't anything that Kate actually wanted, as when she was being picked up after school, but in some cases there may be something specific: animal crackers in the supermarket, ten minutes of your undivided attention. Then again, the child may not even know what she wants. I once saw a nursery school teacher ask a whining child in a nice polite voice: "Is there something that you want?" The child looked exasperated. "How should I know?" he said.

The after-school pickup is a common situation for whining. Kate whined instead of screaming at her mother. My hunch is that she was angry with her mother for having left her all day, yet she didn't want to risk having her mother turn around and say, "If you're going to be a miserable brat and angry with me, I'll just leave you here!" Kate can't be angry with the person she depends on. And, by the way, Kate doesn't know she's furious when she whines. It's protective to herself as well.

Ambivalence is very difficult for a child. In a sense Kate was saying, "I'm angry at you for leaving me here, but I'm glad you picked me up. I can't deal with these two conflicting emotions. I'm too young." As we get older we learn to deal with ambivalent feelings, but a two-and-a-half-year-old child can't possibly cope with them. My advice to Kate's mother was to pick Kate up, hug her and say, "I'm really glad to see you. I missed you today." And possibly to follow that with, "I think you're mad at Mommy for something. Mommy must have done something to make you angry." Sometime later, when the child has stopped whining, the mother might try to get Kate to discuss it. "You know sometimes you probably get mad at me when I go someplace and you don't come along with me," she could say, and in this way encourage the daughter to express her feelings and thoughts and anger.

It is important that you educate your child about the angry emotions. There are many things you can do in addition to labeling her feelings. For example, you might take every opportunity to point out a disagreement between other people. "They look as if they are mad at each other, don't they?" If you are perturbed about something, you can say, "I am really very annoyed that the delivery has not arrived all morning. It really gets me mad to have to wait here all day when they promised it by noon." In so doing, you will be showing your child that you are comfortable expressing your anger and you will be helping her define and identify the feeling. It is also important to let your child know that it is all right if she feels anger toward you. "I know you are angry with me, that's okay. I did something that got you annoyed with me."

I told Kate's mother all of this, and several weeks later I was rewarded with a piece of good news. Kate's mother reported that she'd begun saying to Kate, "I notice that you're whining. Is there something that you want?" She said that, to her surprise, Kate had begun replacing the whining with saying "No" very loudly and adamantly, and that she had even begun to experiment with hitting her mother, confirming that angry feelings were, in fact, behind the whining. Although the hitting wasn't acceptable either, it was, said Kate's mother with relief, at least something she knew how to deal with.

25

Crying

Anger or frustration can be expressed in a number of forms—not just by whining, as we have seen. In the course of helping your child to grow, you will be in a position of having to frustrate him many times. His response, a natural one, often will be to cry. But many parents make the mistake of disallowing this natural expression of anger and frustration, and the consequences can be very upsetting to the child.

※

When my husband tells my daughter she can't do something she wants to, she begins to cry, and the crying drives him crazy. He's very apt to turn to her and yell, "Stop crying!" I feel that this is wrong because I can see that she gets confused and all bottled up inside. What should my husband and I do?

If your child happens to be crying and you can't stand it, you might be tempted to yell, "Stop crying." But you know, upon reflection, that it's probably not going to be effective—and if it is effective, what is accomplished?

By insisting that the child stop crying you are, in essence, telling the child, "Look, I want you to stifle your feelings. I don't want your feelings to come out and be seen by everybody. I don't want you to express how you feel." Obviously that isn't your goal.

When your child begins to cry, first try to deal with the angry feelings the child may be having. You might say to her, "It's okay for you to be annoyed with us. We know you're unhappy because you can't have another ice cream. But Mommy and Daddy think it's not a good idea for you to have another ice cream right now." If the child starts to cry, you don't have to listen to her. Why can't you walk away from her? Why can't you say, "Look I'm going into the kitchen," or, "Yes, I know you're furious right now, but I'm going outside to pick some flowers. If you'd like to join me, you may." She may trail after you whining and crying, but she's entitled to cry.

Some parents make an additional mistake of telling the child to go cry in her room. But when the child gets to her room and starts slamming things around, the parents barge in and yell, "Don't you dare throw your things around!" When does a child then have an opportunity to get her frustrations off her chest? Instead, children bottle them up inside, which only hurts them.

Plan ahead. You can probably see in advance that if you tell your daughter she can't have another ice cream, she's going to cry. Tell yourself that it's okay for her to cry, and then tell her that. "It's fine for you to cry," you might tell her. "I know that you're upset with me. Go ahead and have your cry. But I'm going to go wash up now because in a few minutes I have to go to the store." Then walk out of the room and let her have her cry. It may infuriate her that you've left, but that's okay, too. It's better for children to scream out their anger and frustration and get it off their chests. Later on, when everyone has calmed down, you might say to your daughter, "I hope you're feeling better. I know that you were mad at me."

Sometimes children will use all the ammunition at their disposal and threaten you with, "I hate you, I won't be your friend." To a child, saying he won't be your friend is one of the worst things he can think of. But don't take it too seriously. If a child says he hates you, it's only for the moment and is a very fleeting feeling. You know the child doesn't really hate you. It's just his anger at the moment. One thing you can do for your child, however, is to show that no matter how angry he is with you, you'll survive his rage. No one ever dies as a result of a child's vicious verbal assault. Stifle the temptation to say, even metaphorically, "You're killing me!" It's very important for a child to see that his parents will survive his anger and rage.

Simply say, "Yes, I can see you're very angry with me. But that's okay. You have to be angry right now, and later we can be friends."

The worst thing a parent can do—and I've seen parents do this—is to hit a child for crying. The child cries even harder; the parent insists that he stop; the child then tries to stop because he's afraid of getting hit again. This is disastrous for the poor child, who will have an implosion of powerful feelings.

※

My two-year-old daughter reacts to almost any loss of my attention with crying and screaming. For instance, if her father tries to put her to bed at night, she screams until I come and demands that I stay there. Even when she is doing something she enjoys, she demands that I remain at her side. This behavior seems manipulative to me and it almost always results in my giving in to my daughter. Is there a distinction at this age between sincere and manipulative crying? How can I break this pattern?

The distinction between manipulative and sincere crying is more often one of perception and not one of intent. In either case, the child wants to communicate feelings. She's trying to tell you something: She's not happy with you leaving.

Now why would she want to have her mother by her side, even when she is doing something she enjoys? And why Mother to the exclusion of all others?

This is all part of the separation process in the course of development. At this age, children want to control Mother—and it's almost exclusively the mother that they want to control. This behavior is similar to the younger child's not wanting to let her mother out of her sight. But in this case, because the child is getting to be more independent and autonomous, the issue is one of fear of losing control over the mother. A child of this age is becoming aware that Mom has a separate life and separate interests. Mom has things on her mind other than the child, and that's really frightening. And even though it gives the child a little freedom, the child simultaneously becomes a bit alarmed about this new freedom. The daughter wants to be sure that Mom is going to do what she tells her to do. In a way, the child is becoming a mini-dictator.

This dictatorial stage will last only a short time. Essentially normal, it's simply a stage connected with the child's growing autonomy. The problem comes in the ability of the mother to tolerate her daughter's behavior. For many mothers, this is a much harder stage to deal with than the earlier period of clinginess that we saw at about nine months of age. By the time the child is two, the parent expects the child to have more logic and to be more reasonable, and for this reason the mother may feel unduly put upon when the child appears to be overly clingy. The fact that the child is also stronger and bossier than she was a year ago doesn't help much either.

To get you both through this stage with as little frustration as possible, use a combination of giving in with the use of distractions and negotiations and compromise. The goal shouldn't be to break the child of this exaggerated dependence on the mother; the goal should be simply to learn to tolerate it. Gradually, children venture out further on their own. If they have an emotionally secure sense of your being there for them, they will be able to move toward independence with greater confidence. By experiencing your physical availability, they will learn to have a mental and emotional security that makes them feel more self-reliant.

26
Setting Limits

My three-year-old son won't take "no" for an answer and hasn't for as long as I can remember. He'll ask, "Can I have another cookie?" I'll answer, "No, I said no and I mean no." And he'll say, "But I want another cookie." And he'll keep pestering and pestering me until I give in or until I blow my stack. He will never just simply say, "Okay."

The answer is simple: Don't give your child "no" for an answer. Before you become alarmed by my answer, allow me to elaborate. All too often parents say, "He has to learn who's boss" or "She'll meet with plenty of frustration later." Teaching a child on the basis of some principle that he ought to take no for an answer isn't worth the struggle.

This doesn't mean that you have to give in either. Make a game of it; don't take the situation so seriously that you're tempted to "blow your stack." For example, before cookie time (because you know there's going to be a problem), let him choose a certain number of cookies out of the box. If the number meets with your approval, wrap up the box and put it away. He's made his choice; he's got the cookies in front of him; the box of cookies is gone. That's it for now. In your own mind, however, you know that you can, if you have to, give him half a cookie more.

When he then says, "Can I have another cookie?" you can avoid the word "no." The dialogue that ensues might go something like this:

"You agreed to have those three cookies you took. What do you mean you want another one?"

"I want another cookie."

"But wait a minute. You agreed to take three cookies. You took the three cookies; now I put the bag away."

"I want another cookie."

"I'll tell you what. If you want another cookie, half a cookie is the most I'm going to give you. Take it or leave it. Which half do you want?"

He takes the bigger half.

"You got it. That's it."

After that, forget about the cookies. Go on to the next activity. You've made a little game out of it; you've given him a choice.

Another approach might be the following:

"I'll tell you what. You want one more? Here's another cookie. I'm putting it in a plastic bag. You can have the cookie, but I don't want you to have it now. Let's have this cookie after supper. We're putting it in a bag. And we're putting the bag up here on this shelf. It's yours. It has your name on it. But you can't have it now. After suppertime, you've got that cookie. It's yours."

To the extent that you can, avoid saying "no." No one wants to be told "no." You go to your boss and ask him if you can leave early. You don't want him just to say no. You want an explanation as to *why* you can't leave early. Perhaps he has a deadline and will be really stuck if you leave. But if he just says no, that makes you angry. Parents say to their kids, "I said no. I meant no." But we wouldn't talk to other adults like that.

It isn't always useful to make analogies between adult relations and child relations, because they're not the same. But it does help from time to time to put yourself in the child's shoes to see how it would feel. You also want to prepare your child to think as he gets older. You want him to be critical in his judgments. Teaching a child, by your example, that there's never any room for negotiating or making choices in life may suggest that you expect blind obedience—but it won't help him in the long run to be discriminating in choices and thinking.

27
Active and Passive Play

My eighteen-month-old son used to love to have me read to him. Now that he can walk and run around, however, he won't sit still long enough to get involved with a book. I find also that when I'm reading, he gets very angry and wants to take the book out of my hands. Is this some hostility he has to books in general or to the fact that I'm reading? How can I encourage him to look at books, or does it matter at this age?

It's best to allow a toddler the freedom to explore. A toddler—with a few exceptions—should not be restrained. Only when the child is in danger of hurting himself or damaging something else should you confine him. Instead, allow him to roam as freely as he can so that he can actively discover and explore and play with various objects and spaces—books included. Keep in mind that, for a toddler, books become objects of action. They are things you spin, throw, twist, tear and occasionally bite. For an eighteen-month-old, a book is not necessarily something you sit and look at—unless you are in the mood.

This isn't to say you can't encourage your child to have an interest in looking at the pictures in books. You may want to have a story time—such as at bedtime, or rest time—but I would not organize the boy's day in such a way that he has to have a reading time, or so that he feels he has to love books. Better to let the child be drawn to books in his own time and his own way.

If the child gets "angry" or disruptive when you yourself attempt to sit down with a book, you have to assume that he is primarily reacting to the lack of "undivided" attention. The phone is another "intruder" that children compete with. Many mothers say they have a great deal of trouble conducting even a short conversation on the telephone. Although the child may be playing by himself quite contentedly, it seems as though the minute the phone rings, the child gets up and has to ask you a million "questions" while you are on the phone. Or the child will begin to demand, "Let me talk! Let me talk!" What the child is really saying is, "Don't talk to anyone but me. I'm the only one you're supposed to pay attention to."

As long as you are around, a toddler doesn't have to care about you. But when you become engaged with someone else, or become involved in another activity, suddenly the loss of your attention is threatening. The fear is that you're going to forget about him.

In the same way, a toddler will very often call out to you: "Mom, watch this." He wants to share every achievement with you. If you can give a child enough attention, eventually he will take on for himself the approval and acceptance you have given him during these early years. If every time your son shows you an achievement, you say, "You did that very carefully," or "Wow, you really put a lot of work into that," later he will be able to view his accomplishments with the same positive attitude. On the other hand, if you are constantly bothered by these requests for attention and approval and are more likely to say: "Don't bother me again. Play by yourself," the child will have a much more difficult time being able to internalize any kind of self-approval and may find it very difficult to see his accomplishments in life as valuable. In all likelihood he will continue to demand your attention long past the time he might otherwise have done so.

28
Hyperactivity

My two-year-old son seems to me to be exceptionally active—not at all like his sister was at this age. He won't sit still for even a minute, and I'm always chasing him all over the house and the yard. When I want to hold him in my arms, he wiggles out. He doesn't even like to sit still long enough to watch a cartoon on TV with his sister. Could my son possibly be hyperactive?

Hyperactivity usually refers to problems in controlling the motor system. Before applying this technical term, however, it should be diagnosed by a pediatric neurologist and a child psychologist. No one knows for certain exactly what causes hyperactivity. Occasionally it appears to be the result of diet or emotional factors, or it may have a neurological component. Frequently these three factors work together to cause hyperactivity.

It's very difficult to diagnose hyperactivity in a toddler. You can more easily recognize the condition later when most children have started to settle down. By the time the child has reached kindergarten, he will probably be able to attend to instructions, sit at a table to paint and color and listen to someone read to him. A child who is unable to sit still in order to do these things—at the preschool age—*may* be showing signs of hyperactivity.

When we say a child is rambunctious, we don't mean he's hyperactive. Although the word literally means "too active," it doesn't mean that to a diagnostician. Only with a pediatric neurological examination and a developmental assessment by a psychologist can we then speak of hyperactivity in a young child. It is extremely difficult for a parent who is untrained in diagnosing hyperactive children to pick out a hyperactive toddler.

If your toddler seems overly active, let him have the freedom to exhaust his energy. It's important that a toddler not be overly confined or restricted. Children this age should be given an opportunity to explore space—indoors or outdoors, and to be allowed to do things like running, rolling and climbing. To be penned up is frustrating for them.

This is also a good age to move a child from his crib to a bed. Toddlers like to wander, and you may find them sleeping all over the place. If so, let them. Give them the freedom to explore without harming themselves.

We should not confuse hyperactivity, which is a technical term, with impulsiveness, spontaneity, restlessness and impatience. Young children don't like to delay when they want something. They're very quick and demanding; their attention spans are remarkably short. Allow them their spontaneity, but control them, guide them and protect them as you would in any other situation. As toddlers learn to talk, speech gradually helps them to control behavior and will, to some extent, replace action.

If your child gets to nursery school, and the teacher says he is awkward and clumsy, bangs into things, knocks them over and is distractable, then it would be appropriate to consult a pediatrician. If the hyperactivity is the result of something physiological, medication sometimes helps. If it's the result of an emotional difficulty, interventions of a psychological nature may be of use. And if it's the result of a nutritional imbalance, you will be given guidance as to how to change the child's diet.

29
Phobias

During the toddler age, children often develop irrational fears of monsters, lions, tigers or even insects. They won't go happily to bed at night, because they are afraid that these terrifying animals will come out of the closet and get them in their cribs. They cry for you to make the monsters go away, but you feel helpless in the face of such an inexplicable terror.

These irrational fears are called *phobias* by psychologists. They are very normal and common during this age. Almost all children, to a greater or lesser extent, will have some brush with phobic behavior.

There are many theories about what causes a phobia, but the first step toward understanding this phenomenon is to acknowledge that a phobia may be a sign or a symptom of some struggle that's going on inside the child. Although you will want to help your child deal with the specific fear itself, you probably won't be very successful in eradicating it unless you understand it and what's keeping it going.

Naturally, phobias that children have tend to defy logic. Even though you can talk to the child about the lions he fears, and take him for a guided tour through his room so that he can see there are no lions there, and even though you can explain to him logically that a lion is too big to get into his crib, or that there aren't any lions for hundreds and hundreds of miles around (except perhaps in the zoo), the child will still fear the lions. The child isn't kidding you or manipulating you or merely trying to get you to come into his room—although that may be part of it. He is genuinely scared to death of this imagined menace. For a child persistently to maintain that some beast is in his room, despite all evidence to the contrary, something very powerful must be going on inside him.

Sometimes a phobia is the result of a momentary fright or trauma—such as the child who fears all animals because he was recently bitten or badly scared by a dog. More often than not, an irrational fear is a complex way for a child to manage an uncomfortable feeling. The basis for many phobias is the emotion of anger. Children who are temperamentally placid, or who live in a family that doesn't tolerate expressions of anger, hostility, criticism or aggression, may find that they are unable to acknowledge feelings of anger inside them.

This is quite different from saying that a child can't *express* anger. It's one thing not to be able to express anger—perhaps you can't get mad at your boss because he will fire you—but it is quite another not even to *know* you are angry. If you know that you are angry, but you are unable to express it, chances are the anger will find a way to get out. You may sit around having fantasies of getting even with your boss, or you may even sabotage his efforts by not sending a memo out on time. There are lots of things you, as an adult who knows that he is angry, can do. But a child is still developing and needs help identifying his emotions. If the child is not permitted to understand that he is angry, then it won't get to the point of being acknowledged.

Put yourself in the place of the little child who is angry at his parents for something they did. You're angry, but you can't really risk being angry with them, because they won't tolerate it. Instead, the angry feelings *inside* take on concrete embodiment *outside*. Suddenly spiders are potentially lethal. Lions and tigers, which represent raw emotion, are created. These lethal insects and animals are an attempt on the part of your mind to do something about these angry feelings that you have. They are no longer your feelings, in effect, but objects outside of yourself.

At the same time, these lions and tigers also present a threat to the child. The child creates potentially dangerous creatures in order to bypass his own anger, yet the creatures threaten him. The creatures, like the anger, are out of his control and can hurt him.

Children frequently play games that show how important this phenomenon is. They play at being lions, tigers and monsters, and they also play at being lion tamers or monster killers. These little games serve an important purpose. Being a lion allows a child to express angry raw feelings— without even being aware he is doing so—in the guise of the lion's roar and ferociousness. But because the lion play is a game, he has some control over these feelings. The child can start and stop the game whenever he chooses. And if the child can play the part of the lion tamer, so much the better. Then he is really able to exercise control over the lion—or the anger.

As a parent, you can help a child to deal with his phobias. Don't force a child to confront the feared object. Confrontation will increase the terror—not decrease it. Imagine being afraid of the water, and having someone bigger than you dangle you over a pool, saying, "Well, let's learn to swim." You'd be so petrified you would hardly be able to speak. The same is true for a child. Parents often think they can make the phobia go away by pointing out to a child that the fear is nonsensical. "Oh, that's silly," they say. "Nothing's going to hurt you." That's like telling an acrophobe he shouldn't be afraid of heights.

Confronting a child is something parents should not do, but there are a number of ways in which a parent can take *positive* action to help a child deal with an irrational fear. Starting with the assumption that there are underlying reasons for the phobia, you can now begin to talk to the child about angry feelings. You don't necessarily want to do this while he is in the grips of the fear, but perhaps during the day, in an innocuous way, you might say to him: "Gee, look at those people over there having an argument. Boy, they sure look mad at each other, don't they?" Or perhaps the child is frustrated because he can't get the zipper up on his jacket. The frustration leads to anger. It will help the child if you point out to him what he is feeling. "Well, you seem frustrated. It probably gets you mad that you can't do that as well as you would like to." This labeling of feelings for the child will help him to recognize his anger and frustration and is better for him than denying them. The parent who says to his child, "Oh, dear, don't worry. There's nothing to be upset about. Don't get mad," really isn't helping the child to acknowledge his feelings.

It also helps the child if you can label anger in yourself. "Boy I was really angry today when I went to the store and some man got in line in front of me. I told him he'd better get back in line where he belonged." Use the words *mad, angry, upset,* or *furious* so that the child will understand these words and be comfortable using them. To the extent that he can see it's okay to experience such feelings, he doesn't have to hide them from himself.

The crux of the issue, however, is the child's feelings about you, the parent. As a parent, you will often be in the position of having to frustrate your child. When a child is frustrated, he becomes angry at you. But children don't experience gradations of anger in the way that adults do. We can feel mildly irritated, mad, enraged, or completely furious at someone or some situation. A child knows only one feeling: total anger. When he is mad at you, he wants to smash you. For him it's an all-or-nothing proposition. "I'm angry. Bam. You should be dead. You should vanish. You should be chopped up into little pieces and flushed down the toilet." These feelings are, of course, terrifying. What if Mom should actually vanish? What would happen to the child? Who would take care of him? In the child's mind, the unmodulated feeling of anger can lead to destruction that's tremendous, that will ultimately imperil him. This is one of the major reasons for developing a phobia.

How do you help a child with his anger toward you, the parent? First, talk to him about his anger. Say to the child, in language he can understand, "It's okay to be mad at me. You can't hit me or bite me, but you can certainly tell me if you're mad at me. That's okay, and when it's over we can continue doing what we were doing." By talking about his anger, you are not only helping him to get it out in the open, but you are also telling him that he is allowed to talk about his anger and can even tell you that he is mad at you.

You can also reassure a child during his bouts of fear by saying that Mommy and Daddy love him so much that they're not going to let anything happen to him. You can make a show of going around the room and checking to make sure that nothing is hidden in a closet or a toy box. You could even yell at the monsters in the child's presence and tell them to go away. This may seem silly to you, and it may even appear that you are going along

117

with the idea of monsters being real, but since children inhabit a magical world anyway, there isn't any harm in joining them in their fantasies from time to time. Besides, we already know that the monsters are quite real to the child and that telling him otherwise won't do much good.

Gradually you can help the child defuse the powerful feelings the animal represents by allowing him to grow more comfortable with the animal itself. Do this in stages. First, expose the child to the animal in its most harmless, powerless, distant form—perhaps a picture in a magazine. Then offer the child an opportunity to construct a model or draw a picture of the animal with paper. Finally, invite the child to accompany you to a museum of natural history or even to the zoo, to see the animal stuffed or behind bars—still in a nonthreatening environment. Very slowly, you are helping the child to move toward an acceptance of the thing that frightens him. Another useful method is modeling. If a child fears something very tangible like a dog, viewing other children playing with a dog can help. Gradually the child can be invited to interact very briefly with the animal until the fear is overcome. This approach must be done very slowly, prudently and without criticism of the child.

❦

My daughter seems to have a phobia about clowns. Recently she went to a birthday party, and the parent of the birthday girl had hired a clown to come and do a magic show. My daughter was so petrified of the clown that she hid in another room, face down on the floor, and wouldn't come out until the clown show was over and he left.

Children are often afraid of clowns and puppet shows. This may strike a parent as a little odd, since clowns and puppets are meant to be fun and entertaining—certainly not scary. Yet if you ever go to a parade, and happen to see a dog at the sidelines, you will notice that when the clowns come, the dog begins to bark furiously. He, too, seems to be afraid of clowns. Why?

A clown is wearing a mask over his real face. Children have so recently begun to understand what "real" is, that seeing something that is clearly not real—a face painted over another face—can trigger a reaction of alarm. It may be upsetting to a child to see the mask on a clown or a puppet and not completely understand why it should be so. An older child, who is more comfortable with his sense of what is real and what is not, will probably be better able to enjoy the clown.

Being afraid of a clown in this way is probably not a phobia in the sense that it masks the child's anger—but you can help the child overcome his fear by talking to him about clowns and puppets, and about the way that clowns get made up before they go "on stage." Perhaps you could have the child draw a clown's face, or put clown makeup on a papier-mâché blank face. Or the child can be made up. But do it in front of a mirror so the transformation doesn't frighten him. Later construct some masks together. Let your child put them on and take them off while looking at his reflection in the mirror. This will reinforce that it is he that is in control of this awesome metamorphosis. Once the child understands that a real boy or a real man is only "pretending" to be a clown in order to be funny, perhaps the fear will subside.

30
Waking at Night

My two-year-old daughter has suddenly begun waking up in the middle of the night, crying for us to come for her. But even when we go in to her, she remains awake and won't let us leave her. It's as if she is terrified that we won't be there. Last night she woke up at two and stayed awake until six in the morning. The night before that, she was up between the hours of three and five. It's been going on for a couple of weeks now, and it doesn't show any signs of letting up. I'm concerned for her, since she isn't getting enough sleep, and I am also concerned for my husband and myself who are dragging around all day from exhaustion. The problem seemed to start one night when my husband and I went out to a movie. We had a baby-sitter here, and when my daughter woke up, the baby-sitter went in to her. She panicked and cried for a long time that night. And ever since, we've been having this problem.

The close proximity of the night out and the onset of the sleeping problem lead me to believe that one caused the other. Even though the child seems not to remember the night itself (when she woke up and her parents weren't there), we have to start with the assumption that she's afraid that if the parents leave her room, they are going out and abandoning her.

There are several techniques parents can try to help a child feel more reassured. Accomplishing this will take several weeks, and it will require that the parents not go out and leave the child during this time. Not until the child is *convinced* that the parents won't leave her will she be able to sleep through the night. It's a hardship on the parents to be so confined during this period, but sleep for both the child and the parents seems to be a greater priority.

Begin by talking to the child, during the daytime, about the child's fears. "Mommy and Daddy have noticed that you're afraid at night and that you are waking up. We've been thinking about it, and we think you seem to be worried that we're going to go out. Well, we're *not* going out tonight. We're going to be here *all night*. There won't be any baby-sitters or anyone strange here at all. You're safe and sound." Talking to the child during the day, when she is not so afraid, may stimulate her into hearing what you are saying more clearly than she can at night.

Secondly, when the child goes to bed at night, stay with her until she falls asleep. You won't have to do this *forever*, but if you can do it for a couple of weeks, it may pay off in dividends of extra sleep. When the child wakes in the night and calls for you, go to her at once, and comfort her by rubbing her back. Try gradually to wean her of your attention by stepping out of the room for very short breaks. "I'm just going to get a glass of water. I'll be right back. I'm not going out. I'm right here." Keep saying to the child that you are not going out, over and over again, almost in a singsong tone of voice. Tell her that you'll stay with her until she falls asleep, and then you are going to go to your own bed.

The important ingredients to success are patience and perseverance. It's essential that once you've started on a course of action you don't go back on it. Hang on. The problem should wane with several nights of this treatment. Take alternate watches so that you won't go crazy from lack of sleep. Perhaps one night it can be the husband's turn; the next night the wife's.

Make sure, however, that no matter who goes in to the child, that the routine is the same and that you are in accord as to what you are going to tell the child.

When the child makes it through her first night without waking, change the routine slightly. When she goes to bed, give her a kiss and tell her that you will be there if she needs you, that you are not going out, and that she is safe and sound. Try leaving the room before she falls asleep. If she won't let you leave without crying, stay with her until she is reassured or until she falls asleep. Fairly soon, you can begin to wean her of this habit, by leaving the room for longer and longer periods of time and by calling to her from outside her room.

Some children develop fears about their cribs, and you may solve the problem simply by moving her to a bed, or allowing her to sleep elsewhere. Perhaps she would enjoy a sleeping bag? Perhaps the novelty of sleeping on the couch for a couple of nights might get her over the hump. Toddlers often have the desire to sleep in really strange places—under the crib or alongside the bed, in the doorway or perhaps camped out on the living-room rug. In all likelihood, this will abate after a couple of months. Beware, however, of letting her come into your room to sleep. Sleeping in your bed will make it that much more difficult for her to readjust to her own bed and her own room.

After several weeks of consistent reassurance, it may be safe to try another night out. Many parents think it best to have the baby-sitter come after the child has gone to bed in order to avoid a messy goodbye. In general, however, it's far better to have the baby-sitter come before the child goes to bed, so that she will not be startled by not having you there should she wake up during the night. The baby-sitter can be instructed to allow the child many liberties you would not ordinarily permit (see Part I, Baby-sitters). She can let the child play a few extra games, or have some popcorn, stay up very late or fall asleep in the living room. These treats will make it more palatable for the child to tolerate your absence. It is very important that the child be fond of the baby-sitter. She may prefer one or two over all the others. I would go along with the child's preferences so long as you approve of the baby-sitter and know that his or her judgment is good and can be trusted.

31
Self-Dressing

Many children insist on selecting their own clothes and, if you are lucky, they want to dress themselves, too. (Usually the reverse is true—you have to get them out of the house, and they don't want to get dressed.) The child's desire to select his own clothes is a sign of his growing sense of being an individual, having personal preferences and wanting to be an independent character. Some children will wear horrendous combinations, and you will be embarrassed because the play-group might think you have bad taste. But anybody who knows little kids will understand. Try not to think too much about appearances.

One child would wear only clothes that were purple. This drove her mother crazy, partly because she didn't have enough purple things, and she had to keep washing the same clothes every day. She was also afraid that people would think the child had only these same four outfits to wear. For six weeks, the child was absolutely adamant about wearing purple. After that time, however, her desire to wear purple predictably diminished, and the problem abated.

A parent may indulge a child and go along with her preferences in dressing. I would certainly encourage a child to dress herself, no matter what she wants to put on. If you think about it, what's the big deal? There are so many battles to fight with toddlers, this may not be one in which you want to engage.

Occasionally the child will want to dress inappropriately for the weather. (See The Ubiquitous *No.*) There's no easy solution to this problem. Let's say it's time to leave; you have to get to the day-care center and then off to work. It's also raining cats and dogs. Your daughter decides she won't wear a raincoat, or even a jacket. She also announces that she won't wear her shoes. What do you do?

One possibility, if you can bring yourself to do it, is to say, "Okay, let me have your shoes and socks and your raincoat. I'll put them in a bag and then when we get to school, you can put them on." You can either then carry her to the car, or let her walk across the wet lawn. It's unconventional. So what? Parents are afraid that if they let a child do a thing one time, the child will want to do it for life. But as erratic as children are about everything else, they are about this obstinacy too. Chances are she'll step on a twig on the lawn, or get wet and complain that she should have her shoes or her raincoat on. (And why didn't you let her?!)

If it's very cold out and the child insists on wearing only a short-sleeved shirt, there's a good chance she'll come back in. In this way, you can sometimes let natural consequences help you. But for the most part, you will have to go with the flow of the child's resistance. Ask yourself, what's the worst thing that can happen? The child getting her feet briefly wet or showing up at school in gaudy colors may not be as important as the issue of developing her individuality.

32

Speech and Stuttering

Language develops from day one. By language, I mean the symbol system that a child creates in order to communicate with his parents. Children begin to associate sounds and actions and feelings right from birth; some children show, even as early as three or four months of age (as mentioned in Part I, Stimulating), an ability to recognize words by moving their heads toward an object that you name.

Speech is a subdivision of language. When we talk about speech, we refer to the ability to verbally convey a message. Most children can understand more than they can say at first and will gradually close that gap. The more the child can say in words, the more he can reduce the need for trial-and-error behavior. The more a child can convey his needs, disappointments and feelings, the less likely he will be frustrated.

Speech is one of the most interesting aspects of a child's development, because the normal limits are so wide; you can't easily pinpoint when a child is behind in learning to speak. Some children talk at ten months. Other children don't say anything for years, and suddenly at age three begin talking in whole paragraphs. Then there are children whose language proceeds by learning one word, then another word, then another, and finally saying little two-word utterances. Other children talk in gibberish for months. It sounds like they're speaking the native tongue, because they have the same inflections and syntactical structure as adults, but even if you bend down and listen very closely, you won't hear a single recognizable word. Then quite suddenly, out of this gibberish, come words and sentences and paragraphs.

Many children, mostly boys, begin to stutter during the toddler age. We tend to refer to these speech difficulties as stuttering and stammering, but speech therapists call them "speech disfluencies." They are thought of as normal developmental disfluencies, because they are so common at this age. Some children can't get out the first letter; some repeat the first word over and over and over again. Most of these disfluencies clear up by themselves within a few months. Within a year of onset, 90 percent of all disfluencies have disappeared. They may recur again for brief periods, however, when the child is under particular stress.

There are several theoretical explanations for speech disfluencies. The most common is that they are related to stress. People experience stress in different parts of their bodies. Adults, for example, may have stress pressure points in the lower back or stomach; they may get headaches or indigestion when tense. Others experience tension in the throat, larynx and neck. If you have tension in your throat area, you may have difficulty articulating words. Children who are experiencing tension may develop speech disfluencies.

Another theory about the cause of speech disfluency concerns the rapidity of a small child's thoughts in conflict with his unskilled and unpracticed motor coordination. Children who have recently acquired speech are not very proficient at this new task. Their minds race too fast for their motor skills. They can't form the words to fit the ideas. Because toddlers are impulsive and fast moving, and since speech is a new motor development, trying to say a lot of things quickly might cause a disfluency.

Speech disfluencies may also be related to power struggles. Since this is the age of autonomy, breaking away, being contrary and miscellaneous fears, and because all of these struggles are related to the holding back and the expression of emotions, stuttering can be linked with maintaining control over the body. Speech, to some children, is equivalent to aggression. If the child is experiencing angry feelings, he may also be having difficulty being able to speak out what he feels—trying to hold on to his emotions. I use the concepts of control and release here deliberately since the issue of toilet training is very pertinent at this age, and many of these emotional issues overlap for the toddler.

Most stuttering, *if you leave it alone,* corrects itself. Don't call your child's attention to his stuttering and stammering. Don't ask the child to repeat. Don't have the child repeat after you. Don't perform any amateur speech therapy. Your best bet is to overlook it. If it bothers you a lot (and since one of the theories is that stuttering is related to tension), many speech therapists recommend that you take a deep breath yourself and talk slowly, intimately, soothingly and in a relaxed manner to your child—as if you were relaying a confidence to a friend. The goal is to get the child to relax and to slow down by imitating you. If the child is able to relax the throat and larynx area, it will be easier to get the words out.

Calling attention to the stuttering only creates secondary problems: self-consciousness, worry about whether he's going to stutter and more tension. This should be avoided at all costs, since worry about whether you are going to stutter is something that characterizes true adult stutterers.

Stuttering and stammering are common between the ages of two and four. If speech disfluencies persist beyond that point, then you should seek professional help. Since speech is so intimately tied to hearing, any language evaluation you seek should include a comprehensive hearing examination as well. Do not rely on your impression that the child's hearing is normal based on some informal "tests" like whispering or clapping your hands. Children very often compensate for subtle hearing impairments, and only a specially designed series of tests can detect them. Peculiar speech patterns and odd pronunciation can signal a hearing impairment.

33
Bathing and Shampooing

Children want to be in control. Having their hair washed or lying down in the bathtub can be a threat to feeling in control. It isn't just that your child is being contrary to spite you; some children are truly afraid of the vulnerable position that having their hair shampooed puts them in.

Most of the time when shampooing a child's hair, you ask her to lie back and cradle her head so that the water runs over her hair. That requires that she put herself into someone else's hands with her eyes shut. She's floating there, and someone else is entirely responsible for her—at an age when she's trying to become a separate individual in control of herself. A child who is just beginning to establish a sense of competence and self-control will find this position extremely uncomfortable, particularly in such a menacing spot as the water. If you can remind yourself that her resistance isn't designed just to give you a hard time but has a real emotional component behind it, you'll become much more ingenious in solving the problem.

A child in the bathtub could perhaps have her hair shampooed while crouching on all fours rather than lying back in a more passive position.

127

And by so doing, she can hold her hand to her forehead as if shielding her eyes from the sun, and ward off the water that way. The eyes may be able to be kept open, the child isn't lying on her back, and she will feel like a more active participant in the whole procedure.

Why not give her a washcloth and allow her to shampoo her own hair? The first time you try this, she could shampoo just the back of her head. That's enough for the first day. The front of her head will probably still be a little dirty, but there's probably no harm for a while. The next time, the child can be encouraged to wash the sides and the back of the head. Then the third time, perhaps you could do the front of the head together. As you are doing this, say to the child, "One, two, three, that's it." Make it quick and snappy. If the child cries a little bit, pick her right up, wrap her in a towel, and don't laugh at her. "Look in the mirror. You're fine." Usually that's the end of it. The next time she has to take a bath or a shower, she may complain again. But after several months, she will probably get over it.

Some children don't like to get into the bath because they are afraid they are going to lose control of their bowels or their bladder. They relax in the warm water, and they fear they will void into the tub. Other children take a sudden dislike to the bath about the time that they are being toilet trained. The issue of dirty or clean suddenly looms very large for them. "I'd rather be dirty," the child will say when you suggest a bath. What the child may be expressing is some conflict about conforming. Conformity threatens individuality, and being a separate, competent, autonomous person is a major issue for the toddler. It may also convey some emotional conflict over having to succumb to toilet training, which implies "cleanliness." So, as a child becomes more reliably toilet trained, he may show some resistance to being clean in some other ways. It's a kind of "I'll give in here, but not there!"

34

TV Watching

My two-year-old daughter likes to join her older brother when he watches TV. I don't mind when they watch programs like "Sesame Street" or "Mister Rogers' Neighborhood," but I am concerned when she watches with him some of the more violent cartoons and other shows. Is TV bad for children? Are there some programs that are okay? How much TV is too much at this age?

I'm not in favor of a lot of television for children. In order for children to practice certain skills, they need opportunities to do so—and sitting passively and watching television won't provide these opportunities. I don't mean to make a blanket indictment of television: The medium, used wisely, can be useful. But I do think parents have to be very careful about what they allow their children to watch and for how long.

Rather than having the television on in the background all the time, and encouraging the habit of "television watching," you should preselect and screen the programs your child watches. Offer the child one short program a day with the words, "Let's watch 'Sesame Street' now." Or, "It's time to watch 'Mister Rogers' Neighborhood' on the television now." You are offering not the habit of watching television to your child, but rather a particular *event*. The fact that the event happens to be on television is irrelevant. In this way, the child will come to see watching "Sesame Street" as an event similar to her reading time, or breakfast time or bedtime. It happens at a certain hour, and it has finite limits.

Exploration, physical activity, being read to and using all forms of media—including phonograph records, tapes and picture books—are important activities you as a parent should encourage your child to engage in.

TV can be included among these activities if it is used properly. But make sure TV is not used exclusively, and that it is not used as a baby-sitter. You may be tempted to say to yourself, "She sat so quietly for that half-hour. I have this one more thing to do. What's the harm in letting her sit for another half-hour?" Avoid that temptation. When the program is over, turn off the television.

A two-year-old child should not be allowed to view any program that is violent in content. There has recently been a great deal of debate as to the long-term effects of violent programs on children who watch them. Some experts maintain that video violence stimulates violent play in children; others say that watching violence on television offers the child vicarious relief, and that the child will be a less violent person. As far as I'm concerned, violent content is not good for a young child—not only because it may teach him violence—but because it desensitizes him to the inhumanity of the violence. Two-year-olds are too young to separate fantasy from reality.

Watch cartoons very carefully. Many seemingly innocuous cartoons feature violence as a way of life: the cat who bangs the mouse over the head with the frying pan; the character who falls off a cliff into a ravine and then gets right up. Cartoons can also overstimulate a child. The fast cutting of the scenes and the frenetic pace of the music, can, for some children, be too stimulating.

There are useful animations as well as other programs on television for children. Such programs can teach toddlers and preschool children pro-social behaviors: altruism, sharing and getting along with others. They can also teach some of the learning skills—numbers, letters, shapes and colors. Screened carefully, some of these programs may be beneficial to your child. Today, many schools use electronic media materials.

Many parents ask how much TV a toddler should be allowed to watch. My answer is always the same: the less the better. More specifically, try to limit TV watching to a half-hour a day. All too often, the television is a piece of furniture. If you can, think in terms of putting it away when it is not being watched, and rolling it out on casters when it is time for the child's program—much as you would put other learning materials away when the child was finished with them.

Some parents worry that their children will not only be deprived of certain educational fundamentals but may be out of touch with their peers when they talk about superheroes and TV shows. For toddlers, this is not important. But if your preschooler expresses a concern over not knowing whom his friends are discussing, then some compromise may be necessary. Put up some resistance at first. You might say that just because others watch the show, that doesn't mean that he has to, too. Eventually, moderate exposure to some of these popular shows can be arranged. Watch them with your child and detoxify any violence or poor judgment by interpreting the action and expressing your views. In so doing, you will educate your child to be a critical observer.

Part Three

I'll Be You; You Be Me
Three to Five Years

Introduction

Having achieved in the previous stage of development a somewhat stronger sense of self, a preschooler now begins to experiment with different roles. Prior to age three, a child struggled with the concept of just exactly where you left off and he began. Now that this issue is somewhat more settled, and the child is comfortable in his knowledge that he is a separate person from you, he can begin to try on different roles, to play at being different people and to act out many parts.

One of the most important parts that the child wants to try on is yours. Simply put, he wants to be an adult just like you. In his struggle to give up babyishness and to prepare himself for a more grown-up way of being, your child will look to you to be his primary role model. Of course, a three-year-old isn't ready to assume the postures of an adult—and it's often comical to watch him try—but this won't stop him from acting out roles as he sees adults playing them.

In the trying on of roles, a child begins by imitating those he observes. One notices in nursery school that three- to five-year-olds play games pretending to be the Mommy and the Daddy. At home, you'll begin to see that your child has started to copy your walk, your gestures, your facial expressions and your figures of speech. This practice of imitating is an extremely important one—as humorous as it will sometimes appear to be. As a child passes through this stage he will need you to be his guide.

Another vital task of a child this age is to identify with his proper sex role. A child between the ages of three and five has to make his psychology fit his biological givens. The gestures and clothing and behavior that imitate the parent of the same sex serve a critical function: The child is learning whether he is a boy or a girl. He is just now becoming aware of different sexual characteristics and will be fascinated by them. In fact, for a child in this stage of development, sex is very nearly an all-consuming concern. He

135

wonders about his own body parts, he demonstrates sexual behavior, he is fascinated by life-cycle issues such as sexual reproduction, birth and death, and he is curious about the facts of life. Part of his curiosity will be satisfied by an exploration of his own body and his sexuality. For the rest of it, he will look to you for straightforward and honest answers. Your task as a parent is to guide your child through these fascinating discoveries and to provide valid signposts as he develops both a conscience and a firm sex-role identification.

But where does the "You Be Me" part of the equation come in? In a child's way of thinking, if he gets bigger, that must mean that you get smaller. If a child is going to assume the adult role, then you have to become the child. More to the point, a boss needs a slave. Used to being pushed around and told what to do for all of his life, he now wants to turn passive into active. This means becoming the Boss, the Leader and Number One. And to do this, a child believes there has to be an exchange of power.

Preschoolers are bossy, egotistical and desperate to be included in everything an adult is doing. Their sense of their own importance is exaggerated, but if you can have a sense of humor about it, it's amusing. In essence, they boss you around, telling you what to do for them, because they still can't do very much for themselves. They're like helpless bosses. "Tie my shoes. No, don't tie that one. Tie this one first." "I'll say this story, and you write it down. Read it. No, don't read it that way, read it this way." "You be the baby. I'll be the Mommy."

As preschoolers discover the thrill of being the boss, they also discover competition. You'll suddenly find your four-year-old wanting to compete with you at everything. This, too, borders on the absurd at times, for while they very much want to compete, they're happy only if they win. Losing is devastating. A three-and-a-half-year-old girl decided to race her mother from the back door to the car one morning. But it occurred to her, as she surveyed the distance from the house to the car, that winning against her mother probably wasn't all that feasible. "I have a good idea," she announced to her Mom. "You stay here. And then when I win the race, you can start."

Parents often wonder how to handle a bossy, competitive preschooler. I think it's best if you try to encourage your child's exuberance, and not try to quash it. Even though your child wants to be the boss and win at everything, and even though he will at times get on your nerves, fight off the temptation to overpower him. Tell yourself frequently, "I know I'm the boss really; I'm not going to lose my inherent authority—but I don't have to over-whelm my child into submission, either." In a competition, be a helper and a guide to your child. Let him have success at his endeavors. Point out how he can win, and in that way you'll be helping him to achieve something for himself. Eventually as the child progresses through this stage of develop-ment, the struggle for dominance eases up and gives way to a more cooper-ative and easygoing manner.

Despite the intermittent bossiness, preschoolers are delightful and charming as well—a fact no parent should lose sight of. They're more like people now than ever before, and they have many winning ways. They may be coquettish, or Mr. Personality or very affectionate. They're developing a sense of humor and will begin to say things that are clever rather than merely cute. They have at their command more language and the begin-nings of logic. They believe they live in a world in which everything is pos-sible—and this grandeur is endearing. One three-year-old girl approached a huge tree with no lower branches. The girth of the tree was about five times the span of her arms. "Mommy," yelled the child with great expecta-tions. "Watch how I can climb this tree!"

Preschoolers acquire new skills every day—and take great pride in their accomplishments. "Mommy, watch this!" may be the single most oft-repeated phrase in a preschooler's repertoire. They will begin to recognize letters, words, colors, shapes and numbers, and will make progress in read-ing, painting, cutting and drawing skills. Preschoolers are also sociable at this time and will be much more responsive to social games.

At around three years of age, children can assume a number of small responsibilities. You will find that they enjoy being asked to put some toys away, throw a paper towel into the garbage pail, pour drinks for themselves, pass food at the table, fold and put away clothes and carry small packages.

The ages between three and five are quite dynamic in a child's life and you will find your son or daughter acquiring daily new social, verbal and motor skills with almost head-spinning rapidity. Toward the end of this stage of development, however, children settle down and do actually be-come more like you. They demonstrate better behavior and a more coopera-tive spirit. They show the beginnings of an understanding of the concept of justice and the difference between right and wrong. Eventually, as they move toward elementary school, they become more attuned to the acquisi-tion of academic skills and more accepting of convention and social mores. For both parent and child, one stage in a long journey will be over—and with it its pleasures as well as its irritations. Pay more attention to the joy than to the aggravation. A preschooler's years will be gone almost before you realize you've got them.

35

Sex: The Joy of Discovery

My three-and-a-half-year-old daughter and I were in the kitchen. I was doing the dishes when I noticed that she had stuffed a small pillow into her sundress. When I looked at her, she pulled the pillow out and said, "A baby just came out of my tummy!" She looked really cute, so I laughed. Then she said, "Mommy, how does a baby get into your tummy?"

I took a deep breath and dried my hands. This was IT. She had asked the Big Question. I was prepared for this, right? I made a few mental notes as to how to proceed. I got down on the floor next to her and said, "Well . . ." But she interrupted me. "Mommy," she asked, having forgotten her previous question, "do sheeps have lips?"

The moral of the story is: When your child asks the Big Question, wait ten seconds—it will probably go away.

But not for long.

Children at this age are intensely curious about birth, death and the entire life cycle. This is the age when they begin to wonder where they came from and what happens to people when they die. This is also the age when they realize the differences between the sexes and start to think of themselves as being male or female. Consequently, questions about sex and reproduction are very likely during this stage of development.

If you are pregnant or have recently been pregnant, your child is even more likely to ask you about birth and reproduction. Some parents find it extremely difficult to imagine explaining the sexual nitty-gritty to their young children. "Isn't a four-year-old too young to understand all this?" they ask, hoping the answer will be yes. Sorry. The answer is no. If your four-year-old asks you questions about where babies come from, you had better be prepared with some answers. Children don't like to be deceived. If they suspect you're fabricating an explanation—especially about something as important as sex and reproduction—they may begin to distrust you in other areas as well.

For children in the three-to-five age group, sex is an all-consuming concern. They begin to delight in their own bodies and many will begin to masturbate. They are fascinated with different sexual characteristics and will want to know all about penises and vaginas and why they have one and not the other. They will enjoy nudity and may even appear to be exhibitionistic. They may go to visit Grandma and, to your chagrin, start to fondle themselves. You may come upon your child and another "playing doctor." You will observe that your four-year-old seems to have his hands in every conceivable orifice—down the back of his pants, down the front of his pants, in his mouth, up his nose. Whether we wish it were so or not, the truth is that children in this stage of development are very "sexy." Some have even called this particular age a "minipuberty" because many of the sexual issues that concern teenagers surface in three-to-five-year olds. The two stages are quite different, of course. One really is puberty and is fueled by hormones and the need to experience one's sexuality. The other, with its intense curiosity and pleasure of discovery, merely mimics puberty. But this stage of sexual development is extremely important—indeed critical—for the healthy growth of your child and should not be minimized or ignored and certainly not repressed.

Ignoring or repressing a subject can be taken incorrectly by the child to mean that the subject is something that has to be kept furtive because it is somehow bad. Since adult sexual adjustment seems to be an outgrowth of childhood sex education, it is enormously important that sensible, constructive and healthful attitudes be conveyed. Many of the fears and guilt and shame that we feel as adults derive from misinformation about sex that we received as children.

Many parents feel that when a child learns about sex, he is no longer the sweet little "innocent" cherub he previously was. Poets throughout the ages have referred to the gulf between "innocence" and "experience," and we have commonly come to understand "experience" to mean sexual awareness. For many parents, sex is a loaded issue. They remember their own secret fascination with sex and occasionally, for some, the way sexual activity or curiosity was squelched with the idea that it was "naughty." Why is it so hard to be cool when you come upon your child "playing doctor" or when your son begins to masturbate in the supermarket? Why are we embarrassed? Why does our anxiety level immediately go up? Why do we wish the behavior would vanish? Why did the mother need a gulp of air before answering her daughter's question about where babies come from? Why do we call it the "Big Question"?

Before we as parents can educate our children about sex, it is probably useful to try to understand some of our own feelings about it and why it is such a charged issue for most of us. I think it's probably true that the better we understand the underlying motives for our parental behavior, the better parents we will be.

Some psychologists have suggested that our inability to speak comfortably of three-year-olds and sex in the same breath stems from experiences in our own childhood that we can't remember but which are triggered in our unconscious when we see our children go through this stage. When you see your child "playing doctor," for example, or masturbating, this activity suggests a loss of "innocence." If you are not innocent, then, by implication, you are guilty. Guilt is the function of a conscience, of believing that something you are doing or thinking about is wrong. But how exactly did we come to think of sex as a "wrong" activity, particularly in regard to children?

A baby is a very sensual little creature whose early life is a continuum of one intimate physical experience after another. He is constantly being bathed and nursed and changed and powdered—by his parents. Many of these sensual feelings are quite intense and akin to feelings we think of as sexual in nature. It is the parents who are touching the child, who are providing him with this pleasure. These sensual (sexual) feelings grow and develop and begin to blossom between the ages of three and five. More important, because these feelings have been associated with the parents, at this stage of development the feelings and thoughts are generally directed toward the parents. Mommy and Daddy are the central characters in the child's dramatic play and fantasy life.

At the same time, a child is getting a sense of his maleness or femaleness and is learning to "identify" with the parent of the same sex. Little girls may begin to want to dress up like Mom, even caricaturing a womanly appearance by wearing garish earrings and bracelets and nail polish. A little boy will mimic his father's gestures and walk and facial expressions. He may even try "shaving" with a pretend razor in the mirror when no one is looking. These attempts to identify are delightful and very important. As silly as they may sometimes seem to be, do not be tempted to squash the child's fantasies by saying, "Don't do that. You don't have a beard." Since these activities represent rehearsing to be a grown-up, trivializing them might give the child the impression you don't think he can grow up to be a competent adult. In many ways, four-year-olds are like little clones of their parents.

Because a child so wants to be like his parent—a son wanting to be like Dad, for example—he also wants his parent's privileges, prowess . . . and his woman too. Normally, as the child develops an attraction to the parent of the opposite sex, he will soon begin to think of himself in competition with the parent of the same sex for the affections of the opposite-sex parent. "Don't you think I'm prettier than Mommy?" a little girl will say to her dad. "Whew! Now Mom and I can be alone," a little boy says, as soon as his father goes off to work. "Mommy, will you marry me?" a small boy asks. A mini-love affair is going on in the child's mind, and it's actually quite touching if you're alert to it. If your child begins to indicate to you that he's experiencing just such a love affair, you can gently deal with him by suggesting, "When you get older you can have a wife of your own," or "You may feel differently about marrying me when you get older."

Preschoolers mimic their parents in other ways, too. This is the age when they begin to adopt and absorb your values, and your sense of right and wrong. And once this happens, they begin to develop a sense of morality, or conscience. With a conscience comes guilt. A two-year-old can't feel guilt. Nor can a four-year-old. Not until a child has thoroughly identified with the parent and incorporated inside himself the parent's sense of right and wrong can he be said to have a conscience.

The conscience that a child absorbs from his parents eventually pushes the romantic feelings away. And that's where you get the bridge, or the tie-in, between feeling guilty and matters that have to do with sex. A child begins to develop a conscience at the very point that he's competing sexually for the opposite-sex parent. But as a child develops a conscience—identifies with the values of the parent of the same sex—he gives up the sexual competition.

All of us went through something similar to this, even though we may not be able to remember it. But when we see our kids "playing doctor," something inside of us is triggered, and we feel—somehow, somewhere—a vestige of our own guilt. We are tempted to feel that there's something "wrong" about a child's sexual curiosity. We mourn a loss of "innocence."

At the very least, we feel uncomfortable. These feelings are reinforced by social sanctions and sexual taboos, not to mention threats and scare tactics that some parents impose on their children—threats such as, "If you play with your penis, you will hurt it." We are also often irrationally fearful that children will become consumed by sexual appetites and perhaps even become promiscuous.

Nonetheless, being uncomfortable with or ignoring sexual curiosity is not going to do much for your child. I believe that children should get simple, clear, direct answers to their questions about sex and birth and reproduction. This isn't to say you should foist all this information on a child if he hasn't asked for it. Wait until he is ready and curious. But if we can manage not to perpetuate our own inhibitions and irrational fears in our children, the chances are they will develop healthier attitudes toward sex and toward themselves.

36
How to Tell Your Child the Facts of Life

"Mommy, what's this?"
"That's your vagina."
"Oh. Does Daddy have a Jemima too?"

Your child's sexual education isn't going to be accomplished in one fell swoop or on one momentous day. One morning your daughter may ask why she doesn't have big breasts like yours. On another afternoon, your son may want to know why the baby doesn't have a penis as he does. If you are pregnant, or you and your child know someone who is, it's very likely your child will begin to ask you questions about where babies come from.

No matter when these questions first appear, no matter what the circumstances are, and no matter how long it takes to get the record straight, if you follow a few simple precepts, the task will be easier: Name the sexual activities and parts of the body correctly; explain what happens in such a way that your child can understand it; and don't volunteer more information than your child is asking for.

Sex education begins almost from day one. In the first year of life, infants explore their own bodies in the bath or when they are naked. Curiosity about one's own body should not be inhibited, because inhibition teaches a child there's something strange about his body. Rather, help your child to understand his body by naming the parts for him. Naming the parts correctly is absolutely essential. Parents often make up cute or bizarre names for body parts—"wing dillies" for penises, for example, or "boobs" for breasts. Why do we do that? Perhaps we feel that to use the correct terms is too "technical." But doesn't slang convey to a child that there's something wrong with the correct language? Using slang removes you one step from the actual thing and suggests a "coverup." I think a parent is much better off not using euphemisms with a child.

Little boys have an easier time with their sex characteristics because penises and scrotums are easier to see than vaginas. For little girls, it's important to make a special effort to name all the parts—vagina, clitoris—correctly, because they're not as obvious. It is also important to tell a little girl that women do not urinate from the same opening that babies come from. I've had female patients tell me they didn't know all the parts of their own genitals until they were grown women. And as for men, their lack of knowledge about female anatomy can sometimes be astonishing.

Stressing correct words is especially important when telling your child where babies come from. Let's say you're five months' pregnant and beginning to show. Your four-year-old wants to know what's happening.

I would tell the child that in a special place inside Mommy's abdomen, called the uterus, a baby is growing. I wouldn't say stomach or tummy. It's just as easy for a child to learn a correct word as an incorrect one. As far as pronounciation is concerned, uterus is just as easy to learn as stomach and will mean the child needn't learn another word later on. More important, to say a baby is growing in your tummy is misleading. Doesn't that then get mixed up in the child's mind with two other bodily functions—eating and eliminating? Children have their own theories about where babies come from—and it usually has to do with what's on their minds. They often think that women get babies into their bodies by eating something, and that the babies leave the body just as excrement does. This can be confusing and upsetting to a child, and it is best to clear up quickly any of this confusion. Explanations are further complicated by the general use of the word "egg" for ovum and "seed" for sperm. Think for a minute what the child must imagine if told there is an egg in Mommy, and Daddy puts a seed in Mommy. (An image of a child trying to figure out how a sunflower seed and scrambled eggs make a baby comes to mind.)

To allay some of this confusion, simply say, "Inside of Mommy, there is an ovum—a little round egg-shaped thing—and inside of Daddy there's something called sperm. Daddy puts the sperm inside of Mommy, and that starts the baby growing."

The child may or may not ask the next question, and I wouldn't volunteer any information until he does. But eventually he may ask: "How does the sperm get inside of Mommy?" To answer, simply say: "When a boy grows to be a man, inside of his testicles he makes sperm in order to help make a baby. The sperm comes out through his penis and it's put into Mommy's vagina. From there it goes into Mommy's uterus. Once inside Mommy's uterus, a baby grows." Again, I wouldn't volunteer all of this at once unless the child asks it all at once—which is fairly unlikely.

Be particularly careful about telling a child tall tales and weird stories, such as "the stork brought you," or "I got you at the store." If you lie about where babies come from, it teaches a child that adults cannot be trusted—especially regarding something as important as sex. It's a question everybody asks. It's one of the great mysteries of life: Where do we come from?

37

Masturbation

Young children touch themselves all the time. It's pleasurable and it also often serves as a soothing activity. It's true that children do actually become sexually excited and sexually stimulated with masturbating. Even a child as young as eighteen months old can engage in self stimulation and become sexually excited. Keep in mind, however, that this is nothing to be concerned about, and it's completely natural and normal. This masturbatory activity usually reaches a peak during the middle of the three-to-five age group and then diminishes until puberty.

There are several reasons why young children masturbate. First of all, it feels good and brings pleasure to the child. Second, it is a self-soothing activity that reduces tension. Frequently when children are watching television or daydreaming they will begin to masturbate without really even being aware that they are. Third, masturbation is sometimes a sign of overexcitation from having witnessed a lot of sex. And finally, occasionally children masturbate in order to deal with a specific fear—such as a fear of the loss of a penis. One little boy, for instance, whose mother had just given birth to a little girl, began masturbating excessively. The mother didn't understand why, but the answer wasn't hard to find. He had been examining the new baby when the diaper was off and had grown frightened about why some people didn't have penises. Would he lose his? To reassure himself, he began to devote a lot of attention to this special body part.

Fortunately, most parents today understand that masturbation is normal and not harmful, and they don't scold their children for engaging in it. But let's assume that you're going to visit Grandma. You suspect that your child is probably going to masturbate at some point during the visit. You also know that Grandma is likely to be shocked. What do you do about it?

If it disturbs you when your child touches himself in public, try to give him something else to do with his hands. A child is easily distracted and will quickly engage in a different activity if invited to do so. If you're in a store, ask your child to hold a bunch of carrots for you. If you're at Grandma's, engage him in a game that requires the use of his hands. If you think you can do it, I would try saying to Grandma—and this is a good stock phrase to use about anything—"Mom, he's just going through a phase."

Another alternative is to say to the child, "Don't do that here at Grandma's, because Grandma finds that upsetting." But this suggests to the child that there's something wrong with it. Incredibly some people to this day still believe there is something wrong with it and will say to a child, "If you touch yourself, you'll make yourself sick." Or, "Your penis is going to fall off." Clearly such "warnings" can only hurt the child in the long run.

38
Menstruation

If your child happens to discover a tampon or sanitary napkin, and has a question about it, you should be prepared with an answer. But first of all, it is very important to reassure the child that the blood on a discarded napkin does not mean that anyone is sick; rather that it is a healthy sign that everything is happening just as it should each month.

One of the things you can say to a child to explain menstruation is this: "In Mommy's body every month an ovum is produced. Those times when the ovum is going to grow into a baby, we call that being pregnant. But there are times when the ovum is not going to become a baby, so it has to come out of Mommy's body. Mommy uses a tissue or a napkin for the ovum as it comes out." Try to keep the explanation simple—something you know your child will understand. When he is older and more capable of understanding, you can give a more complicated answer. For girls, be sure to emphasize: "Only when you grow up does this happen." Also, be careful not to say things like, "This is something you'll find out about when you get married." Children create elaborate and sometimes frightening explanations for things they do not understand if left to their own devices. Therefore, it is important to give a child accurate information in a nonemotional manner.

39
Exhibitionism

I'm worried that our four-year-old son is turning out to be a flasher. He runs around the house opening his bathrobe real wide and saying, "Ta da!" as if he is showing us something special. He's naked underneath. How can I get him to stop?

Children of about three to four years of age can be quite uninhibited about showing off their bodies. There are a number of reasons why they do this. Children have a wonderful lack of self-consciousness about themselves, and often in the summer when it is warm they like to be naked simply because it feels good to be naked. For other children, being naked and wanting to see others naked indicates a normal and healthy curiosity about sex and sex characteristics. For them, running around naked is simply part of the joy of discovery of themselves and their bodies.

There is a third reason, however, why a little boy might want to open his robe and exclaim, "Ta da!" to whomever will watch. And that's to reassure himself that he's "okay." In this case, that's exactly what was happening. Like the little boy in the previous chapter who was masturbating excessively, this little boy had seen his little sister naked and was worried about why she did not have a penis while he did. To allay his fears, he was running around the house showing off his body. He was trying to reassure himself that all his parts were still there, because if someone else did not have a penis, did that mean that maybe someday he would lose his? His exhibitionism was protective. For a little boy who has discovered that little girls do not have penises, it really is a big event to keep discovering that his is still there—and to let everyone else admire his important "gender" statement.

The same psychology applies to little girls as well. They too need to make their own "gender" statements. Sometimes little girls will ask, "Why does Jonathan have a penis when I don't?" Or "How come he urinates standing up and I don't?" As I have mentioned earlier, it's much more difficult to teach a young girl about her sex characteristics because hers aren't as obvious. Special attention needs to be paid to teaching a young girl about her body and to reassuring her that she's made exactly the way she's supposed to be. Find an appropriate time to say to your daughter, "There is nothing wrong with your body. You are not missing anything that you are supposed to have. What you have is very special, and someday you will be able to have babies."

Little girls may also observe how their brothers and fathers urinate and may want to try standing up themselves. If your daughter does this, you needn't make a big deal about it—simply explain that it's easier for boys to do it one way and easier for girls to do it another. If she still wants to stand up, let her. She herself will lose interest in this way of doing it as she realizes how impractical it is. What you don't want to do is to convey that she lacks something important or that she's somehow inferior for not being able to urinate like Daddy. Most important, don't make fun of her. Very often little girls, as well as little boys, want to play as many different roles as they possibly can. Why wouldn't a girl, who observes a boy, want to try the same thing? Why wouldn't she wonder why she can't do what the boys do? Don't get terribly upset and nervous about your daughter's sexual adjustment. For most girls, trying to be a boy is fairly common and temporary. In some girls there may be some amount of envy that boys can do things they can't. Not all girls feel it, nor do they remain feeling that way forever. Reassure the girl that boys and girls are made differently and that she's made perfectly fine and right.

40
Parental Nudity

Because sex is such an all-consuming concern for three- to five-year-olds, habits in the family that may have been of no particular interest or anxiety at age one and a half may now take on a special meaning.

※

As many modern parents, we have been fairly relaxed about nudity in our house. Our son, four and a half, seems to be very interested in my breasts. Quite often Tom wants to touch them when I'm getting undressed or even at times when we are sitting fully clothed. When he is on my lap, for example, his hands often wander to my breasts. My husband and I want to give him a healthy attitude about sex and the human body, yet at the same time we don't want him to think that he can grab for any woman's breasts any time he feels like it. Should I discourage his curiosity? Should I not allow him to see me naked anymore?

This mother's concerns are important ones. While parental nudity during the child's first year of life may be insignificant, by age four, it takes on a heightened importance. What's right at one time is not necessarily the best thing at another—often a hard concept to adjust to, and to adjust a family's habits to. While I'm not against nudity in a rigid sense, I do think that a certain concern for privacy ought to be shown. Parents who are very open about parental nudity have a greater likelihood that their children are going to be freer in their exploration of the body. This is only logical. But at age four, I think your child needs an example of restraint, and you therefore have to be that model.

One of the things you can do is put something on when you are walking

149

around the house. There's no reason for you to expose yourself deliberately to your child at this age. If your child happens to walk into your room, you don't have to make a mad scramble to cover yourself up, but you can nonchalantly go and put your clothes on or ask your child to please excuse you. Simply say—without hysteria—"Please excuse me, but I'm not dressed." And while you are saying that, put something on.

In the case mentioned above, Tom clearly had the impression from his parents that the body was quite normal and healthy. But he was at a stage when sex was dominant in his mind—a major concern.

It is, however, easier for children to learn about their bodies and the differences between boys and girls from children their own age than from comparing themselves with a parent. For some children, it can be distressing to see an adult body because the sex characteristics are so different—not just in size, but qualitatively as well. Comparisons are going to be unfair—and may even be frightening. Little girls, for example, are very often afraid when they see their father's genitals. If they've been told about how babies are born, they wonder how a man's penis can fit into a vagina when they compare it with their own genitals. You can tell her that when she gets older her genitals will be bigger, but such an explanation doesn't really mean much to a child.

So what should the mother of a four-year-old do about parental nudity? Particularly a parent who has been, as in the case just mentioned, quite relaxed about it? In my opinion, a bit more discretion should be exercised at this point in the child's development. Since this is a terribly complex matter that may have far-reaching implications for a child's future personality development and sense of sexual identity, I would rather err on the side of conservatism. As for Tom touching her breasts, I think she could say to her son: "I'd rather you don't do that right now." She could find some polite way of discouraging him. The important message to get across is that people can't just touch bodies whenever they want to. And one way of showing that is by safeguarding your own body, showing your child that he can restrict what people do to his body by asking them to stop touching him when he doesn't want them to.

The way in which you convey this to your child is very important. Don't be overly concerned about frustrating him; you have an important lesson to teach him here, and you should be consistent about it. On the other hand, do not tell your child that he is bad, or convey in any way that sex is dirty. Simply say, "I know how hard it is for you not to touch Mommy right now, but I'd really rather you didn't. It's a little uncomfortable."

Concerns of this sort may be short-lived. Many children quite naturally become modest without your having to do anything. And I think, when this happens, you should respect this new-found modesty. This sudden shyness doesn't indicate any problem; it simply means that your child now has some sense of his being different from you and of his wanting to safeguard his own separateness. When children are using the bathroom, for instance, they often plead, "Please don't come in." If your child requests privacy, respect it. I always wince when I hear of parents who just laugh and then barge right in. Stop and think not just about the moment at hand, but about the kind of future behavior you want to instill in your child. Of course your child is not your equal, and you can overpower him by barging in. But you want to demonstrate you'll practice what you say about being able to do what you want with your own body.

※

I can understand not allowing my son to see me naked, but what about my three-year-old daughter? Is nudity with the same sex okay?

I would limit nudity—even with the same sex. Nudity can be over-stimulating for a child, which is not so helpful. Many parents shower or bathe with their young children. While it may be argued that this practice is a matter of personal taste, I think one should be prudent—even with a child of the same sex.

Don't forget that to a child our bodies look very different from theirs. The idea that they're going to grow up to be like us seems too far-fetched for them to comprehend. And they may not find that idea so appealing either. Sagging bodies or different-looking genitals can be scary for a child. There also can be problems of inferiority that last into adult life if a child compares his own genitals with his parent's. One little boy, for example, became extremely anxious when watching his father urinate. His father's output so outmatched his own that he felt inferior in comparison. Children may feel puny or develop performance anxieties.

If your child walks in on you and your spouse during lovemaking, it is understandable that you might become flustered. Children misunderstand the sex act because it is something beyond their personal experience. They may interpret the noise, posture or activity in strange ways. Not infrequently, they think that something violent is happening. Although it is the intensity that affects them, they also seem to realize that it is something very private and intimate. While recovering your composure, mildly explain that Mommy and Daddy were being "affectionate" with one another. Try not to be abrupt despite your having been startled and interrupted. If you are harsh, your child may feel he did something wrong. If you are more courageous, you may want to explain more about sexual activities between Mommy and Daddy. Remember that sex is something that is normal and healthy and how you convey your ideas to a child will have an important effect on his development. You can say that sex is something that feels good and that you do with someone you care about and love. In your daily life, it will be helpful to the child if you can be physically demonstrative with your spouse or use pet names of endearment. It is good for children to experience firsthand this richest of human emotions.

41

Playing Doctor

I walked into my living room the other day and Jonathan, four, was playing doctor with a neighborhood girl—also four. By the time I came in, they had their pants off. I was in a quandary about what to do. Should I discourage this? I wondered. I don't want to ruin my son's curiosity or sensuality, but on the other hand I don't want the other little girl going home to her mother and saying, "Jonathan's Mommy lets me play doctor at his house."

Playing "doctor" is universal. It's been going on for centuries. It's an expression of a perfectly normal and natural curiosity and is no cause for alarm. But it did, in this case, seem to be presenting a problem. As we mentioned earlier, many parents are bowled over by their children's sexuality and find it very hard to deal with.

What was Jonathan's mother's goal? It seemed to be in her interest to discourage her son, because she didn't want the little girl to go home and say something that would be embarrassing to her. Okay, that's one consideration. As a parent, always ask yourself: In whose interest am I making these child-rearing decisions? Sometimes it's fine to choose an action that's in your interest alone—but don't fool yourself into believing that it's solely in the child's interest.

In the best of circumstances, the interests merge. Although her own concerns were primary, Jonathan's mother also had the child's interests at heart as well. Should she discourage her son's curiosity? She had an instinctual sense that this might not be to his benefit. But should she stop a doctor game that she finds in progress?

Parents can't prevent doctor games. The children will find other ways and other places to play them. The urge is too strong. Yet at the same time, parents should represent, to some extent, an example of a certain decorum or restraint.

Remember that the game is normal and natural, but in a quiet, matter-of-fact way—without being overwrought or angry—invite the children to put their clothes back on. Tell them it's time for the doctor game to be over, and that you're all going to do something else for awhile. You don't want to convey the impression that what they're doing is wrong, and you don't have to fill them with guilt. Your invitation to do something else simply means that you're suggesting that they pursue more socially acceptable activities rather than intimate sexual play. You're not discouraging intimacy—but you're not promoting it either.

Jonathan's mother also has a responsibility to make sure that her son's playmate is playing doctor with the same enthusiasm as her son. If the girl appears to be uncomfortable, the mother could help the girl—and at the same time also teach her son a valuable lesson. In this case, she might say to her son, "Mary doesn't seem to be interested in playing that game right now. I think we should respect Mary's wishes. If you didn't want to show your body, I wouldn't force you to. After all, it's your body and you can decide if you want to show it to somebody else or not." This ties in nicely with attempts to teach a child that one's body is private and one should respect another's desire for privacy in the same way that Tom's mother might earlier have said, "I'd rather you didn't touch my breasts right now." There's no reason to make a child feel that his actions are something to be ashamed of, or that he's "dirty"—simply indicate that as we grow up we need to learn some restraint and also to respect another's wishes.

If you come upon your children playing doctor, and during the course of the game you see they are in some way harming themselves, then, of course, you must stop the game immediately. Sometimes children put things into their genitals. This must be discouraged. Again, simply and directly say to the children that their bodies are not made for putting toys or other objects into them.

42
Preparing a Child for a New Baby

My son is four and a half, and I'm three months' pregnant.
What's the best way to prepare him for the arrival of the new baby?

You don't want to tell a child too soon that you are pregnant, because eight or nine months is a long wait for a four-year-old. On the other hand a child is very sensitive to changes—even if he can't put his perceptions into words. If you're more excited than you have been in a while, or you're talking to your friends on the phone about the upcoming event, or if there are changes in your body, a child will feel cheated if no one tells him what's going on. He knows something is different and wonders what it is.

When you're beginning to show a little bit, and it's obvious that you've changed, you can begin by saying to your child that inside Mommy's uterus (be clear about correctly naming the parts) a baby is growing. If you've never had an opportunity to explain to your child where babies come from, this may be a good time to do so—if your child seems curious and asks you to tell him about it. As I have said earlier, be clear and honest in your discussions about sex with your child.

If you have already tackled the question of sex education (and at four and a half, this may well have happened), remind the child that it takes nine months for the baby to get ready to come out. You can try to get your child to remember other babies he may have seen recently. Talk about their little fingers and toes and about how the baby will grow inside of you until it's perfectly formed and ready to be born. Be sure to emphasize to your child that when babies are born, they are very small. This is important, because you will want to remind him that the baby will come out of your vagina—a special opening in Mommy. It should be made clear to the child

155

that the opening the baby comes out of is not the urethra or the anus. Children create theories that are based on their personal experience. One little girl was having her mouth examined by a companion. As she opened wide, he exclaimed while peering in, "Well, I see you are going to have a baby girl."

Tell your child that Mommy will be going to the hospital and that Daddy and the doctor will help you to get the baby out. Add, "That's how I was born, that's how you were born, and that's how everyone was born. That's even how little kittens are born." By age four, many children in nursery school have seen gerbils or guinea pigs give birth, too.

Frequently parents make the mistake of saying that the new baby will become a playmate for the child. Saying that to an older child is probably not a good idea because the baby isn't really going to be a playmate—not for many years. On the contrary, the baby will be a troublesome and demanding interference in the older child's life. Quite naturally, the older child is going to feel disturbed by the presence of the infant. In fact, the question that's probably uppermost in the child's mind is: Why do my parents want to have a baby? Don't they love me? And, if they love me, why do they need another one? Aren't I enough?

Imagine, for a minute, yourself in a similar situation. Your husband comes home and says: "Honey, I love you so much, I've decided to go get another wife, so I can have two." How would you feel?

Try to soft-pedal the news. You can say, "Our family is going to get larger and that will be nice." Present the news in a positive light, but don't expect the child to grasp the consequences. Of course, I wouldn't tell your four-and-a-half-year-old that he's going to be annoyed with the new baby—but I wouldn't make a big to-do about how fabulous it's going to be either. Children often say they want a little brother or sister, but they have no idea what that entails—that it will mean having to share their parents' attention, that Mother will have to go away for a few days, that they themselves will have to be more responsible.

Not too long before—only when you are fairly certain that in a week or ten days you'll be having the baby—you can mention to your older child that you will be away for a short time to have the baby. If you're going to be gone for a day or two, make arrangements for someone your child knows very well (a relative may be best) to stay home with him. Because more husbands now participate in the births of their children, there will probably be a twenty-four-hour period during which someone else will have to take care of your child.

Make careful provisions for the time you will be away. Write up the routine your child is accustomed to because children feel much better if the routine is the same. Remember that it's going to be upsetting to a child to be left by both Mom and Dad—even temporarily—so find out from your hospital if they'll allow visits from children. Wait a bit, however, until you're ready to put on a cheerful robe and you don't look too overwhelmed or sick or tired. The visit shouldn't be a scary one because usually the maternity wing of the hospital is friendly and attractive. Show your child how glad you are to see him, and tell him how much you missed him. Obviously, don't make too big a deal about the new baby.

If a pregnancy is aborted, a child will need to be told. Keep in mind that you've spent a great deal of time preparing the child for the birth, and the child will need to know that it's not going to happen as expected. The child should have a clear explanation. Simply say, "This time it didn't work. Mommy was pregnant and was ready to have a baby, but it didn't work. Mommy is going to have to try again to have another baby." When the child asks questions, try to answer them as simply and as factually as you can. Expect that the child might be a little frightened or temporarily upset. The clearer you are and the more factual you can be, the better off the child is going to be.

If the baby is stillborn, simply say, "The baby wasn't really ready to be born. We will put her in a special place." That's it. Simple and straightforward. But don't ignore it. Don't make believe it didn't happen. Children know something happened. They saw that you were pregnant for nine months, and they will wonder what happened to the baby. If they think you lied to them about this, there may be repercussions later in the form of not trusting you about other things.

Fortunately, such tragedies are rare, and it is much more likely that you will be coming home from the hospital with a nice healthy baby. But regardless of how smitten you are with the new baby, when you get home, try to make a big fuss over the older child. Again tell him how glad you are to see him and how terrific it is to be home again. Be particularly careful not to emphasize that he's now the big one. Because you have an infant, you will be tempted to see your older child as being older than he really is. The contrast between the two is vivid and startling. But remember that for your four-and-a-half-year-old nothing has changed. Although it will be graphically apparent to you how much your four-and-a-half-year-old has accomplished when compared with a newborn, he won't see it that way. Telling him he's such a "Big Boy" can frighten him.

You especially don't want to try rushing an older child through his various stages of development now—or try to rush your child from his crib to a bed. Many mothers with new babies want to get their children toilet trained before the infant comes. Quite naturally they don't want two children in diapers. But by doing that you're in essence saying, "I'm going to overlook my child's needs and put mine first." This could potentially cause the child a problem, because you're not pacing the development according to the child's abilities. Always ask yourself, "In whose interest am I doing this?" Occasionally it is fine to say you're making a decision in your own interest—as long as you know that you are. But when the issue is as important as toilet training, it's too risky to the child to rush him through it.

After the new baby is brought home, I think you can anticipate regressions in the older child. A fully toilet-trained child may suddenly begin to have "accidents." Your four-and-a-half-year-old may whine, "Carry me. I can't walk." Why can't he walk? Obviously because the baby can't walk. Resist the temptation to snap back: "You have two feet. Walk on them." This is an important time to try to understand what your older child is going through. Instead, show your child you empathize with his predicament. "I know you're pretending you can't walk because you want Mommy to carry you, too," you might say good-naturedly, adding, "You poor thing. You'd like to be carried like a baby, too. It's not possible all the time, but once in a while I'll give you a carry."

Expect that every time you nurse the baby, the older one is probably going to demand, "I want a drink now." Try to anticipate these needs and requests so that they won't take you by surprise. The reasons for them are fairly clear. Your four-year-old sees you as taking valuable time away from him and giving it to the little one. Whenever you administer loving care to the baby, the older one feels this as a deprivation. He wants his share. More to the point, he wants it as it used to be before the baby came. "Feed me first. After all, I was here first." And isn't it true? Your four-year-old was there first, and he always took priority. Then along came a new baby and you're looking after the baby first. Who needs this? thinks your older child.

Commiserate with your child and tell him you know it's terrible to have to wait for things he might need when the baby cries. Try to convince him of the advantages of being an older child—but without frightening him or overselling the idea of being the "big one." Say to him, "Gee, there he goes again. Isn't it awful how he cries and can't talk the way you can? What a nuisance!" (Remember, the baby can't understand what you're saying.) Or, "Gee, isn't this fun! You and I can have peanut-butter-and-jelly sandwiches—

but he can't." Get conspiratorial with your older child and let him know you're on his side.

Another tactic is to encourage your older child, particularly if it's a first child, to be a helper to you—but not an indentured servant. Children want to do what you're doing anyway—they like to model themselves after you—so you might as well have them help you. "Would you mind, please, handing me that diaper?" you might ask, and add, "Thank you for being such a help." If he declines the invitation to help, accept it as the right of the child to refuse. Do not count on his assistance.

You can be pretty certain that when the baby is screaming, that's exactly when your older child is going to demand that you read him a story. Find a way of helping the older one to tolerate the necessary delay. Again, be conspiratorial. "Oh, darn," you might say, "there he goes again. What a pain. Let's take care of him, and then I can read you a story." By doing this, you're voicing to the older one that you're on his side, that although you have an unavoidable obligation to take care of, you really would rather be with him. It makes it easier for the older one. Keep in mind that this won't work 100 percent of the time. It's a rough period for a child, and you will have to let him express some of his anxieties and dismay.

In addition to regressions, you may also see overt hostility to and rivalry with the new baby. Some children are overly solicitous with the baby and then show alarming symptoms of hostility in other areas—behavior you might not think is linked with the baby but probably is. Some children will begin by being "loving" and gentle with the new baby, stroking him softly, and then will turn that stroking into a heavy pounding. Try to recognize that your child is in the throes of a very active and important conflict. On the one hand, he wants to love the baby because you love the baby and because you want him to love the baby, too. On the other hand, he's very annoyed that this baby is absorbing so much of your attention. Be vigilant. Never allow a young child to be alone unsupervised with a baby, because he certainly cannot control himself. If you observe hostility, just remove the older child, or take the child's hand away and say, "Let's be gentle with the baby." If that's not feasible, move the baby into another part of the house. Reactions are sometimes very delayed. When the younger child reaches seven or eight months and is more of a person, otherwise indifferent older children may begin to show their resentment for the first time.

If your child shows overt hostility—like wanting to toss the baby out of the crib or throw things at him—always be around when the older child is near the baby. But rather than scolding the older child, you should try to show that you empathize with him. Keep saying over and over again, "I know it really can be awfully tough for you to have a new baby in the house. Sometimes it's such a nuisance. It must make you pretty angry sometimes." Or perhaps you can tell your child stories about "other people" that will help. "Hey, I know a boy who is three and a half years old whose Mommy just had a little baby girl. He is just so annoyed because that baby is crying all the time. I don't blame him, do you?" Sometimes a parent must speak for the child—to allow the child's feelings to come to the surface. But it is also important to add: "But no matter how badly you feel, you may not hurt the baby. I do not hurt you and I do not want any of my children to be hurt. You can tell me when you've had enough of him and we'll find something fun for you to do, but no hitting or squeezing is allowed."

43
From the Crib to a Bed

A mother of a three-year-old boy asked if her son was now old enough to move from his crib to a bed. The crib would soon be needed for an infant, she said, due to arrive in a month. "What's the best way to move my son to a bed in these circumstances?" she asked.

A three-year-old is certainly old enough to move into a bed. In fact, I think one can even consider moving a twenty-month-old child into a bed, even if there isn't another baby coming along. And when we speak of a bed, by the way, it doesn't have to be an elaborate and expensive production. A simple box spring and mattress on the floor will do nicely—especially if you are worried that your child might fall off of the bed in the night.

But first ask yourself: In whose interest are we considering moving the older child to the bed? In this case, put the child's considerations first. You know that the infant can use a bassinet for a while, and after that perhaps a portable crib. Because there are other alternatives for several months, don't rush your older child into a bed. The older one should not be made to feel as though the little one is robbing him of things that are his. He's going to feel that way soon enough, so why cause distress when it isn't necessary?

A child should be prepared for the eventuality of a move from his crib to a bed. If you have ample room, it's a good idea to introduce the bed into the child's room while he is still in the crib. In this way, he can practice using the bed during the day by sitting on it or reading on it, and it will become part of the feeling of the room. Children experience pieces of furniture not just as inanimate objects but as adding to the ambience of a place.

After the child has become accustomed to the bed in the room, you might begin to invite him a little more enthusiastically to try it overnight. In the beginning, he may spend some nights in the bed and some in the crib. Generally the child will gravitate toward the bed. Most children who are normal and healthy want to grow up. If you don't make a big deal about taking the crib away from him, and you don't specifically mention taking it away to give to somebody else, the chances are he will like the idea of sleeping as Mom and Dad do.

Later, when he's secure in the bed, you can invite him to take the crib down with you. Disassemble the crib and put it away, even if it's only for two weeks (the longer the better, however). By doing this, you can avoid his feeling that you gave his precious crib away even before it was cold, so to speak. When you bring it out again for the new baby, you might want to paint the crib another color, so that it's made over in a different way. But don't lie to the older child. Simply ask him to remember when he had this crib and it was another color, or when he was just a baby and used this crib himself. This makes the transition easier and also makes giving it away easier.

There's one other thing you might try to facilitate this move. When you introduce the idea of a bed to the child, take the child to the store with you so he can choose some interesting sheets, pillowcases and blankets. Even if you're not crazy about the choices he makes, try to let him have his way. Allowing him to make some choices about his own bed will give him some sense of control and thus may allow him to adjust better to the new situation.

44

Competition: Winning and Losing

Lately, my four-year-old son has been hypersensitive in relation to his father. They used to wrestle and play together every evening when my husband came home from work, and it was a fun and friendly activity. Now, however, when our son falls down on the ground, he starts crying, claiming that his dad has hurt him. Then he comes running to me for sympathy. One night, when his father grabbed him by the wrist, our son yelled, "Stop! You're killing me!" My husband felt terrible. Is my son turning into a crybaby?

As I mentioned earlier, preschoolers can be very romantically involved with the parent of the opposite sex and very competitive with the parent of the same sex. This little boy probably wants his mother to see him as Number One, rather than allowing his father to occupy the more important role. The little boy wants Mom all to himself, so he feels competitive with his father. He becomes angry with him and wants to show his father up.

There's one big problem, however. This is a losing proposition. His father is clearly bigger and stronger and smarter. The little boy can't beat Dad at very much, although he dearly wants to. He begins to be very provocative with his father now and appears to be very hypersensitive at the slightest opportunity. Why?

The boy is full of anger and annoyance at his father for occupying the number one role. But he is also a little bit afraid of his anger. He fears it will be turned against him. The child perceives the father's roughhousing as retaliation and is suddenly "hurt" and "injured" in the play because he thinks his father is trying to hurt him. And how typical that he would run to Mom—his true love—for sympathy!

The best advice in this situation is to try to keep your cool. If a child tries to provoke you into a fight, take it with a grain of salt. Don't overpower him or push him around. Try to understand why he is acting the way he is. Fathers often ask, "What do I do when the kid wants to play checkers and always wants to win?" The answer is that it's much better to nurture your son than to beat him. If it looks as if he's going to lose a competitive game, point out how he can make a better move so he can win. It isn't important that you win, but it is very important that you let him have some success. And keep in mind that cheating at games or changing the rules in the middle of a game is not at all unusual for a child this age. When appropriate, gently point out to the child that it isn't as much fun for you if he changes the rules in the middle of the game or cheats—but don't be tempted to scold him for it.

You don't have to let a child win every time, of course. Sometimes, realistically, you will win. If this happens, make a joke out of it. Say, "Oh, oh, I think I'd better cover my ears, because I think I'm going to win this game, and you're going to be pretty upset." Or, "Well, look at that! I won this time. But I bet you'll win next time. Let's play again." In this way, you are allowing your child to see you as a helper, not as a threat—someone he can model himself after.

Little girls experience similar conflicts. They want to be like their mothers, but at the same time they're competitive with them. They want to be Daddy's girl, to sit on Dad's lap, to have Dad caress them instead of Mom. When they see Mom and Dad hugging, they run right over and try to get between the parents and push them apart. They're very concerned about losing their place. They want to have both parents sewed up, so to speak. In their eyes, each parent should love the little girl—not each other.

Mothers, too, have to be careful and cautious about coming down too hard on their little girls in a competitive situation. Try to get involved with the child in such a way that she participates with you rather than competes with you. You can teach her to be like you without beating her into submission. Unfortunately, there can be very bad long-term consequences if fathers browbeat their sons or mothers their daughters.

Keep in mind that this competitive, feisty stage is temporary. As the little girl or little boy begins to identify with the parent of the same sex and incorporates some of the parent's values and morals, the romantic love affair will come to an end, and the hypersensitive competition will die down.

45
Sleeping with the Parents

My daughter will be five next month. For seventeen months, she's been getting into our bed every night—one, two, sometimes three times. Each time, we get up and put her back in her own bed. We've asked her what's wrong. Sometimes she says she's scared of the crickets; sometimes she says it's noises outside that frighten her. But I think it's not really the crickets. We want to stop this, but how?

In this case, the problem seems to have started when the child was three and a half. At this age, as we have discussed earlier, the child wants to separate the parents. A child literally wants to get between the mother and the father and share in the parents' intimacy. So it's fairly typical for children to want to share the parents' bed. This is the age when children want to be included in everything. They feel very hurt if you exclude them. They want to be just like one of the grown-ups.

Parents should encourage children to be separate individuals with their own privacy. It's important to teach a child that she can be alone and not be lonely. Being able to sleep in her own bed is an important milestone in achieving this. Keep in mind, also, that there's a certain seductiveness involved in a child's sharing a bed with her parents. Even if the parents aren't engaged in a sexual activity, it may be too stimulating and suggestive for a child to be part of this intimate and close personal contact.

It would have been best, of course, to have dealt with this problem when it first started seventeen months ago. But now the parents are in a situation where something that started out as a fairly typical developmental pattern is now a habit that's been reinforced for a year and a half.

Solving the problem will take a couple of weeks, during which time one parent isn't going to get much sleep, because he's going to have to stick to his procedure if he wants to get the child out of the habit. So first of all, pick a two-week period of time when you can afford not to sleep.

Begin by asking the child just exactly what the reasons for her waking up are. Perhaps there is a real reason, such as a nightmare, an illness or a frightening noise that is causing the sleeplessness. When you have satisfied yourself that there is no manifest reason, then you can concentrate on breaking her of the habit.

Every night when the child wakes up, walk her back to her bed, sit in a chair next to her bed, and wait for her to fall asleep. When she is asleep, go back to your bed. She may get up twenty minutes later. If she does, repeat the same thing. Don't be tempted to yell at her or scream at her. Simply say, "This is your bed. You sleep here. I have my bed and I sleep there."

If you find that she sometimes slips into your bed and you didn't hear her, put some bells on your doorknob and hers, so you'll be awakened. No matter how tempted you are to catch up on some sleep, you have to wake up and deal with the problem. You have to be persistent but not harsh. Just be matter-of-fact so that she knows in no uncertain terms that she cannot sleep in your bed.

After the first night, talk to your child during the day about the incident.

Say to her, "I want you to sleep in your bed, not in our bed. Is there anything that would make it easier for you to stay in your own bed?" Listen to what she tells you. She may have a suggestion. Perhaps it's a night light or a new set of sheets.

If you're so inclined, you might consider compromise. You could offer your child an alternative. "If you don't want to sleep in your bed—but remember that you can't sleep in my bed—how about sleeping in a sleeping bag in your room?" you could ask. Some kids get a kick out of that. You could put the sleeping bag in the hallway between the two rooms—just as long as it's not in your room.

Keep in mind that children do develop fears at different ages. Suddenly your child may begin to speak of monsters—lions and tigers out to get her. Children do develop phobias, and one way of looking at this is to try to figure out what could prompt such fears. Many psychologists believe that these fears are a result of thoughts children have for which they feel they deserve punishment. It could be that a child is unable to express or acknowledge in herself some angry feelings toward you. Because she cannot even acknowledge them, her mind may play a trick on her: the angry feelings that she has return to her in the form of something that's going to do harm to her. As I discussed earlier in Part II, Phobias, these angry feelings are turned against the self.

So how can you help? In addition to reassuring your child that you're not going to let the crickets or whatever is frightening her get her, that you love her very much and that you won't let anybody hurt her, you should look around during the day, when things are calmer, for reasons why she might be angry with you. You could say to her, "Perhaps I did something to make you annoyed with me." Try to encourage her to express any angry feelings she may have. She may be angry because of her own competitive strivings or maybe she resents you for bringing home a baby. Whatever her reasons, it is essential that she be told that it is understandable to be angry with you and that you help her to express her dissatisfactions in words. Since children frequently are unable to articulate the reasons for their worries, engaging them in fantasy play can be helpful to get more of a handle on what's happening. You might make up stories together or draw pictures and discuss the thoughts and feelings of the person in the drawing. Sometimes playing with dolls and hand puppets is a good way to encourage children to reveal fears and concerns through their dramatic play. Very often, however, without any intervention, some of the anger begins to subside, and children pass through this phobia stage.

166

With the subsiding of fears and phobias, and the consistent handling on your part of your child's sleep problems, the nocturnal disturbances should cease. I might add that if you're fortunate enough to have one night when the child doesn't come into your room, a friendly comment to that effect and maybe a small reward to acknowledge her courage might be an added incentive.

46

Am I a Boy or a Girl?

A friend of mine gave my three-and-a-half-year-old son a tea set for Christmas. I was a little surprised when she did, but I let my son play with it. I don't know why, but it makes me nervous somehow watching him making tea and playing such a girlish game. It drives my husband crazy. What I want to know is—is there any way that playing "girl" games can turn my son into a homosexual?

Sex roles and sex stereotypes are undergoing a radical change in our society. Many women have assumed stereotypical masculine roles in their careers and leisure activities. Many men have discovered the joys of nurturing their children in a way their own fathers did not. But how does this translate into child-rearing practices? Do we want our little boys to engage in "feminine" sex-role stereotype behavior—and vice versa, do we encourage our little girls to play with trucks?

One of the achievements of the women's movement of the 1960s is that traditional sex stereotypes are falling away. In nursery school, for example, it is often hard to distinguish the boys from the girls. They all have their hair cut the same length; they're all wearing jeans and sneakers. But interestingly, although it is seen as adding to a girl's repertoire to teach her to use tools or allow her to play with trucks and motorbikes, we as a society still have trouble being comfortable when we see little boys playing with tea sets and dolls.

Recently, in a parenting group in a New York nursery school, this very issue was the topic of discussion. While the majority of the parents felt that it was fine for their little girls to strive toward "masculine" endeavors, they were hesitant and reserved when it came to wanting their sons to strive toward "feminine" activities. Trucks for girls were fine. Tea sets for boys were a bit of a problem. One of the mothers pointed out that some men do grow up to become chefs and waiters, but it still bothered the majority to think that their sons would want to play at serving tea. As the discussion progressed, some of these mothers confessed that they feared their sons might become homosexual. What was interesting was that no one felt that if their girls played with trucks, they would become homosexual. But why? Why would it work for one sex, and not for the other?

Society thinks it's a disservice to a boy to make him more like a girl, whereas it's a credit to a girl if she's able to share in masculine activities. Some have suggested a political motivation for these feelings. Because our society tends to value masculine activity more than feminine activity, we think we are adding to a girl's development to have her take on masculine roles. Conversely, we think we are taking valuable time away from the boy's natural masculine endeavors if he pursues so-called feminine play. This doesn't necessarily explain, however, why parents immediately hop to the thought of homosexuality when they see little boys playing with dolls. Why? Where did the sexual connection come in here? The thinking is so illogical that it suggests an underlying unconscious meaning.

One point of view is that in the unconscious mind a homosexual male is missing some essential male ingredient. Some people may think of a homosexual as symbolically missing a penis and therefore like a woman. Although this is obviously not true and is a prejudice, this primitive idea is a potent one lodged in our unconscious. When adults look at a boy playing with teacups, they may unconsciously think that something has been subtracted from him and that he has become a "girllike boy." Our fear that a little boy somehow symbolically loses his penis may explain why we become irrationally nervous and anxious when we see him engaging in "feminine" behavior.

Once we understand our irrational fears, it is easier to address the question the mother asked: Should a parent buy teacups for her son? I'm in favor of developing the nurturing aspect of a boy's character. One has to develop nurturing attitudes—such as loving and caring and giving—and to squelch those attitudes is to shut off a very important part of a person. Take the average little boy who may be rough and tumble at times but at other times may be very giving and caring. To show abhorrence to his giving, paternal, parental role as he is playing with another child or a doll would be a mistake. Cutting off the nurturing part of a child's personality can make him very vulnerable as an adult.

The mother's question really went beyond this, however. She wanted to know to what extent she should allow a boy child to play with dolls and teacups. Is there any possibility that you are allowing or even encouraging that boy to grow up to be a homosexual?

In some sense you could be. Here's how. If a parent encourages a boy to play with predominantly feminine sex-role toys, then he does the child a serious disservice. If a parent conveys to the child that being a boy is inherently dangerous, bad or undesirable, the parent is saying to the child he doesn't like the gender the boy was born into. Clearly, this is going to cause a child to wonder if he should be a boy. Maybe, he thinks, it's better not to be a boy, to be a girl instead.

Children are very concrete and need clear markers to help them live comfortably with their gender. A child's task at this age is to align his psychology with his biological givens. And he needs some help doing that. I don't think it's a bad idea for little boys to play with dolls and teacups, or to help Mom serve the food, but at the same time, I think it's desirable for boys to be exposed to some of the male markers in our society which will help them fit their psychology to their gender. For this reason, I'd rather see a boy wearing a cowboy outfit than a cowgirl outfit. Even though these markers—such as lace panties or boyish briefs—seem superficial and trivial, from the point of view of helping your child learn to be what he is, they are important signposts for a child. It is less confusing during periods of uncertainty to have such clear markers. Later, when there is no doubt about one's sexual identification, sex-role stereotypes can be cast aside.

Children go through a phase when they want to be everything and don't want to give up anything. They want to be a boy *and* a girl. A little girl is told she's a girl, but she resists having to make the choice. If you pick one, you have to give up the other, right? A little girl has to give up the hope of ever being a boy. As silly as that sounds, in her mind, she's given up something very important. Little boys go through a similar phase of wanting to have babies. They have to give up that idea, too, and it's a big deal for them. Of course, we know they were limited as soon as they were conceived, but they don't know that. Their emotions and wishes have to catch up with their gender. Children resist this process and for a while a residue of this struggle remains. A little girl may not want to wear dresses because she is not ready to give up her option.

❧

With about four exceptions in the past year, my three-year-old daughter won't go near a dress. She's insistent about wearing pants. Earlier in the year, she was equally insistent that she was a boy. Should I be concerned?

A parent has to help a child to be comfortable with her physiological role. But pushing a girl toward wearing a dress may not be the best way to do it. The markers in our society are changing. Clothing—as a marker—

has undergone a revolution. If Mom wears pants, why wouldn't her daughter want to wear them? "Mom doesn't wear dresses; I want to be like Mom," a child thinks. But if some clothing in our society is now a confused marker, parents have to search for other signposts to help their children. We have to find the socially acceptable markers that demonstrate the undeniable differences between the sexes and reinforce them.

The central question is: How can we make it easier for a child to identify with proper sex roles and at the same time not be sexist or oppressed? Is that possible? It's an interesting dilemma. Your goal as a parent is to encourage your child to grow up comfortably in her physiological role. Regardless of how arbitrary they may appear to be, there are certain markers that can help your child move in the right direction: some clothing, some activities, some toys and some behaviors. You want to help your child be comfortable with her own reality, but at the same time, you don't necessarily want to curtail any attempts to explore other roles, too.

The answer, I think, lies partly in the way we explain play with tea sets or dolls or trucks to our children. You can say to a boy who is washing a doll, "Isn't it nice you're pretending to be a daddy." Not Mommy but Daddy—because fathers, too, give baths to babies. Why can't a boy do the same activity but pretend to be a daddy instead of a mommy? Why can't a boy serve food just as Daddy does? Doesn't Daddy ever cut up an apple and give it to him? Doesn't Daddy ever pour the milk? Then the boy can identify with the father and still play out a number of "nurturing" roles. It will be clear to him that he's going to grow up to be a man—like Daddy—and that fathers do lots of things, many of which are loving and caring and giving.

47

Haircuts

I took my son to the barbershop to get him a haircut, and he got completely hysterical. He was crying so much and squirming around so much, the barber had to give up. What am I going to do? His hair is almost to his shoulders.

Not all children—but some children—go through a phase when they're deathly afraid of having their hair cut. It's very important to sympathize with them during this time and to remember that having a haircut is not a life-and-death matter. If the child is truly petrified, try to put off the haircut as long as you can.

There are a number of reasons why a child might be frightened. First of all, the child is in a strange place with a strange person who's handling him, who's pinned something around him, and who is about to alter the child's appearance. This can make a child feel very uncomfortable. By and large, children don't like changes of any kind. Besides, it is annoying. Having a haircut requires that the child sit still, that he put up with having hair get in his nose, eyes and down his back. From a child's point of view, it's all a big pain.

More important, the barber is clipping and snipping something from the child's body. Although we know that hair and nails don't hurt when cut, young children don't know that and are sometimes terrified that a part of the body is being cut away. This irrational fear occurs during a stage of development when children are very concerned about their bodies being intact. It's a time when they worry a lot about their bodies being the way they're supposed to be. They fret that parts of their bodies will fall off or will be lost or hurt. Anything that even symbolically suggests that one's body can be mutilated is frightening. Cutting fingernails, for example, can be terrifying. Although it is irrational, don't yield to the temptation to make a joke of the child's fear or to ridicule him. Such humiliation can be a crushing experience for a young child.

But what can you do? When one mother took her son to have a haircut, every time he opened his mouth to protest, she stuck a chocolate-chip cookie into it. This got them through the haircut, which just goes to show that sometimes bribery works. But as with most problems you solve with bribery, it only works for that one instance. What you really want to do is to help your child deal with his fears.

One way to do this is to let your child watch when you give yourself a manicure. If you're clipping your fingernails, let your child observe you. He may even want to experiment by using an emery board himself.

When you have your own hair cut, let your child go with you one day, just to see what's going on. Remind him that this visit has nothing to do with his having his hair cut.

Another tactic to try is to take the child to the barber for a One-Minute Quickie. Tell the barber what you're up to, and that you'll come back tomorrow to get the haircut finished. Just put the child in the chair. Have the barber work like lightning. Snip, snip, snip, haircut's finished. The next day, go back for another little visit.

At home, play games of pretending you're going to the hair stylist. Let the child be the barber. One of the most important ways to help children overcome fears is to let them perform the active role. If there is a period of time when the fear is very intense, I would not force a child to have a haircut, or even to have to think about it. It's not worth it. Try to wait as long as you can, and then when the haircut is unavoidable, do it yourself at home to minimize the fear.

Incidentally, for many of these same reasons, children are often afraid of people who are handicapped. They see someone on crutches or in a wheelchair and they fear that such damage to the body is contagious. It scares them. After all, if it happened to somebody else, it can happen to them! Often, to a parent's chagrin, a child won't have anything to do with a handicapped person. To a child, such a person brings bad news.

To help your child understand handicapped people, explain matter-of-factly that this particular person needs an appliance or a crutch or a wheelchair to help him get around—in the same way that, when the child was smaller, he himself needed a stroller or a carriage to get around. By relating the tools of a handicapped person to something the child can remember and understand, you will be minimizing the scary quality of such persons. At home you may even play a game with your child: Have him wrap a "pretend" brace around a leg or an arm and show him how such a device helps hold an injured limb in place.

173

48
Surgery

Surgery at this age is to be avoided if it's at all possible. If a child is particularly concerned about his body parts, as we have just discussed, having surgery is really not such a great idea. Sometimes, however, it's unavoidable. If that's the case, invest some time in preparing your child for the event.

There are a number of good books you can read to your child which explain what a hospital is and what doctors do. These books explain, in language a child can understand, what is likely to happen to him during surgery and can begin to demystify the whole experience for him.

You should be very honest with your child and tell him that certain things do hurt. It doesn't pay to lie. Rather say, "It will hurt as it would if I were to pinch you." Pinch the child a little bit, or have him do it himself, and give him some idea of what it will hurt like—and for how long it will hurt. Also explain, as best you can, what the doctor will be doing to him. Try to minimize any surprises. It might be a good idea to buy your child a doctor's kit, and to let the child practice the various medical tasks on you. Pretend to take blood pressures; pretend to take temperatures and to give injections.

Next, visit the hospital. Be sure to pick a children's hospital or a child-oriented hospital. This is very important, and you should tell your doctor this. You want to be able to stay overnight with your child—if you can—and you want the hospital to be colorful and cheerful. Take your child to visit the hospital in advance so he will know what a hospital looks and sounds and smells like. You've already introduced him to the idea of a hospital through books. Now let him see it—the ambulances, the flashing lights, the doctors and nurses.

During the actual hospital stay, remain with your child as long as you can, right up until the anesthesia is given. If your child is awake and getting stitches, stay with him. Talk to him. If the doctor doesn't seem to have much patience for this, speak up for your child. Tell the doctor, "Wait a minute. Let's take our time. Let's discuss it." Go slowly and tell the child about each step of the way: "This may feel cold; this may hurt a bit; you look the other way; I'll tell you what the man is going to do; squeeze my hand as hard as you can." Your primary task is to give the child as much support as you can. The doctor will take care of the rest.

After the surgery, be with the child in the recovery room; he may be upset from the anesthesia. Studies have shown that children whose mothers stay with them at the hospital seem to do much better than those whose mothers don't. They weather the storm quite nicely, because they feel there is someone there for them.

You can indulge a child with treats a little bit when you get home, but don't let him blackmail you into letting him sleep in your bed or into changing his bedtime to midnight. If you let him get away with a great deal, he's going to think there really is a good reason for all this indulgence, and that maybe he is very sick, indeed. Besides, you don't want to start a tradition you'll be sorry about later.

You should tell your child that the experience was very scary for you. "It was scary for Mom and Dad, too. It must have hurt." Give your child an opportunity to talk about the whole experience. Tell the child, "You were very brave, even though you were scared. I understand you were afraid and that's normal, but I'm very proud of you because you were brave. You see, you can be scared and brave at the same time."

The child should have an opportunity to play out as much of the experience as he can. Parents often think they shouldn't dwell on unpleasant experiences, because it will make the problem worse and worse. Sometimes parents think that if no one mentions it, it will go away; or that it's not really bothering the child. I think that if a child isn't saying something about a trauma, it's not because it isn't still bothering him; he's just not talking about it.

A child should practice playing the doctor—being the active one. A child has just gone through an experience during which he was a passive recipient. Turn passive into active. Doing so will better help the child to adjust to and understand many of the unpleasant experiences he's just been through. He will go from having been the helpless victim of an assault to a person with a sense of mastery.

49
Thumb-sucking

If you're the parent of a thumb-sucker and you've tried to discourage the habit, by now you're probably feeling pretty frustrated. Some parents complain that thumb-sucking may cause problems in a child's dental health, but many dentists say that thumb-sucking during the first three or four years is not necessarily harmful. Another reason parents worry is that thumb-sucking makes a bad impression—"It looks babyish," they say. And after all, don't we want our children to be mature and well-behaved? Otherwise we tend to think it reflects badly on us. This is often a situation in which our own embarrassment is more the issue than any real harm thumb-sucking can do.

There are some very strong forces behind a child's thumb-sucking habit. Sucking is first and foremost a reflex that helps a newborn take in food. As mentioned earlier, prenatal photographs have revealed that sometimes even fetuses have thumbs in their mouths. Gradually the sucking reflex becomes a soother and a comforter even when the baby is not hungry. In a way, this self-soothing helps your child become slightly independent of you. When a child is tired or worried or cranky, a quick self-help method is the trusty and familiar thumb. You yourself may catch yourself chewing on your fingers when you're under stress.

Our three-year-old daughter recently started sucking her thumb. She never did it as an infant, but recently she saw her friend do it, and now my daughter continually does it. We have tried turning off the TV when she does it; we've said, "Big girls don't do that"; we've tried to reason with her that she may have to have braces. But nothing works.

If your preschooler's a thumb-sucker, there is probably nothing to worry about. If it persists into the school years, it may be a sign that your child feels stressed or insecure. It could be a new baby in the house or trouble in school or family tensions.

This mother was right in one regard. Almost all methods of discouraging thumb-sucking don't work. Bandages, bitter-tasting solutions and nagging tend to make matters worse. There is, however, one thing that may work.

If you can find the right motivator—so that the child wishes to do that thing more than suck her thumb—that may be the one way you're going to get her to stop. By a motivator, I mean any activity that has greater reward than the pleasure of sucking her thumb. Perhaps the child feels embarrassed in front of friends and wants to be accepted by these friends more than she wants the reward of the thumb-sucking. Or perhaps the suggestion of a manicure will do it. You might introduce the idea that if she can give up her thumb-sucking, you'll put polish on her nails. If that pleasure is more important to the child, that's what will make her give it up. You might offer small rewards for brief periods of non–thumb-sucking in the hope that rewards motivate better than punishments.

Unfortunately there's very little else you can do. If the child walks around with the thumb in her mouth day and night, then you know she is nervous about something and needs additional security. Your only option as a parent is to try to figure out why the child needs extra reassurance and to give it.

50

Imaginary Companions

Children live in a magical world—a world of wishes, fantasies and make-believe. Separating fantasy from reality at this stage of development is a long, slow process. Often for a preschool child perceptions of what's real and what isn't overlap and become confused.

Even as adults, we occasionally experience the blurring of what's real and what's in the mind. Sometimes we have a dream and the dream is so vivid and so "real" we find ourselves the next day questioning whether it was a dream or if it actually happened. There are even more subtle ways we as adults blur fantasy and reality. We may, for example, in a relationship with another person, ascribe to that person thoughts and feelings he or she doesn't have. We think those ascribed thoughts and feelings are "real" because we feel they're real or wish they were, but they may, in fact, be simply products of our imagination.

For children, making the distinction between fantasy and reality is considerably more difficult. Children live in a world in which fantasy serves many important functions. Fantasy is deeply woven into their play, their interactions with others and their own emotions.

One of the most obvious ways a parent can see a child involved with fantasy is when a three-year-old suddenly scolds the parent for stepping on

"Candy's" toes. "Candy?" the parent asks, looking at the thin air where the "toes" are supposed to be. "Yeah," says the child. "She's my friend. She's three, too."

Imaginary companions, while not present in every child's development, are fairly common. It can be alarming to a parent to see his child behave in such an irrational way, talking to someone who's clearly not there, insisting that he give the imaginary companion some juice, too. But imaginary companions can be very useful to a child.

Imaginary playmates may be a way of expressing anger toward the parents. Imaginary companions can say things that may be rude or hostile and "get away" with it, thus giving the child an outlet he may not otherwise feel he has. Motives can be attributed to the imaginary companion rather than to the child himself. If the child does something "naughty," the imaginary companion can take the blame. "Candy spilled my juice. That was naughty," you might hear your three-year-old say. Also, imaginary companions can bolster a child's confidence—on the principle that there's strength in numbers. Rather than having to try something alone, your child now has a "buddy" with whom to meet a new challenge.

༅

My four-year-old daughter has an imaginary girlfriend and, at the moment, her "girlfriend" is having a baby. Should I be concerned about this imaginary playmate? Why do you think she is saying her "friend" is having a baby?

As we have seen earlier, four-year-olds are very interested in birth and reproduction, so it is not surprising that concerns of this sort would surface in this child's play with her imaginary companion. In fact, four-year-olds often use imaginary companions to explore issues or feelings that are threatening to them. Perhaps the child finds it easier for the imaginary companion to get involved with the mysteries of birth than it is for her. Frequently we see children using imaginary companions to discuss a subject that is painful or awkward.

Having an imaginary playmate is like playing a game of "pretend," and as a parent you need not feel uncomfortable about going along with the game. If a child brings up the idea that her playmate is having a baby, ask her what she has in mind, and this may lead to an interesting discussion about birth. In general, it's good to play along and to get involved with the fantasy from time to time. Respect the playmate as an alter ego of your child. If you treat the companion badly, the child is going to feel badly. If you have to serve a little extra food to the companion, fine. If you have to bring along an extra toy for the companion on a trip, well and good. Be careful not to embarrass or humiliate your child for having an imaginary companion, nor to humiliate the imaginary companion itself. Try to keep in mind that the playmate is serving a useful purpose in the growth and development of your child.

Imaginary companions are nothing to be alarmed about; many children go through a stage when one is ever-present. In most cases children give up the imaginary playmates by the time they reach kindergarten.

51
Security Blankets

Imaginary companions are one way in which we can see the worlds of fantasy and reality merging in a child's emotional life, but there are other, more subtle ways as well. What happens when the "companion" is not an imaginary playmate but a tangible item, such as a doll or a blanket? What if one of your child's deepest relationships is, temporarily, not to a person but to a thing?

※

When my daughter was an infant, I nursed her, and in the evenings or at night, I was often wearing a nursing nightgown. Later, when she had trouble putting herself to sleep at night, I gave her the nightgown in her crib, and this soothed her. She's three now, and the nightgown has become a security blanket for her. Lately, however, she's been asking for it when she's upset or tired or hurt. My husband is concerned about this and wonders if we should try to take it away from her.

In the same way that fantasy and reality blend for a child with an imaginary companion, they can also mesh when the child forms an attachment to a blanket or a doll or a piece of fluff. In this case, however, the attachment is associated with the mother and with nursing. Even if the mother had not provided her daughter with the nightgown, the child may have developed an attachment to some other object herself. Some children suck their thumbs while holding a finger next to their noses. In this way, they're imitating the feel of the breast against their faces while they suck. Other children like to hold on to a little piece of fluff, because it's reminiscent of the nap from a diaper or a blanket. Others get attached to an actual blanket. Some children make this connection with hair. You'll often notice them pulling and twirling their own hair, which reminds them of playing with their mother's hair during nursing.

These objects or activities are called "transitional objects," and they are pleasurable, soothing and calming for the child. A transitional object is something that's associated with the mother and nursing and comforts the child as the mother and nursing did. Because the child can now be comforted by something other than her mother—yet associated with her—it enables the child to separate from her mother. The object is one step removed from the primary person, the mother, and as such it stands for something—it's a symbol. This is a big mental and emotional milestone for a child. Because she can adopt this early symbol, she can free herself from the mother and be comforted by a mother substitute. Such attachments to transitional objects at three years of age are still within the realm of normal and expected behavior. Not every child, however, gets so obviously attached to a tangible transitional object. Some children have their own special sources of comfort, and you might not even know about them. It might be a thought or an idea or a sound that is comforting to them.

Usually the transitional object is put to rest by the child herself. At some point the child will lose interest in the object; she won't forget about it, exactly, but it will lose the lifelike qualities it has possessed. A child may say, "Remember how I used to drag around the little teddy bear?" but it won't have an emotional investment anymore. This may happen as the child approaches four years of age.

If the child is older, and the use of a transitional object bothers you, you could, gently, encourage the child to give it up, but it's better to wait until she herself puts it away. You could, of course, restrict its use by suggesting that the child use it only in the house or in her room.

One of the ideas that psychologists have about the importance of these transitional objects is that the child can take out angry feelings on the object. This is particularly true if it's a doll (see Part II, Anger and Emotional Honesty). You may observe the child slamming the doll around or poking it. Sometimes this may seem alarming, but psychologists believe this provides a positive emotional outlet for the child because her rage is often disproportionately great and cannot be directed toward her parents or other loved ones.

Usually the object will start to fall apart: It becomes shabbier and shabbier until there's hardly anything left of it. There's something endearing to the child about this shabbiness—as the mother will discover if she tries to mend the object—or worse, wash it. The child likes it shabby. It's as if the child appreciates the object's endurance—in a way perceiving it as a companion that's gone through a lot with her.

52
Lying and Stealing

Imaginary companions and transitional objects are understandable aspects of a child's fantasy life. But it comes as a surprise to most parents to learn that certain so-called antisocial or immoral behavior, such as lying or stealing, is also a manifestation of a child's magical world.

❧

My son, Patrick, who is four and a half, has begun to tell lies. How concerned about this should I be? He lies when it comes to getting out of trouble. I try to word my questions carefully so that I don't put him on the spot and make him feel accused before I find out the truth, but he still lies just the same. Frequently, I'll hear a cry in the next room and go in to find his sister, Eileen, fourteen months old, sprawled on the floor. "I didn't do it," Patrick will say, when, of course, he did.

The first thing to ask here is this: Is it possible for a four-year-old really to lie? Children at this age may not represent the truth the way we do, but it may not be fair to call their responses lies. To lie, you have to be aware of purposely distorting reality. A four-year-old lives in a world very different from ours, and when he "lies" he may not be purposely distorting reality. He may feel as though someone else spilled the milk. Because he may wish that someone else had done it, he says that he didn't do it. He doesn't have the same logic we do, so it's not fair to call his words a lie.

At four, a child also doesn't have a fully developed system of ethics or a conscience. And without that, it's very hard to hold somebody to being truthful. It isn't because the child is a criminal psychopath in the way that some adults are. He simply hasn't developed a reliable conscience yet. At four and a half, he's too young to have incorporated the ethical principles that we believe one should have—a sense of right and wrong. Moral judgment develops slowly through different stages.

So what should a parent do when a four-and-a-half-year-old appears to be "lying"? I think this mother was instinctively correct not to accuse her son out of hand. If a parent insists on a confession from a child, she's not really helping him. Many parents feel they have to back the child against a wall and make him confess. "Who started this fight?" they'll ask. "How did those crayons get broken? No one else was in the room with you. Who broke the crayons? But I saw you peeling the paper off the crayons and breaking each one. Did you break the crayons?" And, of course, the poor child continues to say no.

Ask yourself this question: Toward what end am I trying to get a confession of guilt? Let's say, as in the case of Patrick and Eileen, the older child has pushed the younger one. Patrick's mom comes in and finds Eileen sprawled on the floor. Toward what end does she try to extract a guilty confession? Suppose Patrick says, "Yes, Mom, I cannot tell a lie. I did it." Then what should she do? Punish him? Reward him? It's a no-win situation. The only thing a parent can do here is to deal with the situation with dispatch. Pick up the crying child and comfort her. Find something else for Patrick to do. If necessary, try to avoid leaving the two of them alone together in the future.

On the other hand, if you actually see Patrick pushing Eileen, you do have to talk to the older child about it. Say to Patrick: "Please do not hurt your baby sister. I don't want anyone to hurt you because I love you. I don't want anyone to hurt her because I love her. If you don't like something she's done, just tell me."

183

If the conflict is between two friends, the parent, rather than trying to find out who started it, might teach the child about taking turns and negotiation. If the conflict is over a toy, for example, try to engage your four-and-a-half-year-old in a discussion of what would be a fair way for each of the children to use the toy. Instead of trying to pin the child against the wall by demanding that he tell you who had it first, turn the event into a positive learning experience by showing him how they might take turns, trade one toy for another or otherwise negotiate a settlement.

Extracting a confession of guilt from your child is quite different, however, from helping your child with honesty. There are a number of positive ways to do this. Keep in mind that you won't help a four-year-old with honesty in the sense that he will then become an honest four-year-old. He's not capable of it. Instead what you are doing is planting the seeds in a child so he will have good moral judgment later on. And one of the best ways to do this is to use yourself as a learning device. Be a model for honesty. Specifically, you might go to the store with your child. If you get incorrect change, turn to your child and say, "Look, Mr. Jones gave me an extra dollar. Mr. Jones made a mistake. This is his dollar, not mine. I want to return it. It may be tempting to keep something that doesn't belong to me, but I know he will feel bad because it is his."

Or you might ask your child to think about how it would feel if someone kept a toy of his and didn't tell him. Remind him of a time when a possession of his was mislaid or perhaps stolen, and how he felt about it then. To reinforce this, if you see a child drop something in the playground, make a big deal of giving it back. If possible, have your child return it and then reward your child with praise. "I'm proud of you for returning that toy," you can say.

It's also important to show honesty in your dealings with your child. If your child forgets about something he has earlier requested, remind him of it and ask if he still wants it. That way, he won't later come to think he was tricked out of it.

You've now demonstrated honesty. Later you can talk about these experiences with your child and explain to him how important it is to be honest. But be patient. Learning to be honest won't happen overnight. The news reports on television and in the papers are filled with stories of dishonesty. Even presidents and police officers are sometimes caught giving in to temptation. Honesty is an ideal most of the time. The ability to love and empathize with other people is, to my way of thinking, a more effective means of promoting honesty than the fear of punishment. In other words, you can demonstrate to your child that you wouldn't hurt someone you care about, and you should care about people.

One of the main tasks of this age is the development of a conscience—but it's a slow process. As one sage once put it: "Even with understanding, self-control in the face of temptation is a life-long struggle."

※

My daughter is four and a half. Incredibly, when I make a chocolate pudding, she sneaks into the fridge when I'm not looking, lifts up the "skin" on the top of the pudding and scoops out the pudding to eat. Then she puts back the skin to make it look as if she never did it. Later, when we confront her at the dinner table, she swears up and down she didn't do it, becoming enraged and indignant that we could even think of accusing her. She's done this a couple of times now and won't admit her guilt, even though it's obvious to her that neither her father nor I did it.

In this case, I see an inability to exercise sufficient self-control. The little girl is acting on the impulse that if I want it, I should have it. She shows little tolerance for depriving herself or delaying getting something that would satisfy her. I wouldn't technically call it stealing—she's just taking something that she wants.

A child has to be helped to conform and to resist temptation, but this has to happen gradually and not harshly. In this case, the mother might engage the child in the making of the pudding—no reason why a child of four can't help at this task—and the mother could say, as they put it in the fridge, "You can have a big dish of pudding but not before dinner. If you want to, why don't we scoop some out into a special bowl and it will be yours—it has your name on it—and you can have it as soon as you've finished dinner."

The mother might ask herself: What's going on in this relationship that the daughter feels she has to sneak things? Maybe there's a larger issue here that needs to be explored. She might also ask herself, does it make any difference if the child has the pudding now or after dinner? For some children, eating before a meal doesn't really interfere with their appetite. If it's a matter of principle, be clear about it. Sometimes you might not want to have a fight over a matter of principle. Pick your battles. Don't set yourself up for twice as many conflicts as you need to have.

As with lying, to speak of someone under the age of five or six as stealing is not altogether accurate. Technically, if you take someone else's property, you steal it, yes. But from the point of view of knowing in your heart that you're doing something wrong—having a conscience to be your guide—at four and a half, that's impossible. The conscience isn't fully developed yet. Likewise, the girl cannot be accused, strictly speaking, of lying to her parents about what she did. Because she wishes she hadn't done it, in some way she comes to believe she hasn't—as is evident in her moral outrage and indignation, which, by the way, are very common at this age. It's kind of comical, actually, to watch the way these kids bristle with indignation. Sometimes parents become enraged at being lied to so blatantly and do not want to be "taken for a fool" by an equally indignant four-year-old. But, as hard as it is, try to rise above the desire to show that you are smarter and "more right" than your child.

Stealing can also be a symbol or statement of something else. A four-year-old girl in nursery school was "stealing" another little girl's drawings and taking them home. Later it was discovered she was also taking things out of the little girl's pockets, and once she took a hat that belonged to the girl, who was talented and fairly affluent. When she was found out, there was a big uproar. The child was stealing! Horrors! Later when everyone calmed down, they realized that the girl wasn't stealing from everybody, just from this one little girl. A child who was poor and lived in a deprived section of town was taking objects from a girl she admired. The items did not have real or monetary value. Her stealing was a statement that she wanted to be that other little girl. She wanted to have that other little girl's drawings so she could pretend she was that child and receive the recognition and praise she so desperately wanted.

Children are not perfectly clear about the fact that they are taking something that belongs to someone else. Remember that this is the age of magical thinking. If a child takes another's drawings and hat, will she not be transformed into a child she likes better than herself—and that everyone else seems to like better, too? A child believes that if she can wish hard enough she can make something happen—and conversely, as with lying, that if she wishes hard enough, it didn't happen.

53

Bossiness

Between the ages of three and five, children become very social creatures. Up until this point, you've been their best and perhaps only friend, but now they are learning to make other friends and to interact with other children their own age. Having friends and playmates is extremely important at this age, and you may find you have to seek out children for your own to play with when neighborhood kids aren't readily available. By the time a child is ready to enter elementary school at age six, he will need to have had plenty of opportunity to interact with other children and to know how to get along. Your task as a parent is to guide your child through this all-important socialization process—helping him to learn to give in to others when appropriate and not to be too bossy.

❄

My four-year-old daughter is extremely bossy with her friends. Whenever they play, she's very aggressive and has to be in control. She has to have it her way all the time. She wants to win. She wants to be the leader. Some of her friends no longer want to play with her. This hurts her, and I want to protect her from this hurt, but I'm not sure how to handle it. Should I step in?"

At this age, children want to be the boss. For years, they've been pushed around, told what to do, how to behave. Suddenly they begin to assert themselves. They no longer want to be the passive "done-to" child. They want to be you—a grown-up person with power and influence. Conversely, as we discussed earlier, they want you to be them—little slaves they can boss around. They want to reverse roles.

At play with other children, this translates into their wanting to be the

187

boss, or the mommy, or the daddy, or the leader while the other kids are the "babies," or "second," or losers or, essentially, slaves. They see in their play with others an easy opportunity to take their passive position and turn it into an active—assertive role. This is very common behavior, and in general it's a healthy attitude.

In this child's case, however, her bossiness is a bit exaggerated, which suggests that she may be having some problems with her sense of helplessness and powerlessness at home. Possibly the girl has no opportunity to make any choices or decisions about her own life. She may perceive herself as powerless—as being bossed around all the time by her parents. If the girl had some opportunity to make some choices, and to demonstrate some preferences, she might not feel the need to be so bossy at the playground. Four-year-olds can make choices about simple things—what to wear that day, what to eat for lunch, where her toys go in her room—little things that might give her a feeling of power, some belief that her actions can effect change.

I should point out another cause for the bossiness, although it is a less common one. This might be a child who has never really had to follow anyone else's rules. Perhaps at home the girl is overly indulged and never expected to give in to someone else's demands or needs. Consequently when the time comes in a social situation to give in to other people, the child finds the concept abhorrent. Such a child is used to having everything her way.

This particular mother wants to know if she should "step in." My hunch is that it's better for a parent not to moralize or to tell the child it's bad to be so bossy. It's probably not a good idea to force a child to give in to the other kids or to make her be second instead of first. Let the other children handle it. Peer pressure can be quite effective. By the age of four, most children won't put up with a superbossy kid and will let the child know this in no uncertain terms. They'll see the child coming and make it clear they don't want anything to do with her.

Naturally your child may be hurt or defensive. When that happens, you might say very gently, "I notice that some of the other children are afraid that you're going to be mean to them. They don't want to play with you because they don't like to be treated that way." It's a nice way to introduce the subject. It may not change the child's behavior right away, but it will plant an idea in her head. The child may become angry or defensive, but at least you've opened up the subject with her.

If the problem persists, then I think you can step in once or twice to act as a model for proper behavior. You can't just say to a bossy child, "Go

play," and hope the problem will go away. You have to be an active participant in a way that will help your child learn the proper behavior. One way
to do this is to invite one friend over for your child and arrange an activity
for both of them to do together—going to the playground, getting an ice-
cream soda. Go with them and participate in their activities. Generally it's
not advisable to insert yourself in the middle of their play, but this is an
artificial kind of a set-up. Because you're trying to teach your child something, it requires ingenuity.

Let's take the example of having a soda. When you get to the soda foun-
tain, ask each of them where she wants to sit. If it happens that they both
want to sit in the same chair, see if you can come up with a clever idea as
to how to share or cooperate so that your child can begin to learn how to
deal with another child and not always have to be the boss. Perhaps you
could say, "You both want the same chair? Let's see if you both can fit in
the chair together." Of course, that won't last very long, since they'll start
wiggling around. (And remember that the soda is incidental; you have a
hidden agenda.) After that, try another way of sharing. You might say,
"Kate, you sit there for thirty seconds. Now, Mary, you sit there for thirty
seconds. Now we have two ways of sharing something, don't we?"

There are a number of ways you can model problem solving for a child.
You can teach her how to be polite and how to take into account another's
needs and wants and feelings. Later, go on to another activity and try it
again. But remember that you've got to get involved. You can't expect a
four-year-old miraculously just to "get it" without some help. You need endless patience. At this stage of development, your child is soaking up your
values like a sponge. If you can demonstrate in your dealings with others
the principles of taking turns, sharing and giving in, your child will find it
easier to adopt some of these ways of interacting with her own friends. In
the long run, your investment will pay off.

54
Playing Alone

Raising a young child requires a lot of patience—often when we feel as if we have none left. There are moments, hours, days when you simply wish your child would go off and play by himself for a while so you could get something done around the house. And at the preschool age, you can expect a child to be able to do a few things independently of you—but his period of independence or his attention span may seem exasperatingly short, particularly if you are busy with other tasks.

Our son will not play by himself. He seems to be happy only when we supply him with a playmate or he goes to a friend's house. There are days when there are no friends to play with, and on these occasions he gets upset and cries. Short of literally playing with him all day or letting him watch TV all day, he is miserable. What should I do?

I sympathize with this mother's predicament because I do think a child this age ought to be able to spend some period of time entertaining himself. But I wouldn't expect him to play all day by himself. It's not realistic. And his need for friends is very healthy and normal. Nevertheless you do want to start encouraging your child toward some independence, and there are a number of things you can do to begin this gradual process.

First of all, to be doing something on his own doesn't mean he has to be doing it alone—or even away from you in another room. The first step in helping a person to do a task on his own is to begin it with him. Does he enjoy putting together a puzzle? Or coloring? Whatever it is that turns him on, sit down with him and help him get started on the task. You might complete a couple of puzzles with him at the table and then start him out on another. While he is putting it together you can do a different task right there with him at the table: open your mail, peel carrots or read a magazine. Because you're close by, you can help him in a friendly way if he gets stuck. Or if he finishes the puzzle successfully himself, you're right there for him to show it to. The next step would be for you to move away from the table for a few minutes at a time while he is playing a game and then come back to the table to check on him. But don't expect him to stay alone for twenty minutes at this age.

If your complaint is that you can't ever get anything done, then let your four-year-old help you with your chores. Four-year-olds want to be just like you. If you're dusting the furniture, they want to dust the furniture. If you're vacuuming, they want to vacuum. Give them tasks to do that are real and helpful. The work may not be done as well as you would do it, but give it to them anyway. There's no reason why a child can't set a table, put some pots and pans away or dust the furniture. You'll be rewarded with their sense of delight and pride in their accomplishments.

If your goal is to free up some time for yourself when your child temporarily doesn't have anyone to play with, consider exploring some of the afternoon and weekend activities that may be available to you in your community. Local libraries often have Story Hours for preschoolers, and children's museums may have special indoor programs or nature walks. Nursery school is also a fine alternative to being at home with Mom. Many children thrive in the structured atmosphere of a nursery school setting, enjoy the company of other children and can participate in learning projects that may not be feasible for you to do at home.

If your child is able to spend time away from you visiting a friend or a relative without signs of distress, this may indicate a readiness for some preschool experience. Being able to spend time away from you, fairly well-developed verbal skills, an interest in other children, some social adaptability and independent toilet habits suggest that it may be a good time to initiate some group experiences for your child.

55
Talking to Strangers

I have two sons, ages three and a half and one and a half. What I'd like to know is at what point do you start talking to children about strangers? You hear so many crazy stories about children being taken, and my older son is quite outgoing. Is it too soon to start to teach him to be careful?

This is a very important question. We recoil in horror when we hear on the news terrible stories of children being lost or stolen from their parents. Every parent, at some point, experiences this fear. We spend so much time trying to teach our children to trust people and to like them, and then all of a sudden we are faced with the task of trying to teach them not to trust people they don't know.

There is, however, a natural period of disillusionment in children. This is a term psychologists use to indicate a certain point in a child's development when he simply becomes more realistic about life. If you forget about something you've promised to do, for example, your child will experience a moment of disillusionment about your "perfection." This also happens when you get sick. Suddenly the child may feel that his Rock of Gibraltar is no longer so sturdy. But if the parents have instilled in the child feelings of self-confidence, trust and security, then this disillusionment period is easier to deal with.

Teaching your child about strangers can coincide with this time of disillusionment. This is not to say that we should terrify our children. But we should explain that there are some people out there who have "something wrong with them." And because when we meet a stranger we don't know if he's good or bad, we shouldn't trust someone we don't know. If Mom and Dad say it's okay to be friendly, then you can trust the person. The main task here is to keep the explanation simple. If your son is only three and a half, he probably can't understand any explanation more complicated than that.

I know that this confuses some parents. "But if a man or a woman comes up to my son in the supermarket and says, 'Hello, how are you?' I want my child to be respectful," one woman said. In response to that, I would suggest that a three-and-a-half-year-old child doesn't have to be respectful in that situation. If a stranger comes up to you and your son in the supermarket and says, "Hi, Buster, how ya doin'?", you can answer for your child. Simply say, "He likes to come to the store with me. We have a good time." Then pat your son on the head.

Children at this age often have a natural aversion to strangers anyway. Encouraging kids to talk only to people that Mom and Dad approve of will frequently mesh with the child's inclinations and may not turn out to be a big problem after all.

Most children get a firm message from their parents. The message is: You have to obey grown-ups. You have to obey the baby-sitter, your parents, the nursery school teacher, even the police officer. That's what you want them to do. At the same time, however, how can they critically distinguish between a person they should obey and someone who's up to no good?

This is very hard, and I don't think you can expect a child between the ages of three and five to be able to do this without any guidance. To help a child, talk to him about situations in which he may notice something peculiar going on. For example, if the child is playing ball and there is a man standing behind the fence watching, ask the child what is peculiar about this scene. Why is the man not working? The man may have a perfectly benign reason for watching the children play, but it is better to alert your child to a possible problem than have him be totally ignorant.

If a person says to the child, "Hey, come here," tell the child that he doesn't have to. "Just because a grown-up calls to you, you don't have to go over there. If a stranger asks you a question about how to get somewhere or asks you to go with him to show him the way, tell him no and run away." Have the child ask himself why this stranger is asking a little kid for directions rather than an adult. Tell your child that if he feels he is being followed, he should run to the nearest store or public place. If someone should touch him or grab him, tell him to scream and run away immediately.

If something should actually happen to your child, encourage him to tell about it. Remind him that he hasn't done anything wrong, and that he should always tell you if something strange has happened to him or if someone has told him to keep a secret. Even if it turns out that the person in question was innocent, no harm done. Better to check it out.

One suggestion, which came to me from a mother of a five-year-old boy, was to teach a child, if he were accosted by a stranger, to yell out, "This is not my parent." The reasoning behind this is that a passerby might see an adult pick up a screaming child and think to himself, "Oh, the kid's having a temper tantrum," and that the adult was merely the child's parent. Telling a child to yell that the adult is not the parent may make a passerby more alert to trouble.

Even a young child can be told that although his family and friends love him and care about him, there are some people out there who have something wrong with them. Their minds don't work right. Their thinking is sick thinking, and they sometimes do things they're not supposed to do. It also helps to read stories to children about this subject. In all likelihood your local librarian will be able to help you find some appropriate books. But don't overdo it. A certain amount of caution is vital, but exaggerated concern can distort a child's perception of his vulnerability.

56
Guns and Violence

My son, Brian, just turned four years old. For his birthday, a friend of ours gave him a gun. As soon as Brian opened it, I gently found a way to distract his attention and removed the gun and gave it back to my friend. I explained to him that I didn't want Brian to have a gun. I hoped he wasn't offended, but it was a matter of principle I strongly believed in.

Our daughter is just three. She's an extremely sweet, gentle child. The other morning at breakfast, she was eating a piece of toast and discovered after she had taken several bites that she had fashioned the toast into the shape of a gun. Then she started aiming it at us and saying, "Pow, pow." I've noticed lately that with any "found" object that resembles a gun, she begins to shoot it. Should I discourage this?

I think it goes without saying that children should not be encouraged to accept violence as a means of resolving differences. By having guns around the house as part of your standard everyday equipment, you're really saying to a child that you're promoting the use of violence to solve problems.

You can explain to a child that you're opposed to the idea of people shooting each other, and you can add that in certain circumstances—such as with the police or with hunters—guns are a part of reality. But make it clear that you believe there are other, better ways to resolve conflict than by the use of guns.

But what do you do if your son is begging you to give him a ray gun or a cap pistol for Christmas? Suppose all the other kids have them, and your son wants one? Suppose your son fashions a gun out of a stick and plays with that? Does that mean your child has violent tendencies you should discourage?

To some extent it's a matter of taste whether a parent gives a young child a gun for a present. But it is easier to make that decision if you understand the nature of the relationship that a small child has to a gun.

First of all, small children have no sense of doing damage to another person when they "shoot" a gun. (Which is why it's extremely important never to leave a real gun anywhere where the child can get at it.) When children say, "Bang, bang, you're dead," that really doesn't mean much to them. A child can just as easily say, "I'm a little bit dead," or, "I'll be dead for a minute, then I'll get back up." They have no sense of death's finality. When they play with guns, they're not really expressing violence or killing as we think of it.

What they are experiencing is a sense of power. In fact, shooting a gun is one of the child's first experiences with remote control. If he pulls the trigger right here, something appears to happen over there. A friend falls down and pretends to be dead. The child discovers that he can control somebody from a distance. If you don't look upon the act of shooting a gun as violence, it's an achievement on the part of the child to make something happen far away from him. It's practicing power. Similarly, a very young child will experience this same sense of power when he or she throws a pebble or some sand. Something happens over there. For a child it's fascinating to be able to do that.

It's particularly appealing for children because they have so little real power. Children often feel vulnerable, powerless and exploited by others. We push them around, tell them what to do, and most of the time they feel we do not treat them fairly. Any opportunity to exercise power is going to be attractive to them.

I think you should point out to a child from time to time that there are ways to resolve conflict other than by fighting or shooting with guns. But when a child is deeply involved in a fantasy game of cowboys and Indians or cops and robbers, such a discussion will be useless. When a child is involved in a fantasy game, he's not really fighting, nor is he really experiencing violence. If, however, in the course of the game a child should pick up a stick and hit another child, then you do have to step in. But to the extent that they're using their fantasy and imagination, you should be cautious about interfering.

Later, when the game is over, you might try a little brainwashing. You might introduce the subject by saying, "I noticed earlier that you were playing with guns. I wonder if there isn't some other way besides shooting the bad guy to solve the problem." But for the most part it's beyond the child's comprehension that he's being violent.

The true lessons about violence will come from you and your values and perceptions about the world. If you read in the newspaper of an assassination, for example, say to your child, "Oh my goodness, isn't this awful that there are people in this world who would actually shoot or kill another person? That's outrageous. If we are angry with someone, what could we do instead?" That kind of a conversation in the proper context can be useful.

57
Swearing

Have you ever been shocked by a preschooler who's come up with newly acquired four-letter words?

Children have an uncanny knack of picking up precisely those words you'd hoped they'd never hear. Naturally if you openly use profanity, it's more likely they will too.

The other day my daughter and I were playing in the kitchen. I was cooking, and she was playing with some pots and pans. Suddenly I heard her drop one of the pans and saw her bend to pick it up. "Oh Ka-wheist!" I heard her say. I had to laugh. I know where she got that one.

If you're presented with some colorful language, it's probably best to minimize your reaction to it. If they see it gets a rise out of you, they'll keep at it. Young children find sexual and bathroom terms exciting and great fun to use.

Don't laugh or convey the idea that it's cute because then you'll have a really tough time discouraging it when it's lost its novelty. Likewise, don't immediately become outraged and punitive. It's best to overlook it the first time. It may be just a trial balloon that doesn't reappear.

If it recurs, then calmly ask your child if she knows what the word refers to and explain it to her to make sure she does. Let her know you've heard all those words before and they're not as interesting to you anymore. In fact, it's boring to hear them over and over again. Sometimes when a child sees you face the issue squarely and deal with it technically and correctly, it takes the wind out of her sails. It also embarrasses her.

It can also be helpful to tell a child that everyone says these things at times and that it's okay to use them in private, or to think it to themselves, or even to use with their friends in the park—but not in public or with you. You certainly don't want your child to be disrespectful to you. You might point out that it's not polite and that people don't like to hear those things—especially Grandma!

If you're matter-of-fact with your children, and view their excursions into profanity as nothing more than child's play, I think you'll find fewer occasions to cover your ears.

58

Night Terrors

My five-year-old son wakes in the night with loud piercing cries, full of terror and fear. My husband and I rush into the room to comfort him and discover he isn't really even awake. He doesn't seem to know us, nor does he seem to emerge from his awful "nightmare." We hold him, and gradually the screams subside. He lapses back into a peaceful sleep.

A nightmare? No. This is a night terror—and it is often just as terrifying for a parent as it appears to be for a child.

A night terror is different from a nightmare. It has different causes and different characteristics. Usually when a child is having a night terror, he screams, seems to be very panicky, may flail his arms and legs and won't necessarily recognize you. If you sit down on the bed with him to calm him down, you find he can't be consoled. Even though his eyes may be open, he never fully wakens. Normally a child won't remember the terror the next morning.

Most research suggests that night terrors are not serious. Nobody knows why children have night terrors, and they don't seem to be related to problems in everyday life. Some research has suggested that if a child has been overly stimulated before going to sleep, has engaged in a wild activity, has seen a scary film on television or has been read something frightening, that might cause it. But again, there doesn't seem to be any positive correlation.

The best thing to do for a night terror is to follow your instincts. Go in to your child. Try to calm him down. Don't try to wake him up. Just comfort him until he stops.

Recently, it's been discovered by people who monitor children and dream states that night terrors seem to be related to nondream sleep. Bed-wetting at night also seems to occur in nondream sleep. This suggests that something physiological triggers the terror. It's not really a question of self-control. Nor is it a product of bad dreams.

Typically night terrors occur around the ages of four and five and usually stop at age eight. Although so little is known about them, it can't hurt to sit with your child, to talk softly in a calm reassuring way and to tell him where he is. Eventually the terror will subside and the child will go back to sleep.

If the terrors persist and/or become very frequent, then you might consult your pediatrician. There are some medications that can be used. Because terrors seem to be a sleep-related issue, medication can change the level of sleep and may help your child.

59
Bed-wetting

When we speak of bed-wetting (the technical term is nocturnal enuresis), we refer to a child who urinates in his sleep overnight—a very different problem from wetting during the day. Frequently parents think that bed-wetting is a toilet-training issue, but it's not always accurate to link the two. In general, bed-wetting problems occur long after good toilet-training habits have been established. One can't really speak of a bed-wetting problem in a two-and-half-year-old who is just learning to control urination and may have accidents on occasion while he is asleep at night. Bed-wetting, as a problem, more frequently refers to a child who has been dry at night for at least six months and all of a sudden begins to wet the bed during sleep several times a week.

Before I go into the several causes of bed-wetting in children, I want to point out that it's important first to consult with your pediatrician to ascertain that there is not a bladder or other organic disorder at the root of the problem.

Bed-wetting can be the result of a number of different causes—one of which is an emotional response to stress. Typically something stressful happens, such as Dad losing his job, Mom going off to work or a new baby arriving in the family, and the previously dry child begins to wet the bed. The bed-wetting appears to be a clear signal that the child is experiencing stress but cannot acknowledge it. If you think your child is wetting the bed due to an emotionally stressful situation, you have to deal with the underlying cause of the stress, and once successfully tackled, the bed-wetting symptom will disappear. You can discuss the bed-wetting with the child by saying, "I notice that you're wetting the bed, and I've been wondering about that. Perhaps something is bothering you. Perhaps you have a worry. Perhaps something happened." Try to figure it out together. More often than not, of course, the child doesn't know what the worry is. If he knew, he'd bring the worry to you and you'd be able to help him with it, and he wouldn't have developed the bed-wetting problem.

Bed-wetting can also be related to other emotional issues for the child—not necessarily stress but issues related to this particular stage of development. For example, in this age group, children go through a phase of wanting control over their environment and trying to master ambitions that far outreach their abilities. Bladder, genital and urinary tract symptoms can sometimes be related to the emotional issues involving control and mastery. Once these matters are resolved, as they will be during this phase of development, the bed-wetting should stop.

More recently, researchers have suggested that some forms of bed-wetting may be more a sleep-related issue than a toilet-training matter. This usually applies when the child has never had an extended dry period despite being well trained during the day. Some children go into a deep level of sleep that is referred to as non-REM (rapid eye movement) sleep, which interferes with the child's natural impulse to wake up when the bladder is full and needs to be emptied. During this level of sleep, the message that the child needs to wake up and go to the bathroom never makes it into his consciousness, and he then wets the bed. This type of bed-wetting really represents a physical immaturity, which will resolve itself once the child's nervous system becomes more fully developed.

Some doctors have suggested ways to cure a child of this sleep-related bed-wetting, but personally I am not in favor of them. One is to have the pediatrician prescribe medication that would alter the child's state of consciousness. I'm generally opposed to introducing medication to the child's body unless it's absolutely necessary, because we never really know all the side effects and consequences to the nervous system of a young child. The other method is to wake the child on the hour all night for a number of weeks. By doing that, you train him behaviorally so that he can never really fall asleep quite as deeply as he normally would, thus ensuring that the child gets the signal to get up to go to the bathroom.

Some researchers have linked bed-wetting with food allergies. While it is highly speculative at this point, I think you might do well to talk over this possible connection with your pediatrician and perhaps a child nutritionist as well.

Since the child can't do anything about his problem, no matter what the cause, you should not shame or humiliate him. Rather reassure him that he will soon be dry, and that it's not his fault. Most children will automatically, without any help from anybody, stop wetting the bed by the time they are three. In those children with a bed-wetting problem the wetting will probably cease by the age of five. In some children, the problem persists until puberty. In even fewer instances, it goes on past puberty. You might also keep in mind that sometimes it runs in families, so that if you or your husband were bed-wetters, it may well be that your children will follow suit.

I've had so many questions concerning bed-wetting through the school-year ages that I realize it's a much wider concern than was previously thought, which calls into question just how much a "problem" it is at all if so many children appear to experience it.

60
Cleaning His Room

I ask my four-year-old to clean up his room after he's finished playing with his toys. He'll say yes, and then he won't do it. He'll just fool around and continue playing. I lose my temper and we have an argument. How can I get him to clean up his room?

You can't expect a four-year-old to respond to a verbal instruction like "Clean up your room." To hope that a preschooler will heed such a command will lead only to frustration on your part and escalation of conflict between the two of you.

A parent should give a child a specific task. Cleaning the room may sound like a specific task to you, but it's too large a request for a child to comprehend. The specific task at hand should be smaller and simpler: "Would you please put your toy cars away in the toy garage?" "Would you return the puzzle pieces to their box?" And leave it at that. In this way, the child will know exactly what the beginning and end of the task is and what *specifically* has to be done.

After giving the child the request, don't automatically leave him on his own and expect him to follow it. Follow him into his room and call attention to the next activity so that the cleaning up isn't the end of something he likes doing but rather a transition to something he looks forward to. No one wants to stop doing something that's enjoyable. Make putting back the toys a shared activity, even a game. "You hand me a car, I'll drive it into the garage"; "I'll hand you a puzzle piece, you put it in the box."

I think you'll find that the combination of clear instructions, participation and calling attention to the next activity will make cleaning up a lot easier. These tips won't entirely solve the problem, however, because no four-year-old likes to do a chore. And don't be afraid that if the child doesn't quickly do the task at hand you are losing your authority. A parent doesn't demonstrate authority by shouting out commands. It won't be effective anyway, and that will threaten your authority even more. It's much better to be a leader and a participator—you get much more done that way.

Incidentally, there shouldn't be just a big bin, or big toy chest, to dump toys in. In the old days everyone used to think it was nice to have a toy box in the child's room for all his toys. But it is probably more suitable if there's a special place for everything, and if all the toys can be seen. A series of shelves or a stack of boxes, for example, is much better for the child. Arranging the toys in such a way helps a child with his concepts of organization. This will be useful in school, where he will be expected to begin to organize his learning tools.

One mother, who had a big toy chest for her daughter, remarked that she often felt badly since some toys were "lost" at the bottom of the chest and not seen again for months. Her daughter couldn't make a good selection and tended to play with the same "visible" toys over and over again. Of course, it's more convenient for a mother to have a big box to dump everything into, but it won't be better for the child. And the child may find it easier to "clean up his room" if he knows exactly where each toy is supposed to go.

61
Starting School

Going off to school for the very first time can be an emotional experience for both children and their parents. For children who have been at home with their mothers since birth, the idea of going off independently of Mom can be particularly trying. But for most it will be a tremendously rewarding time—full of excitement and new challenges.

In order to make sure that the first several days of school are pleasant and happy ones for your child, give some thought to preparing her for this new experience. There are a number of things you might try, and in the process you may find that they help *you* prepare for this separation as well.

First, take your child for a school visit and a preview. The unknown is always frightening to a child, and it helps her if she can see firsthand exactly what is in store for her. Spend some time looking at the classrooms, and tell her what the different objects in the room are for. If possible, try to make an appointment to visit the new teacher as well, so that this person won't be a completely new face on the first day. And if the teacher can join you on your "tour" of the new classroom, this too will help your child feel more comfortable about entering school. If she will be taking a bus to school, walk down to the bus stop with her one morning and together watch the kids getting on the bus. Explain to her that the bus will be taking her to school in the morning and bringing her home in the afternoon.

Secondly, have your child discuss school with an older child—perhaps an older brother or sister, or perhaps a neighbor who would be willing to talk about the way things are done in school and what can be expected. This kind of "peer" talk is often quite effective since, in general, most little kids want to grow up and be like the "big kids."

At home, you can provide your child with puzzles and games like those used in school. Introduce her to cutting and pasting and drawing shapes on paper. Practice with her some of the letters in her name, for example. Give the directions slowly and patiently, and stay with her so she can show you her accomplishments. Allowing the child to gain some experience in following directions and in working with pencil and paper will give her a feeling of security and familiarity when she is first asked to do similar tasks in school. The request won't be so alien or frightening to her, and she will feel she has a better chance to succeed.

Finally, read stories about school to her. There are many books on this subject available at your public library that are written in an appealing way for children.

The way in which you demonstrate your feelings about the new experience will also be quite important in the child's adjustment to school. Some mothers weep and convey a sense of dread to their children on that fateful first day. Some feel a deep sense of loss; others may feel that they are being supplanted by another important figure in their child's life—and they do not like losing the position of ultimate authority. In some, depression may result from the feeling that they no longer have a useful role to play.

When these emotions take over, parents can sabotage the independence and autonomy they claim to value in their children. Under these circumstances, the normally mild apprehension a child feels when embarking on a novel experience can become a frightening separation. It is important for parents to prepare themselves adequately for that first trip to school. Parents must be able to make an honest appraisal of their feelings so that their children are not burdened with the fears or self-interest of their parents.

This isn't to say that the feeling of loss isn't real or valid. Of course it is. But my advice is to send your child off to school cheerily and enthusiastically, and then go home and have a good cry all by yourself.

Once you make your child's needs primary, you will be able to encourage mastery and instill confidence and self-esteem in her. Enabling a child to take the necessary steps toward emotional separateness is one of the most important roles a parent can play in the child-rearing years.

Part Four

Special
Family Considerations

62
Grandparents

If you are fortunate to have them, grandparents can be an important addition to a child's life. Not only can they be a welcome relief for both you and your child, but they can also give the child an opportunity to have another intimate "family" relationship and can provide him with a sense of life's continuity.

Having grandparents on hand breaks up the intensity of the relationship you and your child have together. The child is able to form a relationship that, although "family," is often more relaxed than the one he has with you. The proverbial Grandma, for example, always indulges and spoils the child and doesn't worry too much about discipline. Why should she? Because she is not the primary care giver of the child, she can experience "parenting" in a more relaxed and easygoing manner than she did with you perhaps, or than you can with your own children. And if she should "spoil" your child while he is in her care, so what? Such "spoiling" is easily corrected once the child returns to you. Simply say, "That's how Grandma does it in her house. But we don't do that here. Next time you go to Grandma's you can do that again, but right now, you can't."

Another appealing aspect to having grandparents is that they do help, as your child grows older, to give him a sense of continuity—of his place in the world and in the generations. Not only do grandparents help him intellectually to comprehend that there are parents of parents, but they also aid him in understanding where he fits in the succession of things. Even a very young child can begin to feel a sense of rootedness and history.

While grandparents are generally a big plus in your child's life, occasionally problems will arise. Competition, for example, may and often does develop between you and your own mother or your mother-in-law. Grandparents sometimes have the tendency to think that *their* way is the right way because with age comes wisdom. While that may be true in other situations, much of child rearing is a matter of opinion. As a parent, you have to stand by your own opinion. It's your child, and you will have to live with the consequences.

If you find yourself in such a competitive situation, make sure that you and your spouse are united in your decision to do it *your* way. If the Grandma in question is your spouse's mother, then it may be up to your partner to speak to her for the both of you. If it is your own mother, you will have to do the talking. Explain that in your house you are going to raise the child your way. If this makes the grandparents uncomfortable, then you can request that they keep their opinion to themselves. If they are extremely uncomfortable, perhaps visits should be kept to a minimum until the situation rights itself.

Remember, however, that when your child is visiting the grandparents' house, the tables are reversed. You can ask them to conform to certain of your likes and dislikes, but since you can't monitor their behavior, there isn't really very much that you can do. You can insist that the child not be kept up until all hours of the night or be fed things that you know will cause an upset stomach. But you can't guarantee that these things will not happen. Make your requests clear and hope they'll listen. If they don't, you can express your disappointment, but that's probably as far as you want to go. (Secretly, everybody believes that he knows best.)

A much more subtle problem is that you may feel that the grandparents are treating your baby better than they treated you. You may have noticed, for example, that your father or mother is much more tolerant of certain behaviors in your child than he or she was when raising you. You might find that you feel secretly competitive with your own child—obviously an uncomfortable feeling. Or you may be angry with your parents because *now* they put up with a particular behavior. Why didn't they let you do that when you were a kid? These are very common reactions. Being aware of them will enable you to see them for what they are and to avoid having these feelings dominate your actions. Examine your feelings and be careful not to compete with your own child.

At times, grandparents handle children in a way that children are not comfortable or familiar with. Or they can have ideas or habits that are so alien to the child that they are distasteful. Obviously this can lead to all sorts of tensions and hurt feelings. "Kiss Grandma goodbye," you say, but your son doesn't want any part of Grandma. After all, the child doesn't automatically love his grandparents unless a relationship has had enough time and contact to develop. Whatever the reason for the child's aversion to the grandparent in question, don't force a child to conform to your desires. Respect the reasons the child has for not wanting to be intimate with Grandma. It would be much better in this case to say to your mother, "Look, Mom, he's just going through a phase. He'll pass through it soon." Or you could try negotiating a compromise with your child. "I know you don't like to kiss Grandma," you could say before you go into Grandma's house. "But how about doing me a favor? At least say hello. If Grandma wants to kiss you, I'll say, 'Oh, he's not in a kissing mood right now.'" Perhaps by attempting a compromise, you can get your child to shake hands instead and keep everybody happy.

63

Twins

Throughout history, twins have been a source of fascination. In some cultures, twins were regarded as having special powers; in others, they were killed at birth because they were believed to bring bad luck to the village. Even in our culture, we are still fascinated by twins. They catch our eye on the street and we wonder what it would have been like to grow up with our own replica.

One of the main concerns in twin development is how to help each of them gain a strong individual identity. For practical reasons, in early childhood, the children are often treated as a *unit*. They are wheeled around in a double stroller; they are fed together in a double highchair; they will probably, as infants, share the same room. Although their individual needs and preferences may vary at times, these may be overlooked because they are going through the same stages of development together. One can imagine, for example, the difficulty one twin might experience if he was not yet ready for toilet training, while the other had already mastered it. Some twins are bathed together, fed the same meals, dressed alike, named similar or rhyming names, and referred to as "them," or "the twins." Identical twins may suffer even more. For years, friends and acquaintances are unable to tell them apart. Think for a moment how it would feel if people who were talking to you weren't sure who you were.

When raising twins, fight the urge to play up the novelty of their similarity. The similarity is already apparent enough; what twins need are for their differences to be distinguished. They should receive separate but equal treatment. I lean toward providing separate rooms, camps, schools, clothing, friends, toys, musical instruments—as much as you can practically and financially manage.

Some twins will find their own ways to maximize their individuality. Athletic twin boys whom I know developed the complementary roles of pitcher and catcher on the baseball team and offensive and defensive line positions in football. A less desirable method is for one to take on the role of the "bad" kid while the other assumes the role of the "good" kid. To the extent that you can emphasize, from birth, the positive ways in which they are different from each other, you may be able to forestall the development of such undesirable identities.

The physical demands on the parents of twins are tremendous. Feeding two, carrying two, running after two, cleaning and dressing two and comforting two can be exhausting. It is important to have as much assistance as you can and to try to give one another some free time to be out of the situation. For practical advice and a support network, the Mothers of Twins organization is a very good source.

64
Adoption

When do you tell a child that he has been adopted?

It seems to me it's never too soon to introduce the word *adoption* into the family's everyday vocabulary. If you do this, there never has to be a time when you will have to say, "When am I going to sit down with my child and tell him that he's been adopted?" Right from the beginning, even before the child is verbal, he will have heard the word and will be familiar with the concept.

You can introduce the idea casually and as soon as you want to. If someone should happen to say to you, for example, "Gee, your child looks just like you," you can say later to your spouse, in the child's hearing, "Isn't that funny? Mrs. Jones said Tommy looks just like me. I didn't tell her that Tommy was adopted." Even before Tommy knows what you are talking about, he will know the word. The idea will be part of his everyday life.

Later there will be a time when he will begin to ask questions about where babies come from, how they are born, was he born this way, and did you give birth to him. This typically happens at about three years of age. When it does, you will have a perfect opportunity to say that he was born like all other babies and that while you did not carry him around inside of you, he was in another woman's uterus. She wasn't able to take care of him, but she wanted someone else to care for him the way he should be taken care of—someone who loved him, and that was you. Tell him that you wanted a baby very much, and you wanted someone who needed your love. When you found out that Tommy was such a baby, you arranged to get him. And ever since that time, you have been his parents, and you will be his parents forever. Only when a child is much older do you have to explain the differences between psychological parents and biological parents.

It's easier to deal with a concept that's always been part of your reality. Imagine what it feels like to a child to be told suddenly, after thinking otherwise, that he was adopted. If the child has heard the word, and people talk about it freely in his presence, he will be comfortable and familiar with the idea. Once in a while, you might say to someone on the phone, "Gee, I'm so glad we adopted Tommy. Life wouldn't be the same without him." You don't have to do this every single day, but just enough to familiarize him with the concept and to lessen the possibility of overwhelming surprise when you finally explain to him what it means.

Almost inevitably, the child will at some point begin to ask more difficult questions. "Why did my mommy not want to keep me?" is a very common question for a child to ask and a very difficult one for you to answer. If you have certain basic information about the biological parent, you can share that with the child. You might say to your son that his mother felt she was too young to take care of him. Or perhaps the child has come from a war-torn country. You can say to the child, "There was a war, and people died, and later some children were found who didn't have parents anymore."

Although I am always in favor of telling a child the truth, I think there is one occasion when stretching the truth is better for the child. If the child asks if his parents loved him, you should say that yes, he was loved, but his parents couldn't take care of him. A small child—even an older child—cannot easily deal with the idea that he was not loved. (Besides, we may not know whether or not it is true!)

Children often fantasize about finding their parents someday and being reunited with them. Remember that this is natural and that just because the child wants to find his biological parents you needn't take this to mean he doesn't love you. It's just curiosity on the child's part. You can even make light of it. "Hey, we're stuck with you, and you're stuck with us. Too bad. You're our kid. And that's it for life." In this way, the child will know he's not going to be returned or sent away.

It is also natural for a child to wonder what life would have been like with his biological parents. You can engage in this curiosity with him. "Where do you think you would be now?" Try not to shy away from these questions. If you do, it conveys to the child that there's something wrong with his being adopted. He may feel guilty about it, or hurt, or just confused. It's better to pursue it as far as the child wants to go with it and to help him express his feelings so he doesn't bottle them up.

Lately there have been several changes made in adoption procedures. One of these is the introduction of the idea of "open adoption." In open adoption, biological parents and adopting parents know one another right from the beginning. The two sets of parents negotiate visitation rights, and the biological parents are part of the child's cast of characters. From his earliest days, the child knows there are biological parents and adopting parents. There is also new legislation that allows children of a certain age to ask for information about where their biological parents are. Because these two ideas are so new, nobody knows yet the psychological consequences of these changes in adoption practices.

65
Spacing Children

We have a two-and-a-half-year-old girl now and are thinking of having another baby. How much space is optimal between children? Ideally, how old should my daughter be when the baby is born?

It's hard to dictate what the optimal space between children should be. There's no hard and fast research that says what's best. In some families children who are very close together in age manage to get along with each other very well. In other families children are widely separated in age and get along well because they are widely separated.

If the child has been an only child for five, six, seven years, she may find it very difficult—virtually intolerable—to put up with a little one. But not necessarily. If there are many children in the family—ranging in age from infants to teenagers—the older ones may wonder why their parents keep having babies. On the other hand, the teenager might be getting pleasant vicarious parenting experience from the new baby.

In general, the rule of thumb is that, for practical reasons, the spacing of the children should conform to the various stages of development, so that you don't have more than one child in a particular stage at any given time. Let each child progress through each stage of development at her own pace. It can be confusing to a parent to be introducing a younger child to a particular task which the older child is just growing out of. Some parents say, "Let's do it all at once." They like the idea of having all the diapers and toilet training and bottles over with as fast as possible. But to do this is to risk having two children in the same stage of development— and to risk not being able to give any one individual child the attention and guidance she needs.

215

Most researchers feel that if your child is off the bottle and out of diapers—so you don't have to deal with those anymore—it's a good time to have another if you are planning a larger family. This will probably occur at three years of age. At three, a child often goes to nursery school, has friends of her own and is able to do a number of things independently. Younger than three, children are not so self-sufficient, and you risk having more than one child in a single stage of development.

ONLY CHILDREN

Many parents worry about having only one child. They are concerned that being an only child will produce undesirable traits such as selfishness, a lack of sociability, an exaggerated sense of importance and even loneliness. I do not know of any hard and fast evidence to support those worries. The way an only child develops depends largely on your outlook. You need to provide an only child with ample opportunity to play with others his own age. Occasionally, an only child will ask for a baby brother or sister. Some parents express guilt over not having another child. Just tell your child that you are quite happy with the family the way it is. Perhaps you could say, "Maybe someday we will decide to have another child, but right now we love having just you." Without the conflict of adjusting to a sibling, only children can grow into quite nice and nurturing adults.

66

Helping Siblings to Get Along

How can I foster love and friendship between my son, four, and my daughter, two? Our daughter worships her brother, but my son is often nasty and unkind to his sister. I've been careful not to compare the two children, yet usually it's my son who gets punished for pushing and shoving his sister or for being just plain rotten to her.

In general, an older child looks with thorough disdain at a younger one, while a younger sibling looks up to an older one with adoration. It's a distressing situation for the parents but a fairly common pattern.

Although there may be some unwritten ideal that says that children should love each other and develop a warm close relationship that will last for the rest of their lives, I'm not sure this goal is always attainable. Some children quite naturally manage to get along with each other and sustain a good relationship. Others, however, fight like cats and dogs as children and develop a good relationship only when they are adults. But I don't think you can predict at ages four and two what's going to happen at eighteen or twenty.

Instead of focusing on a far-off ideal, deal with your children in the here and now, at ages four and two, first by respecting the fact that they have different needs because they're in different stages of development. A four-year-old doesn't want a two-year-old hanging around touching his stuff or getting involved with his friends. And he certainly doesn't want to have to share his toys with the little one.

Remember that almost every child who inherits a sibling has to grapple with a very important question: "Does my mother still love me?" When another child is born, the first child is going to have some resentment and be threatened. His reasoning goes like this: "If they love me, then what do they need another one for?" A child can't see the issue from your point of view—how nice it would be to have a large family with lots of happy children. He's a four-year-old. There he was, the apple of your eye; no one else was around. Wonderful. It was sublime. Now, suddenly, there's this other kid whom people think is adorable. You give her a bottle; you change her; she wakes during the night. He's not supposed to have a bottle, yet she's allowed to luxuriate in being an infant.

A parent has to try to understand the way a child sees things. You can't expect a four-year-old to love the next in line. He may eventually learn to love his sibling (more likely he will both love and resent his younger sister), but don't expect it. If the family relationships generally are positive, he will probably in time come to terms with the fact of another child.

To help your son cope with the second child on a day-to-day basis, have his friends over to the house and permit him to play with his friends without her. In turn, let him go visit his friends—again without her. When she does something typical of younger siblings, like interfere with his toys, don't say to him: "Well, she's just a little kid. Let's let her borrow them." This makes the older child feel as if he's not worth anything when com-

217

pared with the younger one, and that he's supposed to give up everything for her. This is a particularly harsh thought to deal with at four years of age, when most children are possessive about their toys. Rather, say to your son: "I know it's really annoying that she's bothering your stuff. Let me try to help you bring your toys to a place where she can't get to them. I'll try to restrict her so she doesn't touch them. Every once in a while, though, she's probably going to find them. If she does, come to me and tell me."

One thing you might try with the older child who is anxious about his toys is to suggest making labels or name tags for his things. "Let's put your name on all of your toys," you can say to him, "so we'll know that these things are yours and not hers." In this way the child can have some pride of ownership as well as an alleviation of some of his anxiety.

You can encourage friendly relations by saying to your older child: "Shall we invite your sister to play with us? Which of your toys would you like to let her borrow while you're playing with this toy?"

As for the two-year-old, there's little you can do to get such a young child to stop interfering with her older brother's things. She's too impulsive at this age. The only way to avoid trouble is to be physically on top of the situation so that the younger one doesn't damage the older one's toys or annoy him too greatly. Give the younger sibling toys that are appropriate for her age. And if you have to, buy her some duplicates to avoid unnecessary conflict.

67
Moving

Moving is a traumatic experience for adults—never mind children. In the old days, parents just picked up and went, and never gave a thought to what their kids might be feeling about the transition. Today, however, parents are aware of their children's anxieties in stressful situations and need guidelines as to how to lessen this stress. It's a good idea to prepare your child for a move, to include him in moving day and to be aware of certain changes in behavior after the move.

If you can save moving day for the summer vacation, the move may be easier for your child especially if he is school age. Summer vacation is a "natural" transition time—a kind of in-between period. School's out, and your child will have a better chance to become acclimated to the new home.

There are a number of things you can do to help make the switch a smooth one. First, let your child know about the move as soon as "funny" things or "strange" things start to happen, such as people coming to see your house, dishes being packed and telephone calls being made to real estate agents.

Next, tell him about the new home and the neighborhood and remind him that he'll be able to visit the old house and friends after the move (if that's feasible). If the new home is not too far away, take him to visit it. Remind him that the furniture in this strange home will be replaced by your own. A visit gives reality to the move; nothing can be more scary than the unknown.

Let your child get involved in the decision making. Let him choose the color he would like his room to be, or ask if he would prefer bookshelves or a bookcase. Keep the options within your range of acceptability while giving your child a sense of participation.

After preparing your child for a move to a new home, your next consideration is the moving day itself. No matter what age the child, seeing all of his possessions packed up and carted away can be a pretty harrowing experience. You needn't pack up absolutely everything. On moving day, keep some special items like a favorite doll or blanket or stuffed animal with you for ready access. You don't want to have to scrounge through cartons to find a comforting object on that very first night in the new place. Better yet, let your child help you pack up his things. Not only will it keep him occupied; it will give him a sense that he's involved in the moving. Many parents ship the children off to Grandma's on the day of the move. I think it's better to let them be involved in the process—if not for the whole day, then at least for a portion of it.

Next, let your child be at the new place when the old furniture shows up so he can watch his new home begin to take shape. We sometimes think we ought to spare our children certain painful experiences, and "goodbyes" seem to rank high among them. But I think departures and arrivals should be properly punctuated for children so they can develop a clear grasp of what's going on around them. In this way they can learn that moving is not some magical and mysterious occurrence that just happens to them but rather a logical process with a beginning, middle and conclusion.

When you've completed the move into your new home, you may find that your child is coming up with some puzzling new behavioral patterns. Don't be surprised if your son or daughter shows some disturbance in an otherwise regular routine. He or she may develop some sleeplessness, or a normally good eater may become finicky about foods. These are most likely temporary reactions to a new set of living conditions. Be patient. In all likelihood, they'll disappear as quickly as they appeared in the first place.

Comfort your child at bedtime, and maybe give him a little extra treat or a slightly extended curfew. But avoid temptations like taking him into your bed or rocking him to sleep in your arms. Try not to get into habits you'll regret later.

After the move has been completed, help your child familiarize himself with the new environment. Meet the shopkeepers, visit the bank, locate the playground, library and other neighborhood places. Make it feel like home as soon as possible.

Another helpful idea is to phone or write to friends from the former neighborhood. If possible, invite an old friend to visit and perhaps stay over. All of these tactics help reestablish continuity after the move.

Making new friends, exploring a new environment and maintaining old ties are all lessons in becoming adaptable and if handled properly will stand your child in good stead for future adjustments.

68
Helping a Child Through a Divorce

Divorce and separation are for a large number of children a painful reality. Fifteen or twenty years ago, in the average first-grade class, one might have had trouble finding even a single child from a broken home. Today, in a suburb north of Boston, a mother reports that exactly half of her son's first-grade classmates live with only one parent.

Divorce is painful for everyone—for the children and for the parents. And what makes it so terribly difficult is that it's very hard to do what's right for your children when you're in a situation filled with painful—almost unbearable—feelings. A parent must deal with his own anger, grief, loneliness and sense of disappointment and at the same time help his child with his or her feelings, too.

Parents whose marriages are unhappy often ask themselves: Would it be better to stay together, despite the tension, the fights, the silence and the sadness? Unfortunately, we don't have a definitive answer to that question.

There simply isn't enough research data comparing children in homes where the marriages are unhappy with children in homes where the marriages are thriving.

One thing we do know, however, is that if there's trouble in the home, children will react. Attuned to the subtle interactions between parents, children will show behaviors that are, in essence, attempts to make things right. If a child senses that Mom is unhappy, for example, he may come over to her as soon as Dad has left for work and in an exaggerated, conciliatory manner try to make her feel better.

Even if you don't think your child notices the trouble, it's almost certain he does. It's not so much that children are altruistic, although they do show a certain amount of empathy. Rather it's primarily a concern for their own well-being. If you're upset because your marriage is in trouble, the child perceives that something is wrong with Mom or Dad. "What does this mean?" he asks himself. "Am I going to be all right? Am I going to have to take care of Mommy and me?" These concerns may seem preposterous, but children do worry about just those things. They want to be sure they are going to be taken care of. They know, in their hearts, they can't take care of themselves.

Although a divorce is extremely painful for a child, we have to keep in mind that we don't know what toll would have been exacted from a child had his parents stayed together. What do the torment, the silence and the tears do to a child whose unhappy parents stay together? He is not upset by the wrenching experience of his parents separating, but he very well may have experienced other deeply upsetting feelings.

I think it goes without saying that you should make every effort to get your marriage in good working order, for the simple reason that it's your responsibility to do so. Couples in trouble should try to work out their personal grievances in the context of the marriage. This may include getting professional help in the form of a family or marriage counselor, a psychologist, a clergyman or a divorce-mediation specialist.

Sometimes, however, the only option is divorce. If this is the case try to remember, as hard as it may be, that your greatest concern has to be for your child during this very difficult period. It's easy to say you're not going to use the children in the struggle, but in more cases than not, children inadvertently get caught in the middle. Although it may be your goal to have an amicable separation, that goal is seldom reached.

When you're involved in a divorce, there are many hard feelings: misery, anger, disappointment and shame. These feelings can provoke, or evoke, motives and behaviors a person might not otherwise have acted on. The most civilized people, whose hostilities are kept well in control and sublimated in their normal lives, often find themselves doing outrageous things when they go through a divorce. They feel they are out of control. This is understandable, if not desirable.

Children see their parents in the throes of an emotional conflict transformed into people whom they haven't seen before, and whom they will probably never see again. Sometimes inadvertently, and sometimes in an exploitative way, the children are victims of these emotional conflicts. There's no excuse for the opportunistic use of children during a divorce. Although you may be very upset, fight back the urge to say: "Mommy said something very nasty to me." Or, "Daddy did something unforgivable." Think of the effect such phrases might have on the child.

Start out with the understanding that your child has inherited the two of you. To your child, you're a package deal. He assumes Mommy and Daddy go together. In fact, young children find it fascinating and exciting to learn that when you were a little girl you didn't know Daddy, that you grew up in a different state or that you didn't go to the same school. Until a child gets a bit older, he just assumes that Mommy and Daddy come together. The idea of his parents separating is almost incomprehensible to a child.

If a divorce is inevitable, a child has to be informed. Begin by pointing out that Mommy and Daddy are not feeling friendly toward one another. "Friendly" is a word that children understand. This isn't to say that children will understand everything you tell them about a divorce. But you will have to tell them certain things, even though they aren't capable of digesting all of it. You might say, "Mommy and Daddy aren't friendly. You've probably noticed that there has been a lot of screaming and yelling going on." Or, "Mom and Dad haven't been talking to one another. It's been silent and sad here." Whatever the reality has been, articulate it so the child knows.

One father told his daughter that he was going to pick her up after school. "There's something I want to tell you," he said. The girl, in suspense, asked, "What? What?" But the father said, "Wait until after school." All day she kept thinking of the surprise and fantasized that it might be a present or a party for her. When her father picked her up, he took her for a snack and told her, "Mom and Dad are going to get divorced." The news, after her pleasant expectations, hit her, she said years later, like a ton of bricks. She simply refused to believe it.

Obviously this is not the way to tell a child about a divorce. Rather do it as a unit. Together sit down and say, "This is something we've discussed. We want to hear your questions." Quickly reassure the child that the divorce has nothing to do with him. This message has to be repeated often. Children, being egocentric, think that had they acted otherwise, things might have turned out differently. They have to be told this isn't true. "You were not a bad girl. Daddy and Mommy will always love you. Daddy will always be your Daddy, and Mommy will always be your Mommy. You'll be taken care of and your life will go on as it ought to." Although this may not be entirely true, start by telling a child that his life won't change for the worse. This is a child's primary concern, and he will need constant reassurance. Also, your child needs to be reassured that when you and he disagree that he will not be thrown out—or "divorced" from the family.

Expect that your child will be angry with you. After all, you're upsetting something very important to the child—his family. You're imposing a change he didn't ask for. You're imposing the experience of the parents' emotions, which he probably finds hard to deal with. In short, you're upsetting his whole life. It's understandable that he'll be mad at you.

Try to be careful about using that anger and turning it against the other parent. Because a child is mad at you anyway for messing up his life, it's tempting to make him blame the other parent. If each of you blames the other, the child is eventually going to feel like a Ping-Pong ball. One minute he's going to hate Mommy, the next he's going to hate Daddy. It's very confusing. The poor child feels pulled apart. Children even do this to themselves without your assistance. If you're fighting, a child will try to get in between you to stop you from fighting. Have you ever looked at your child's face when you're having an argument with your spouse?

To the extent that you know some of the facts about the practical arrangements, you should inform your child. You don't have to go into the gory details about why you're getting divorced. There may have been a love affair or gambling or alcoholism, but unless the child has witnessed these events, you don't have to go into detail with him. Save it for when he is older, if at all. But once you know the practical arrangements, you should explain to a child what they are. If the mother is going to leave with the children, she has to say, "We're moving. We're going to live in such and such a place. Daddy is going to stay here in this apartment." If the father is moving out, then say, "Daddy will be moving out, but we'll still be here, and you will have the same nursery school, the same friends and Daddy will come to visit you." If a move is involved, which is very often the case, go take a look at the new home, after it's been furnished a bit and doesn't look too gloomy or lonely. Take your child to look at the neighborhood and the school and the playground. Tell him that he'll have a special place in the new house or apartment all his own.

Although you're dealing with your own wounds, during a divorce you have to put the children first. Children want to know what's going on and what will happen to them in the future. To the extent that a child lacks information and lives in a world of uncertainty, he's going to be upset.

Be clear and honest about your feelings if you can. I know this is hard to do. But if you can, and if a child knows you're feeling lousy, you might say, "Mommy is feeling a little sad today." If a child sees your pain and experiences it, then it worries him. It's helpful to label the feelings a child sees. If you try to tell a child that nothing is the matter, and attempt to go through life with a happy face, he will know it's a lie and be very confused. You say one thing but clearly you feel another. Emotional honesty is very important for children. You can't really fool them too much. You can fool them to the extent that their intellect can't grasp all the details, but you can't really fool them about how you feel. This doesn't mean you have to say you're deeply depressed. Simply say, "I'm feeling a little sad today."

If the child's response is to blurt out: "I hate Daddy [or Mommy]," the chances are he's saying that to you to make you feel better. But if he does say that, you have to help him because he's going to feel terribly guilty for these feelings and words. Point out to the child that he doesn't have to hate Mommy (or Daddy). "Just because Mommy [or Daddy] and I are having an argument, and aren't getting along, you can still love each of us, because each of us loves you." A child isn't capable of grasping that if you both love him, and he loves both of you, why you don't love each other. He learns that over time.

The concept of "family" is a very precious one to a child. And anything that threatens that security is necessarily going to frighten him. I saw this graphically demonstrated one evening when a three-year-old girl was in tears because her mother was going out to have dinner with a friend. The father was going to stay home and take care of the girl. "But, but, but . . ." sputtered the girl. "But we won't be a family!"

Even in a situation such as this one, where separation and divorce aren't imminent, children are very attached to the idea of family—of being together and not being lonely. Children experience divorce as the loss of the family.

Many people say children are incapable of depression, but I don't think that's true. They can feel depressed. Sometimes they show it as depression, and sometimes it manifests itself in other ways. When they show the depression as depression, it has the same signs as in an adult: a depressed demeanor, a low-keyed attitude, a lack of energy, fitful sleeping or too much sleeping. Other children, instead of acting depressed, counteract this feeling by being belligerent or provocative. Some become clowns, laughing on the outside but inwardly crying. Older children—four to five years old—may show accident proneness. Be alert to signs of depression or guilt feelings. Try not to berate a child for not eating or not having any energy or being accident prone. Try not to be annoyed if he doesn't want to go to sleep at night. Although you may be tempted to feel that you've got enough on your hands without a child acting up on you, realize that this is his way of reacting to the stress, and that he needs reassurance. Bad behavior just doesn't happen coincidentally. It's very much a part of what you're going through.

Address these issues with your child. Say that you know how sad it is for him. Ask if he wants to call the other parent and talk to him. Try to make the child feel as comfortable and reassured as possible. When things are quieter, and you're not feeling terribly emotional, you could explain some of the facts of the divorce: the lawyers, the courts, what alimony and custody mean. Within limits, the more a child knows, the better off he will be.

※

After my divorce, whenever I went to visit my children, I was filled with a sense of futility. I would get incredibly tense before each visit. I wouldn't know what to expect, who might be there, how long I would have with the children. I felt I was never "with" the kids. I was just making my presence known, that's all. Later I would get very depressed. I considered from time to time forgetting them altogether. None of it was enjoyable.

I can understand why a parent might sometimes wish to stay away from his children after a divorce. But even though I am sympathetic to these feelings, I think a parent in this situation should seek help, either from a friend or from a psychologist. There are some situations in life that require sacrifice, and this is one of them. The child has to come first. The child needs to know that the parent who is not living with him cares enough to maintain a relationship over time. While it's understandable that a parent might be tempted to drift off, it's important to try as hard as possible to be there for your children.

Look at it from the child's point of view. "My father left me. Why?" he wonders. "Obviously he doesn't care enough about me." The child experiences ambivalence. He loves the parent, but he is also angry at the parent for leaving him and rejecting him.

Even when there is no question of abandonment, the child feels a loyalty to the parent he is living with. Likewise he feels disloyal if he misses the absent parent. It is sometimes so difficult for a child to live with these mixed feelings that he closes off his feelings toward the absent parent. It's not only to appease the parent he is living with but to help himself tolerate the mixed feelings. It's easier for a child not to care about somebody than to feel ambivalence.

If you are the custodial parent and the other parent isn't showing up to visit your child, you have to deal with the problem head-on. First give the parent every benefit of the doubt. There may be an illness or it may be an exceptionally busy time at work for the other parent. Don't jump at the opportunity to put your ex-spouse in a bad light. But if the absences do continue, and it looks as if the other person is being irresponsible, talk with your child about it. "I know how badly you feel," you can say. "I know how hurt you are, and I know how upset you are. You have every right to be upset. I don't think it's right either that your father doesn't keep his word and come visit you. I think that's irresponsible. There's no good excuse for that. Let me try and do something for you." Show the child you're writing a note to the other parent. Make a phone call with the child listening. You don't have any control over the other parent except to make an appeal, but you do have a responsibility to calm your own anger and to tell your child that his feelings are understandable.

69

Custody

Your decisions about custody will depend, to some extent, upon prevailing laws and practices. But whatever you choose, the child should be informed as to how the decision was reached and why. Again, the more a child knows the better off he is. Dispel any strange ideas and fears that the child may have about why it turned out the way it did. Point out that the person who has custody isn't necessarily the one who loves him more.

I believe that children should have maximum opportunity to be with both parents. Parents have devised various ways to share custody. One of the ways is for the child to spend half of the time with one parent and half with the other. This may work out to three-and-a-half days with one parent and three-and-a-half days with the other; a week with one and a week with the other, or even a month with one and a month with the other. The child can either go back and forth from one parent to the other—which is only possible if the parents live close to each other—or the parents can move in and out of the child's house. In this situation, the child stays put. One month the father lives with him. The next month the mother. Such discontinuity is very difficult for an adult, but on the other hand, the other alternative requires that the child live with discontinuity. Shared custody arrangements require a good deal of logistical planning. Whom does a teacher call on a given day? In the case of a medical emergency, which parent is authorized to make decisions? Many problems will emerge that will require forethought and responsible planning.

It is commonly believed that it's probably better for one parent to be the custodial parent while the other has the freedom to see the child as much as possible. The noncustodial parent could arrange to walk the child to school everyday, or go out for desserts together every evening. From the child's point of view, it may be best to live in one place with one parent, and to see the other on a daily basis. This offers the child a greater sense of rootedness.

Presently, the most common arrangement is for the mother to obtain custody and for the father to have visitation rights. But don't be hesitant about trying to negotiate whatever arrangement is best for you and your child. Within limits, the better you feel about your arrangement, the better it will be for your child.

Although I have pointed out that a parent must have the child's feelings uppermost in his mind during a divorce or separation, I do not want to minimize how difficult it is for a parent to deal with his own grief and anger and at the same time deal with a child's feelings. Aside from the tragic or sudden death of a family member, there is probably no harder parenting situation than a divorce or a separation. Seek help, get good advice, comfort your child and take comfort in him as well. Children are remarkable tonics.

I think that given the enormity of separation and divorce, and the feelings that such an action stirs up, some psychological or professional help should be made available to all family members—even if only briefly.

The quality of a child's life after a divorce is probably the key to his adjustment. It is not simply the divorce itself that has a significant impact on a child, but the circumstances that the child finds himself in after the breakup as well. How you replace what has been taken away deserves a great deal of consideration—both for your child as well as yourself.

70
Helping Your Child to Deal with a Death in the Family

Death has to be dealt with as we would any life cycle issue—with the understanding that children have their own way of looking at these things. Children do not perceive death in the same way adults do. When a little child tries to imagine death, he thinks it's something that can be changed—when you're dead, it's a temporary state. You're not dead forever. If you ask a child what death means, he'll get all scrunched up and make himself smaller, or he'll lie down and show you what it looks like to be dead. But a child has no sense of the finality of death. In fact, often children say, "I wish you were dead" (see Part II, Anger and Emotional Honesty). What they really mean is, "Go away."

If someone close to you and your child dies, tell your child of the death by giving him matter-of-fact, straightforward information. Try to avoid idiosyncratic explanations, such as, "An angel took Grandpa up to heaven." Even if we are religious, we understand that an angel doesn't literally take a person to heaven, but a child doesn't, and this image may confuse him for years. One boy wanted to know if his brother were mailed up to heaven in an envelope. After all, the child wondered, how did his brother get there? A woman wrote to me that when she was eleven, her father died, and she was told he "went to heaven." Later, throughout her childhood, she was deathly afraid of getting ill. She had a horrible fantasy that things in the sky would "get" her.

Sometimes parents use analogies such as, "Grandpa went to sleep." But these can be counterproductive, too. You may find that very night that the child is afraid to go to bed.

Each kind of death will require a special way of handling. The death of a grandparent is an easier situation for a child to tolerate than that of a parent. Although the grandparent may have been very close to the child, it is not the parent—and it's the parent that the child is mainly concerned about. The child cares primarily about one thing: What will happen to me if everybody dies? This is a crucial question and the nucleus of the whole issue.

If a grandparent dies, be very clear and simple in your explanation. Begin by saying, "Grandma was very old and died." To us, of course, our parents may not seem very old, but to a child who's four or five, someone who's fifteen times his age is very old. Hasten to add that none of us is planning on dying for quite a long time, not until we're very, very, very old. Fortunately our children don't see us as being old like grandparents. You can convince the child that he is safe for a long, long time to come by adding that you're going to be around to take care of him for a long, long time. Children can't possibly conceive of the fact that one day they won't need you.

If you are sad and grieving because of the death, don't hide this from your child. "Yes, I'm very sad," you can say, "because I will miss Grandma. I love Grandma. I'm sad because of that." Reassure the child that you're not sad because of anything that he did and you're not angry with him. Make sure the child understands that you will be fine. But right now, you're sad.

If the death is very sudden or tragic, and people are out of control, the child should be shielded from this. An emotion that's out of control is terribly upsetting to a child. But a child can see and tolerate normal mourning.

I think it's fine to take a child to a funeral service. It's probably not a good idea to have him view the deceased, but he certainly can come to the services. Keep in mind that if he's very young, he won't be able to stay very long, because of his short attention span. Bring along a baby-sitter who can take him for a walk or to the bathroom. The child should know that he's going to a memorial service where people want to remember the person who died.

You can also take a child to a cemetery. He should be told that it's our custom when people die to be buried. Tell him, simply and truthfully, that to be buried means to be put into the ground. Sometimes we think a child should be shielded from such knowledge—but why? Why would we give our children a false explanation unless we think there's something wrong with burying the dead? Like sex, if we do it, then why can't we talk about it? If you pass a cemetery, and the child sees all the stones and asks you about them, don't pretend you don't know what he's talking about—which a lot of parents do. Don't pretend there's nothing there, because then he'll know something's amiss. Simply say, "That's called a cemetery. That's a place where, when people die, they're buried." The child may ask you a lot of questions. If so, you can answer them. "Yes, there's a special container that people are put in, and that's called a coffin. It's usually made out of a pretty wood and it looks nice. Because we respect and love the people who die, we place them in this comfortable container. Then the coffin is placed in the ground and we put a stone on the grave. Why? So we can remember where they are buried. The stone helps us remember how long they lived and who they were."

To help your child prepare for death, you might bury a pet who has died at home and explain to your child what you are doing each step of the way. If a bird or a gerbil dies, get a shoe box, place the dead pet in the box and say a few words about the pet as you bury it in the backyard. "Let's remember Squeaky. Squeaky has died. Remember how we loved to play with him?"

Deaths of famous personalities are also useful in helping your child to learn about death. If such an event occurs, mention it to your child. "Gee, so and so, the famous actor, died today. He was very, very old. Remember all the movies we saw him in?" This will help the child get accustomed to the idea that death happens. In this case, however, it happens to distant people and doesn't affect his life at all. But by learning of these deaths, he's already beginning to deal with the issue.

The most significant loss to a child is the death of a parent. Explanations about the death have to be handled in the same way as other deaths, with careful attention paid to the services and the grieving process. It's very important for a child to experience the funeral and burial so that the death has a reality to it. Because they don't know what death means, little children fantasize that the parent is not really dead. They think a parent can come back from the dead. Because they play dead-and-alive all the time, that means a parent can come back, too, right? But if a child at least has an anchor, some tangible recognition that he went to a funeral, when he gets older, he can remind himself, "I did go to the funeral. I did see the services. I did go to the cemetery. I did see them lower her coffin into the ground. I know that really happened." If a child is shielded from these events, he may always harbor the secret wish that the parent will come back or that the parent somehow mysteriously vanished.

A child should be permitted to be angry as well as sad. Mourning is a process during which you learn to give up someone you've lost, and you're entitled to be resentful and angry at the person you've lost. This is a difficult thing to do. After all, how can we be angry at someone who died? They didn't want to die, so how can we feel this way?

But rage is an integral part of the mourning process. It's just plain unfair when a parent dies on you. You're left with only one parent. Financially and emotionally there may be problems. You've lost the support of this parent; he or she has deprived you of being proud of you. Even adults often say, when they have an achievement, "I wish my mother and father were here to see this." Why? Because we all have inside of us a wish that our parents be proud of us. Anger, fury and rage at being denied this must not be underestimated. Such feelings must be introduced to the child—gradually and not all at once. It's very hard for a child to come to grips with his rage. Because he feels guilty for feeling rage at the lost parent, he supresses it and doesn't allow it expression. You can help him with these feelings.

Another very difficult matter to handle is the death of a sibling. A good rule to follow is to be matter-of-fact about the loss of the other child but not to pretend to be unemotional about the untimely death. Some discussion of the facts involved in the other child's dying should be mentioned. It is advisable to use simple terms while trying not to instill undue fear in the child. Moreover, I would try to avoid moralizing. For instance, if the child drowned because he didn't follow instructions and went to the lake despite warnings not to, or if the child was hit by a car because he crossed an off-limits street, do not use the death as an example to the living child. It's also not a good idea to reproach yourself in front of the child. Do not say that you wish you had been more careful or that you wish you had insisted that the child not go to the lake, since this may shake the living child's confidence in you and cause needless anxiety.

After the death of the sibling, be careful not to overindulge the living child. Nor should you idealize the child who has passed away, even though the temptation to do so is perfectly normal. Rather reassure your child that he is not at fault. Help him to assuage his potential guilt feelings by pointing out that it's okay for him to go on with his life and to be successful. There's nothing wrong with his having survived.

A child needs to be reassured that although his life is going to change—such as with a divorce or a separation—he will be taken care of. Make sure he understands that you will see to it that he is taken care of to the best of your ability.

Afterword

While it's true that a lot of important ingredients go into the making of a personality in the very early years of a child's development, that doesn't mean that the case is closed after the age of five. Although we often need to plant the seeds for certain behaviors and beliefs early on, most of them won't come to fruition until the child is older. Major personality changes can also take place in the adolescent years, when the struggling child is trying to accommodate himself to his changing body, and even later, in parenthood, when the adult will have an opportunity to relive certain conflicts, anxieties and worries he had as a child and perhaps resolve them once and for all. Having said that, however, it is true that many of the behaviors and attitudes inculcated in your child between birth and five years of age will, in the long run, be part of the child's thinking and personality.

Child rearing is hard. When a problem arises there may not be a simple solution. Success depends on being loving and thoughtful, but it also requires a great deal of perseverance. Although the hard times are unavoidable, I hope my thoughts about the issues you must deal with on a day-to-day basis have helped to reduce some of the guilt, confusion and frustration that so often cause needless difficulties.

Once you've been launched into parenthood, you'll need all your best skills, self-control, good judgment and patience. But at the same time there is nothing like the thrill and exhilaration that come from watching that bright, cheerful, inquisitive, creative, eccentric and even goofy child you have raised flourish and shine. That's what keeps you going, and what, in the end, makes it all worthwhile.

Bon voyage.

INDEX

ABOUT THE AUTHORS

Dr. Lawrence Balter is Professor of Educational Psychology at New York University and director of NYU's WARMLINE, a telephone counseling service for parents. He is a practicing psychologist and psychoanalyst in New York City and has been honored by the National Media Awards Committee of the American Psychological Association for his television series "Children and All That Jazz."

Dr. Balter hosts a nationally syndicated ABC TALK-RADIO program and is the resident child psychologist on the CBS-TV *Morning News*. His articles have appeared in numerous scientific journals as well as such popular magazines as *The Ladies' Home Journal* and *Parents Magazine*.

Anita Shreve is a prolific writer on child care and parenting. Her articles have appeared in magazines such as *Redbook* and *The New York Times Magazine*. She is the author of a forthcoming book on working mothers and their children and another on working women and health.